Mastering Django

The original, best-selling programmer's reference completely rewritten for Django 2 and 3.

Nigel George

Mastering Django

Published by GNW Independent Publishing, Hamilton NSW, Australia

ISBN: 978-0-6488844-1-5 (PRINT)

22 21 20 1 2 3 4 5 6 7 8 9

Acknowledgments

As always, my thanks go out to my family for putting up with the months of absences and insanity that comes with completing a project like this around working for a living.

To the Django community, without your input and enthusiasm, I would never find the motivation to even complete a web tutorial, let alone a 600-odd page textbook.

In particular, I would like to make special mention of my beta testers, who were (in no particular order):

> Didier Clapasson, Dominic Bühler, Maria Hynes, James Bellis, Rick Colgan, Simon Schliesky, Lourens Grové, Derrick Kearney, Adrian German, Raphael Thanhoffer, Jan Gondol, David Price, Jaap Onderwaater, Georges Samaha, Bogdan Górski, Hans Hendrick, Martijn Dekker, Alberto Nordmann G., Peter Boers, Robert Helewka, Phil Moose, Jean-Patrick Simard, Gerald Brown, Daniel Coughlin and Hermann Kass.

Thank you all—your feedback and suggestions have helped me make this a far better book than it would have been otherwise.

Table of Contents

1

Introducing Mastering Django

When Django 2 was released, a lot changed in the Django world.

Not just because we finally got rid of the complications with having to deal with both Python 2 and 3, but also because of the many new features, tweaks, updates and optimizations that ensure Django keeps getting better and better. Django 3 continues the tradition of continual improvement in Django's codebase.

What many of you may not know, is the original *Mastering Django:Core* was an update of the original book written by two of the creators of Django—Adrian Holovaty and Jacob Kaplan-Moss. Given the original book had been around since Django 1.1, it got dated. There are also a lot of similarities to the Django docs in several chapters.

(Funny aside: I have had a couple of people email me and take me to task for copying the docs. Lol! Given that the guys who wrote the original book also wrote the original docs, that will happen folks!)

I have decided to start with a clean sheet of paper for *Mastering Django*. This means you don't just get an update; you get a new book, written from scratch to meet the needs of today's programmers.

First and foremost, the book remains a plain-English, easy to follow deep-dive into Django's commonly used core functionalities. It covers both Django 2 and Django 3.

Second, the book complements the existing docs; it doesn't just reproduce them in a different format. I have removed all the original material from Jacob and Adrian's book and all the content from the Django documentation. There are lots of topics not covered adequately in the docs, which provide ample opportunities for me to create resources that will make you a better Django programmer. I have done my best to include them in this book.

Third, the book takes a more practical approach, with less emphasis on theory and more exploration of working code. It's impossible to put all Django's functions into a single book, but I have done my best to include the functions, classes and tools you will use regularly. With each major function or class, I expand them into functioning code examples. Source code is also available for *Mastering Django.*

And finally, while I will not be releasing the book as open-source, the early chapters will remain free to access and read on djangobook.com. As with the previous book, all income from sales support the Django Book project, allowing me to keep the core content ad-free and accessible to all.

Exciting times ahead! :)

All the best with your programming journey!

Cheers,

Big Nige

Who This Book is For

This book is a programmer's manual targeted at intermediate to advanced programmers wishing to gain an in-depth understanding of Django.

In saying that, it doesn't mean beginners can't get value out of the book. Since the publication of the first edition of the book, roughly half of the readers I have spoken to identified as being a beginner when they started out with the book.

The way I write—building on simple concepts and explaining every step—is highly accessible to beginners, so if you are a beginner, you will still learn a great deal about Django from the book.

Where the book can challenge beginners is all the peripheral stuff—HTML, CSS, Python and web development in general—that I don't explain in any detail. The book is big enough as it is, without me trying to teach you all the stuff you need to know that isn't Django-related!

I do, however, give you lots of references so you can easily get more information if you need it.

Structure of the Book

I've broken the book up into two parts:

- **PART 1: Fundamentals**—A high-level overview of Django, how it's structured, and its core components, so you can grasp how Django brings together each element to create powerful and scalable web applications.
- **PART 2: Essentials**—This is the meaty part of the book where we take a deep and detailed dive into the core modules of Django so you can gain a thorough and practical understanding of all the most commonly used modules in Django.

Throughout the book, I will use snippets of code from a fictitious website for a social or sporting club called MyClub.

It was my original plan for this book to end up with a complete website for MyClub. However, it was apparent halfway through that a book that teaches you as much as possible about the popular parts of Django has very different goals to a book that teaches you how to create a complex, professional website.

In the latter case, no more so than the need to write tests. Tests, while necessary for developing a professional application, distract from learning the core functions of Django. If I wrote proper tests for all the code in this book, I would double the size of the codebase and add little to your learning. For these reasons, I have kept the code in this book to illustrative snippets.

Required Programming Knowledge

The book assumes you have little to no experience with Django.

I expect you to have a basic understanding of web technologies like HTML and CSS, and a basic understanding of how to structure code. You should also be familiar with your OS's terminal or shell program. Absolute beginners shouldn't be too concerned, as it's easy to learn the basics, and that's all you need to get value out of the book.

As Django is written in Python, I also assume you have a basic understanding of Python. Although, since Python is so easy to learn and there are such great resources available online for Python, I haven't heard from a learner yet who said not knowing Python was a barrier. You will learn a lot about Python just by learning Django, and all the extras you need to know are easy to find online.

Software Versions

As the book only covers core Django, you don't require any special functions or libraries, so the latest versions of Python 3 and Django 2 or 3 are OK. At the time of writing, this is Python 3.8.3 and Django 2.2.12 (for Django 2) and Django 3.0.6 (for Django 3).

Django 2 or 3??

There is very little difference between Django 2.2 and Django 3.0, which can be confusing for programmers new to Django. What small differences exist, I have noted in the book.

Django 2.2 is a Long Term Support version, so is older, more stable and better supported than Django 3.0. In saying this, the differences between the two versions are sufficiently small that 99% of the code in this book will work on either version.

Code that only works on Django 3 is clearly marked in the text, so you shouldn't have any problems identifying the parts specific to Django 3.

I provide installation instructions for Windows and Mac users. Linux users can refer to the 90 million Linux installation tutorials online (OK, so that's maybe an exaggeration, but there are *lots*).

All the code in this book will run on Windows, macOS or Linux. While the code and screenshots are all from a Windows machine, the fundamentals remain the same—all three have a terminal or command window and management commands like `runserver` work the same on all three platforms.

Coding style is also identical across platforms with one exception—I use Windows-style backslashes in file paths. This is to assist Windows users to differentiate between Windows' native use of backslashes and Django's implementation of forward slashes in path names. Linux and macOS users, simply need to substitute forward slashes in these cases.

All browser screenshots are taken from the latest version of the Chrome browser. If you are using FireFox, Safari or some other browser, your screen may look different than the screenshots.

The images are in full-color in the PDF and eBook versions, but are grayscale in the printed book (color is *way* too expensive to print). Paperback users are encouraged to run the code to see the full-color effect in your browser.

Source Code

You can download the source code and resources in this book from `https://djangobook.com/mastering-django-source/`.

The included source has been written in Django 3.0. All source code has been tested and will run unmodified on Django 2.2, except for the MariaDB configuration files as MariaDB support was not added until Django 3.0.

The source has been tested against the version of SQLite that comes with Django. While the data structures used in the book are simple and shouldn't cause problems if you decide to use another database, there are no guarantees. If you find any database-related quirks, refer to the database engine documentation.

The source is broken up into folders, one for each chapter of the book. Rather than delete code that changes from chapter to chapter, I have commented out lines of code in the source so you can see where the code has changed.

Code line numbering in the book is provided so you can easily cross-reference my explanations to individual lines of code in the book. In most cases, line numbering in the book does not match line numbers in the source files.

The source is not designed to be executed as-is. The SQLite database file and migrations for each chapter have been removed from the source. While copying the source code from a chapter and running it inside a virtual environment will work in most cases (after running the migrations), there is no guarantee it will. The source code is for your reference and to assist your learning, it's not fully functioning code that you can just copy and use in your projects.

Found a Bug or Typo?

With a book project the size of Mastering Django the odd bug or typo will slip through. This is even after countless edits from me and plenty of feedback from my awesome beta testers (you know who you are :)).

In a perfect world, I'd be able to pay the megabucks for professional editors, but there's a reason why those of us who support Django all have day jobs; it ain't exactly a meal ticket.

So, if you find a bug or a typo, get in touch with me via the Djangobook website[1] and let me know so I can fix the error. The major plus of self-publishing is that I can make changes quickly and send updates to everyone as soon as I have a batch of edits completed. I will even make sure you get a free electronic copy of the updated version if one of your edits makes it through to a published version of the book.

Errata and Django 3 Updates

I will be publishing errata (bugs and typos) information and updates for future versions of Django 3 on the website here:

```
https://djangobook.com/mastering-django-errata-and-updates/
```

Getting Help

For any other questions regarding the book, you can contact me via the help page on the Djangobook website. Note that, due to working full-time, it's very difficult for me to find time to answer Django questions that don't directly relate to my books and courses.

1 https://djangobook.com/django-help/

Your first points of contact for general information on Django and answers to "how do I…" questions should be Stack Overflow[2], your favorite search engine, and any one of the dozens of social media groups relating to Django.

2 https://stackoverflow.com/questions/tagged/django

Part 1

Django Fundamentals

2

Installing Python and Django

Before you can start learning Django, you must install some software on your computer. Fortunately, this is a simple three-step process:

1. Install Python
2. Install a Python Virtual Environment; and
3. Install Django

I've written this chapter mostly for those of you running Windows, as most new users are on Windows. I have also included a section on installing Python 3 and Django on macOS.

If you are using Linux, there are many resources on the Internet—the best place to start is Django's own installation instructions[1].

For Windows users, your computer can be running any recent version of Windows (7, 8.1 or 10).

This chapter also assumes you're installing Django on a desktop or laptop computer and will use the development server and SQLite to run all the code in this book. This is by far the easiest and best way to set up Django when you are first starting.

1 https://docs.djangoproject.com/en/dev/intro/install/

Installing Python

A lot of Windows applications use Python, so it may be already installed on your system. You can check this out by opening a command prompt, or running PowerShell, and typing `python` at the prompt.

If Python isn't installed you'll get a message saying that Windows can't find Python. If Python is installed, the python command will open the Python interactive interpreter:

```
C:\Users\Nigel>python
Python 3.6.0 (v3.6.0:41df79263a11, Dec 23 2016, 07:18:10) [MSC
v.1900 32 bit (Intel)] on win32
Type "help", "copyright", "credits" or "license" for more
information.
>>>
```

You can see in the above example that my PC is running Python 3.6.0. Django 2.2 is compatible with Python version 3.5 and later. Django 3.0 is compatible with Python version 3.6 and later. If you have an older version of Python, you must install Python 3.7 or 3.8 for the code in this book to work. If you have Python 3.5 or 3.6, I still recommend you install Python 3.8 to ensure you have the latest version installed on your machine.

Assuming Python 3 is not installed on your system, you first need to get the installer. Go to `https://www.python.org/downloads/` and click the big yellow button that says "Download Python 3.8.x".

At the time of writing, the latest version of Python is 3.8.3, but it may have been updated by the time you read this, so the numbers may be slightly different. Once you have downloaded the Python installer, go to your downloads folder and double click the file `python-3.x.x.msi` to run the installer. The installation process is the same as any other Windows program, so if you have installed software before, there should be no problem here; however, there is one essential customization you must make.

By default, the Python executable is not added to the Windows PATH. For Django to work correctly, Python must be listed in the PATH statement. Fortunately, this is easy to rectify—when the Python installer screen opens, make sure "Add Python 3.8 to PATH" is checked before installing (Figure 2-1).

Do Not Forget This Step!

It will solve most problems that arise from the incorrect mapping of pythonpath (an important variable for Python installations) in Windows.

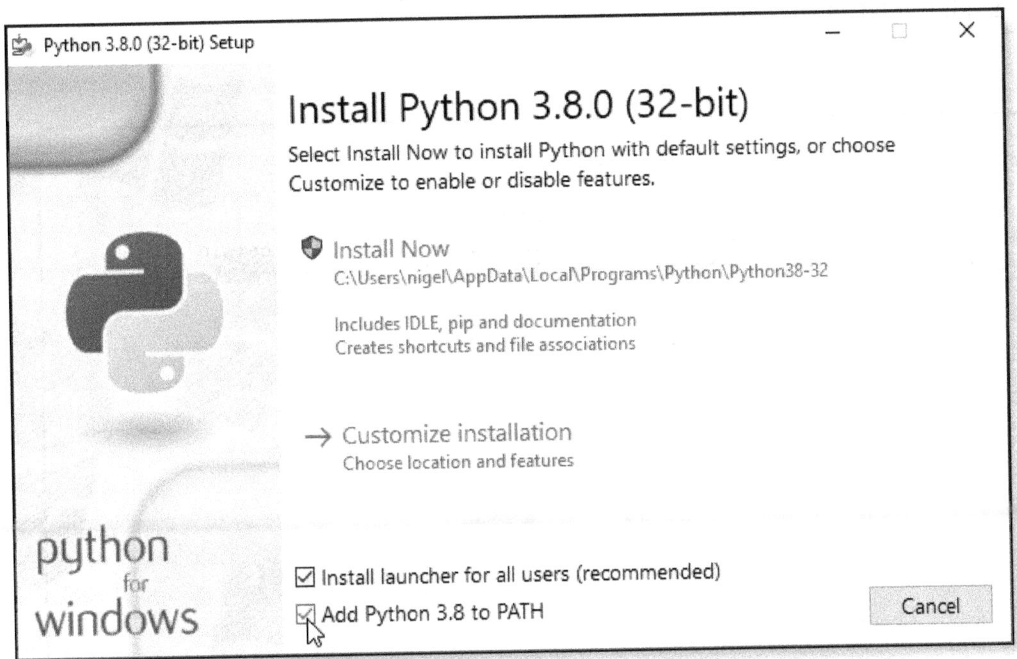

Figure 2-1. *Check the "Add Python 3.8 to PATH" box before installing.*

Once Python is installed, restart Windows and then type `python` at the command prompt. You should see something like this:

```
C:\Users\nigel> python
Python 3.8.3 (tags/v3.8.3:6f8c832, May 13 2020, 22:20:19) [MSC
v.1925 32 bit (Intel)] on win32
Type "help", "copyright", "credits" or "license" for more
information.
>>>
```

Installing Python on macOS

If you open a terminal and type `python` at the prompt, you will see that the system version is Python 2 (Figure 2-2). Django is not compatible with Python 2, so we need to install the latest version of Python 3.

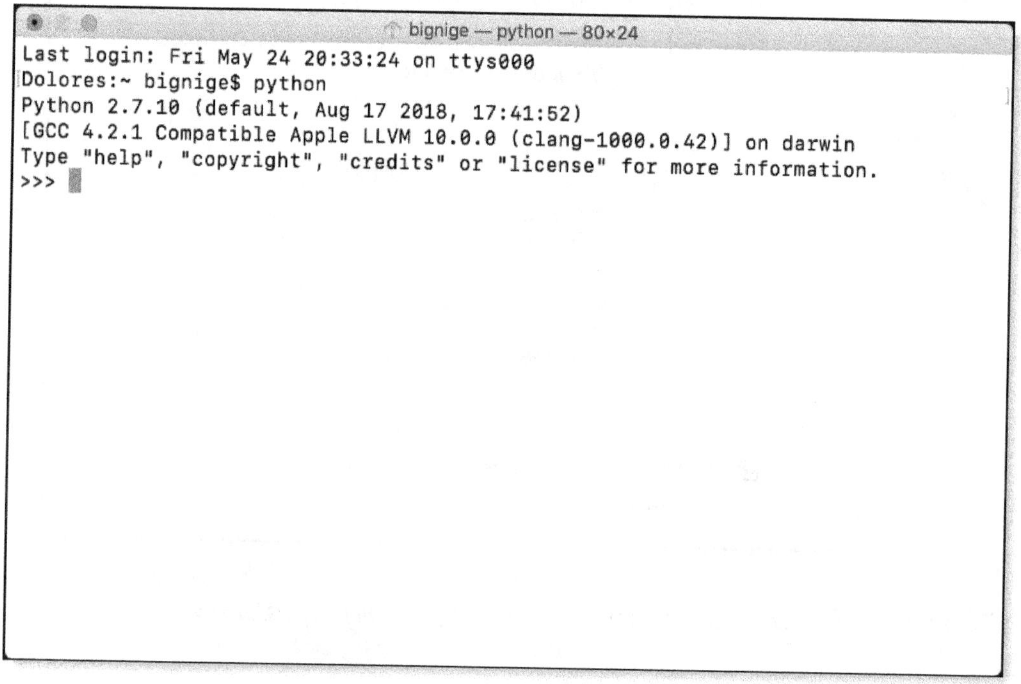

```
bignige — python — 80×24
Last login: Fri May 24 20:33:24 on ttys000
Dolores:~ bignige$ python
Python 2.7.10 (default, Aug 17 2018, 17:41:52)
[GCC 4.2.1 Compatible Apple LLVM 10.0.0 (clang-1000.0.42)] on darwin
Type "help", "copyright", "credits" or "license" for more information.
>>>
```

Figure 2-2. *macOS uses Python 2, which is incompatible with Django.*

Downloading a copy of Python 3 follows the same process as Windows—Go to `https://www.python.org/downloads/` and click the big yellow button that says "Download Python 3.x.x". Your browser should automatically detect that you are using macOS and take you to the correct download page. If it doesn't, select the correct operating system from the links below the button.

The Mac installer is in `.pkg` format, so once it's downloaded, double-click the file to run the package installer (Figure 2-3). The screenshot is for Python 3.7, but the process is identical for Python 3.8.

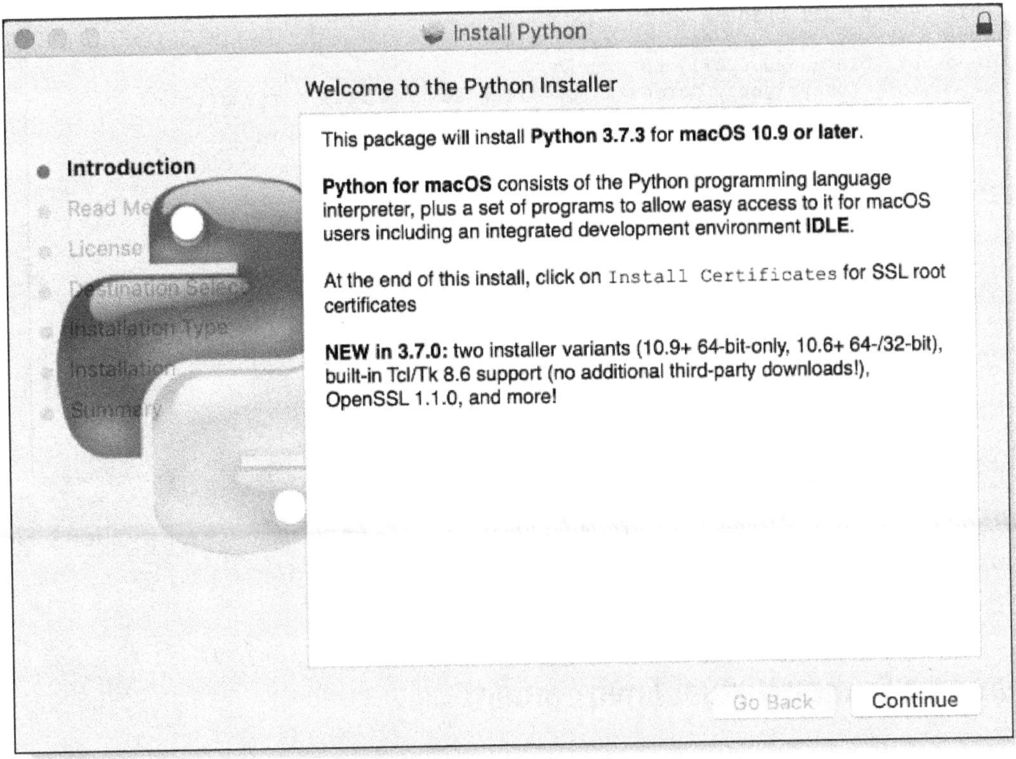

Figure 2-3. *Follow the prompts to install Python 3 on macOS.*

Follow the installations steps and, when Python 3 has been installed, open a new terminal window. If the installation was successful, typing `python3` at the prompt will open the Python 3 interactive shell (Figure 2-4). Note that macOS will happily run multiple versions of Python on the one machine, you just need to make sure you select the correct version when running the terminal.

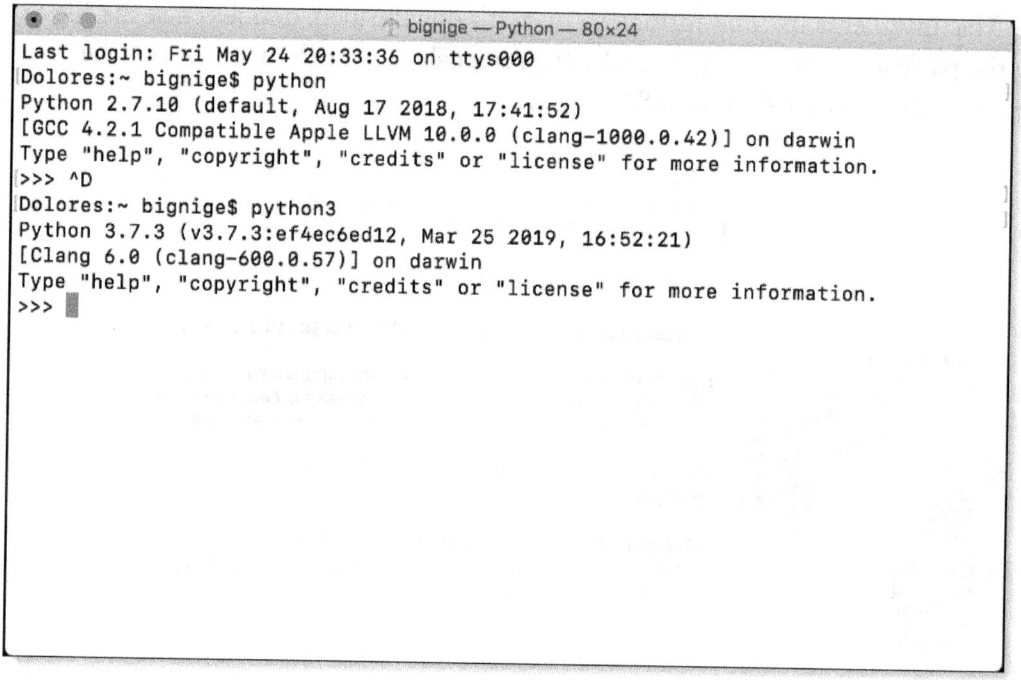

```
bignige — Python — 80×24
Last login: Fri May 24 20:33:36 on ttys000
Dolores:~ bignige$ python
Python 2.7.10 (default, Aug 17 2018, 17:41:52)
[GCC 4.2.1 Compatible Apple LLVM 10.0.0 (clang-1000.0.42)] on darwin
Type "help", "copyright", "credits" or "license" for more information.
>>> ^D
Dolores:~ bignige$ python3
Python 3.7.3 (v3.7.3:ef4ec6ed12, Mar 25 2019, 16:52:21)
[Clang 6.0 (clang-600.0.57)] on darwin
Type "help", "copyright", "credits" or "license" for more information.
>>>
```

Figure 2-4. *Once Python 3 is installed, run it from the terminal with the* `python3` *command.*

Creating a Python Virtual Environment

When you are writing new software programs, it's possible (and common!) to modify dependencies and environment variables that your other software depends on. This can cause many problems, so should be avoided. A Python virtual environment solves this problem by wrapping all the dependencies and environment variables that your new software needs into a filesystem separate from the rest of the software on your computer.

The virtual environment tool in Python is called `venv`, but before we set up `venv`, we need to create our club site project folder.

Create a Project Folder

Our project folder will house not only our virtual environment, but all the code and media for our Django club site.

The project folder can go anywhere on your computer, although it's highly recommended you create it somewhere in your user directory, so you don't get permission issues later on. A good place for your project in Windows is your *My Documents* folder. On a Mac your *Documents* folder is also a logical choice; however, it can go anywhere in your user directory.

Create a new folder on your system. I have named the folder `myclub_project`, but you can give the folder any name that makes sense to you.

For the next step, you need to be in a command window (terminal on Linux and macOS). The easiest way to do this in Windows is to open Windows Explorer, hold the SHIFT key and right-click the folder to get the context menu and click on **Open command window here** (Figure 2-5).

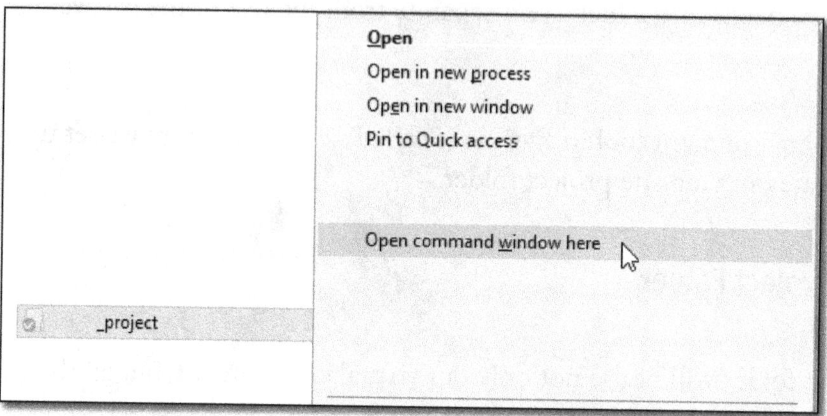

Figure 2-5. Hold the shift key and right-click a folder to open a command window.

Terminal in Windows 10

If you are running newer versions of Windows 10, the command prompt has been replaced by PowerShell. For the examples in this book, the command prompt and PowerShell are functionally the same, and all commands will run in PowerShell unmodified.

Create a Python Virtual Environment

Once you have created your project folder, you need to create a virtual environment for your project by typing the following at the command prompt you just opened:

On Windows

```
...\Documents\myclub_project> python -m venv env_myclub
```

On Mac

```
...$ python3 -m venv env_myclub
```

Remember, you must be inside the project folder!

The function of this command is straightforward—the `-m` option tells Python to run the `venv` module as a script. `venv` in turn requires one parameter: the name of the virtual environment to be created. So this command is saying "create a new Python virtual environment and call it *env_myclub*"

Once `venv` has finished setting up your new virtual environment, it will switch to an empty command prompt. When it's done, open Windows Explorer (Finder on a Mac) and have a look at what `venv` created for you. In your project folder, you will now see a folder called
`\env_myclub` (or whatever name you gave the virtual environment). If you open the folder on Windows, you will see the following:

```
\Include
\Lib
\Scripts
pyvenv.cfg
```

On a Mac, it's:

```
/bin
/Include
/Lib
pyvenv.cfg
```

On either platform, if you look inside the `\Lib` folder, you will see `venv` has created a complete Python installation for you, separate from your other software, so you can work on your project without affecting other software on your system.

To use this new Python virtual environment, we have to activate it, so let's go back to the command prompt and type the following:

On Windows

```
env_myclub\scripts\activate
```

On Mac

```
source env_myclub/bin/activate
```

This will run the activate script inside your virtual environment's `\scripts` folder. You will notice your command prompt has now changed:

```
(env_myclub) ...\Documents\myclub_project>
```

On a Mac, the prompt looks like this:

```
(env_myclub) ... <yourusername>$
```

The `(env_myclub)` at the beginning of the command prompt lets you know that you are running in the virtual environment.

Oops! Script Error!

If you are using PowerShell and running this script for the first time, the `activate` command will throw a permission error.

If this happens to you, open PowerShell as an administrator and run the command:

```
Set-ExecutionPolicy remoteSigned
```

Once you have run this command, the activation script will run.

If you want to exit the virtual environment, you just type `deactivate` at the command prompt:

```
(env_myclub) ...\Documents\myclub_project> deactivate
...\Documents\myclub_project>
```

Installing Django

Mac Users Note

Once Python 3 and the virtual environment are installed, the installation steps for Django are identical on both Windows and macOS.

The critical thing to remember with macOS is that system Python is version 2 and Django requires Python 3, so you *must* be running the Python virtual environment on macOS to run any of the code in this book.

Now we have Python installed and are running a virtual environment, installing Django is super easy, just type the command:

```
pip install "django>=2.2,<3"
```

For Django 3, the command is:

```
pip install "django>=3.0,<4"
```

If you are not familiar with the `pip` command, put briefly, it's the Python package manager and is used to install Python packages. To keep with Python programming tradition, `pip` is a recursive acronym for "Pip Installs Packages".

This will instruct pip to install the latest version of Django 2 or Django 3 into your virtual environment. Your command output should look like this (for Django 2.2):

```
(env_myclub) ...\myclub_project> pip install "django>=2.2,<3.0"
Collecting django<3.0,>=2.2
Downloading .../Django-2.2.12-py3-none-any.whl (7.5MB)
    |################################| 7.5MB 2.2MB/s
Collecting pytz (from django<3.0,>=2.2)
Downloading .../pytz-2020.1-py2.py3-none-any.whl (510kB)
    |################################| 512kB 3.3MB/s
Collecting sqlparse (from django<3.0,>=2.2)
Downloading .../sqlparse-0.3.1-py2.py3-none-any.whl (40kB)
    |################################| 40kB 2.6MB/s
Installing collected packages: pytz, sqlparse, django
Successfully installed django-2.2.12 pytz-2020.1 sqlparse-0.3.1
```

The Django 3 installation output is identical except for the version numbers.

To test the installation, go to your virtual environment command prompt, start the Python interactive interpreter by typing python and hitting Enter. If the installation was successful, you should be able to import the module django:

```
(env_myclub) ...\myclub_project>python
Python 3.8.3 (tags/v3.8.3:6f8c832, May 13 2020, 22:20:19) [MSC
v.1925 32 bit (Intel)] on win32
Type "help", "copyright", "credits" or "license" for more
information.
>>> import django
>>> django.get_version()
'2.2.12' # Your version may be different.
>>> exit()
```

Don't forget to exit the Python interpreter when you are done (you can also use CTRL-Z).

You can also check if Django has been installed directly from the command prompt with:

```
(env_myclub) ...\myclub_project>python -m django --version
2.2.12 # Your version may be different.
```

Starting a Project

Once you've installed Python and Django, you can take the first step in developing a Django application by creating a Django *project*.

A Django project is a collection of settings and files for a single Django website. To create a new Django project, we'll be using a special command to auto-generate the folders, files and code that make up a Django project. This includes a collection of settings for an instance of Django, database configuration, Django-specific options and application-specific settings.

I am assuming you are still running the virtual environment from the previous installation step. If not, start it again with `env_myclub\scripts\activate\`.

From your virtual environment command line, run the following command:

```
(env_myclub) ...>django-admin startproject myclub_site
```

This command will automatically create a `myclub_site` folder in your project folder, and all the necessary files for a basic, but fully functioning Django website. Feel free to explore what `startproject` created now if you wish, however, we will go into greater detail on the structure of a Django project in the next chapter.

Creating a Database

Django includes several applications by default (e.g., the admin program and user management and authentication). Some of these applications make use of at least one database table, so we need to create tables in the project database before we can use them. To do this, change into the `myclub_site` folder created in the last step (type `cd myclub_site` at the command prompt) and run the following command:

```
python manage.py migrate
```

The migrate command creates a new SQLite database and any necessary database tables, according to the settings file created by the `startproject` command (more on the settings file later). If all goes to plan, you'll see a message for each migration it applies:

```
(env_myclub) ...\myclub_site>python manage.py migrate
Operations to perform:
  Apply all migrations: admin, auth, contenttypes, sessions
Running migrations:
  Applying contenttypes.0001_initial... OK
  # several more migrations (not shown)
```

The Development Server

Let's verify your Django project works. Make sure you are in the outer `myclub_site` directory and run the following command:

```
python manage.py runserver
```

This will start the Django development server—a lightweight Web server written in Python. The development server was created so you can develop things rapidly, without having to deal with configuring a production server until you're ready for deployment.

When the server starts, Django will output a few messages before telling you that the development server is up and running at `http://127.0.0.1:8000/`. If you were wondering, 127.0.0.1 is the IP address for localhost, or your local computer. The 8000 on the end is telling you that Django is listening at port 8000 on your local host.

You can change the port number if you want to, but I have never found a good reason to change it, so best to keep it simple and leave it at the default.

Now that the server is running, visit `http://127.0.0.1:8000/` with your web browser. You'll see Django's default welcome page, complete with a cool animated rocket (Figure 2-6).

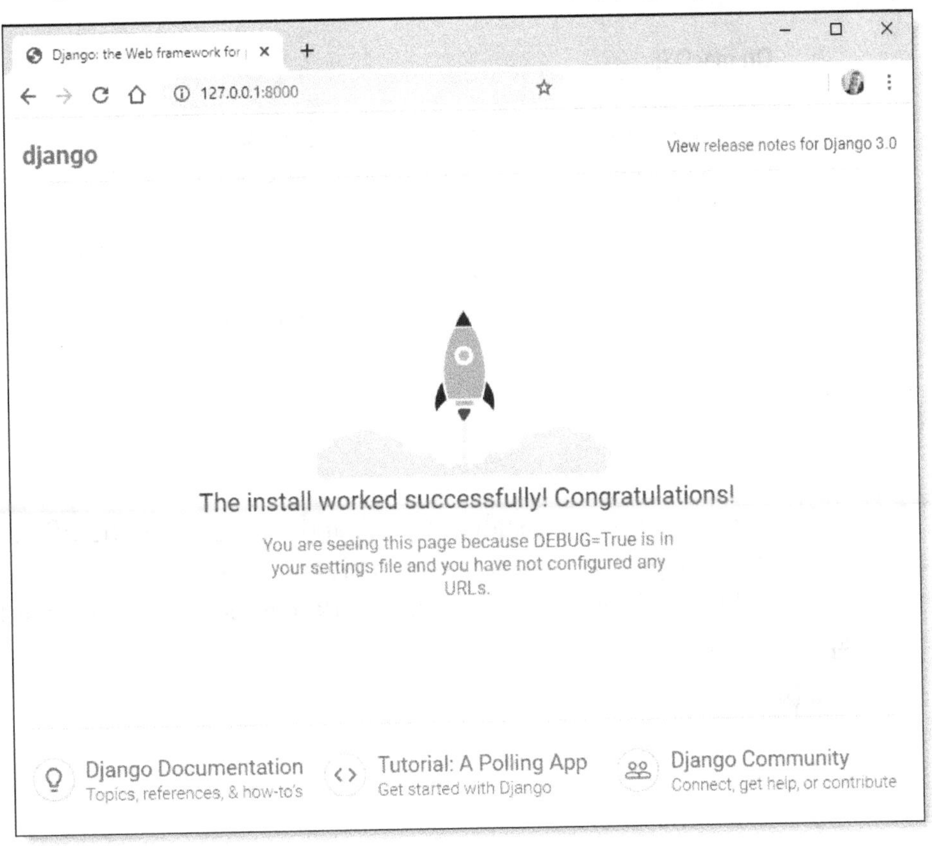

Figure 2-6. *Django's welcome page. The welcome page is the same for Django 2 and 3.*

TIP: Remember the Startup Sequence

It will help to make a note of this sequence, so you know how to start your Django project each time you return to the examples in this book:

On Windows:

1. Shift right-click your project folder to open a command window.
2. Type in `env_myclub\scripts\activate` to run your virtual environment.
3. Change into your site directory (`cd myclub_site`) to run `manage.py` commands (e.g., `runserver`).
4. Type `deactivate` to exit the virtual environment.

On macOS:

1. CTRL-click your project folder to open a terminal window.
2. Type in `source env_myclub/bin/activate` to run your virtual environment.
3. Change into your site directory (`cd myclub_site`) to run `manage.py` commands (e.g., `runserver`).
4. Type `deactivate` to exit the virtual environment.

Chapter Summary

In this chapter, I showed you how to install Python 3 and Django on both Windows and macOS. In the next chapter, we will step back a bit and have a big-picture look at Django's structure and how all the parts of Django work together to create powerful, scalable web applications.

3

The Big Picture

Django's Structure—A Heretic's Eye View

The most common complaints from those new to Django is "it's too hard to understand", or "it's too complex". You may even be thinking this yourself right now.

At the fundamental level, Django isn't complicated. Yes, it has its quirks and, yes, big Django projects can be very complex beasts, but bottom line: Django is a logically structured framework built on the easiest to learn programming language available (Python).

As an educator, I have spent countless hours trying to work out why people find Django complex and hard to learn. Thinking on this has led me to commit heresy #1: it's not your fault, we've just been teaching it wrong.

Remember all the books and tutorials that start with "Django is a Model-View-Controller (MVC) framework..."? (This is cut and paste from one of my books, so I am as guilty as anyone in this).

Stating up front that Django is an MVC framework gets one of two responses:

1. Beginners say "What the heck is MVC? *groan*. Guess that's one more fricking thing I have to learn!"

2. More experienced programmers say "Aha! It's just like Framework X."

In both cases, they're almost entirely wrong.

Django is a Loosely Coupled Framework

If you can indulge me a minute, and purge your brain of your favorite Three Letter Acronyms (TLAs), there's an easier way to understand this.

The first step is to understand that Django is not the result of an academic exercise, nor is it some guru's idea of cool—Django's creators designed Django to solve a particular set of problems in a busy and complex news organization. At the center of this set of problems were three very different needs:

1. The data guys (and gals) needed a common interface to work with disparate data sources, formats and database software.
2. The design teams needed to manage the user experience with the tools they already had (HTML, CSS, JavaScript etc.).
3. The hard-core coders required a framework that allowed them to deploy system changes rapidly and keep everyone happy.

Crucial to making this all work was ensuring each of these core components—data, design and business logic—could be managed independently, or to use the correct computer parlance—the framework had to employ *loose coupling*.

Now, it's important to understand that I'm not trying to say Django is doing anything magic or new here, nor were the problems Django's creators faced unique. The creators of Django are brilliant guys, and they certainly knew MVC was a well-established design pattern that would help solve their problems.

My point is it's highly unlikely any of them ever said, "Hang on boys, we need to change this code because Wikipedia says a controller should ...".

You need not get hung up on semantics—you can safely forget about the confusing TLAs and whether Django is like Framework X and concentrate on what Django is.

Django's architecture comprises three major parts:

- **Part 1** is a set of tools that make working with data and databases much easier.
- **Part 2** is a plain-text template system suitable for non-programmers; and
- **Part 3** is a framework that handles communication between the user and the database and automates many of the painful parts of managing a complex website.

Parts 1 and 2 are instantly relatable:

- **Django Models** are the tools we use to work with data and databases; and
- **Django Templates** provide a designer-friendly plain-text template system.

But what about Part 3? I hear you ask, isn't that the controller, or a Django view?

Well, no. Which leads me to heresy #2:

A Django View is Not a Controller

Check out Figure 3-1 on the next page, does it look familiar?

This is one of my diagrams, but there are plenty of similar versions out there. A common way of explaining Django's architecture in terms of MVC is to describe it as a Model-Template-View (MTV) or Model-View-Template (MVT). There's no difference between MTV and MVT—they're two different ways to describe the same thing, which adds to the confusion.

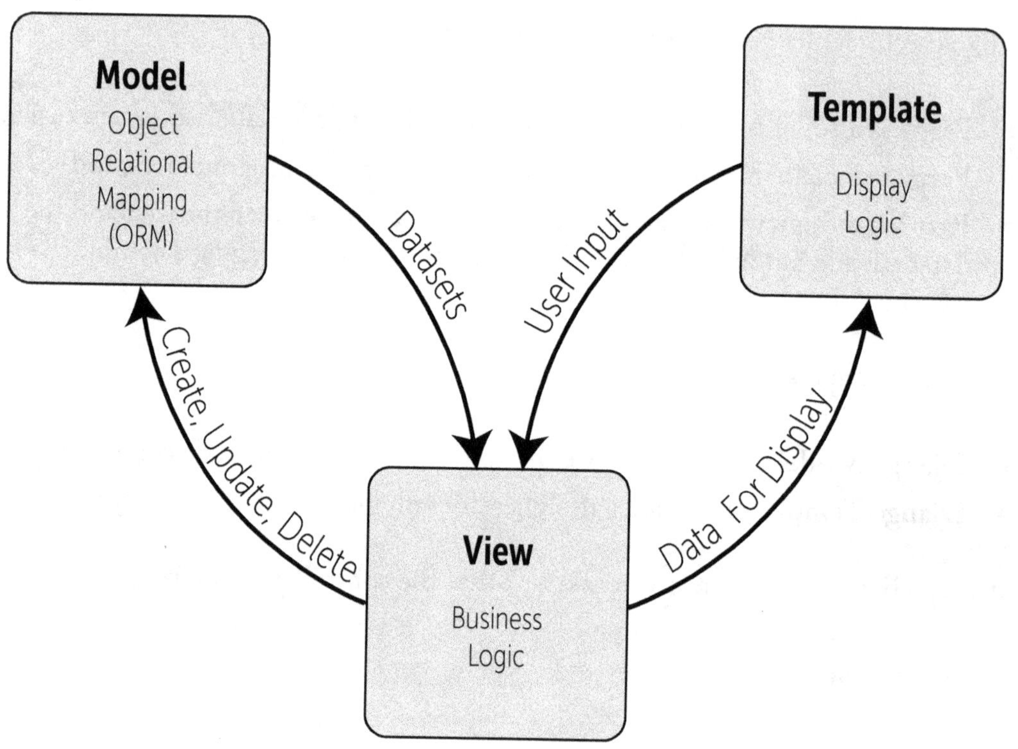

Figure 3-1. *The somewhat misleading Django MTV diagram.*

The misleading part of this diagram is the view. The view in Django is most often described as being equivalent to the controller in MVC, but it's not—it's still the view.

Figure 3-2 is a variation on Figure 3-1 to illustrate my point.

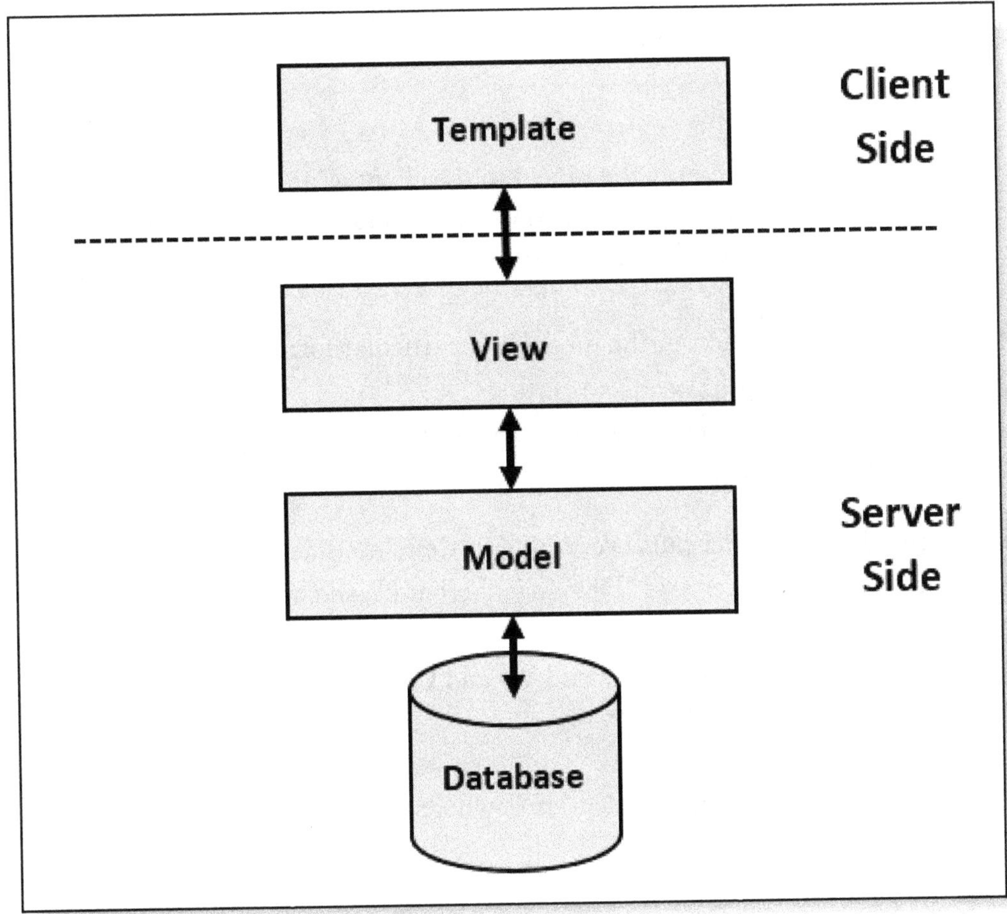

Figure 3-2. *A slightly different view of Django's MTV "stack".*

Note how I have drawn a line between the client- and server-side.

Like all client/server architectures, Django uses request and response objects to communicate between the client and the server. As Django is a web framework, we're talking about `HTTP` request and response objects.

So, in this simplified process, the view retrieves data from the database via the model, formats it, bundles it up in an HTTP response object and sends it to the client (browser).

In other words, the view presents the model to the client as an HTTP response. This is also the *exact* definition of the view in MVC, or to quote Wikipedia (not the most definitive source, I know, but close enough):

"The view means presentation of the model in a particular format"

Trying to bend the definition of a Django view to fit a particular viewpoint inevitably leads to one of two things:

1. Confused programmer puts everything in views module; or
2. Confused programmer says "Django is too hard!", and watches TV instead.

So getting away from our M's and T's and V's and C's, Figure 3-3 presents a more holistic view of Django's architecture.

The first point of confusion we can clear up is where to put a particular function or class:

Does the function/class return a response?

- **YES**—it's a view. Put it in the views module (`views.py`).
- **NO**—it's not a view, it's app logic. Put it somewhere else (`somewhere_else.py`).

We'll discuss the somewhere else part in the next section of this chapter.

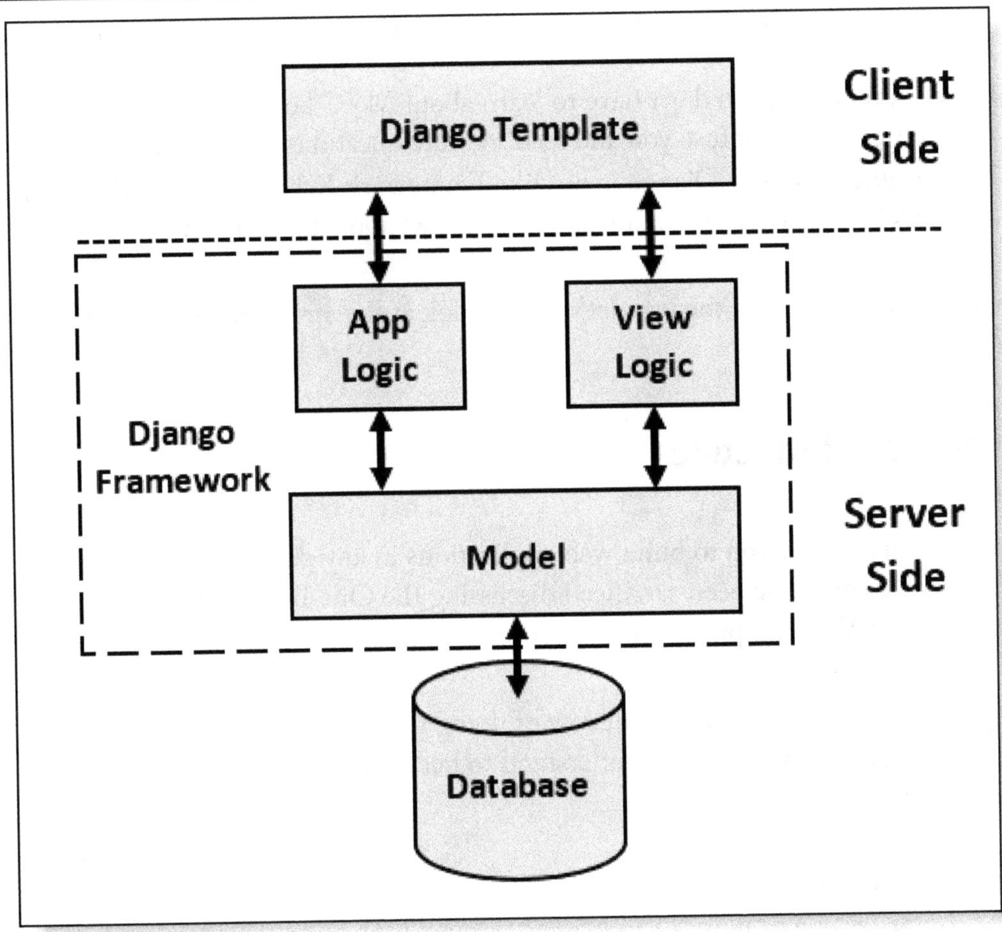

Figure 3-3. A more holistic view of Django's architecture.

The next point to note is that the Django framework encapsulates the model, view logic and business logic. In some tutorials, it's said that the Django framework is the controller, but that isn't true either—the Django framework can do much more than respond to user input and interact with data.

A perfect example of this extra power is Django's middleware, which sits between the view and the client-side. Django's middleware performs critical security and authentication checks before sending the response to the browser.

So, returning to the two confused responses from the beginning of the chapter:

1. **Beginners**—no, you don't have to learn about MVC because it's more than likely going to confuse you and lead to more questions than answers.
2. **Programmers**—no, Django is not like Framework X, and trying to think it is, is likely to confuse you and lead to more questions than answers.

Now we've got that out of the way, let's have a look at the structure of a Django project.

Django Project Structure

Django doesn't require you to build web applications in any particular way. In fact, billions of electrons have been sacrificed discussing the One Best Way to structure a Django project. We're all pragmatic programmers here, so we won't play that game.

Django does, however, have a default way of doing things, and there is a definite underlying logic to it you need to understand to become a professional Django programmer.

The fundamental unit of a Django web application is a Django project. A Django project comprises one or more Django apps (Figure 3-4)

A Django app is a self-contained package that should only do one thing. For example, a blog, a membership app or an event calendar. Notice at the bottom of Figure 3-4, there's an extra package called Django Apps.

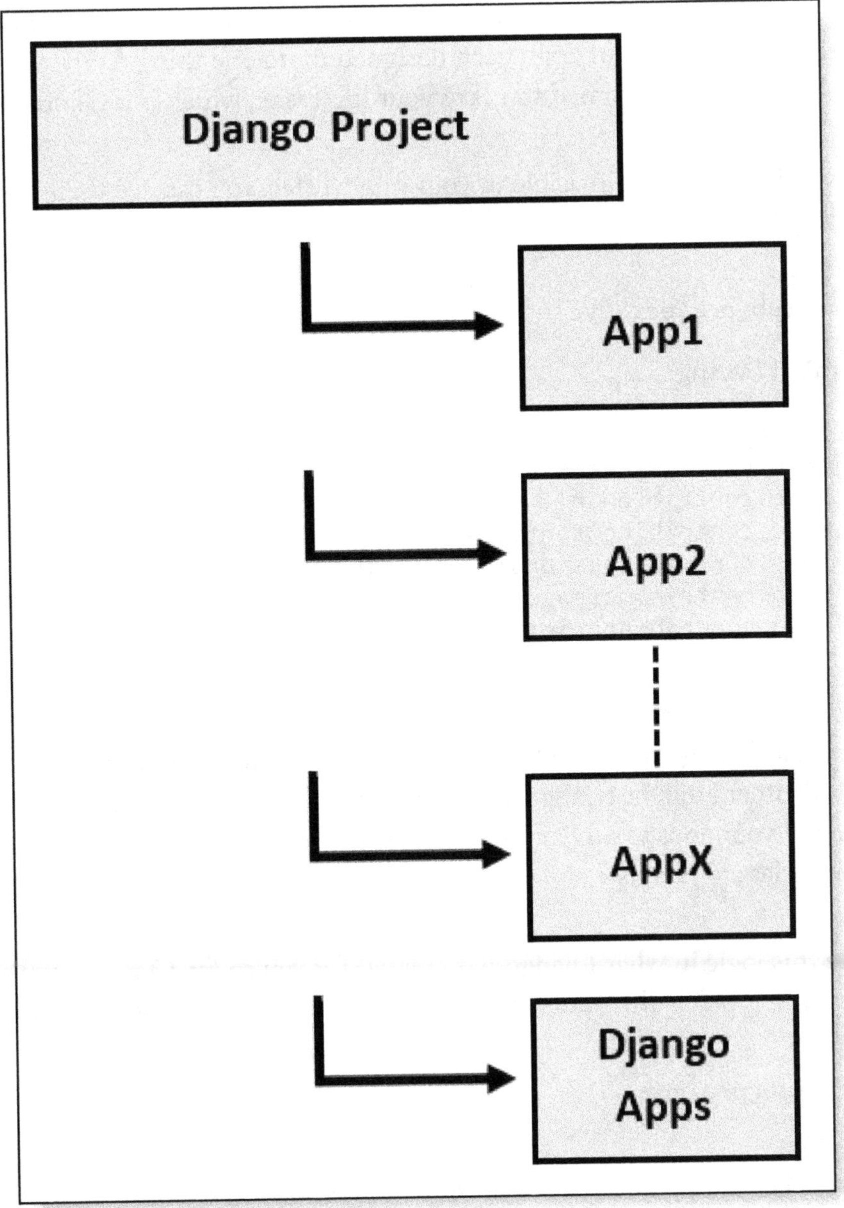

***Figure 3-4.** Django's project structure.*

This is another case where Django's logic carries right through the framework—Django itself is a collection of apps, each designed to do one thing. With Django's built-in apps, they're all designed to make your life easier, which is a Good Thing.

While the built-in apps are invisible in your project tree, you can see them in your `settings.py` file:

```
# ...\myclub_project\myclub_site\myclub_site\settings.py

# partial listing

INSTALLED_APPS = [
    'django.contrib.admin',
    'django.contrib.auth',
    'django.contrib.contenttypes',
    'django.contrib.sessions',
    'django.contrib.messages',
    'django.contrib.staticfiles',
]
```

You can see that Django has added several apps to your project automatically. There are also many other built-in Django apps you can add to the `INSTALLED_APPS` list. When you add your apps to a Django project, you also add a link to the app configuration class to this list.

You can see this logic in what Django has created for you so far. Open up your `\myclub_project` folder. The folder structure should look something like this:

```
# ...\myclub_project

\env_myclub
\myclub_site          <= This is your Django project
    \myclub_site      <= This is a Django app
    db.sqlite3        <= Your project database
    manage.py         <= Django project management utility
```

Let's examine these files and folders in more detail:

- The **env_myclub** folder is where Django stores your virtual environment files. Generally, you should leave everything inside this folder alone.
- The outer **myclub_site** folder is your Django project. Django created this folder and its contents when you ran the `startproject` command in the last chapter. Django doesn't care about the folder name, so you can rename it to something meaningful to you.
- Inside the outer `myclub_site` folder are two files:
  - **db.sqlite3**. The database created when you ran the `migrate` command; and
  - **manage.py**. A command-line utility for executing Django commands from within your project.
- The inner **myclub_site** folder is your Django website application. This is the one application that Django creates automatically for you. Because Django is a web framework, it assumes you want a website app.

This should make more sense by now, but I bet there is one thing that's still a bit confusing—the two `myclub_site` folders.

A very common complaint from programmers new to Django is how confusing it is to know which folder they should work in when there are two folders named the same. Django is not alone with this convention—Integrated Development Environments (IDEs) like Visual Studio create a project folder and application folder with the same name. But just because it's common, that doesn't mean it isn't confusing.

As I said a moment ago, Django doesn't care what you name this folder—so let's commit heresy #3, breaking thirteen years of Django tutorial convention while we are at it, and rename the folder!

Here, we're renaming it to "myclub_root".

Once you have made the change, your folder structure should go from this:

```
\myclub_project
    \myclub_site
        \myclub_site
```

To this:

```
\myclub_project
    \myclub_root
        \myclub_site
```

Now we've taken care of that source of confusion, let's have a look inside the `myclub_site` website app Django created for us:

```
# \myclub_project\myclub_root\

\myclub_site
    __init.py__
    asgi.py # Django 3 only
    settings.py
    urls.py
    wsgi.py
```

Looking closer at these files:

- The **`__init__.py`** file tells Python that this folder (your Django app) is a Python package.
- **`asgi.py`** enables ASGI compatible web servers to serve your project (Django 3 only).
- **`settings.py`** contains the settings for your Django project. Every Django project must have a settings file. By convention, Django puts it in your website app, but it doesn't have to live there. There are proponents for other structures as I mentioned earlier, but here we're using the default.

- **`urls.py`** contains project-level URL configurations. By default, this contains a single URL pattern for the admin. We will cover more on URLs later in the chapter, and in great detail in Chapter 5.
- **`wsgi.py`** enables WSGI compatible web servers to serve your project.

Now that we've had a good look at the basic structure of a Django project, it's time to take the next step and add our own Django app.

Creating Your Own Django Apps

You might have noticed that there is no real program code in your project so far. There is a settings file with configuration information, an almost empty URLs file, and a command-line utility that launches a website that doesn't do much.

This is because to create a functioning Django website, you need to create *Django applications*. A Django application (or app for short) is where the work gets done. Apps are one of Django's killer features. Not only do they allow you to add functionality to a Django project without interfering with other parts of the project, but apps are designed to be portable so you can use one app in multiple projects.

So, let's create our first custom Django app. Our social club website needs an events calendar to show upcoming events for the club, so we're creating a Django app called `events`.

Fire up your Python virtual environment, switch into the `\myclub_root` folder and run the command:

```
python manage.py startapp events
```

This is what your command shell output should look like:

```
(env_myclub) ...> cd myclub_root
```

```
(env_myclub) ...\myclub_root> python manage.py startapp events
(env_myclub) ...\myclub_root>
```

Once you have created your app, you must tell Django to install it into your project. This is easy to do—inside your `settings.py` file is a list named `INSTALLED_APPS`. This list contains all the apps installed in your Django project. Django comes with a few apps pre-installed, we just have to add your new `events` app to the list (change in bold):

```
1 INSTALLED_APPS = [
2     'events.apps.EventsConfig',
3     'django.contrib.admin',
4     # more apps
5 ]
```

Inside every app, Django creates a file, `apps.py`, containing a configuration class named after your app. Here, the class is named `EventsConfig`. To register our app with Django, we need to point to the `EventsConfig` class—which is what we are doing in **line 2** of our modified `INSTALLED_APPS` list.

If you were wondering, `EventsConfig` contains a single configuration option by default—the name of the app ("events").

Line Numbering in Code Examples

Throughout the book, I use line numbering to make it easier for you to follow along with the explanations.

As I often use code snippets from your application files, the line numbering in the example is not the same as the line numbering in the actual source code file.

Now let's look inside the `\myclub_root` folder to see what Django has created for us:

```
\events
    \migrations
    __init__.py
    admin.py
    apps.py
    models.py
    tests.py
    views.py
```

- The **`migrations`** folder is where Django stores migrations, or changes to your database. There's nothing in here you need to worry about right now.
- **`__init__.py`** tells Python that your `events` app is a package.
- **`admin.py`** is where you register your app's models with the Django admin application.
- **`apps.py`** is a configuration file common to all Django apps.
- **`models.py`** is the module containing the models for your app.
- **`tests.py`** contains test procedures that run when testing your app.
- **`views.py`** is the module containing the views for your app.

Now we have a complete picture of a Django project, we can also answer the question from earlier in the chapter: "well, if it's not a view, where does it go?"

When you have code that isn't a view, you create a new Python module (`.py` file) inside your app and put *related* functions and classes inside the file. Note the emphasis on related. If you have a bunch of functions that provide database management utilities, for example, put them all in one file. Functions and classes not related to database management should go in another file. You should also try to be descriptive in naming modules—after all, it's more sensible to put your database functions in a file called `db_utils.py` than a file called `monkeys.py`...

When creating new modules for your Django project, you should also consider scope. While adding custom modules to apps is far more common (and more portable), you can have project-level modules (e.g., Django's `manage.py`) and site-level modules. In the latter case, your custom modules should go in the same folder as your `settings.py` file.

The last couple of points might seem blindingly obvious, but it's important to understand that, while Django has a default logic to its structure, nothing is cast in stone. Django is flexible and allows you to expand and change your project structure to suit the logic of your web application.

Now we have a thorough understanding of the structure of Django's projects and apps, the next obvious question, given we are building web applications is "how do we navigate a Django project?"

To answer this question, we need to check out the final piece of the Django big picture puzzle—URL configurations.

URLconfs—Django's Navigator

There's one last piece to the Django framework puzzle—the critical communication pathway that matches a request on the client-side with a project resource (the arrows between the view and the template in Figure 3-3). Like all web applications, Django uses Uniform Resource Locators (URLs) to match content with a request.

Django's `urls` package provides dozens of functions and classes for working with different URL formats, name resolution, exception handling and other navigational utilities. However, at its most basic, it allows you to map a URL to a function or class within your Django project.

A Django URL configuration (or URLconf for short) matches a unique URL with a project resource. You can think of it being like matching a person's name with their address. Except in Django, we're not matching a street address—we're matching a Python path using Python's *dot notation*.

Assuming you're not familiar with dot notation, it's a common idiom in object-oriented programming. I like to think of the dot like a point because the dot points to something. With Python, the dot operator points to the next object in the object chain.

In Django classes, the object chain is like this:

```
package.module.class.method
```

Or with functions:

```
package.module.function.attribute
```

Some real-life examples:

- `forms.Form` points to the `Form` class in the `forms` package.
- `events.apps.EventsConfig` points to the `EventsConfig` class in the `apps` sub-package of the events package (i.e., the `apps.py` file in your `events` app).
- `django.conf.urls` points to the `urls` package inside the `conf` package inside Django, which is also a Python package!

This can sometimes get a bit confusing, but if you remember to join the dots (sorry, a bad pun there), you can usually find out what the dot operator is referring to.

With a URLconf, the path points to a function or class inside a module (`.py` file). Let's look at our Django project diagram again (Figure 3-5).

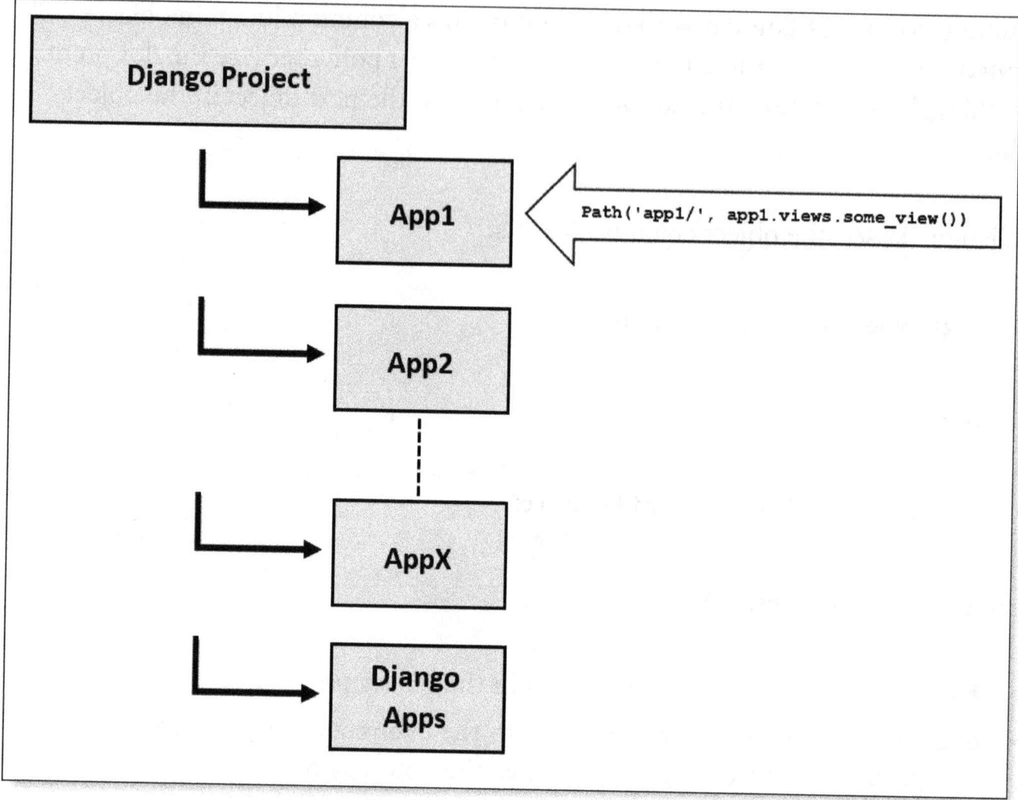

Figure 3-5. Finding functions and classes with Django's URLconfs.

To create a URLconf, we use the `path()` function. The first part of the function is the URL, so in Figure 3-5 the URL is `app1/`. The `path()` function then maps this URL to `app1.views.some_view()`.

Assuming your site address is `http://www.mycoolsite.com`, in plain English we're saying:

"When someone navigates to `http://www.mycoolsite.com/app1/`, run the `some_view()` function inside `app1`'s `views.py` file"

Note a URL doesn't have to map to a view—it can map to any module in your Django app. For example, you may have a set of wireless environmental sensors that post data back to the server. You could have a custom module called `sensors.py` that has a function or class to record the sensor data to your database, all without ever touching a view.

And that's all there is to it. Of course, URLconfs can do a lot more than map a static URL to a function or class, but if you can understand the basics—that Django's incredibly fast and powerful navigation system is based on the simple concept of matching a URL with a resource—then you have all you need to tie all your Django apps together into a navigable web project.

A Final Note on Writing Django Apps

A common and inevitable question arises once you get your head around Django's basic structure:

"Where do I start? Should I start with writing my models, the URL configurations, my views? Or what?"

Well, here's your final heresy for the chapter: *it doesn't matter*.

Some people like to start by building all the models so they can see how the data structure looks; others prefer to build the visual layout first, so they start with templates. Others might like to get the basic communication framework in place, so they start with views and URLconfs. Others will start at whatever point seems logical for the project.

Being pragmatic to the bone, I am usually in the last group. I try not to get fixated on what someone else thinks is the right or the wrong way to do things and try to find the simplest and quickest way to achieve the result I want. I also like to work incrementally starting small getting the flow right and building on it to create the complete application. This approach means I inevitably end up jumping from one element to another as the application grows.

Your brain is wired differently to mine and every other programmer. This is a Good Thing. Just remember, an imperfect start to a project is *way* better than not starting at all. Do what works for you.

Chapter Summary

In this chapter, I gave you a high-level overview of how Django projects are structured, how each component works with other parts of Django to create a web application, and how to create a Django app.

In the next chapter, we will start diving into the inner working of Django's core modules by exploring the fundamentals of Django's models.

4

Django's Models

Unless you are creating a simple website, there is little chance of avoiding the need to interact with some form of database when building modern web applications.

Unfortunately, this usually means you have to get your hands dirty with Structured Query Language (SQL)—which is just about nobody's idea of fun. In Django, the messy issues with SQL is a solved problem: you don't have to use SQL at all unless you want to. Instead, you use a Django *model* to access the database.

Django's models provide an *Object-relational Mapping* (ORM) to the underlying database. ORM is a powerful programming technique that makes working with data and relational databases much easier.

Most common databases are programmed with some form of SQL, but each database implements SQL in its own way. SQL can also be complicated and difficult to learn. An ORM tool simplifies database programming by providing a simple mapping between an object (the 'O' in ORM) and the underlying database. This means the programmer need not know the database structure, nor does it require complex SQL to manipulate and retrieve data (Figure 4-1).

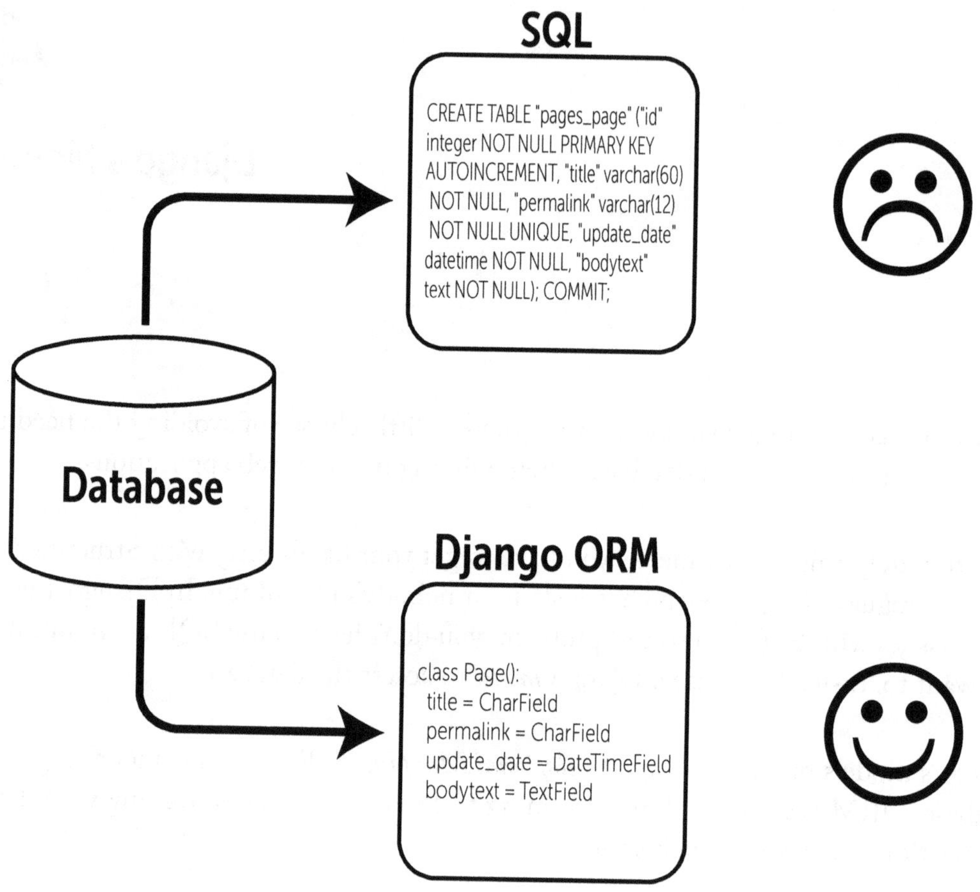

***Figure 4-1.** An ORM allows for simple manipulation of data without having to write complex SQL.*

In Django, the model is the object mapped to the database. When you create a model, Django executes SQL to create a corresponding table in the database (Figure 4-2) without you having to write a single line of SQL. Django prefixes the table name with the name of your Django application. The model also links related information in the database.

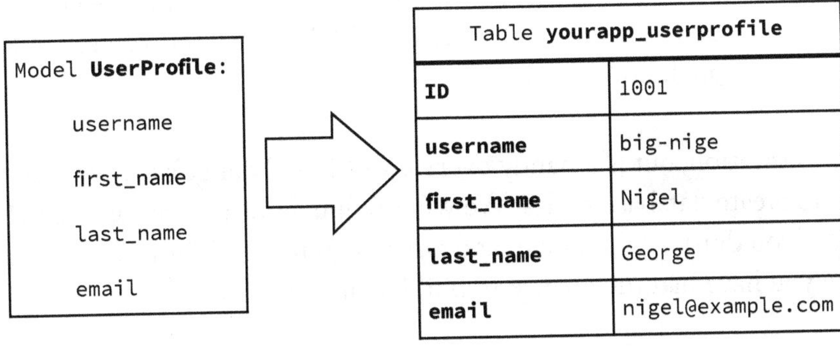

Figure 4-2. Creating a Django model creates a corresponding table in the database.

In Figure 4-3, a second model keeps track of a user's course enrollments. Repeating all the user's information in the `yourapp_Course` table would be against sound design principles, so we instead create a relationship (the 'R' in ORM) between the `yourapp_Course` table and the `yourapp_UserProfile` table.

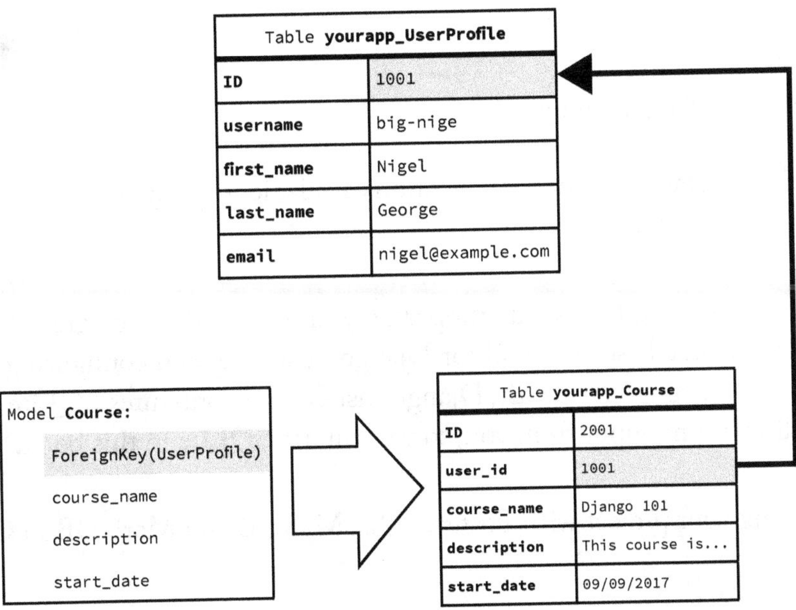

Figure 4-3. Foreign key links in Django models create relationships between tables.

This relationship is created by linking the models with a foreign key—i.e., the `user_id` field in the `yourapp_Course` table is a key field linked to the `id` field in the foreign table `yourapp_UserProfile`.

This is a simplification, but is a handy overview of how Django's ORM uses the model data to create database tables. We will dig much deeper into models shortly, so don't worry if you don't 100% understand what is going on right now. Things become clearer once you have had the chance to build actual models.

Supported Databases

Django officially supports five databases:

- PostgreSQL
- MySQL
- SQLite
- Oracle
- MariaDB (Django 3 only)

There are also several third-party applications available if you need to connect to an unofficially supported database.

The preference for most Django developers, myself included, is PostgreSQL. MySQL is also a common database back end for Django. Installing and configuring a database is not a task for a beginner. Luckily, Django installs and configures SQLite automatically, with no input from you, so we will use SQLite in this book.

I cover running your project with PostgreSQL, MySQL and MariaDB in Chapter 16.

Which Database is Better?

Easy one first—SQLite is for early development and testing. Do not use in production. Ever.

Next easiest answer—Oracle is for big corporations with deep pockets. You are unlikely to need to decide whether to use Oracle unless you join a big enterprise, and then you might find it's your only choice.

As for PostgreSQL, MariaDB (Django 3) and MySQL, there are specific reasons PostgreSQL is a better database than MySQL. However, by the time you have learned enough programming to understand why, you can judge for yourself. Most often, you don't get a choice because the client, your employer or the web host makes it for you.

MariaDB is a fork of MySQL. Other than reminding you that it only works with Django 3 and up, my advice is the same as MySQL.

Smart programmers avoid this kind of argument—use PostgreSQL if you can; otherwise, MySQL or MariaDB are fine too.

Defining Models in Python

Django's models are written in Python and provide a mapping to the underlying database structure. Django uses a model to execute SQL behind the scenes to return Python data structures—which Django calls *QuerySets*.

Writing models in Python has several advantages:

- **Simplicity**. Writing Python is not only easier than writing SQL, but it's less error-prone and more efficient as your brain doesn't have to keep switching from one language to another.
- **Consistency**. As I mentioned earlier, SQL is inconsistent across different databases. You want to describe your data once, not create separate sets of SQL statements for each database to which the application will be deployed.

- **Avoids Introspection.** Any application has to know something about the underlying database structure. There are only two ways to do that: have an explicit description of the data in the application code, or introspect the database at runtime. As introspection has a high overhead and is not perfect, Django's creators chose the first option.
- **Version Control.** Storing models in your codebase makes it easier to keep track of design changes.
- **Advanced Metadata.** Having models described in code rather than SQL allows for special data-types (e.g., email addresses), and provides the ability to store much more metadata than SQL.

A drawback is the database can get out of sync with your models, but Django takes care of this problem with *migrations*. You've already used migrations in Chapter 2 when you created the MyClub application. We'll be using them again shortly when we create the `Event` model.

Also note you can introspect an existing database with Django using the `inspectdb` management command. We'll be diving deeper into introspecting existing databases in Chapter 16.

Your First Model

Now you have an idea what Django models are, it's time to create your first model.

The MyClub website application includes an event planner. In the last chapter, we created the `events` app to manage events within our MyClub web application. If you haven't created the `events` app yet, you need to go back to page 39 and create it now.

There is lots of information we can record for a club event, but we will start with a basic event model. When you are first designing a data model, it's always an excellent idea to map out the table fields before you create the model.

DB Browser for SQLite

Throughout this chapter, and in a few other chapters, I will use an application called *DB Browser for SQLite*. This is an excellent tool for checking out what is going on inside your SQLite database as Django changes things.

If you want to install DB Browser for SQLite on your machine, you can download it from `https://sqlitebrowser.org/`.

There are many approaches to mapping out data structures—from simple tables to complex data maps using special markup. As you have probably worked out by now, my preference is to keep things as simple as possible, so I tend just to use tables (Table 4-1).

Field Name	Field Description	Data Type
`name`	Name of the event	Short Text
`date`	Date and time of the event	Date/Time
`venue`	Location of the event	Short Text
`manager`	Name of the person managing the event	Short Text
`description`	Detailed description of the event	Long Text

Table 4-1. *A simple mapping of our event model fields.*

This should be straightforward—we have database-friendly names for the fields, a description of the field, and the data-type to save to the field in the database. The description is for your benefit when you come back to the model later and need to remind yourself what the field was for. You can also put the field description in your model as comments or in the model's docstring. We won't be adding comments or docstrings to our code in this book; just keep it in mind for when you become a professional programmer—properly documenting your code is a Good Thing.

Now, let's turn our table into a Django model. Open the `models.py` file in your `events` folder and add the following model code:

```
# \myclub_root\events\models.py

1 from django.db import models
2
3 class Event(models.Model):
4     name = models.CharField('Event Name', max_length=120)
5     event_date = models.DateTimeField('Event Date')
6     venue = models.CharField(max_length=120)
7     manager = models.CharField(max_length=60)
8     description = models.TextField(blank=True)
```

Let's have a closer look at your first model, as a fair bit is going on here:

- **Line 1** imports the `models` package from `django.db`. If you used `startapp`, this line will already be in your file.
- **Line 3** is the `Event` class definition. Each Django model must inherit from Django's `Model` class.

Each of our model fields has a related Django *field type* and *field options*. The `Event` model uses three different field types—`CharField`, `DateTimeField` and `TextField`. Let's have a look at the field types and options in more detail:

- **Line 4**. The `name` field is a Django `CharField`. A `CharField` is a short line of text (up to 255 characters). Here, the `max_length` option sets the maximum length of the event name to 120 characters. The `name` field also has a *verbose name* argument. The verbose name is used to create a human-friendly name for the model field. Most model fields accept verbose name, either as the first positional argument or as a keyword argument (`verbose_name`).
- **Line 5**. `event_date` is a Django `DateTimeField`. A `DateTimeField` records a Python `datetime` object. The `event_date` field has a single argument—the verbose name for the field. Note that I have named the field `event_date`, rather than just `date`. This is to avoid confusion with Python's `date()` function.

Django will let you use function names and Python reserved words in field names, but it's always best not to.

- **Lines 6 and 7.** `venue` and `manager` are both Django `CharFields`. As the `max_length` argument is required on `CharFields`, `max_length` is set to limit the size of the field.
- **Line 8.** `description` is a Django `TextField`. A `TextField` is a large text field that can hold many thousands of characters (maximum depends on the database). The final option—`blank=True`—is set so we can create an event without a detailed description. The default for this option is `False`; if you don't add a description, Django will throw an error.

This simple event model only uses a small subset of the model field types and options available in Django. We'll be using many more throughout the book. There is also a complete reference to all the model fields and options in the Django documentation[1].

Now we've created the model, it's time to add it to the database. Make sure the virtual environment is running and then change into the `myclub_root` directory. From your command prompt, run:

```
python manage.py makemigrations
```

Hit enter and then run the command:

```
python manage.py migrate
```

Your terminal output should look something like this:

```
(env_myclub) ...\myclub_root> python manage.py makemigrations
Migrations for 'events':
  events\migrations\0001_initial.py
  - Create model Event
(env_myclub) ...\myclub_root> python manage.py migrate
Operations to perform:
  Apply all migrations: events
Running migrations:
```

1 https://docs.djangoproject.com/en/dev/ref/models/fields/

```
Applying events.0001_initial... OK
```

This is all you need to do to add your new model to the database. Before we go on though, remember how I said Django uses the model to generate SQL? Try this command at your command prompt:

```
python manage.py sqlmigrate events 0001_initial
```

You should get an output that looks like this (I've reformatted the output for clarity):

```
BEGIN;
--
-- Create model Event
--
CREATE TABLE "events_event" (
    "id" integer NOT NULL PRIMARY KEY AUTOINCREMENT,
    "name" varchar(120) NOT NULL,
    "event_date" datetime NOT NULL,
    "venue" varchar(120) NOT NULL,
    "manager" varchar(60) NOT NULL,
    "description" text NOT NULL
);
COMMIT;
```

The `sqlmigrate` command prints the SQL for the named migration. Here, it's printing out the SQL for the initial migration, where Django creates the new table and adds the fields to the table.

We can check out what Django created in the database browser (Figure 4-4).

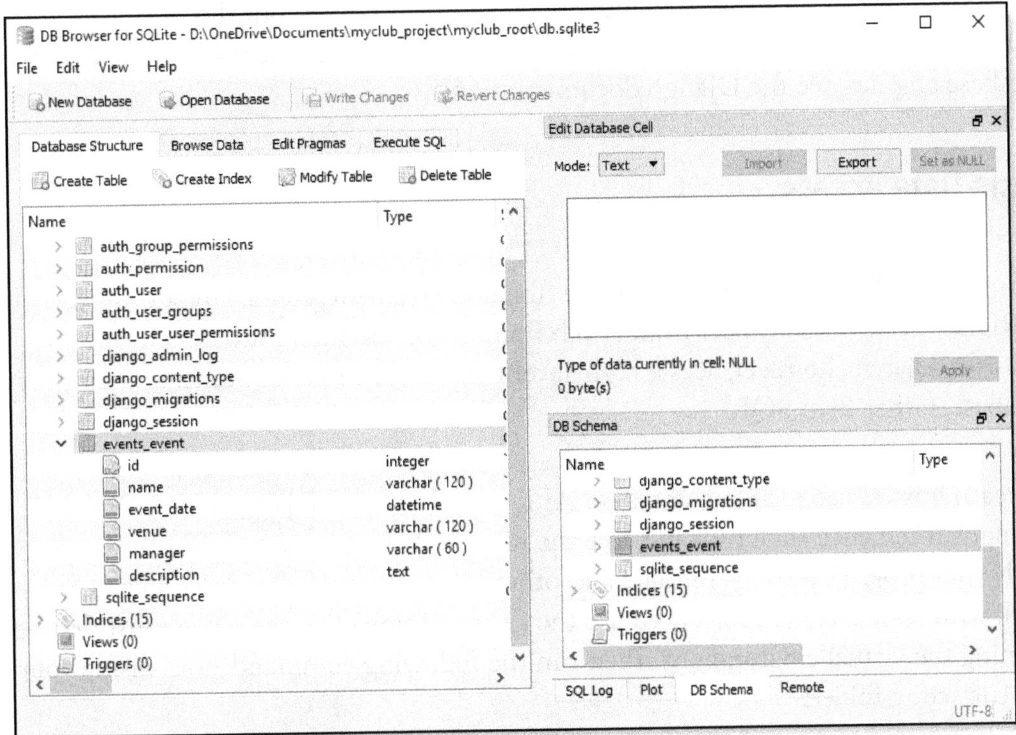

Figure 4-4. *The event table in the database.*

You can see Django's `app_model` naming convention for table names at work in the table name (`events_event`). Also, note how each model field is added as a table field with the appropriate data-type applied. If you are using DB Browser for SQLite, you will also notice the schema for the table is almost the same as the SQL the `sqlmigrate` command printed out.

Finally, note that the SQL, data-types and database schema are different for each database type. This is what's so cool about Django's models—most of the time, you don't have to worry about the underlying database when creating your models.

There are some quirks relating to individual database engines, but this is advanced stuff beyond the scope of this book. If you want to check out the notes on individual database engines, see the Django documentation[2].

Basic Data Access

Django provides the four basic database functions—Create, Read, Update and Delete (CRUD)—you would expect from a web framework designed for data-driven websites. Django, however, uses a high-level Python API to communicate with your database, rather than SQL.

To learn how to use Django's database API, we will use the Django interactive shell. Django's interactive shell runs just like the regular Python interactive shell, except it loads your project's settings module and other Django-specific modules so you can work with your Django project. To use the Django interactive shell, you must first be running the virtual environment. Then run the following command from inside your `myclub_root` folder:

```
python manage.py shell
```

Your terminal output should look like this:

```
(env_myclub) ...\myclub_root> python manage.py shell
Python 3.8.3 (tags/v3.8.3:6f8c832, May 13 2020, 22:20:19) [MSC v.1925
32 bit (Intel)] on win32
Type "help", "copyright", "credits" or "license" for more information.
(InteractiveConsole)
>>>
```

While this looks the same as the Python interactive shell, you can do things like this:

```
>>> from events.models import Event
```

2 https://docs.djangoproject.com/en/dev/ref/databases/

If you try to do this in the standard Python interactive shell, you will get an error because the basic Python shell won't load Django or your project.

Creating Database Records

To create a new event, you must first create a new `event` object:

```
>>> from events.models import Event
>>> event1 = Event(
...     name="Test Event1",
...     event_date="2020-05-22",
...     venue="test venue",
...     manager="Bob"
... )
>>>
```

You can see I have imported the `Event` model class and have created a new `Event` object and named it `event1`. Before we move on, have a look at the database (Figure 4-5). You'll notice Django hasn't saved the object to the database yet. This is by design. Accessing a database is expensive time-wise, so Django doesn't hit the database until you explicitly tell Django to save the object.

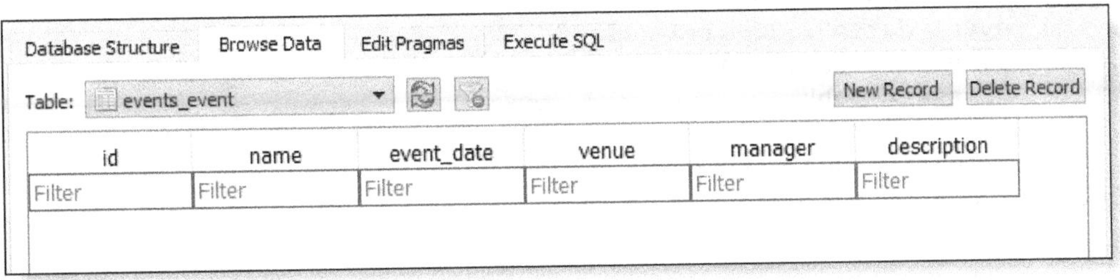

Figure 4-5. Django doesn't hit the database until the record is saved.

To save a record to the database, Django has a model method conveniently called `save()`. So, let's save the record to the database:

```
>>> event1.save()
```

You will probably get a warning from Django about saving a date without a timezone, but you can ignore it for now; we're going to fix this warning shortly. Now, when you check the database, you can see the record has been added to the `events_event` table in the database (Figure 4-6).

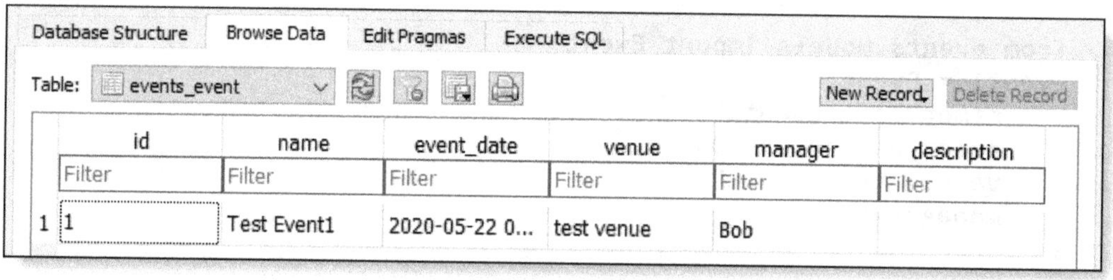

Database Structure | Browse Data | Edit Pragmas | Execute SQL

Table: events_event — New Record — Delete Record

	id	name	event_date	venue	manager	description
	Filter	Filter	Filter	Filter	Filter	Filter
1	1	Test Event1	2020-05-22 0...	test venue	Bob	

Figure 4-6. *The record is added when you call the* `save()` *method.*

As creating and saving objects is so common, Django provides the `create()` method as a convenient shortcut to create and save a record in one step:

```
>>> Event.objects.create(
...     name="Xmas Barbeque",
...     event_date="2020-12-24 12:00",
...     venue="Notareal Park",
...     manager="Bob"
... )
# Ignore the timezone warning
<Event: Event object (2)>
```

You can see in the above example, I have used the `create()` method to create a new event record which Django automatically saves for you.

Django and Naive Datetimes

We've ignored the previous timezone warnings, but this is not recommended. As Django and the databases it supports are all timezone aware, your apps shouldn't use datetimes without timezone information (naive datetimes).

At the moment, Django will accept naive datetimes for backward compatibility, but there is no guarantee support for naive datetimes won't be removed in later versions.

Let's create one more event to use in our examples as we explore models in the Django shell. First, create a timezone-aware event date:

```
>>> from datetime import datetime, timezone
>>> event_date = datetime(2020,12,31,18,0, tzinfo=timezone.utc)
```

Now, we can create and save the event:

```
>>> event3 = Event(
...     name="NYE Party",
...     event_date=event_date,
...     venue="McIvor's Bar",
...     manager="Terry"
... )
>>> event3.save()
```

Or you can use the `create()` shortcut method to achieve the same result:

```
>>> Event.objects.create(
...     name="NYE Party",
...     event_date=event_date,
...     venue="McIvor's Bar",
...     manager="Terry"
... )
<Event: Event object (3)>
>>>
```

Retrieving Records

Retrieve All Records

To retrieve all the records in a database table, you use the `all()` method:

```
>>> event_list = Event.objects.all()
>>> event_list
<QuerySet [<Event: Event object (1)>, <Event: Event object (2)>,
<Event: Event object (3)>]>
```

As you can see, this is not a very useful output—you have no way of knowing which event "Event Object" is referring to. Luckily, Python has a special *string representation* method you can add to Python functions and classes. Let's go back to the `Event` model class declaration and add two lines of code (changes in bold):

```
# \myclub_root\events\models.py

1  from django.db import models
2
3  class Event(models.Model):
4      name = models.CharField('Event Name', max_length=120)
5      event_date = models.DateTimeField('Event Date')
6      venue = models.CharField(max_length=120)
7      manager = models.CharField(max_length = 60)
8      description = models.TextField(blank=True)
9
10     def __str__(self):
11         return self.name
```

The magic is in **lines 10 and 11**. The `__str__` method generates a string representation of any Python object. For the `Event` model, we are simply returning the name of the event. Restart the Django interactive shell for the changes to take effect. After you have added the `__str__` method, your terminal output should look like this:

```
>>> from events.models import Event
>>> event_list = Event.objects.all()
>>> event_list
<QuerySet [<Event: Test Event1>, <Event: Xmas Barbeque>, <Event: NYE
Party>]>
```

Much better.

Retrieve a Single Record

You retrieve single records with the `get()` method. You can retrieve a record using its primary key:

```
>>> Event.objects.get(id=1)
<Event: Test Event1>
```

You can also retrieve a record using one of the field names:

```
>>> Event.objects.get(name="Xmas Barbeque")
<Event: Xmas Barbeque>
```

The `get()` method only works for single objects. If your search term returns multiple records, you will get an error:

```
>>> Event.objects.get(manager="Bob")
Traceback (most recent call last):

# Lots of traceback info

... get() returned more than one Event -- it returned 2!
>>>
```

And if you try to retrieve a record that doesn't exist, Django will throw a `DoesNotExist` error:

```
>>> Event.objects.get(id=999)
Traceback (most recent call last):

# Lots of traceback info

events.models.Event.DoesNotExist: Event matching query does not exist.
>>>
```

Retrieve Multiple Records

Whereas the `get()` method can only return a single record, the `filter()` method allows you to filter your data to return zero or more records.

You can filter with a single search term:

```
>>> Event.objects.filter(manager="Bob")
<QuerySet [<Event: Test Event1>, <Event: Xmas Barbeque>]>
```

You can also filter with multiple search terms:

```
>>> Event.objects.filter(manager="Bob", venue="Notareal Park")
<QuerySet [<Event: Xmas Barbeque>]>
```

In both the above cases, Django translates the search terms into an SQL `WHERE` clause.

By default, the filter method uses exact match lookups. For more control, you can search using one of Django's *field lookups*:

```
>>> Event.objects.filter(manager="Bob", name__contains="Xmas")
<QuerySet [<Event: Xmas Barbeque>]>
```

Note there's a double underscore between `name` and `contains`.

If you're curious, the `__contains` part gets translated by Django into an SQL `LIKE` statement. See Chapter 9 for an in-depth review of field lookups.

If the search string doesn't match, `filter()` will return an empty QuerySet:

```
>>> Event.objects.filter(manager="Fred")
<QuerySet []>
>>>
```

If you want to return all records in the database table with `filter`, you leave the query string blank:

```
>>> Event.objects.filter()
<QuerySet [<Event: Test Event1>, <Event: Xmas Barbeque>, <Event: NYE
Party>]>
>>>
```

This is equivalent to using `Event.objects.all()`.

Ordering Data

In the previous examples, records are being retrieved from the database in table order. If you want to sort the records by a field in the table, you use the `order_by()` method:

```
>>> Event.objects.order_by("name")
<QuerySet [<Event: NYE Party>, <Event: Test Event1>, <Event: Xmas
Barbeque>]>
```

If you want to sort in descending order, you add a minus (-) sign before the field name:

```
>>> Event.objects.order_by("-name")
<QuerySet [<Event: Xmas Barbeque>, <Event: Test Event1>, <Event: NYE
Party>]>
>>>
```

Internally, Django translates the `order_by()` method into an SQL `ORDER BY` statement.

You can also sort by multiple fields:

```
>>> Event.objects.order_by("manager", "name")
<QuerySet [<Event: Test Event1>, <Event: Xmas Barbeque>, <Event: NYE
Party>]>
>>>
```

Model Default Ordering

You can see that this would get tedious if you wanted a default ordering for your model and had to use the `order_by()` method every time you retrieved records from the database.

Django solves this issue with the `ordering` attribute of Django models' `class Meta` method. More about the `class Meta` method in Chapter 9.

It's very common to want to set a sort order on a subset of your database records. You achieve this in Django by chaining lookups. This is best illustrated with an example:

```
>>> Event.objects.filter(manager="Bob").order_by("name")
<QuerySet [<Event: Test Event1>, <Event: Xmas Barbeque>]>
>>>
```

In this example, the `filter()` method first retrieves all events managed by Bob, and then the `order_by()` method sorts them in alphabetical order by event name.

Slicing Data

You can also return a fixed number of rows from the database using Python's list slicing syntax. This is handy for when you are paginating data or want to return the Top 10, say, of a QuerySet.

For example, you can retrieve the earliest event in the database:

```
>>> Event.objects.all().order_by("event_date")[0]
<Event: Test Event1>
```

Or the latest:

```
>>> Event.objects.all().order_by("-event_date")[0]
<Event: NYE Party>
```

You can even specify a subset of records to retrieve:

```
>>> Event.objects.all()[1:3]
<QuerySet [<Event: Xmas Barbeque>, <Event: NYE Party>]>
>>>
```

What you can't do is use negative indexing. So, to retrieve Bob's last event, this won't work:

```
>>> Event.objects.filter(manager="Bob")[-1]
Traceback (most recent call last):

# More traceback info

AssertionError: Negative indexing is not supported.
```

To get around this limitation, you use a reverse sort:

```
>>> Event.objects.filter(manager="Bob").order_by("-event_date")[0]
<Event: Xmas Barbeque>
>>>
```

Updating Records

Earlier in the chapter, we used Django's database API to create a new record. Let's follow the same process and add another record:

```
>>> from datetime import datetime, timezone
>>> event_date = datetime(2020,9,8,15,0, tzinfo=timezone.utc)
>>> event4 = Event(
...     name="Bob's Birthday",
...     event_date=event_date,
...     venue="McIvor's Bar",
...     manager="Terry"
... )
>>> event4.save()
```

You may have noticed our `Event` model class doesn't have a primary (unique) key field defined. This is because Django creates a primary key automatically when it adds a record to the database. Django generates the primary key using the `AUTOINCREMENT` function of your database. In SQLite, `AUTOINCREMENT` returns an integer which you can access via the object's `id` field:

```
>>> event4.id
4
```

You can see in Figure 4-7 that this is the same key used by the database.

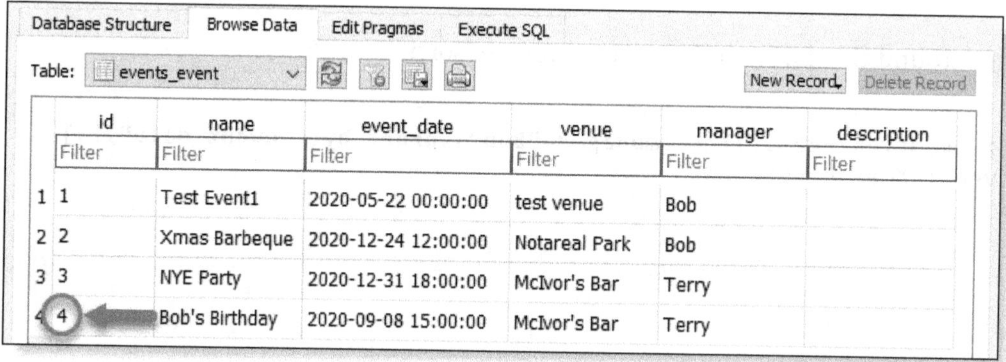

	id	name	event_date	venue	manager	description
	Filter	Filter	Filter	Filter	Filter	Filter
1	1	Test Event1	2020-05-22 00:00:00	test venue	Bob	
2	2	Xmas Barbeque	2020-12-24 12:00:00	Notareal Park	Bob	
3	3	NYE Party	2020-12-31 18:00:00	McIvor's Bar	Terry	
4	4	Bob's Birthday	2020-09-08 15:00:00	McIvor's Bar	Terry	

Figure 4-7. The `Event` *object primary key is the same as the database record unique ID.*

To update records, you change the instance data and call the `save()` method again. Each subsequent call to the `save()` method will update the record:

```
>>> event_date = datetime(2020,9,8,17,0, tzinfo=timezone.utc)
>>> event4.event_date = event_date
>>> event4.save()
```

If you check out the database table, you can see the updated event data (Figure 4-8).

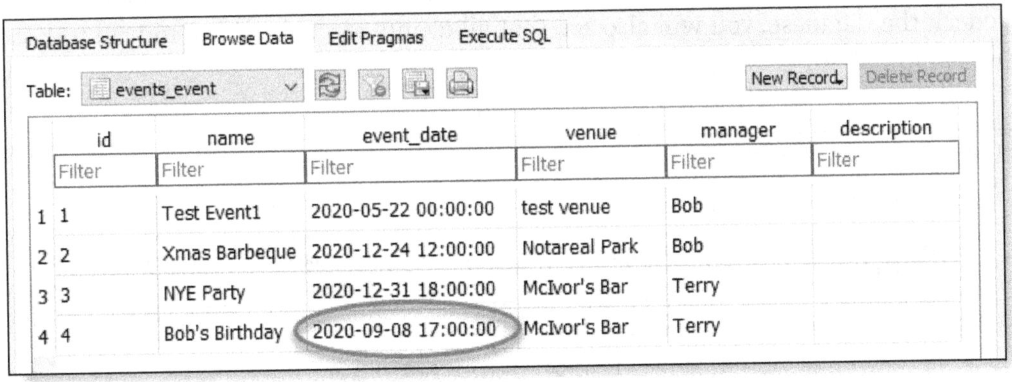

Database Structure | Browse Data | Edit Pragmas | Execute SQL

Table: events_event — New Record — Delete Record

	id	name	event_date	venue	manager	description
1	1	Test Event1	2020-05-22 00:00:00	test venue	Bob	
2	2	Xmas Barbeque	2020-12-24 12:00:00	Notareal Park	Bob	
3	3	NYE Party	2020-12-31 18:00:00	McIvor's Bar	Terry	
4	4	Bob's Birthday	2020-09-08 17:00:00	McIvor's Bar	Terry	

***Figure 4-8.** Changing instance data and calling the* `save()` *method updates the current record.*

While this method of updating a database record is simple, it's inefficient as it will save *all* the field values, not just the event date. To ensure records are updated in the most efficient manner possible, use the `update()` method. Rewriting the above process to use the `update()` method, you get:

```
>>> Event.objects.filter(id=4).update(event_date=event_date)
1
>>>
```

`update()` has an integer return value—the number of records updated.

You can also use `update()` to modify multiple records. For example, say you want to move all the events at McIvor's Bar to Rippemoff Casino, you can use the following code:

```
>>> Event.objects.filter(venue="McIvor's Bar").update(venue="Ripemoff
Casino")
2
>>>
```

The return value tells you that `update()` has changed two records in the database. If you check the database, you will also see that all events at the bar have moved to the casino (Figure 4-9).

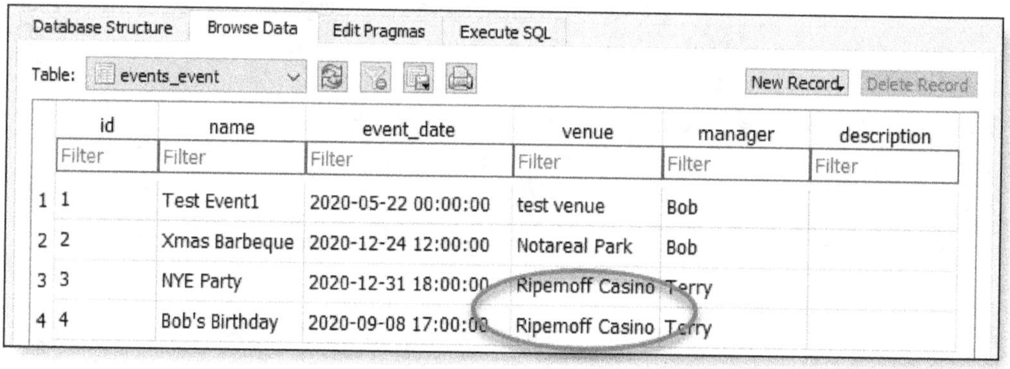

Database Structure | Browse Data | Edit Pragmas | Execute SQL

Table: events_event | New Record | Delete Record

	id	name	event_date	venue	manager	description
	Filter	Filter	Filter	Filter	Filter	Filter
1	1	Test Event1	2020-05-22 00:00:00	test venue	Bob	
2	2	Xmas Barbeque	2020-12-24 12:00:00	Notareal Park	Bob	
3	3	NYE Party	2020-12-31 18:00:00	Ripemoff Casino	Terry	
4	4	Bob's Birthday	2020-09-08 17:00:00	Ripemoff Casino	Terry	

Figure 4-9. *The* `update()` *method makes updating multiple records easy.*

Deleting Records

To delete a record from the database, you use the `delete()` method:

```
>>> Event.objects.filter(name__contains="Test").delete()
(1, {'events.Event': 1})
>>>
```

The return value for the delete() method lists the total number of records affected (one in this example), a dictionary listing the tables affected by the delete operation, and the number of records deleted in each table.

You can delete multiple objects by using a filter that returns more than one record:

```
>>> Event.objects.filter(manager="Terry").delete()
(2, {'events.Event': 2})
>>>
```

And you can delete all the records in a table with the all() method:

```
>>> Event.objects.all().delete()
(1, {'events.Event': 1})
>>> Event.objects.all()
<QuerySet []>
>>>
```

To prevent accidental deletion of all the data in a table, Django requires you to use the all() method explicitly to delete everything in a table. For example, this code doesn't work:

```
>>> Event.objects.delete()
Traceback (most recent call last):
File "<console>", line 1, in <module>
AttributeError: 'Manager' object has no attribute 'delete'
>>>
```

Creating Relationships

In a data-driven website, it's rare to have a table of information unrelated to information in other tables. This is primarily due to well-established database design best-practice.

Let's take the `venue` field as an example. If you were only saving the venue name in the database, you could get away with repeating the name of the venue multiple times in your database records. But what about if you wanted to save more information for the venue?

Your venue records should also include an address, telephone number, website address and email. If you add these fields to your events table, you can see that you will end up with a lot of repeated information, not to mention the nightmare of ensuring you update all records if some venue information changes.

Database normalization is the process of designing your tables to minimize or eliminate data repetition. In simple terms, normalization is keeping related data in separate tables and linking tables via *relationships* (hence the name *relational* database).

Database normalization is also in keeping with Django's Don't Repeat Yourself (DRY) philosophy. So, as you would expect, Django makes creating relationships between tables of related information simple.

With our venue example, it would be good practice to have all the venue information in one table, and link to that information from the event table. We create this link in Django with a *foreign key*. Multiple events linking to one venue record is an example of a *many-to-one relationship* in relational database parlance. Looking at the relationship in the opposite direction, we get a *one-to-many relationship*, i.e., one venue record links to many event records.

Django provides QuerySet methods for navigating relationships in both directions—from one to many, and from many to one—as you will see shortly.

There is one other common database relationship that we need to explore, and that is the *many-to-many relationship*. An excellent example of a many-to-many relationship is the list of people who are going to an event. Each event can have many attendees, and each attendee can go to multiple events. We create a many-to-many relationship in Django with the `ManyToManyField`.

Let's dispense with the theory and make some changes to our `Event` model, add a `Venue` model and add a `MyClubUser` model to our `events` app (changes in bold):

```
# \myclub_root\events\models.py

from django.db import models

class Venue(models.Model):
    name = models.CharField('Venue Name', max_length=120)
    address = models.CharField(max_length=300)
    zip_code = models.CharField('Zip/Post Code', max_length=12)
    phone = models.CharField('Contact Phone', max_length=20)
    web = models.URLField('Web Address')
    email_address = models.EmailField('Email Address')

    def __str__(self):
       return self.name


class MyClubUser(models.Model):
    first_name = models.CharField(max_length=30)
    last_name = models.CharField(max_length=30)
    email = models.EmailField('User Email')

    def __str__(self):
        return self.first_name + " " + self.last_name


class Event(models.Model):
    name = models.CharField('Event Name', max_length=120)
    event_date = models.DateTimeField('Event Date')
    venue = models.ForeignKey(Venue, blank=True, null=True, on_delete=models.CASCADE)
    manager = models.CharField(max_length = 60)
    attendees = models.ManyToManyField(MyClubUser, blank=True)
    description = models.TextField(blank=True)

    def __str__(self):
        return self.name
```

Note the order of the classes. Remember, this is Python, so the order of the models in your `models.py` file matters. The new model classes need to be declared before the `Event` model for the `Event` model to be able to reference them.

The `Venue` model is very similar to the `Event` model, so you should find it easy to understand. Notice how the `Venue` model uses two new model fields: `URLField` and `EmailField`.

This is another cool feature of Django's models—while at the database level these fields are no different than Django `CharField`'s (they're all saved as `varchar`'s in SQLite), Django's models provide built-in validation for specialized fields like URLs and email addresses.

The `MyClubUser` model should also be straightforward. At the moment, it's a simple user model that records the user's name and email address. We'll be expanding this model to create a custom user model in Chapter 14.

There are two important changes to the `Event` model:

1. In **line 27**, I have changed the `venue` field type from a `CharField` to a `ForeignKey` field. The first argument is the name of the related model. I have added `blank=True` and `null=True` to allow a new event to be added without a venue assigned. The `on_delete` argument is required for foreign keys. `CASCADE` means that if a record is deleted, all related information in other tables will also be deleted.
2. In **line 29**, I have added the `attendees` field. `attendees` is a Django `ManyToManyField` which has two arguments—the related model (`MyClubUser`), and `blank` set to `True` so an event can be saved without any attendees.

Before we add the new models to the database, make sure you delete the records from the `Event` table. If you don't, the migration will fail as the old records won't be linked to the new table. Go back to the Django interactive shell and delete all event records like so:

```
(env_myclub) ...\myclub_root> python manage.py shell
...
(InteractiveConsole)
>>> from events.models import Event
```

```
>>> Event.objects.all().delete()
(4, {'events.Event': 4}) # Total records deleted. May be different for
you.
>>>exit()
(env_myclub) ...\myclub_root>
```

Don't forget to exit the interactive shell when you're done (`exit()` or CTRL-Z).

Now, let's add our new model to the database:

```
(env_myclub) ...\myclub_root> python manage.py check
System check identified no issues (0 silenced).
(env_myclub) ...> python manage.py makemigrations events
Migrations for 'events':
  events\migrations\0002_auto_20200522_1159.py
    - Create model Venue
    - Create model MyClubUser
    - Alter field venue on event
    - Add field attendees on event
(env_myclub) ...\myclub_root> python manage.py migrate
Operations to perform:
Apply all migrations: admin, auth, contenttypes, events, sessions
Running migrations:
Applying events.0002_auto_20200522_1159... OK
(env_myclub) ...\myclub_root>
```

After running the migration, you can see that Django has added the `events_venue`, and `events_myclubuser` tables, and the venue field in the `events_event` table has been renamed `venue_id` and is now an integer field (Figure 4-10).

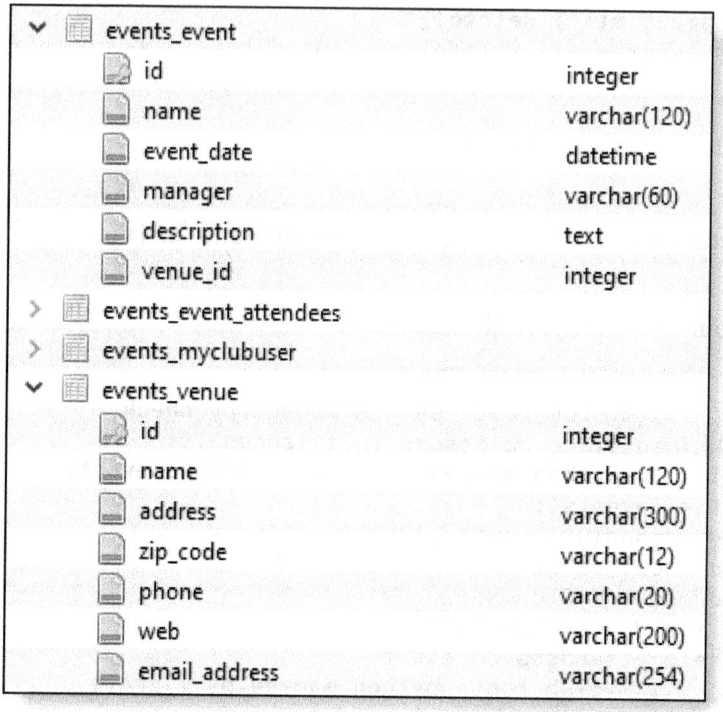

events_event	
id	integer
name	varchar(120)
event_date	datetime
manager	varchar(60)
description	text
venue_id	integer
events_event_attendees	
events_myclubuser	
events_venue	
id	integer
name	varchar(120)
address	varchar(300)
zip_code	varchar(12)
phone	varchar(20)
web	varchar(200)
email_address	varchar(254)

Figure 4-10. *Django has added a new table and created a relationship with the event table. Did you notice there's no* `attendees` *field, but there is an* `events_event_attendees` *table?*

If you look at the event table schema (you can also do this with the `sqlmigrate` command you used earlier in the chapter) you can see the SQL Django uses to create the relationship:

```
CREATE TABLE "events_event" (
    "id" integer NOT NULL PRIMARY KEY AUTOINCREMENT,
    "name" varchar(120) NOT NULL,
    "event_date" datetime NOT NULL,
    "manager" varchar(60) NOT NULL,
    "description" text NOT NULL,
    "venue_id" integer NOT NULL
        REFERENCES "events_venue" ("id")
        DEFERRABLE INITIALLY DEFERRED
)
```

Notice there is no reference to the attendees list in this SQL statement, nor is there an attendees field in the table.

This is because Django handles many-to-many relationships by creating an intermediate table containing each relationship in a simple `event_id` and `myclubuser_id` data pair (Figure 4-11).

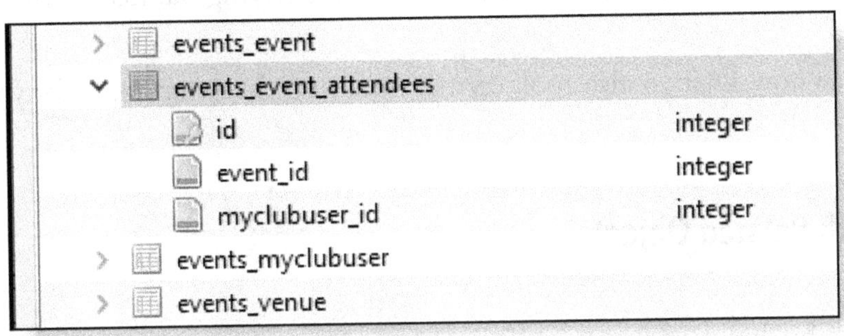

Figure 4-11. *Django records many-to-many relationships in an intermediate table.*

Looking at the output from `sqlmigrate`, you can see Django is not only creating the relationships between the `events` table and `myclubuser` table, but it also sets up several indexes to make search faster:

```
CREATE TABLE "events_event_attendees" (
    "id" integer NOT NULL PRIMARY KEY AUTOINCREMENT,
    "event_id" integer NOT NULL
        REFERENCES "events_event" ("id")
        DEFERRABLE INITIALLY DEFERRED,
    "myclubuser_id" integer NOT NULL
        REFERENCES "events_myclubuser" ("id")
        DEFERRABLE INITIALLY DEFERRED
    );
CREATE UNIQUE INDEX
    "events_event_attendees_event_id_myclubuser_id_d3b4e7a8_uniq" ON
    "events_event_attendees" ("event_id", "myclubuser_id");
CREATE INDEX
    "events_event_attendees_event_id_45694efb" ON
```

```
    "events_event_attendees" ("event_id");
CREATE INDEX
    "events_event_attendees_myclubuser_id_caaa7d67" ON
    "events_event_attendees" ("myclubuser_id");
```

As I mentioned earlier, this SQL will be different for each database. The key takeaway here is Django's migrations take care of creating relationships in your database at the model level without you having to care about the underlying database structure.

Did you notice how Django also took care of updating the event table for you? Cool, huh?

Working With Related Objects

Because of the bi-directional nature of database relationships, and the need to maintain referential integrity, the basic database actions work differently with related objects.

For example, let's try to add a new event in the Django interactive interpreter using the same code from the start of the chapter:

```
>>> from events.models import Event
>>> from datetime import datetime, timezone
>>> event_date = datetime(2020,6,10,12,0, tzinfo=timezone.utc)
>>> event1 = Event(
...     name="Test Event1",
...     event_date=event_date,
...     venue="test venue",
...     manager="Bob"
... )
Traceback (most recent call last):
# ...
ValueError: Cannot assign "'test venue'": "Event.venue" must be a
"Venue" instance.
>>>
```

I've removed the rest of the traceback from this code to keep things simple—so what went wrong?

We have created a relationship between the event table and the venue table, so Django expects us to pass an instance of a Venue object, not the name of the venue.

This is one way Django maintains referential integrity between database tables— for you to save a new event, there must be a corresponding venue record in the venue table.

So, let's create a new venue. I am using the save() method here, but you could also use the create() shortcut method:

```
>>> from events.models import Venue
>>> venue1 = Venue(
...     name="South Stadium",
...     address="South St",
...     zip_code="123456",
...     phone="555-12345",
...     web="southstexample.com",
...     email_address="southst@example.com"
    )
>>> venue1.save()
>>>
```

Now we can create an event using the venue instance (venue1) we just created, and the record should save without error:

```
>>> event1 = Event(
...     name="Test Event1",
...     event_date=event_date,
...     venue=venue1,
...     manager="Bob"
... )
>>>  event1.save()
>>>
```

Accessing Foreign Key Values

Due to the relationship created between the event table and the venue table, when you access the ForeignKey field from an instance of the Event, Django returns an instance of the related Venue object:

```
>>> event1.venue
<Venue: South Stadium>
```

You can also access the fields of the related model object with the dot operator:

```
>>> event1.venue.web
'southstexample.com'
```

This works in the opposite direction, but because of the asymmetrical nature of the relationship, we need to use Django's <object>_set() method. <object>_set() returns a QuerySet, for example, event_set() will return all the events taking place at a particular venue:

```
>>> venue1.event_set.all()
<QuerySet [<Event: Test Event1>]>
```

We are using the all() method here, but as <object>_set() returns a QuerySet, all Django's regular QuerySet slicing and filtering methods will work.

Accessing Many-to-Many Values

Accessing many-to-many values works the same as accessing foreign keys, except Django returns a QuerySet, not a model instance. So you can see how this works, let's first create a new user:

```
>>> from events.models import MyClubUser
>>> MyClubUser.objects.create(
```

```
...     first_name="Joe",
...     last_name="Smith",
...     email="joesmith@example.com"
... )
<MyClubUser: Joe Smith>
```

When we added the `ManyToManyField` to our `Event` model, a special model manager class called `RelatedManager` becomes available. `RelatedManager` has a few useful methods; in this example, we will use the `add()` method to add an attendee to an event:

```
>>> attendee = MyClubUser.objects.get(first_name="Joe", last_
name="Smith")
>>> event1.attendees.add(attendee)
```

You can also use the `create()` shortcut method to add a user and sign them up for an event in one step:

```
>>> event1.attendees.add(
...     MyClubUser.objects.create(
...         first_name="Jane",
...         last_name="Doe",
...         email="janedoe@example.com"
...     )
... )
```

As they are QuerySets, accessing many-to-many records uses the same QuerySet methods as regular model fields:

```
>>> event1.attendees.all()
<QuerySet [<MyClubUser: Joe Smith>, <MyClubUser: Jane Doe>]>
```

And, to follow the relationship in the opposite direction, you use the `<object>_set()` method:

```
>>> attendee.event_set.all()
<QuerySet [<Event: Test Event1>]>
```

To check out the other `RelatedManager` methods, see the Django Documentation[3]

Chapter Summary

In this chapter, we explored the fundamentals of Django's models. We covered how to define Django models in Python, how to create models, basic data access, and how to create relationships between models.

In the next chapter, we will explore the fundamentals of Django's views.

3 https://docs.djangoproject.com/en/dev/ref/models/relations/

5

Django's Views

Django's views are the information brokers of a Django application. A view sources data from your database (or an external data source or service) and delivers it to a template. For a web application, the view delivers web page content and templates; for a RESTful API this content could be formatted JSON data.

The view decides what data gets delivered to the template—either by acting on input from the user or in response to other business logic and internal processes. Each Django view performs a specific function and has an associated template.

Views are represented by either a Python function or a method of a Python class. In the early days of Django, there were only function-based views, but as Django has grown over the years, Django's developers added class-based views.

Class-based views add extensibility to Django's views. Django also has many built-in class-based views that make creating common views (like displaying a list of articles) easier to implement. Don't worry too much about the differences between function- and class-based views now, we will cover both in more detail later in the book.

We covered the basics of Django's models in Chapter 4. In this chapter, we will take a detailed look at the basics of Django's views without getting into any detail on how views interact with models and templates. To help you grasp how views work at a fundamental level, I will show you how they work using simple HTML responses. In the next chapter, we'll cover the basics of Django's templates, and we'll cover class-based views in Chapter 13.

Your First View

Project Files

The following code examples assume you have created your project and app files with the `startproject` and `startapp` utilities. It's recommended you use this default structure throughout the book so your code matches the examples. Also note, the code in this book was written in Django 3.0, so the default file contents may be slightly different if you are using Django 2.2 or a later version of Django 3.

To create our first view, we need to modify the `views.py` file in our `events` app (changes in bold):

```
# \myclub_root\events\views.py

1  from django.shortcuts import render
2  from django.http import HttpResponse
3
4  def index(request):
5      return HttpResponse("<h1>MyClub Event Calendar</h1>")
```

Let's examine this code closely:

- **Line 1**. Import the `render()` method. `startapp` adds this line to the file automatically. `render()` is used when rendering templates, which we will cover in Chapter 6.
- **Line 2**. We import the `HttpResponse` method. HTTP, the communication protocol used by all web browsers, uses request and response objects to pass data to and from your app and the browser. We need a response object to pass view information back to the browser. We cover request and response objects in Chapter 10.

- **Lines 4 and 5.** This is your view function. It's an example of a function-based view. It takes a request from your web browser and returns a response. In this simple case, it's just a line of text formatted as an HTML heading.

Configuring the URLs

If you started the development server now, you would notice it still displays the welcome page. For Django to use your new view, you need to tell Django the `index` view is the view you want to display when someone navigates to the site root (home page). We do this by configuring our URLs.

In Django, the `path()` function is used to configure URLs. In its basic form, the `path()` function has a very simple syntax:

```
path(route, view)
```

A practical example of the basic `path()` function would be:

```
path('mypage/', views.myview)
```

In this example, a request to `http://example.com/mypage` would route to the `myview` function in the application's `views.py` file. Don't worry if this is a bit confusing now; it will make a lot more sense once you have written more views.

The `path()` function also takes an optional `name` argument, and zero or more keyword arguments passed as a Python dictionary. We will get to these more advanced options later in the book.

The `path()` function statements live in a special file called `urls.py`.

When `startproject` created our website, it created a `urls.py` file in our site folder (`\myclub_site\urls.py`). This is the correct place for site-wide navigation, but is rarely a good place to put URLs relating to individual applications. Not only is having all our URLs in the one file more complex and less portable, but it can lead to strange behavior if two applications use a view with the same name.

To solve this problem, we create a new `urls.py` file for each application. If you are wondering why `startapp` didn't create the file for us, not all apps have public views accessible via URL. For example, a utility program that performs background tasks would not need a `urls.py` file. For this reason, Django lets you decide whether your app needs its own `urls.py` file.

First, we need to create a `urls.py` file in our `events` app (new file):

```
# \myclub_root\events\urls.py

1  from django.urls import path
2  from . import views
3
4  urlpatterns = [
5      path('', views.index, name='index'),
6  ]
```

Let's look at this code closer:

- **Line 1** imports the `path()` function. This import is necessary for the URL dispatcher to work and is common to all `urls.py` files.
- **Line 2** imports the local `views.py` file. The dot operator (".") in this case is shorthand for the current package, so this is saying "import all views from the current package (`events`)".
- **Line 4** lists the URL patterns registered for this app. For readability, the list is broken into multiple lines, with one URL pattern per line.
- **Line 5** is the actual URL dispatcher:
    - `''` matches an empty string. It will also match the "/" as Django automatically removes the slash. In other words, this matches both `http://example.com` and `http://example.com/`.

- **`views.index`** points to our `index` view. I.e., the dot operator is pointing to the `index` view inside the `views.py` file that we imported in line 2.
- **`name='index'`**. While it's optional, you should always name your URLs. We name URLs so they can be referred to in code (reverse lookup). URL reversing is common in both templates and views, so you will see several examples as we work through the book.

Now let's look at the site `urls.py` file (changes in bold):

```
# \myclub_site\urls.py

1  from django.contrib import admin
2  from django.urls import include, path
3
4  urlpatterns = [
5      path('admin/', admin.site.urls),
6      path('', include('events.urls')),
7  ]
```

We have made two important changes to the file:

- **Line 2.** We have added the `include()` function to our imports.
- **Line 6.** We have added a new URL dispatcher. In this file, the dispatcher is including the `urls.py` file from the `events` app. The empty string (`''`) will match everything after the domain name.

  This pattern must be the last entry in the `urlpatterns` list, otherwise Django's shortcut logic will switch to the `events` app before trying to match any of the other site URLs.

If you now run the development server and navigate to `http://127.0.0.1:8000/` in your browser, you should see a plain, but functioning home page (Figure 5-1).

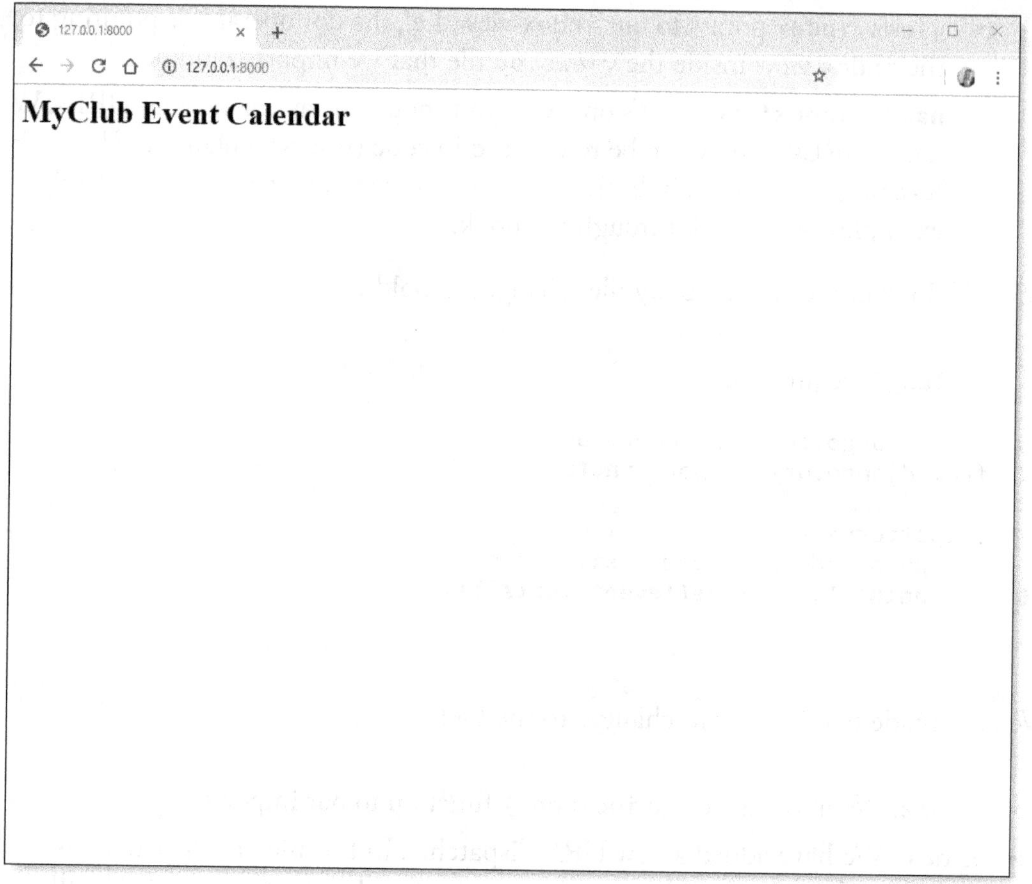

Figure 5-1. A plain, but functioning homepage for your website.

So What Just Happened?

To better understand how Django works, let's build on the generic example from Chapter 3 with a concrete example of what Django did to display our home page:

1. Our browser sent a message to the Django development server requesting it return content located at the root URL (`http://127.0.0.1:8000/`).

2. Django then looked for a URL pattern matching the request, by first searching the site level `urls.py`, and then each of the apps for a `urls.py` file containing a pattern that matches.
3. Django checks the first pattern (`admin/`) in our site level `urls.py` which doesn't match and moves on to the second line in which the empty string (root URL) matches.
4. The matching pattern includes the `urls.py` from the `events` app. Basically, this include says "go look in the `events` app for a pattern that matches".
5. Once in the app-level `urls.py`, the empty string matches again. But this time, the request is sent to the `index` view.
6. The `index` view then renders our simple HTML message to a `HttpResponse` and sends it to the browser.
7. The browser renders the response and we see our page heading.

Every Django application follows this same basic process each time it receives a request from the browser.

Your Second View: Dynamic Content

Our simple index view does an excellent job of demonstrating how content from a Django view is rendered to the browser, but it's not a very good example of a modern web page. That's because it's static, i.e., the page content is always the same.

For a modern interactive site, you want the content of your pages to change dynamically based on interaction with the user and program logic.

With our event calendar, it would be good for the page heading to include the month and year. This can't be hard-coded into the HTML, so we need to develop a way to show the current month and year in the title.

We should probably add an actual calendar too—given it will not be much of an event calendar without you being able to see the calendar!

Static Pages Still Have a Place

Not all pages need to be dynamic. For example, about pages, terms and conditions, and privacy statements don't change regularly and are often saved as static HTML pages.

Django's developers thought of this and made managing static pages from within your Django administration dead easy with the built-in `flatpages` app. We will have a look at the `flatpages` app in Chapter 18.

Before we modify our `index` view, let's use the interactive shell to test out some new code. You can use either the Python interactive shell or Django's shell; the code will work in both:

```
>>> from datetime import date
>>> t = date.today()
>>> t
datetime.date(2020, 3, 22)
```

To start, we're importing the `date` class from Python's `datetime` module. We then assign today's date to the variable `t`. Now we have some useful information we can use to extract the current month and year:

```
>>> t.year
2020
>>> date.strftime(t, '%b')
'March'
>>> month = date.strftime(t, '%b')
>>> year = t.year
>>> title = "MyClub Event Calendar - %s %s" % (month,year)
>>> title
'MyClub Event Calendar - March 2020'
>>>
```

The first line should be straightforward—we're accessing the `year` attribute of the `datetime` object `t`.

The next bit of code is more interesting. We're using the `strftime` (string format) module from Python to format `t`. The `%b` format string converts `datetime` object `t` into a string containing the month formatted to its abbreviated (3-character) name. `strftime` is a handy module for formatting dates and times. If you want to learn more check out the Python `strftime` documentation[1].

In the last bit of test code, we're putting the month and year into two variables and then using Python's string formatting syntax to generate a dynamic title for our event calendar page.

Now we've got some working code, let's jump over to our `index` view and put it to practical use (changes in bold):

```
# \myclub_root\events\views.py

1  from django.shortcuts import render
2  from django.http import HttpResponse
3  from datetime import date
4
5
6  def index(request):
7      t = date.today()
8      month = date.strftime(t, '%b')
9      year = t.year
10     title = "MyClub Event Calendar - %s %s" % (month,year)
11     return HttpResponse("<h1>%s</h1>" % title)
```

Let's have a look at the changes to our `index` view:

- **Line 3.** Import the `date` class from Python's `datetime` module.
- **Line 7.** Assign today's date to the variable `t`.
- **Line 8.** Set the `month` variable to the 3-character month.
- **Line 9.** Assign the current year to the variable `year`.
- **Line 10.** Use a Python string format function to create the dynamic title for our page.

1 https://docs.python.org/3/library/datetime.html#strftime-and-strptime-behavior

- **Line 11.** Use another Python string format to return our dynamic title as HTML.

If you run the development server, you should see the homepage now shows the event calendar title with the current date appended (Figure 5-2).

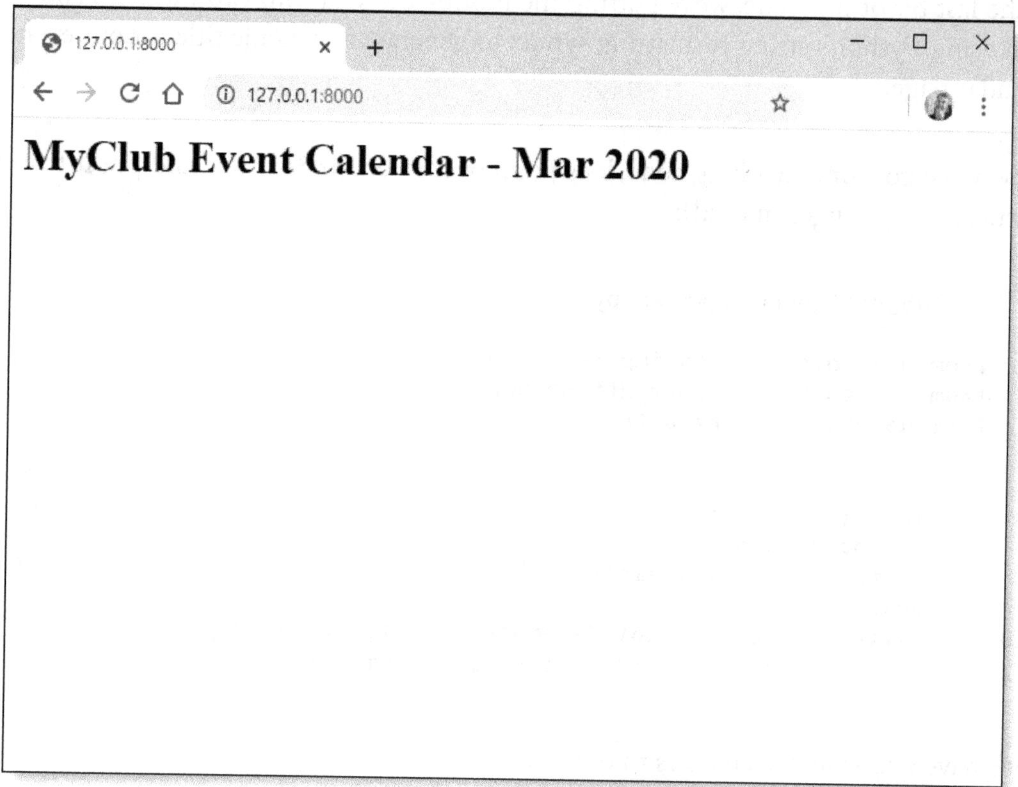

***Figure 5-2.** Your homepage with a dynamic title.*

Your Third View: Dynamic URLs

We've updated our `index` view to include the current month in the title (we'll get to the calendar bit soon), but what if we wanted to show a month other than this month?

In most web applications, dynamic URLs are used to serve different content. For example, an eCommerce site might give each product a unique URL, like `/widgets/green` and `/widgets/blue`.

In Django, we create dynamic URLs with *path converters*. A path converter has a simple syntax:

```
<type:variable>
```

There are five different path converter types:

- **`str`**—matches any non-empty string, excluding '/'.
- **`path`**—matches any non-empty string, including '/' Useful for matching the entire URL.
- **`int`**—matches an integer.
- **`slug`**—matches any slug string. e.g., `slugs-are-text-strings-with-hyphens-and_underscores`.
- **`UUID`**—matches a universally unique identifier (UUID).

Here's an example of a URL containing path converters:

```
/<int:year>/<str:month>/
```

When Django is presented with a URL matching this pattern, for example `/2020/may/`, Django puts the value "2020" into the variable `year` and the string "may" into the variable `month`. If you are familiar with regular expressions, path converters are equivalent to capturing groups.

Let's put this into practice and modify the events app's `urls.py` file (change in bold):

```
urlpatterns = [
    # path('', views.index, name='index'),
    path('<int:year>/<str:month>/', views.index, name='index'),
]
```

A simple change here—we've just added the path converters to the `path` statement in our `events` app. The `events` app will now capture any URL with the format `/year/month` and pass the year and month to the `index` view. I've left the original path statement commented out in the source for your reference, so you can see what's changed.

If you tried to do this now, you would get an error because the `index` view doesn't know what to do with the new variables. Let's fix that now by modifying `views.py` (changes in bold):

```
# \myclub_root\events\views.py

1 def index(request, year, month):
2     # t = date.today()
3     # month = date.strftime(t, '%b')
4     # year = t.year
5     title = "MyClub Event Calendar - %s %s" % (month, year)
6     return HttpResponse("<h1>%s</h1>" % title)
```

You can see on **line 1**, I have added `year` and `month` as input parameters to the view function. We no longer need to calculate the year and month values, so I have commented out **lines 2 to 4**. You can delete these lines if you wish—I left them in to make it easier for you to see what has changed.

To test the new view, navigate to `http://127.0.0.1:8000/2020/may/` in your browser. You should see something that looks like Figure 5-3.

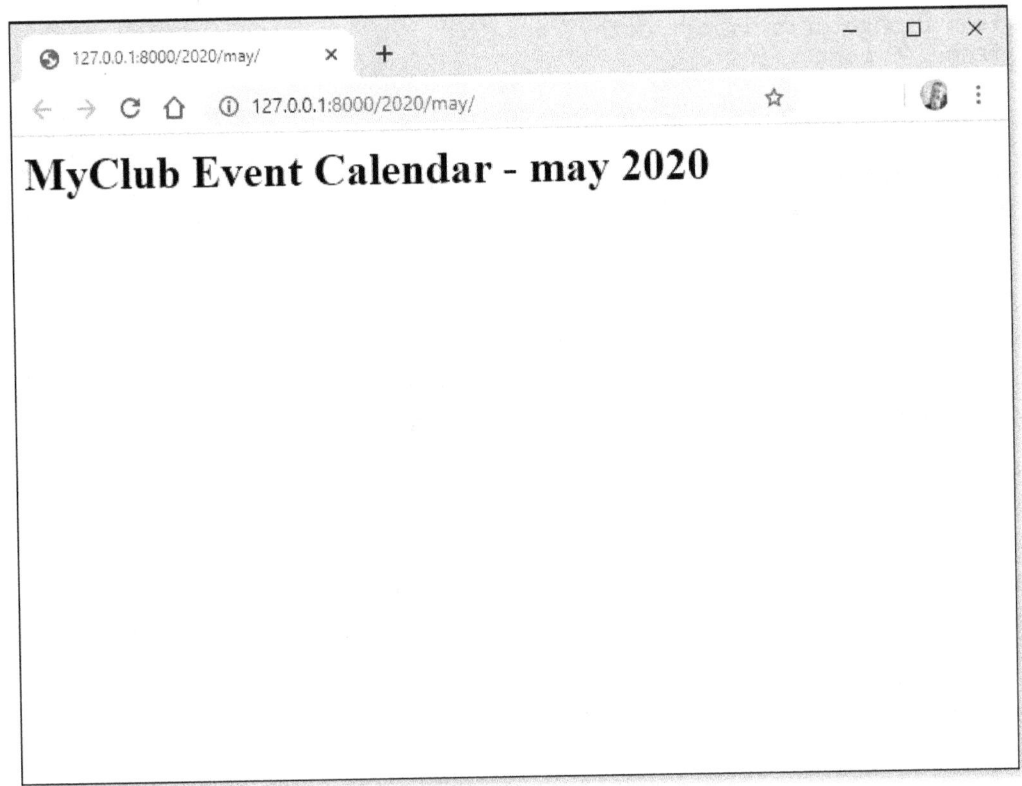

Figure 5-3. *The dynamic title is now being generated from the URL.*

This is pretty cool, but what if you entered some nonsense URL like `http://127.0.0.1:8000/123456/12monkeys`? You can try this URL—the view will still work, but the title no longer makes sense.

Path converters are an easy to understand and simple to code method for capturing URL arguments. However, when you need a more robust option for validating URLs, Django also provides regular expression (regex) matching for URLs.

Let's change our `urls.py` file to use regexes (changes in bold):

```
# \myclub_root\events\urls.py

1 from django.urls import path, re_path
2 from . import views
3
4 urlpatterns = [
5     # path('<int:year>/<str:month>/', views.index, name='index'),
6     re_path(r'^(?P<year>[0-9]{4})/(?P<month>0?[1-9]|1[0-2])/',
views.index, name='index'),
7 ]
```

You can see in **line 1**, I have imported the `re_path` function from `django.urls`. I have commented out the original URL configuration using path converters in **line 5**, so you can compare it to the new URL configuration using regexes in **line 6**.

If you have used previous versions of Django, notice that the regex syntax is very familiar. The `re_path()` function replaced the `url()` function in Django 2.0. This means if you prefer regexes, you can continue to use them with the `re_path()` function just as you did with the `url()` function in Django 1.11 and earlier.

Let's have a closer look at the regexes:

- **`[0-9]{4}`** captures any 4-digit number and assigns it to the variable `year`. This is not perfect because it will still accept an invalid year, but at least it limits the number to 4 digits. We will perform additional validation logic in the view.
- **`0?[1-9]|1[0-2]`** will only capture numbers between 1 and 12, which is the range of valid month numbers, and assign the captured value to `month`. The `0?` at the beginning is an optional leading zero, so (for example) both "1" and "01" are valid inputs for January. Note we are no longer capturing a string here. This is because validating a month as a string is too difficult—you would have to check for all variations of English spelling of the month, plus additional checks for localization.

Try a few URLs in `YYYY/MM/` format to test the new URL configuration. For example, you could try `http://127.0.0.1:8000/2020/01/` to show January 2020 in the title. You should also see that any URL that doesn't match either of the arguments will throw an HTTP 404 (Not found) error, which is the behavior we want.

Note the month no longer shows a string—the title only includes the month number. To fix this, we need to modify the `index` view to work with our new URL configuration (changes in bold):

```
# \myclub_root\events\views.py

1   from django.shortcuts import render
2   from django.http import HttpResponse
3   from datetime import date
4   import calendar
5
6   def index(request,year,month):
7       year = int(year)
8       month = int(month)
9       if year < 2000 or year > 2099: year = date.today().year
10      month_name = calendar.month_name[month]
11      title = "MyClub Event Calendar - %s %s" % (month_name, year)
12      return HttpResponse("<h1>%s</h1>" % title)
```

Let's step through this code in a little more detail:

- **Line 4.** We import the `calendar` module from Python.
- **Lines 7 and 8.** While the URLconf is capturing numbers, they are passed in as strings, so we need to convert `year` and `month` to integers.
- **Line 9.** Validates the year. If the year is less than 2000 or greater than 2099, `year` is set to this year.
- **Line 10.** We're using the `month_name()` function from the `calendar` module to retrieve the month name that matches the month number.
- **Line 11.** Replaced `month` with the `month_name` variable.

Now when you fire up the development server, you should be able to enter any URL in the form `/YYYY/M` or `/YYYY/MM`, and you will see the dynamic title change to match the URL arguments.

Now, all we need to do is add the calendar. Luckily, Python makes this easy with the `HTMLCalendar()` class from the `calendar` module. If you want to explore the `HTMLCalendar()` class and the `calendar` module in more detail, check out the Python documentation[2].

In this lesson, we will instantiate a new `HTMLCalendar` object and pass the HTML formatted content for the selected month to the response. Open up your `views.py` file and make the changes below (in bold):

```
# \myclub_root\events\views.py

1  from django.shortcuts import render
2  from django.http import HttpResponse
3  from datetime import date
4  import calendar
5  from calendar import HTMLCalendar
6
7
8  def index(request,year,month):
9      year = int(year)
10     month = int(month)
11     if year < 1900 or year > 2099: year = date.today().year
12     month_name = calendar.month_name[month]
13     title = "MyClub Event Calendar - %s %s" % (month_name,year)
14     cal = HTMLCalendar().formatmonth(year, month)
15     return HttpResponse("<h1>%s</h1><p>%s</p>" % (title, cal))
```

Let's look at the changes in detail:

- **Line 5.** We import the `HTMLCalendar` class from the `calendar` module.
- **Line 14.** We retrieve an HTML formatted calendar using the `formatmonth()` method and place the HTML content into the variable `cal`.

2 https://docs.python.org/3/library/calendar.html#module-calendar

- **Line 15**. We modify the string formatting to attach the calendar to the response.

To test the changes, navigate to `http://127.0.0.1:8000/2020/1`. Your browser should now look like Figure 5-4.

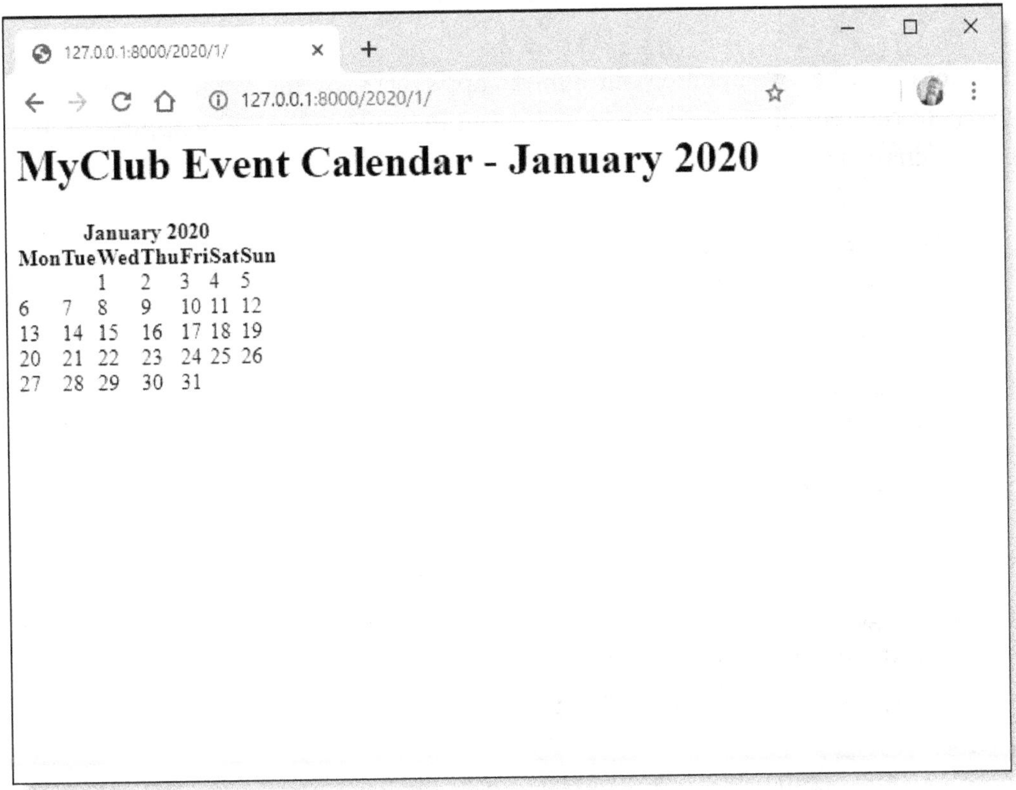

Figure 5-4. *The completed dynamic view.*

Try a few different years and dates to see how your dynamic view is working. Well done!

OK, so our event calendar is not very pretty, but you will learn how easy it is to style Django websites in the next chapter. In the meantime, there is still one thing to do.

A Note About the Site Root

Django does nothing special with the site root (/)—it's just another URL. In fact, if you go to your browser and try to navigate to `http://127.0.0.1:8000/` now, Django will throw an HTTP 404 (Not found) error.

This is because when we updated our `events` app's `urls.py` file, we removed the mapping to the root directory (`''`). Let's fix that by adding the root mapping back to `urls.py` (change in bold):

```
# \myclub_root\events\urls.py

from django.urls import path, re_path
from . import views

urlpatterns = [
    path('', views.index, name='index'),
    re_path(r'^(?P<year>[0-9]{4})/(?P<month>0?[1-9]|1[0-2])/',
views.index, name='index'),
]
```

This is simple enough—I've added the same URL configuration for the root URL we used back at the beginning of this chapter. But we're not finished: if you navigate to the root now, your browser is going to look like Figure 5-5.

This error occurs because the `index` view requires the `year` and `month` arguments to render the calendar. As there are no arguments to capture from the root URL, the call fails.

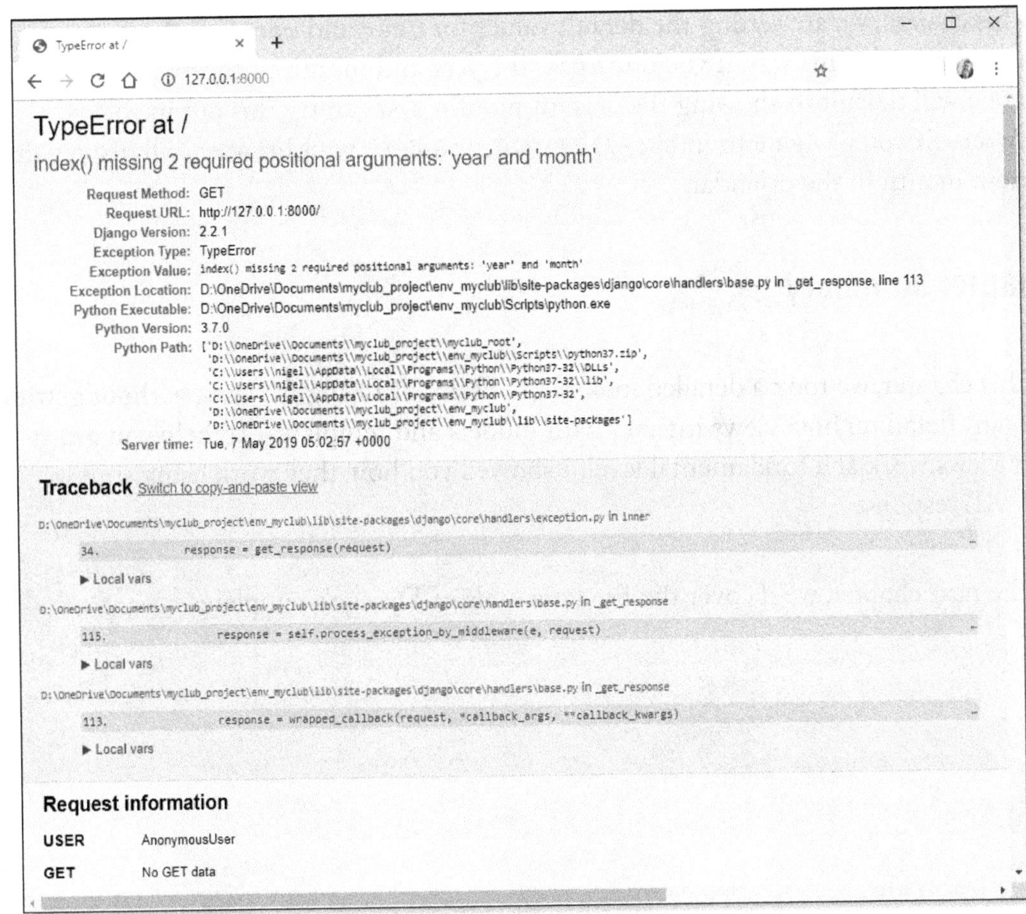

***Figure 5-5.** The* `index` *view requires the year and month arguments.*

We solve this problem by using *default arguments*. Make the following small change (in bold) to the `index` function definition:

```
# \myclub_root\events\views.py

# ...
def index(request, year=date.today().year, month=date.today().month):
    # ...
```

In this change, we are setting the default values for `year` and `month` to the current year and month. This way, if you don't pass the year and month to the `index` function, Django will default to showing the current month. You can try this out in your browser—if you navigate to `http://127.0.0.1:8000/`, your browser will display the current month in the calendar.

Chapter Summary

In this chapter, we took a detailed look at the basics of Django's views, without getting into any detail on how views interact with models and templates. To help you grasp how views work at a fundamental level, I showed you how they work using simple HTML responses.

In the next chapter, we'll cover the fundamentals of Django's templates.

6

Django's Templates

In Chapter 5, we created a view to show a simple title and calendar in the browser. This is a long way from a fully functioning modern website—for one, we are missing a site template.

Site templates, at their most basic, are HTML files displayed by your browser. All websites—from simple, static websites to interactive web applications that work on multiple devices—are built on HTML.

Modern interactive websites are more complex. For example, a modern website will add Cascading Style Sheets (CSS), semantic markup and JavaScript in the front end to create the user experience, with a back end like Django supplying the data to show in the template.

Template Design Philosophy

Django's approach to web design is simple—keep Django logic and code separate from design. It's essential to understand that Django's templates are not Python code embedded into HTML; it's not possible to execute Python code in a Django template.

This means a designer can create a complete front end (HTML, CSS, imagery and user interaction) without having to write a single line of Python or Django code. A designer need only leave HTML comments in the template for a programmer to replace with *template tags*—plain text markup tags defined by the Django Template Language (DTL).

While the DTL is similar to other template languages that embed template code in plain HTML, the original creators of Django had a specific set of philosophies in mind when creating the DTL. These philosophies remain core to Django today. They are:

1. Separate logic from presentation
2. Discourage redundancy
3. Be decoupled from HTML
4. XML is bad
5. Assume designer competence
6. Treat whitespace obviously
7. Don't invent a programming language
8. Ensure safety and security
9. Extensible

1. Separate logic from presentation

A template system is a tool to control presentation and presentation-related logic—and that's it. The template system shouldn't support functionality that goes beyond this primary goal.

2. Discourage redundancy

Most dynamic websites use many common site-wide design elements—a common header, footer, navigation bar, etc. The Django template system should make it easy to store those elements in a single place, eliminating duplicate code. This is the philosophy behind template inheritance.

3. Be decoupled from HTML

The template system shouldn't just output HTML. It should be equally good at generating other text-based formats, or plain text.

4. XML should not be used for template languages

Using an XML engine to parse templates introduces a whole new world of human error when editing templates, and incurs an unacceptable level of overhead in template processing.

5. Assume designer competence

The template system shouldn't be designed so templates display nicely in WYSIWYG editors such as Dreamweaver. That is too severe of a limitation and wouldn't allow the syntax to be as concise as it is.

Django expects template authors to be comfortable editing HTML directly.

6. Treat whitespace obviously

The template system shouldn't do magic things with whitespace. If a template includes whitespace, the system should treat it as it treats text— display it. Any whitespace that's not in a template tag should be displayed.

7. Don't invent a programming language

The template system intentionally doesn't allow

1. assignment to variables; or
2. advanced logic.

The goal is not to invent a programming language. The goal is to offer just enough programming-esque functionality, such as branching and looping, essential for making presentation-related decisions.

The Django template system recognizes designers, not programmers, usually create templates. Therefore, the template language should not assume Python knowledge.

8. Safety and security

The template system should forbid the inclusion of malicious code—such as commands that delete database records. This is another reason why the template system doesn't allow arbitrary execution of Python code.

9. Extensibility

The template system should recognize that advanced template authors may want to extend its technology. This is the philosophy behind custom template tags and filters.

DTL Philosophy—Concluding Thoughts

Having worked with many templating systems myself over the years, I wholeheartedly endorse this approach—the philosophy and design behind the DTL is one of the major advantages of the Django framework.

When the pressure is on to Get Stuff Done, and you have both designers and programmers trying to communicate and get all last-minute tasks done, Django gets out of the way and lets each team concentrate on what they are good at.

Once you have found this out for yourself through real-life practice, you will find out quickly why Django really is the "framework for perfectionists with deadlines".

Remember though, template syntax is highly subjective, and programmers' opinions vary wildly. Python alone has dozens of open source template-language implementations, each created because its developer deemed all existing template languages inadequate.

With this in mind, Django is flexible—it does not require you to use the DTL. All versions of Django since Django 1.8, ship with the popular Jinja2[1] template engine along with the DTL to provide developers with options.

Because Django is intended to be a full-stack web framework providing all the pieces necessary for web developers to be productive, most times it's more convenient to use the DTL; but it's not a requirement.

Django Template System Basics

A Django template is a text file. While in the vast majority of cases this text file is an HTML file, Django templates can also be non-HTML files. Non-HTML examples include email templates and CSV templates.

To turn a plain text file into a Django template, the template designer adds *template tags*, *variables* and *filters*.

A **template tag** is surrounded by `{%` and `%}`. A template tag *does* something. This is deliberately vague because Django's tags are extremely flexible. Some example functions performed by template tags are:

- **Display Logic**. E.g., `{% if %}...{% endif %}`
- **Loop Control**. E.g., `{% for x in y %}...{% endfor %}`
- **Block Declaration**. E.g., `{% block content %}...{% endblock %}`
- **Content Import**. E.g., `{% include "header.html" %}`
- **Inheritance**. E.g., `{% extends "base.html" %}`

1 http://jinja.pocoo.org/

It's also possible to create custom template tags to extend the DTL.

A **template variable** is surrounded by `{{` and `}}`. A template variable *is* something. Template variables are passed to the template at runtime in the *context*. We'll dig deeper into template contexts shortly.

Template variables don't just handle simple data, they work with more complex data structures too. For example:

- **Simple Variables.** E.g., `{{ title }}`
- **Object Attributes.** E.g., `{{ page.title }}`
- **Dictionary Lookups.** E.g., `{{ dict.key }}`
- **List Indexes.** E.g., `{{ list_items.0 }}`
- **Method Calls.** E.g., `{{ var.upper }}`, `{{ mydict.pop }}`

With few exceptions, the methods and attributes available to the Python object are also accessible in the template via the dot operator.

Filters modify a variable for display. You apply a filter to a variable using the `|` (pipe) character. There are dozens of built-in filters; here are some examples:

- **Change Case.** E.g., `{{ name|title }}` or `{{ units|lower }}`
- **Truncation.** E.g., `{{ post_content|truncatewords:50 }}`
- **Date Formatting.** E.g., `{{ order_date|date:"D M Y" }}`
- **List Slicing.** E.g., `{{ list_items|slice:":3" }}`
- **Default Values.** E.g., `{{ item_total|default:"nil" }}`

This is a sample of the template tags, variable methods and filters available in Django. We'll be covering all the most common elements of the DTL in more detail as we work through the book. Chapter 11 includes an exercise covering all common tags and filters, complete with example implementations of each.

How Django Finds Templates

When `startproject` created your Django site, it added a `TEMPLATES` setting to your `settings.py` file that looks like this:

```
1  TEMPLATES = [
2      {
3          'BACKEND': 'django.template.backends.django.DjangoTemplates',
4          'DIRS': [],
5          'APP_DIRS': True,
6          'OPTIONS': {
7              'context_processors': [
8                  'django.template.context_processors.debug',
9                  'django.template.context_processors.request',
10                 'django.contrib.auth.context_processors.auth',
11                 'django.contrib.messages.context_processors.messages',
12             ],
13         },
14     },
15 ]
```

The most important line to note here is **line 5**. When `APP_DIRS` is `True`, the Django template engine will look for templates in a folder called "templates" in each app listed in `INSTALLED_APPS`.

Django doesn't create the folder for you, so let's create one for our `events` app. Once you have added the folder, your directory tree should look like this:

```
\events
    \migrations
    \templates
    __init.py__
    # ...
```

Following on from this, you might think adding templates to your project should be as simple as adding template files to your `\templates` folder. In a single app project, you can get away with this, but it's not recommended.

Why? Because Django uses short-circuit logic when searching for templates. This can be a problem when you have two apps in a project with a template with the same name.

Say you have created an `index.html` template for your events app and you add a 3rd party app that also uses a template called `index.html`. Your folder structure will look like this:

```
\events
    \templates
        index.html
\other_app
    \templates
        index.html
```

When you tell Django to load the template `index.html` it will load the first file it finds (based on the order of your apps in the `INSTALLED_APPS` setting). So, if you want to load the index template for `other_app`, but the `events` app is listed first in `INSTALLED_APPS`, Django will load the wrong template.

We solve this problem by *namespacing* our templates. Namespacing templates is simple—we add a folder named after the app to our templates folder. This is what the above example looks like after namespacing the templates:

```
\events
    \templates
        \events
            index.html
\other_app
    \templates
        \other_app
            index.html
```

Now, when you want to load a template, you include the namespace ("`events/index.html`" or "`other_app/index.html`" in this example), and Django will always load the correct template.

As with most things in Django, namespacing templates is a convention, not a hard and fast rule. But if you want maximum portability for your apps, and to avoid some headaches later on, it is a convention that you would do well to follow.

Before moving on, add the new folder to your events app. When you're done, the folder structure will look like this:

```
\events
    \migrations
    \templates
        \events
    __init.py__
    # ...
```

Creating a Site Template

All modern websites have a site template that creates a common look and branding for every page on the website.

The most common place for storing site template files in Django is in the website app that Django created automatically for you when you ran `startproject`. Django didn't create the `\templates` folder for you, so create it now. When you're finished, your folder structure should look like this:

```
\myclub_site
    \templates
    __init__.py
    ...
```

As your website app is not in `INSTALLED_APPS`, Django won't automatically look for templates in the `\myclub_site\templates` folder, you must tell Django where to look by adding a path to the `DIRS` setting. Let's modify `settings.py` (change in bold):

```
1  TEMPLATES = [
2      {
3          'BACKEND': 'django.template.backends.django.DjangoTemplates',
4          'DIRS': [os.path.join(BASE_DIR, 'myclub_site/templates')],
5          'APP_DIRS': True,
6          # ...
```

Line 4 looks complicated, but is easy to understand—`os.path.join` is a Python command to create a file path by joining strings together (concatenating). In this example, we are joining `myclub_site/templates` to our project directory to create the full path to our templates directory, i.e., `<your project path>/myclub_root/myclub_site/templates`.

The `DIRS` list is not just for letting Django know where your site templates are. It's also useful for listing any template resources that exist outside of your existing apps. Note that Django will search your `DIRS` list in the order listed, so keep in mind my previous warnings about templates with the same name when linking to external resources.

Now we have the template folder created and the folder path listed so Django can find our site template, it's time to create a simple template. We will name this file `base.html` (new file):

```
# \myclub_site\templates\base.html

<!doctype html>
<html>
  <head>
    <meta charset="utf-8">
    <title>Basic Site Template</title>
  </head>

  <body>
    <h1>{{ title }}</h1>
    <p>{{ cal }}</p>
  </body>
</html>
```

This is plain HTML except for lines 9 and 10. In **line 9**, we've created a Django variable tag and named it `title`, and in **line 10**, we've created another variable tag and named it `cal`. If you remember from the view we created in the last chapter, these are the same variable names we gave the event title and calendar respectively.

Displaying a Template

Now we've created the template, we need to tell Django to use our new base template when displaying content on the site. This is done in your `views.py` file. Modify the `index` view as follows (changes in bold):

```
# \events\views.py

1  from django.shortcuts import render
2  from django.http import HttpResponse
3  from datetime import date
4  import calendar
5  from calendar import HTMLCalendar
6
7
8  def index(request, year=date.today().year, month=date.today().month):
9      year = int(year)
10     month = int(month)
11     if year < 1900 or year > 2099: year = date.today().year
12     month_name = calendar.month_name[month]
13     title = "MyClub Event Calendar - %s %s" % (month_name, year)
14     cal = HTMLCalendar().formatmonth(year, month)
15     # return HttpResponse("<h1>%s</h1><p>%s</p>" % (title, cal))
16     return render(request, 'base.html', {'title': title, 'cal': cal})
```

For our new view, we have replaced the call to `HttpResponse()` with a call to `render()`. I have commented out the original `HttpResponse` (**line 15**) so you can more easily see the changes. You don't have to remove the `HttpResponse` import from `django.http` (**line 2**) as we're going to use it in a later chapter.

`render()` is a special Django helper function that creates a shortcut for communicating with a web browser. If you remember from Chapter 5, when Django receives a request from a browser, it finds the right view, and the view returns a response to the browser.

In the example from Chapter 5, we simply returned some HTML text. However, when we wish to use a template, Django first must load the template, create a context—which is a dictionary of variables and associated data passed back to the browser—and return an `HttpResponse`.

You can code each of these steps separately in Django, but in the majority of cases, it's more common (and easier) to use Django's `render()` function, which provides a shortcut that executes all three steps in a single function. Using `render()` is so common that Django added it to the `views.py` file for you when `startapp` created the `events` app (**line 1**).

When you supply the original request, the template and a context to `render()`, it returns the formatted response without you having to code the intermediate steps.

In our modified `views.py` (**line 16**), we are returning the original request object from the browser, the name of our site template and a dictionary (the context) containing our `title` and `cal` variables from the view.

Once you have modified your `views.py` file, save it and fire up the development server. If you navigate to `http://127.0.0.1:8000/`, you should see your simple new site template (Figure 6-1).

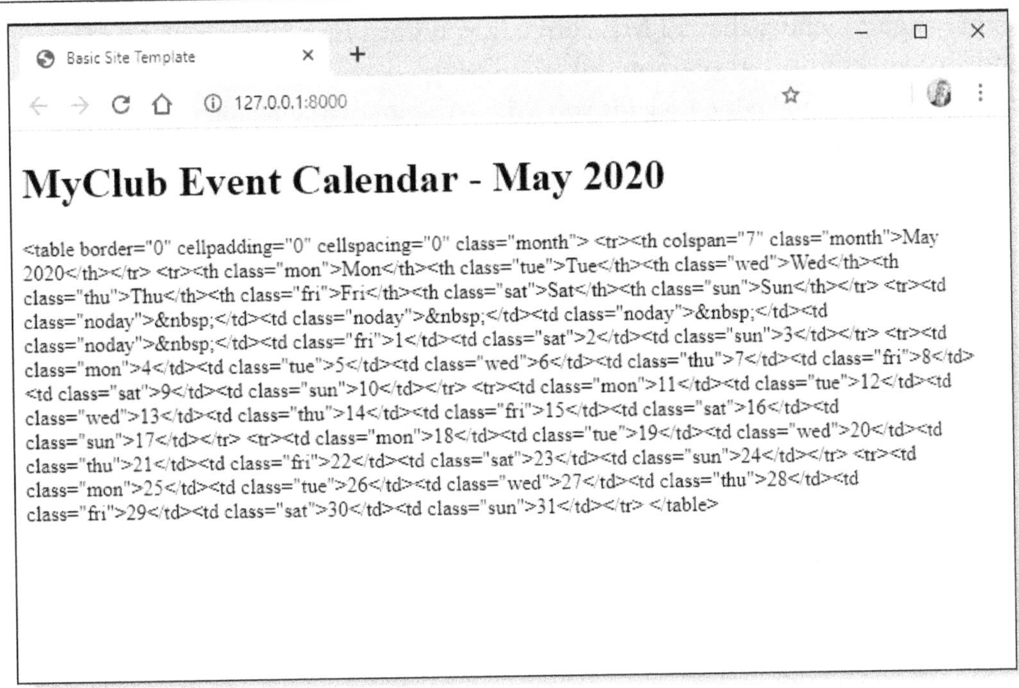

***Figure 6-1.** The unformatted base template.*

Hmm. Something isn't quite right—the calendar is rendering as plain text, not as HTML. If you look at the page source, you can see why:

```
~~ snip

<p>&lt;table border=&quot;0&quot; cellpadding=&quot;0&quot;
cellspacing=&quot;0&quot; class=&quot;month&quot;&gt;&lt;tr&gt;
&lt;th colspan=&quot;7&quot; class=&quot;month&quot;
&gt;May 2019&lt;/th&gt;&lt;/tr&gt; ...
```

All the HTML codes are escaped!

This is because, by default, Django autoescapes all code before sending it to the browser. This is a built-in security feature designed to prevent a hacker inserting malicious code into your site code.

To get Django to render the HTML correctly, you must turn autoescape off for the calendar code. As this is a common task, the Django developers created the `autoescape` tag to make life easy for you. Make the following changes to your `base.html` file (changes in bold):

```
# \myclub_site\templates\base.html

<!doctype html>
<html>
  <head>
    <meta charset="utf-8">
    <title>Basic Site Template</title>
  </head>

  <body>
    <h1>{{ title }}</h1>
    <p>{% autoescape off %}{{ cal }}{% endautoescape %}</p>
  </body>
</html>
```

Now, when you refresh your browser, the site homepage should look like Figure 6-2.

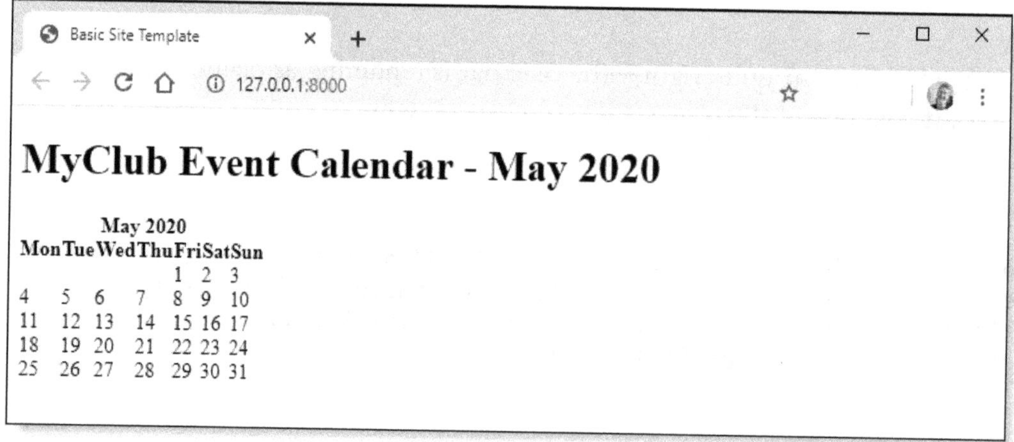

Figure 6-2. *The site template rendered with autoescape off for the calendar code.*

Template Inheritance

While our base template is rendering fine in the browser, it's not an effective site template because it's tied to the `events` app. A site template needs to be independent of all the other apps in your Django project.

This is where Django's *template inheritance* comes in handy.

With Django's template inheritance, you create a parent template containing content shared by every page on the website and child templates that inherit these shared features from the parent. Child templates can then add content and formatting unique to the child.

This is easier to understand in practice. First, modify your `base.html` file as follows (changes in bold):

```
# \myclub_site\templates\base.html

<!doctype html>
<html>
  <head>
    <meta charset="utf-8">
    <title>
      {% block title %}
      {{ page_title|default:"Untitled Page" }}
      {% endblock title %}
    </title>
  </head>

  <body>
    {% block content %}
    <p>Placeholder text in base template. Replace with page content.</p>
    {% endblock content %}
  </body>
</html>
```

Let's have a closer look at what's changed:

- **Lines 6 and 8.** I have added a pair of Django *block tags*. The block tag defines a block of text other templates can replace. I've named the block "title".
- **Line 7.** I've created a new template variable called `page_title`. I have also added a default filter to the variable. If a view passes a value for `page_title` in the context, the template will render the `page_title` variable in the page title; otherwise, it will render "Untitled Page".
- **Lines 13 and 15.** Another pair of Django block tags to define a replaceable block for the page content.
- **Line 14** is placeholder text to render when a child template has not replaced the content block.

If you fire up the development server again and navigate to `http://127.0.0.1:8000`, you will see that Django now renders your base template (Figure 6-3). Note we didn't pass a value for `page_title` to the template, so the page title shows the default.

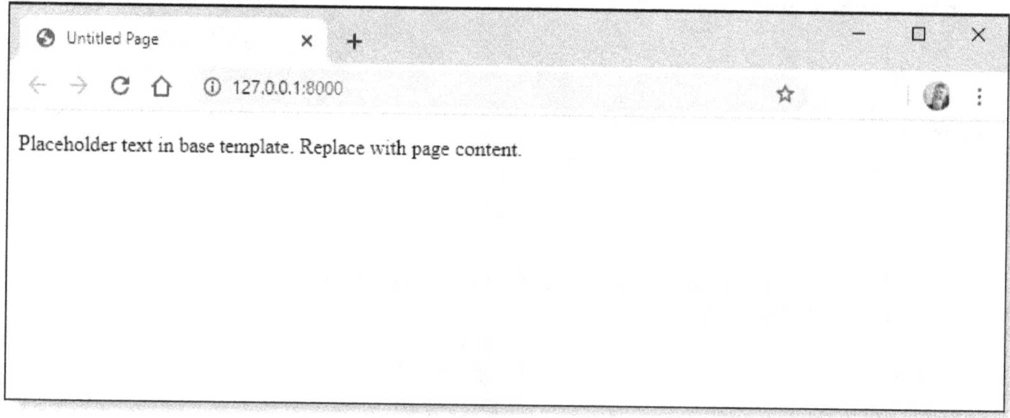

Figure 6-3. *The site base template with no content.*

Next, we will create a child template for the events calendar that inherits common content from the base template and adds new content unique to the event calendar. Create a new file called `calendar_base.html` in your `events\templates\events` folder and add the following (new file):

```
# \events\templates\events\calendar_base.html

1  {% extends 'base.html' %}
2
3  {% block title %}{{ title }}{% endblock title %}
4
5  {% block content %}
6    <h1>{{ title }}</h1>
7    <p>{% autoescape off %}{{ cal }}{% endautoescape %}</p>
8  {% endblock content %}
```

Let's have a look at this file to see what's going on:

- **Line 1.** The `{% extends %}` template tag is where Django's template inheritance magic happens. When you add the `{% extends %}` tag to a template file, you are telling Django to load all the content from the parent template (`base.html`). All you have to do in the child is define what blocks the child replaces and add HTML and code unique to the child.
- **Line 3.** We replace the `title` block tag from `base.html` with a new block that will contain the title variable from the `index` view.
- **Lines 5 and 8.** We're replacing the content block from `base.html` with a new content block.
- **Lines 6 and 7.** These are the same lines that were originally in the base template—they've been moved to `calendar_base.html`, so the site template is not tied to the `events` app.

To display the new child template in the browser, we must modify the `index` view to load the new template (change in bold):

```
# \events\views.py

# ...

1  def index(request, year=date.today().year, month=date.today().month):
2      year = int(year)
3      month = int(month)
4      if year < 2000 or year > 2099: year = date.today().year
5      month_name = calendar.month_name[month]
6      title = "MyClub Event Calendar - %s %s" % (month_name,year)
7      cal = HTMLCalendar().formatmonth(year, month)
8      return render(request,
9          'events/calendar_base.html',
10         {'title': title, 'cal': cal}
11     )
```

Only one change: in **line 9**, I've replaced the `base.html` template with the `calendar_base.html` template. Note the namespacing on the template to ensure Django always selects the right template. I have also reformatted the `render()` function to shorten the line length, but the function remains the same otherwise.

Refresh your browser, and the site should look like Figure 6-4. Note the page title and the content have changed.

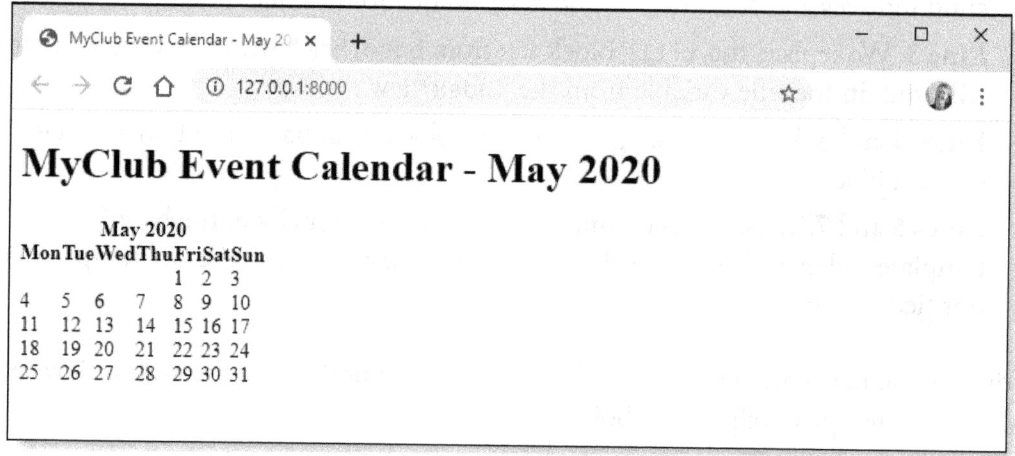

Figure 6-4. *The events calendar is now a child of the site template, and shows the correct title and page content.*

Displaying Database Data

So far, we've been showing dynamic data generated by Python (dates and a calendar). Displaying formatted database data in a browser is also essential in a modern web application. In the previous example, we created an HTML calendar, added it to the context in the view and used a template to display the formatted calendar at a URL set by a URLconf.

We follow exactly the same process for rendering database data to the browser, except we're adding a QuerySet to the context, not HTML. Let's start by adding a simple view to our `views.py` file (new code):

```
# myclub_root\events\views.py

# Add this import to the top of your file
from .models import Event

# ...

1  def all_events(request):
2      event_list = Event.objects.all()
3      return render(request,
4          'events/event_list.html',
5          {'event_list': event_list}
6      )
```

You can see from this view, it takes very little code to render model data to the browser. After importing the `Event` model from `models.py`, the view simply retrieves a QuerySet containing all the event records (**line 2**) and then renders it to a template with the QuerySet added to the context (**line 5**).

While we're retrieving all events with the `all()` function in this example, all the model filtering, sorting and slicing functions we covered in Chapter 4 are available in the view, so you have a great deal of flexibility to decide what records need to be displayed.

For the event records to display in the browser, we still need to add a template and a URLconf. Let's start with adding a template to our `events` app (new file):

```
# \events\templates\events\event_list.html

1  {% extends "base.html" %}
2
3  {% block title %}Displaying Model Data{% endblock title %}
4
5  {% block content %}
6    <h1>All Events in Database</h1>
7    <ul>
8      {% for event in event_list %}
9        <li>{{ event.name }}</li>
10     {% endfor %}
11   </ul>
12 {% endblock content %}
```

This template is not a lot different than the calendar base template, so should be easy to follow. The magic happens in lines 8, 9 and 10. **Lines 8 and 10** are a simple `{% for %}`/`{% endfor %}` set of template tags for creating a `for` loop in the template. We'll cover `for` loops in templates in more detail in Chapter 11, but for the moment, just remember they behave exactly the same as a Python `for` loop.

Line 9 displays the `name` attribute of each event record in the QuerySet as the for loop iterates over the data. In this template, we're showing the event names in a bulleted list.

Finally, we add a URLconf so we can navigate to the event list in a browser (change in bold):

```
# myclub_root\events\urls.py

# ...
urlpatterns = [
    path('', views.index, name='index'),
    path('events/', views.all_events, name='show-events'),
    # ...
```

A simple change—our event list template will show at the URL `/events/`. Navigate to `http://127.0.0.1:8000/events/` in your browser, and the page should look like Figure 6-5.

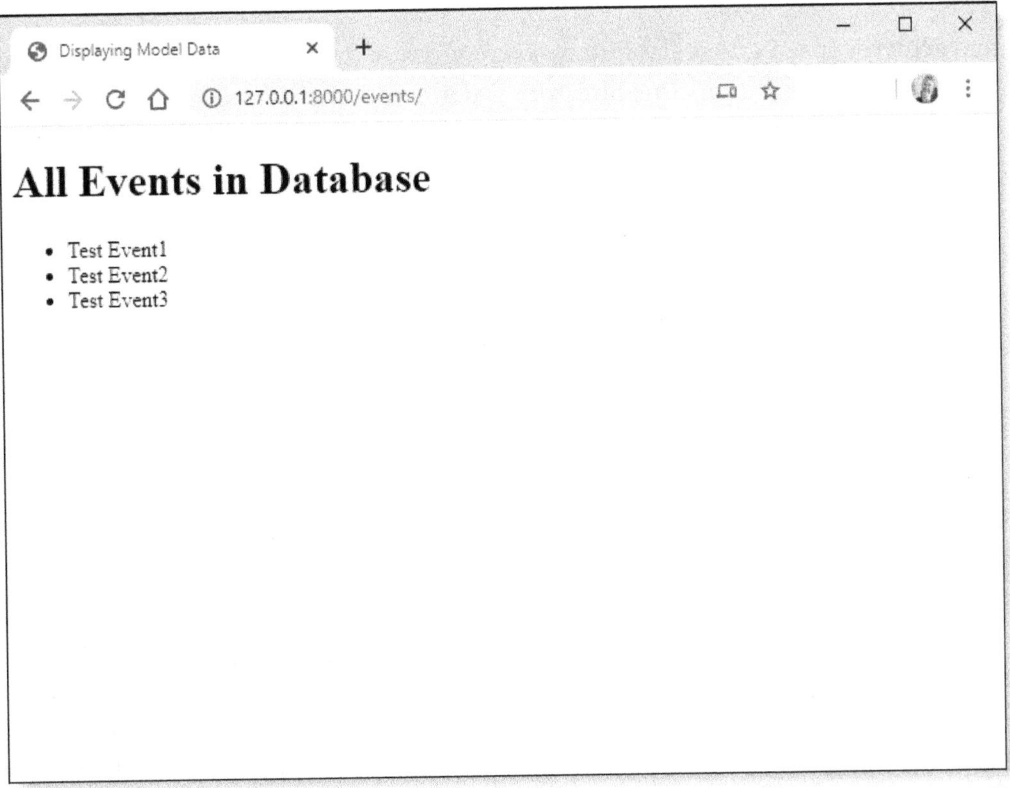

***Figure 6-5.** Rendering database data in a browser with a Django view and template.*

Loading Static Files

The basic site template and event calendar are functioning OK, but they're not very pretty—the site lacks a style sheet, images and other niceties that make up a professional website.

Django treats static files—images, CSS and JavaScript—different than templates. Django's creators wanted it to be fast and scalable, so right from the beginning, Django was designed to make it easy to serve static media from a different server to the one the main Django application was running on.

Django achieves speed and scalability by keeping static media in a different directory to the rest of the application. This directory is defined in the `settings.py` file and is called "static" by default:

```
STATIC_URL = '/static/'
```

This line should be at or near the end of your `settings.py` file. We need to add another setting so Django can find the static files for our site. Add the following below the `STATIC_URL` setting:

```
STATICFILES_DIRS = [
    os.path.join(BASE_DIR, 'myclub_site/static'),
]
```

The `STATICFILES_DIRS` list serves the same function for static files as the `DIRS` list does for templates. In this case, we are telling Django to look for static files in the `static` directory in our site root. Now we need to create a static folder in our site root. Once you have created the new folder, your project directory will look like this:

```
\myclub_root
    \myclub_site
        \static
        \templates
    # more files ...
```

Now we've created a folder for our static media, we will modify the `base.html` template to include static media, create a style sheet, and add a logo and a top banner image to the site. We'll be working with four files:

1. **base.html.** We'll update this file to include media and additional structural elements.
2. **main.css.** A new style sheet for the site.
3. **logo.png.** Create or upload a logo for the site.
4. **top_banner.jpg.** Create or upload an 800x200px banner image for the site.

Listing 1: base.html

Let's start with the modified base template (changes in bold):

```
# \myclub_site\templates\base.html

{% load static %}
<!doctype html>
<html>
  <head>
    <meta charset="utf-8">
    <title>
      {% block title %}
      {{ page_title|default:"Untitled Page" }}
      {% endblock title %}
    </title>
    <link href="{% static 'main.css' %}" rel="stylesheet" type="text/css">
  </head>
  <body>
    <div id="wrapper">
    <header id="header">
      <div id="logo"><img src="{% static 'logo.png' %}" alt="" /></div>
      <div id="top_menu">Home | Calendar | About | Contact</div>
      <div id="topbanner"><img src="{% static 'top_banner.jpg' %}" alt="" /></div>
    </header>
    <aside id="rightsidebar">
      <nav id="nav">
      <ul>
        <li>Menu 1</li>
        <li>Menu 2</li>
        <li>Menu 3</li>
      </ul>
```

```
27          </nav>
28        </aside>
29        <section id="main">
30          {% block content %}
31          <p>Placeholder text in base template. Replace with page content.</p>
32          {% endblock content %}
33        </section>
34        <footer id="footer">Copyright &copy;
35          <script type="text/JavaScript">
36          document.write(new Date().getFullYear());
37          </script> MyClub
38        </footer>
39        </div>
40    </body>
41 </html>
```

Most of the new code in this file is plain HTML5 markup. However, there are few new elements worth noting:

- **Line 1.** The {% load static %} tag links the static elements in the template to your STATIC_ROOT.
- **Line 11.** We're adding a style sheet to the template. Using the {% static %} tag avoids hard coding the URL in the template, which is always preferable. The {% static %} tag is replaced with the full path to main.css at runtime.
- **Lines 15 to 19.** We've added a <header> section to the template and added a logo, placeholder for the top menu and a banner image. Note the use of the {% static %} tag again when loading resources.
- **Lines 20 to 28.** We've added a conventional right sidebar element with a placeholder menu.
- **Lines 34 to 38.** Finally, we've added a footer element that uses JavaScript to render the current year.

Other than a few tags, there is nothing Django-specific necessary to upgrade the template. This is by design. Django is front end agnostic, so it will do nothing to stop you adding whatever you like to the front end—whether that be anything from making the templates responsive with Bootstrap to adding JavaScript frameworks like jQuery and Angular.

Listing 2: main.css

```
# \myclub_site\static\main.css

@charset "utf-8";
#header {
    border-style: none;
    width: 800px;
    height: auto;
}
#wrapper {
    margin-top: 0px;
    margin-left: auto;
    margin-right: auto;
    background-color: #FFFFFF;
    width: 800px;
}
body {
    background-color: #E0E0E0;
    font-family: "Trebuchet MS", Helvetica, sans-serif;
    font-size: 0.9em;
    text-align: justify;
    color: #474747;
}
h1 {
    color: #270c39;
}
#footer {
    text-align: center;
    font-size: 0.8em;
    padding-top: 10px;
    padding-bottom: 10px;
    background-color: #FFFFFF;
    border-top: thin solid #BBBBBB;
    clear: both;
    color: #969696;
}
#nav li {
    padding-top: 10px;
    padding-bottom: 10px;
    font-size: 1em;
    list-style-type: none;
    border-bottom: thin solid #e0e0e0;
    color: #1e9d36;
    left: 0px;
```

```
    list-style-position: inside;
}
#nav li a {
    text-decoration: none;
}
#rightsidebar {
    width: 180px;
    height: 350px;
    float: right;
    padding-right: 20px;
}
#main {
    width: 560px;
    float: left;
    margin: 0 10px 50px 20px;
    padding-right: 10px;
}
#logo {
    padding: 10px;
    float: left;
}
#top_menu {
    float: right;
    padding: 50px 20px 0px 0px;
    font-size: 1.2em;
    color: #270c39;
}
table.month td {
    border: 1px solid rgb(221, 221, 221);
    padding: 20px;
    text-align: center;
}
table.month th {
    padding: 2px 0px;
    text-align: center;
}
th.month {
    display: none;
}
```

This file is standard CSS. If you are not familiar with CSS, you can enter the code as written and learn more about style sheets as you go, or if you want to learn more now, you can check out W3schools[2].

2 https://www.w3schools.com/css/default.asp

logo.png and top_banner.jpg

You can download these files from the book website (they're included in the source code[3]), or you can create your own. Either way, put them both in the `\myclub_site\static\` folder.

If you fire up the development server again and navigate to `http://127.0.0.1:8000`, you will see the results of your efforts (Figure 6-6). I am sure you agree that, while it still has a way to go, the new template is much prettier than the last!

Figure 6-6. *The event calendar template with styling and structural elements added.*

3 https://djangobook.com/mastering-django-source/

OK, if you are using the printed textbook, this will look a lot less impressive as the images are black and white, but if you use my code and style sheets, the site will be in color.

Template Includes

Django also provides you with the ability to insert templates into other templates with the `include` tag. The syntax of the `include` tag is simple:

```
{% include <template name> %}
```

The `<template name>` can be a string or a variable, for example:

```
{% include "events/announcements.html" %}
```

Let's try the include tag out with a practical example. Announcements are a common function of club websites and often show on several pages on the website. The HTML for displaying announcements is a perfect candidate for an include—we can create a template for the announcements and include that template on each page we want to show the announcements. First, let's create the announcements template and save the file with our event templates (new file):

```
# events\templates\events\announcements.html

<h2>Announcements</h2>
<table>
  {% for announcement in announcements %}
  <tr>
    <td><strong>{{ announcement.date }}</strong></td>
    <td>{{ announcement.announcement }}</td>
  </tr>
  {% empty %}
  <tr>
    <td><strong>{% now "m-d-y" %}</strong></td>
    <td>No Announcements</td>
```

```
12   </tr>
13   {% endfor %}
14 </table>
```

We're using some new Django template tags here, so let's have a closer look at some of the important lines of code:

- **Line 3** is the beginning of a Django `for` loop tag.
- **Lines 5 and 6** execute for each item in the announcements list. The HTML code will render each announcement in a table row, with the date of the announcement in bold.
- **Line 8** is a Django `empty` tag. The `empty` tag is an optional, but convenient, way to test if a list doesn't exist, or is empty. It's a neater and faster alternative to using an `if...else` clause to test the list.
- **Lines 9 to 12** only execute if the announcements list is empty or doesn't exist. They show a message saying there are no announcements. In **line 11**, we're using Django's `now` tag to show the current date. The `now` tag takes one parameter—the date format string. For more on date format strings, see the Django documentation[4].
- **Line 13** is the closing tag for the Django `for` loop.

To include the new `announcements.html` template in our event calendar, we need to add one line to the calendar template (change in bold):

```
# \events\templates\events\calendar_base.html

{% extends 'base.html' %}

{% block title %}{{ title }}{% endblock title %}

{% block content %}
  <h1>{{ title }}</h1>
  <p>{% autoescape off %}{{ cal }}{% endautoescape %}</p>
  {% include "events/announcements.html" %}
{% endblock content %}
```

4 https://docs.djangoproject.com/en/dev/ref/templates/builtins/#date

In **line 8**, I have added an include tag which loads the new template into the calendar template. If you load up the development server now, your calendar page should look like Figure 6-7.

Figure 6-7. *The empty announcements list is inserted into the page using Django's* `include` *tag.*

To get actual announcements to display, you must pass a list of announcements to the template. In a real website, you would store information on the announcements in a model in your database, but for the sake of showing how the `for` loop displays announcements in the included template, we will add a hard-coded list to the `index` view (changes in bold):

```
# \myclub_root\events\views.py

# ... partial listing

def index(request, year=date.today().year, month=date.today().month):
    # ...
    cal = HTMLCalendar().formatmonth(year, month)
    announcements = [
        {
            'date': '6-10-2020',
            'announcement': "Club Registrations Open"
        },
        {
            'date': '6-15-2020',
            'announcement': "Joe Smith Elected New Club President"
        }
    ]
    return render(request,
        'events/calendar_base.html',
        {'title': title, 'cal': cal, 'announcements': announcements}
    )
```

Save your `views.py` file and refresh your browser. Your event calendar announcements list should now look like Figure 6-8.

Announcements

6-10-2020 Club Registrations Open
6-15-2020 Joe Smith Elected New Club President

Figure 6-8. *The announcements list now displays all the announcements passed to it from the view.*

You wouldn't hard-code announcements in the view like this in a real website, but it is a handy illustration of how you can use a combination of Django's `include` tag and `for` loop to show list data in templates.

Chapter Summary

In this chapter, we covered the basics of how Django's templates work, how to pass information from a Django view to the browser, and how Django doesn't get in the way of you creating a professional, modern look for your website.

I also introduced you to some of the more common Django template tags and filters. In Chapter 11, I have included an exercise that covers all the most common template tags and filters, complete with example implementations.

In the next chapter, we will take a closer look at the Django admin.

7

The Django Admin

A web-based administrative back end is a standard feature of modern websites. The administrative interface, or admin for short, allows trusted site administrators to create, edit and publish content, manage site users, and perform other administrative tasks.

Django comes with a built-in admin interface. With Django's admin you can authenticate users, display and handle forms, and validate input; all automatically. Django also provides a convenient interface to manage model data.

In this chapter, we will explore the basics of the Django admin—create a superuser login, register models with the admin, customize how our models are viewed in the admin, add and edit model data, and learn how to manage users in the admin.

Accessing the Django Admin Site

When you ran `startproject` in Chapter 2, Django created and configured the default admin site for you. All you need to do now is create an admin user (superuser) to log into the admin site. To create an admin user, run the following command from inside your virtual environment:

```
python manage.py createsuperuser
```

Enter your desired username and press enter:

```
Username: admin
```

Django then prompts you for your email address:

```
Email address: admin@example.com
```

The final step is to enter your password. Enter your password twice, the second time to confirm your password:

```
Password: **********
Password (again): *********
Superuser created successfully.
```

Now you have created an admin user, you're ready to use the Django admin. Let's start the development server and explore.

First, make sure the development server is running, then open a web browser to `http://127.0.0.1:8000/admin/`. You should see the admin's login screen (Figure 7-1).

Log in with the superuser account you created. Once logged in, you should see the Django admin index page (Figure 7-2).

At the top of the index page is the **Authentication and Authorization** group with two types of editable content: **Groups** and **Users**. They are provided by the authentication framework included in Django. We will look at users and groups later in the chapter.

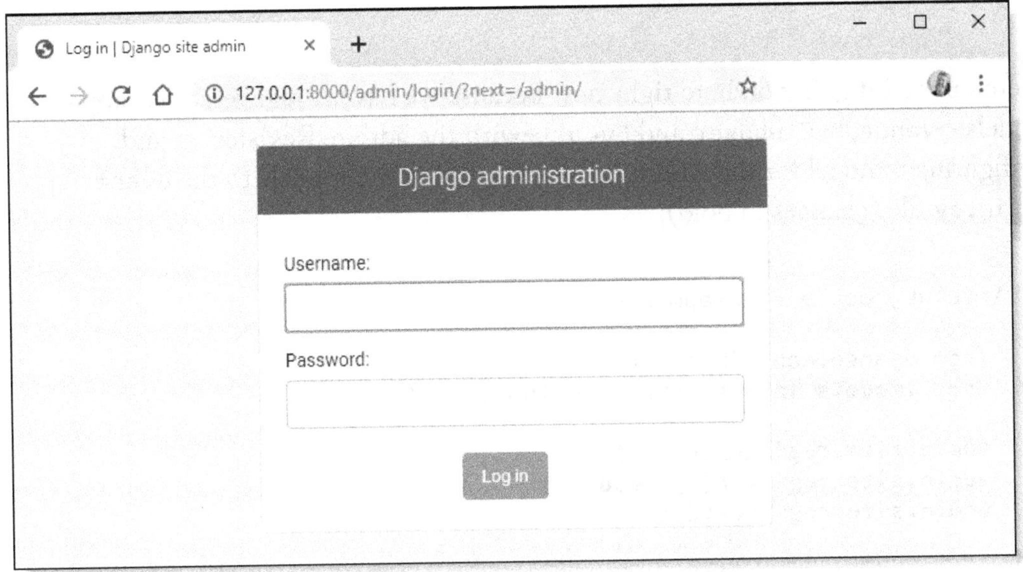

Figure 7-1. Django's admin login screen.

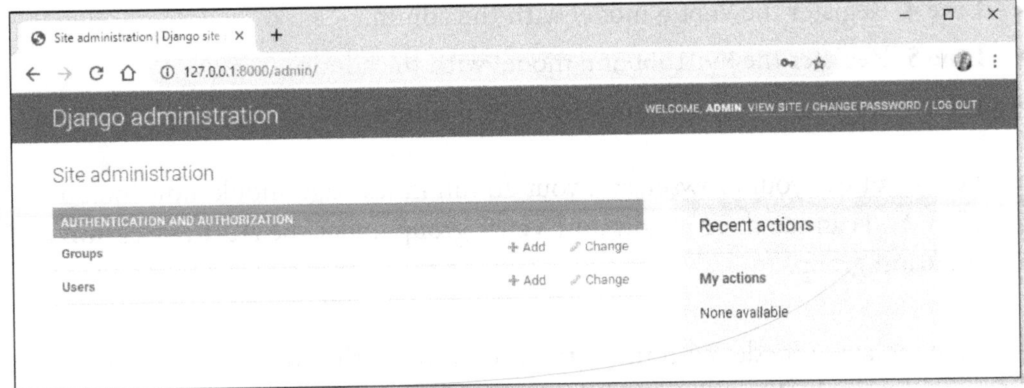

Figure 7-2. The Django admin index page.

Registering Models With the Admin

There's not a lot going on here right now because we haven't registered our app's models—`Venue`, `MyClubUser` and `Event`—with the admin. Registering and configuring a model for the admin is done by adding the models to the `events` app's `admin.py` file (changes in bold):

```
# \myclub_root\events\admin.py

1  from django.contrib import admin
2  from .models import Venue, MyClubUser, Event
3
4  admin.site.register(Venue)
5  admin.site.register(MyClubUser)
6  admin.site.register(Event)
```

We've added four lines of code to our `admin.py` file:

- **Line 2**. Import the `Venue`, `MyClubUser` and `Event` models.
- **Line 4**. Register the `Venue` model with the admin.
- **Line 5**. Register the `MyClubUser` model with the admin.
- **Line 6**. Register the `Event` model with the admin.

Save the file, refresh your browser, and your admin index page should now look like Figure 7-3. You can see there is now an **Events** group under the **Authentication and Authorization** group.

When you register a model with the admin, you can use the admin to add, edit and delete model records. Now we've registered the `Event`, `MyClubUser` and `Venue` models with the admin, we can use the admin to manage venues, users and events for our club.

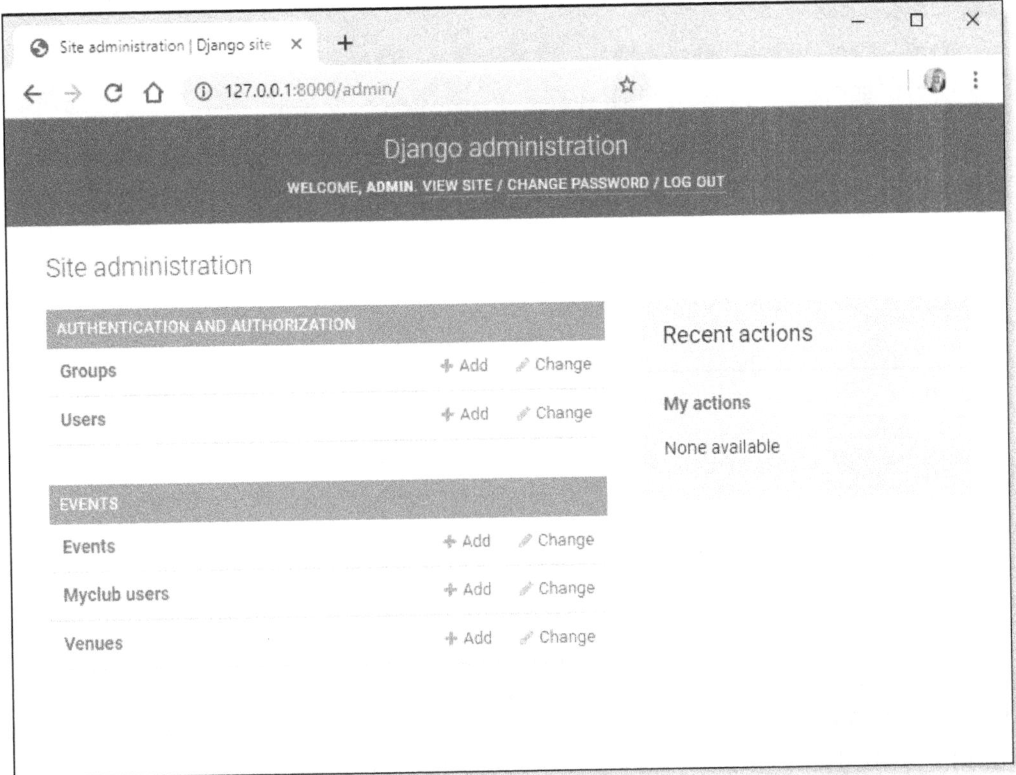

***Figure 7-3.** Once registered, the* `Venue`, `MyClubUser` *and* `Event` *models display in the admin.*

Django's admin is designed to be simple and intuitive for non-technical users. Each model registered with the admin has a *change list* and an *edit form*. If you click on **Venues** in the admin index, this will open the venues change list (Figure 7-4). Your venue list might be empty—I have added some records so you can see the default change list for the model.

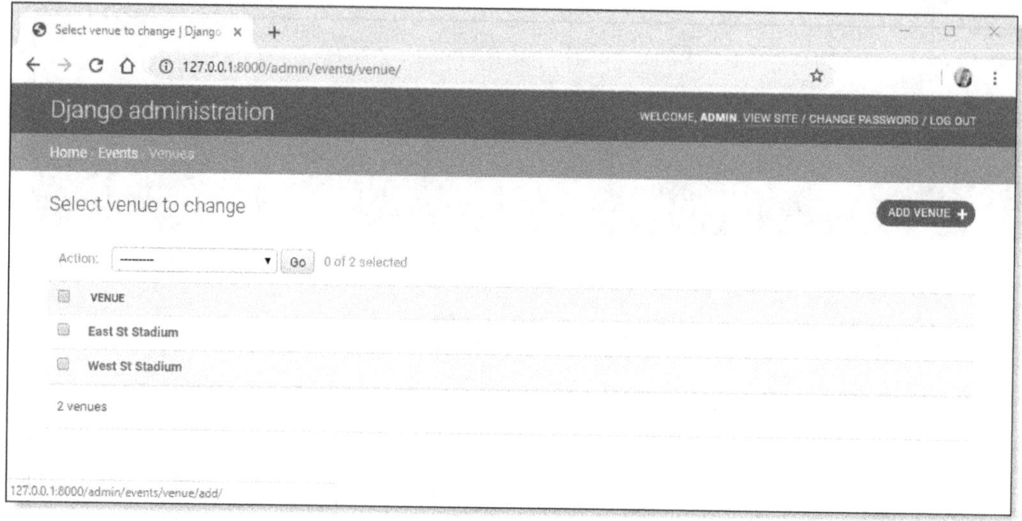

Figure 7-4. *The Venues change list. Click "Add Venue" to add a new venue.*

The change list is a table containing all the rows in the database for that particular model. To open an edit form to edit a record, click on the record title (the venue name in this example). To open a blank edit form to add a new record, click the "Add Venue" button on the top right.

Making Fields Optional

Enter Venue Name, Address and Zip/Post Code in the blank form, but leave the Contact Phone, Web Address and Email Address fields blank. Click "Save". Your screen should look something like Figure 7-5. This error occurred because, by default, all model fields are required.

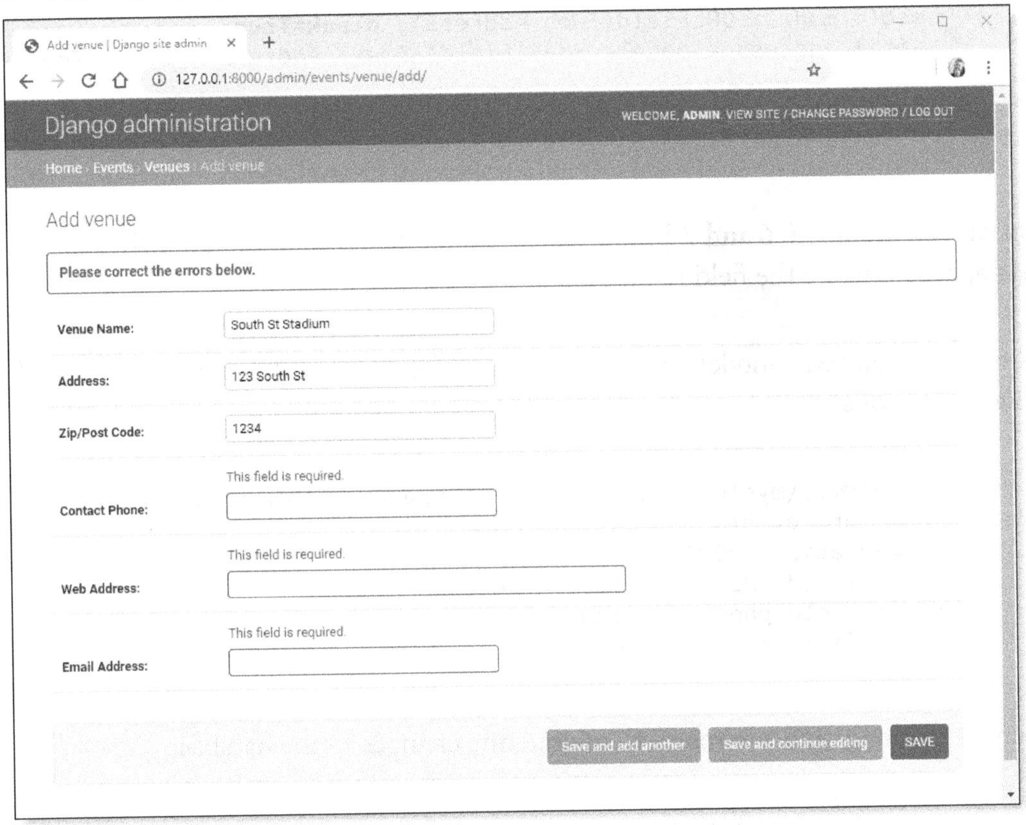

Figure 7-5. By default, all fields are required when adding records in the admin.

This is not always what you want. For example, a venue might not have a web address, and a venue may provide an email address or a phone number, but not both. To correct this error, we need to update the `Venue` model (changes in bold):

```
# \myclub_root\events\models.py

class Venue(models.Model):
    name = models.CharField('Venue Name', max_length=120)
    address = models.CharField(max_length=300)
    zip_code = models.CharField('Zip/Post Code', max_length=12)
    phone = models.CharField('Contact Phone', max_length=20,
blank=True)
```

```
6        web = models.URLField('Web Address', blank=True)
7        email_address = models.EmailField('Email Address', blank=True)
8
9        def __str__(self):
10           return self.name
```

You can see in **lines 5, 6 and 7** I have set the `blank` field option to `True`. The default is `False`, which makes the field required.

As we have changed a model, we need to update the database. First, run `makemigrations`:

```
(env_myclub) ...\myclub_root> python manage.py makemigrations
Migrations for 'events':
  events\migrations\0003_auto_20200523_0740.py
    - Alter field email_address on venue
    - Alter field phone on venue
    - Alter field web on venue
```

Then run the `migrate` command to migrate the changes to the database:

```
(env_myclub) ...\myclub_root> python manage.py migrate
Operations to perform:
Apply all migrations: admin, auth, contenttypes, events, sessions
Running migrations:
Applying events.0003_auto_20200523_0740... OK
```

Restart the development server and log in to the admin. Click on the "Add" link next to the **Venues** listing to open the edit form (Figure 7-6).

The first thing you should notice is that the Contact Phone, Web Address and Email Address field names are no longer in bold text. This indicates these fields are no longer required. Enter some information for Venue Name, Address and Zip/Post Code and click "Save". You should have no problem entering the new venue with the blank fields. Django will display a success message and switch back to the venue change list view.

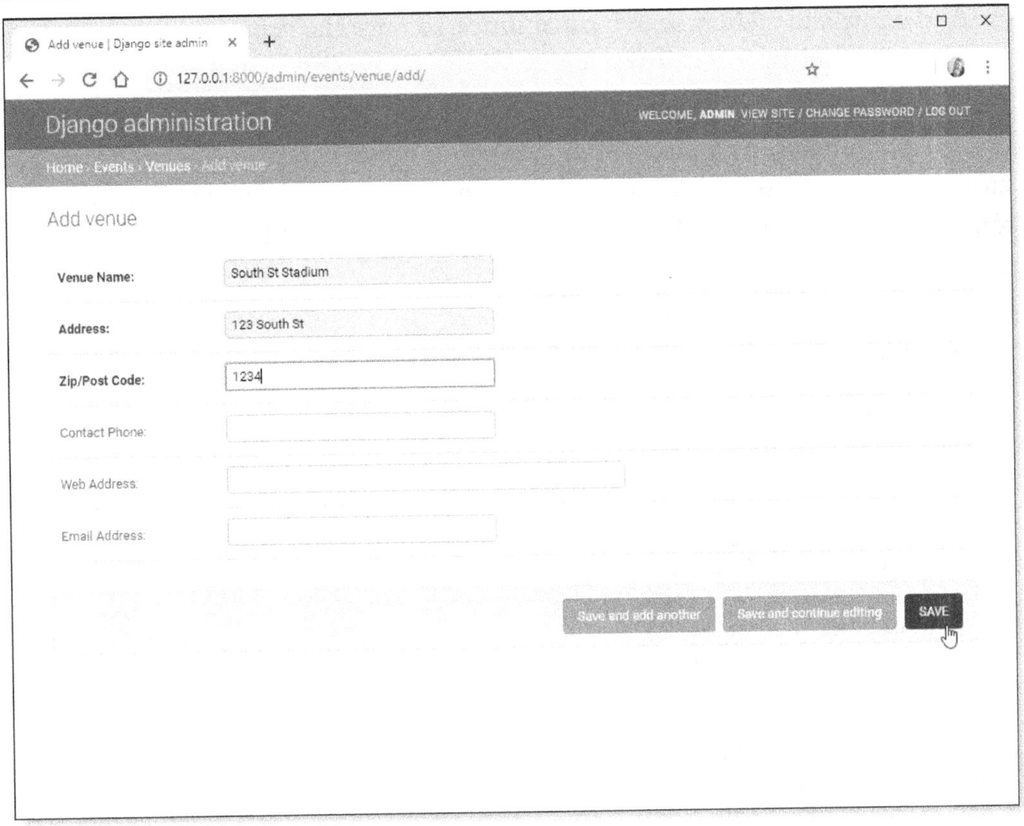

***Figure 7-6.** The venue edit form with optional fields.*

Customizing the Venue Change List

The default change list view is not very user-friendly—it just lists the venue names in no particular order. To make the list display more useful, we will make some customizations:

1. Show the venue names in alphabetical order to make browsing easier.
2. Add the venue address and phone number to the listing to make it easier to access key contact information; and

3. Add name and address search capabilities, so once the venue list gets larger, it's easier to find a particular venue.

In Django, each model is represented in the admin interface by the `ModelAdmin` class. To customize how a model displays in the admin, you can set several options in a custom `ModelAdmin` subclass. Open your `admin.py` file and add a custom `VenueAdmin` class (changes in bold):

```
# \myclub_root\events\admin.py

1  from django.contrib import admin
2  from .models import Venue, MyClubUser, Event
3
4
5  @admin.register(Venue)
6  class VenueAdmin(admin.ModelAdmin):
7      list_display = ('name', 'address', 'phone')
8      ordering = ('name',)
9      search_fields = ('name', 'address')
10
11
12 # admin.site.register(Venue)
13 admin.site.register(MyClubUser)
14 admin.site.register(Event)
```

Let's have a closer look at this new class:

- **Line 5**. We're using the `register` decorator to register the new class with the admin. The `register` decorator is functionally equivalent to the `register` method. I am using the decorator here because most books and online tutorials use the `register` method and I wanted to give you an example of an alternative way of registering your custom `ModelAdmin` subclasses. If you wanted to use the register method, you would delete line 5 and replace line 12 with `admin.site.register(Venue, VenueAdmin)`.
- **Line 6** is your `VenueAdmin` class declaration, which subclasses the `admin.ModelAdmin` class.

- **Line 7** sets the `list_display` option to show the venue name, address and phone number in the venue change list.
- **Line 8** sets the default sort order to the venue name. As `ordering` is a 1-tuple (singleton), don't forget the comma on the end! **TIP:** If you wanted the default sort to be in reverse order, you can use `ordering = ('-<fieldname>',)`. In this example, if you wanted to sort in reverse order by venue name it would be `ordering = ('-name',)`.
- **Line 9** sets the default search fields to the venue name and venue address.
- **Line 12**. As we're using the `register` decorator, line 12 is not needed, so I have commented it out.

If you refresh the admin in your browser, the venue change list should now look like Figure 7-7.

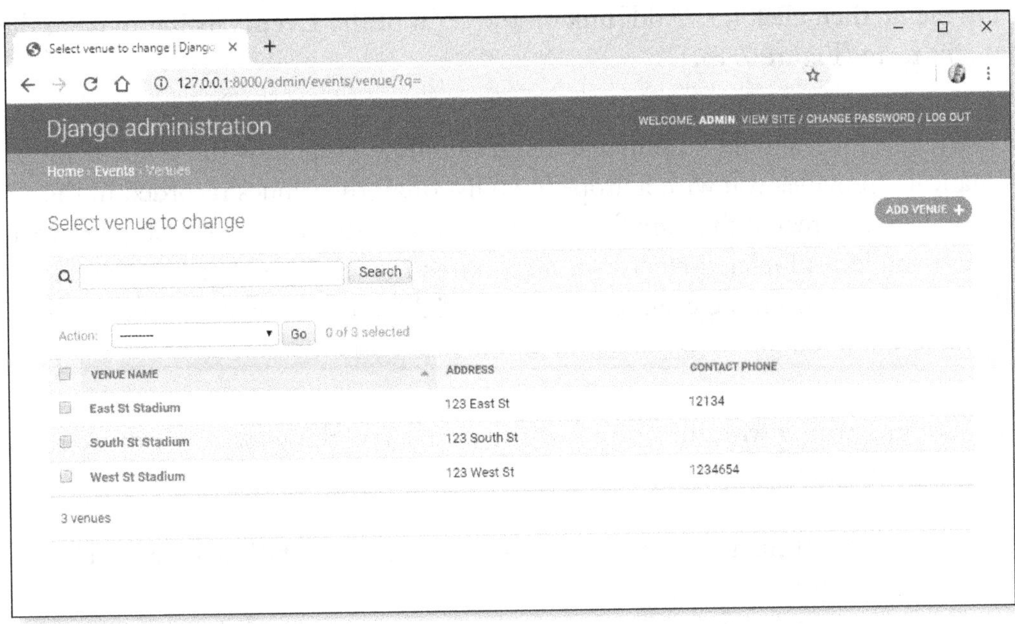

***Figure 7-7.** The venue admin now has search capability, the venues are listed in alphabetical order, and the venue address and phone number columns have been added to the change list.*

Looking at your customized venue change list, you will note that:

1. The venues are listed in alphabetical order.
2. Each venue's address and phone number are listed, along with the venue name; and
3. A search bar has been added to the change list page. Django will perform a case-insensitive search of the venue name and address fields for whatever term you enter into the search box. To show all records again, search for an empty string.

Customizing the Events Change List and Form

Now, we will make some changes to the events change list and form to make it more user-friendly too. Go back to the admin index by clicking **Django administration** in the top menu, then click the "Add" link on the right of the **Events** listing to open the event edit form (Figure 7-8).

The event edit form should be simple enough to follow. Note how the venue field automatically provides you with a drop-down list of all the venues recorded in the database. Django created this link for you when you created the relationship between the `Event` model and related records in the `venues` model. Also, note how you can create a new venue from the event edit form by clicking the green cross next to the field.

There's nothing wrong with this form, but there are a few things we can tidy up to make it easier to use:

1. Link the event manager field to the user database so a staff member can be selected.
2. Remove the attendees list from the form; and
3. Reorganize the fields on the form, including listing the event name and venue on the same line.

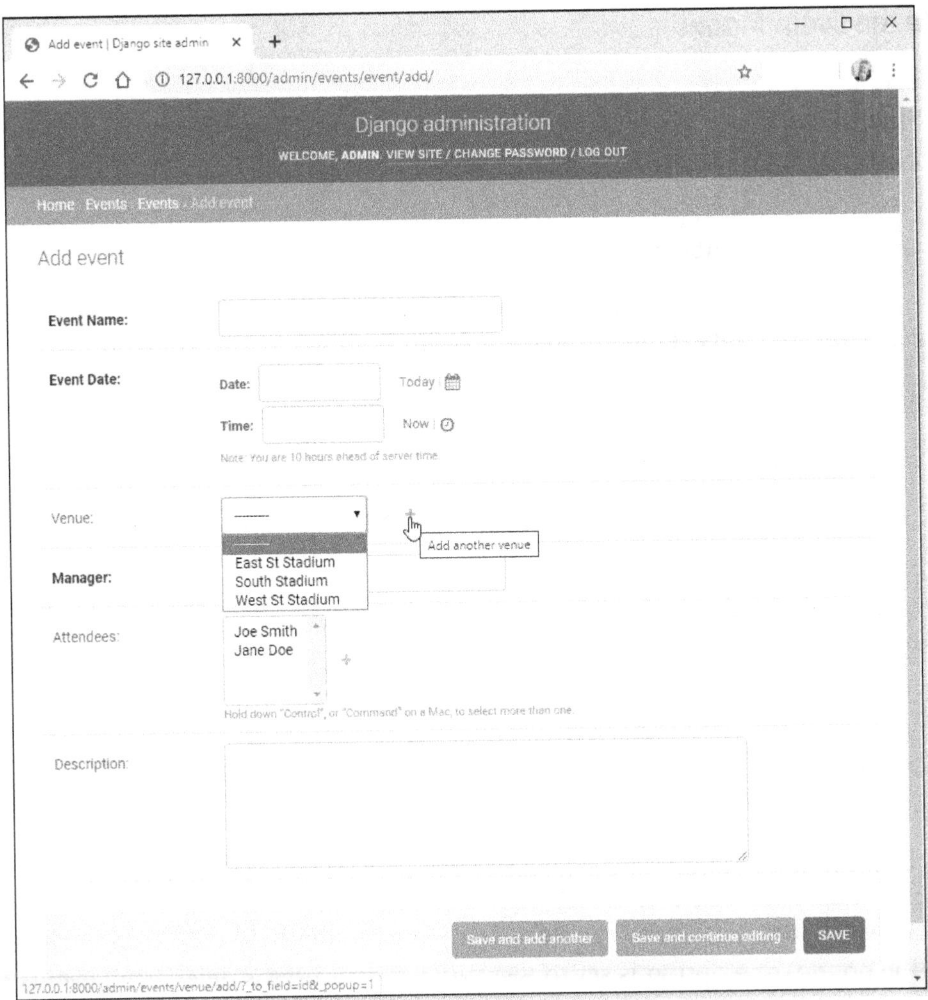

Figure 7-8. *The event change form is automatically linked to venue records in the database through model relationships. To add a new venue from the event change form, click the green cross.*

We also want to make the following changes to the event change list:

1. Modify the event change list to display additional columns; and
2. Add filter by date and filter by venue options to the event change list.

Update the Event Model

To link the `Event` model to the user database, we need to make some changes to the model class (changes in bold):

```
# \myclub_root\events\models.py

1  from django.db import models
2  from django.contrib.auth.models import User
3
4  # ...
5
6  class Event(models.Model):
7      name = models.CharField('Event Name', max_length=120)
8      event_date = models.DateTimeField('Event Date')
9      venue = models.ForeignKey(Venue, blank=True, null=True,
on_delete=models.CASCADE)
10     manager = models.ForeignKey(User, blank=True, null=True,
on_delete=models.SET_NULL)
11     attendees = models.ManyToManyField(MyClubUser, blank=True)
12     description = models.TextField(blank=True)
13
14     def __str__(self):
15         return self.name
```

In **line 2**, we've imported the `User` model from `django.contrib.auth.models`. In **line 10**, we've changed the `manager` field to a `ForeignKey` field that links to the `User` model. The `on_delete` option is set to `SET_NULL` so if a user is deleted, all events they managed have their manager ID set to `NULL`.

Once you have modified the model class, create and run the migration.

Delete All Event Records First!

Make sure you have no event records in the database, or the migration will fail!

This is because you are changing the **manager** field to a foreign key and the migration will break when the data in the field doesn't match a user ID.

```
(env_myclub) ...\myclub_root> python manage.py makemigrations
Migrations for 'events':
events\migrations\0004_auto_20200523_0751.py
    - Alter field manager on event

(env_myclub) ...\myclub_root> python manage.py migrate
Operations to perform:
Apply all migrations: admin, auth, contenttypes, events, sessions
Running migrations:
Applying events.0004_auto_20200523_0751... OK
```

Modify the Event Change List and Edit Form

To customize the admin for the Event model, we will modify admin.py and add a subclass of ModelAdmin, just as we did with the Venue model (changes in bold):

```
# \myclub_root\events\admin.py

from django.contrib import admin
from .models import Venue, MyClubUser, Event


@admin.register(Venue)
class VenueAdmin(admin.ModelAdmin):
    list_display = ('name', 'address', 'phone')
    ordering = ('name',)
    search_fields = ('name', 'address')


@admin.register(Event)
class EventAdmin(admin.ModelAdmin):
```

```
14      fields = (('name','venue'), 'event_date', 'description', 'manager')
15      list_display = ('name', 'event_date', 'venue')
16      list_filter = ('event_date', 'venue')
17      ordering = ('-event_date',)
18
19 # admin.site.register(Venue)
20 admin.site.register(MyClubUser)
21 # admin.site.register(Event)
```

The new `EventAdmin` class is basically the same as the `VenueAdmin` class, with two notable differences:

- **Line 14.** The `fields` option lists all the fields to show on the edit form, in the order they are to be displayed. If two or more fields are listed in parentheses, they are grouped together on the same line. Note the `attendees` field is not in the field list. To hide a field on an admin form, you simply don't include it in the fields list. Be careful though—you can't hide required fields; otherwise, the form won't save!
- **Line 16.** The `list_filter` option is a tuple of fields to add "Filter by..." filters to the right sidebar of the model change list.
- **Line 21.** Don't forget to comment out or delete this line as we're using the `admin.register` decorator.

Figure 7-9 shows the result of the customizations on the edit form and Figure 7-10 the resulting change list.

Figure 7-9. The customized event edit form.

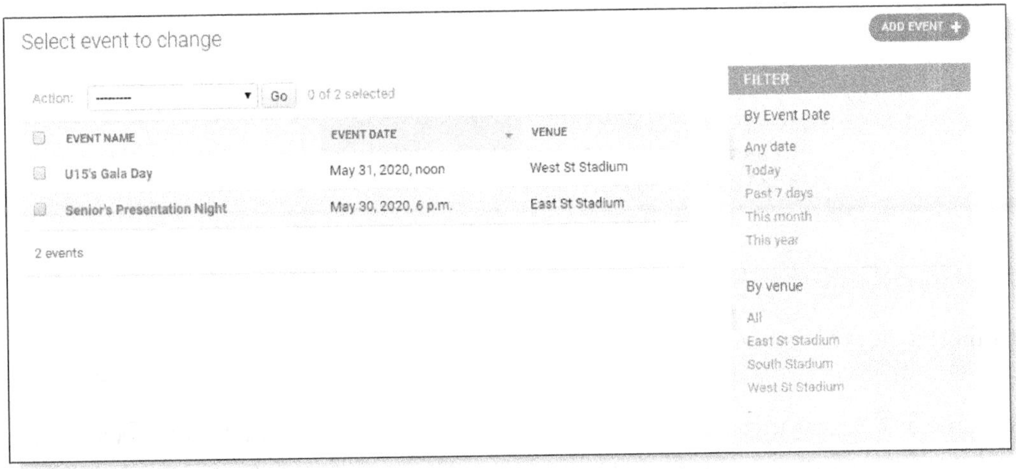

Figure 7-10. The customized event change list.

Grouping Information with Fieldsets

On larger, more complicated forms, it's easier to manage the form if the form fields are in groups. This is accomplished with the `fieldsets` option. An advantage of the `fieldsets` option is it provides some additional options that allow you to customize your model edit form further. To demonstrate, let's make some changes to the `EventAdmin` class (changes in bold):

```
# \myclub_root\events\admin.py

# ...

1  @admin.register(Event)
2  class EventAdmin(admin.ModelAdmin):
3      # fields = (('name','venue'), 'event_date', 'description',
'manager')
4      list_display = ('name', 'event_date', 'venue')
5      list_filter = ('event_date', 'venue')
6      ordering = ('-event_date',)
7      fieldsets = (
8          ('Required Information', {
9              'description': "These fields are required for each
event.",
10             'fields': (('name','venue'), 'event_date')
11         }),
12         ('Optional Information', {
13             'classes': ('collapse',),
14             'fields': ('description', 'manager')
15         }),
16     )
```

Let's have a closer look at the changes:

- **Line 3**. I've commented out the `fields` option for the class. This is because the form field display and layout options are now defined in the `fieldsets` option.
- **Lines 7 to 16** is the new `fieldset`. A `fieldset` is a list of 2-tuples, each of which represents a group of fields on the edit form. Each 2-tuple includes a group name and a dictionary of field options:

- **Line 8.** The first fieldset is named "Required Information".
- **Line 9.** The first option sets the description for the group.
- **Line 10.** This has the same effect as the fields option we commented out: `name` and `venue` are listed on the same line, and `event_date` is added to complete the "Required Information" group.
- **Line 12.** The second fieldset is named "Optional Information".
- **Line 13.** Adds the `collapse` class to the fieldset. This will apply a JavaScript accordion-style to collapse the fieldset when the form first displays.
- **Line 14.** The remaining two form fields—`description` and `manager`—are displayed as a part of the "Optional Information" group.

Save the `admin.py` file and reload the admin and you should find that the event edit form looks like Figure 7-11. Note the required and optional group names, the description for the required group, and the hidden optional fields when the form loads. Click "Show" next to the optional information title and the extra fields will show.

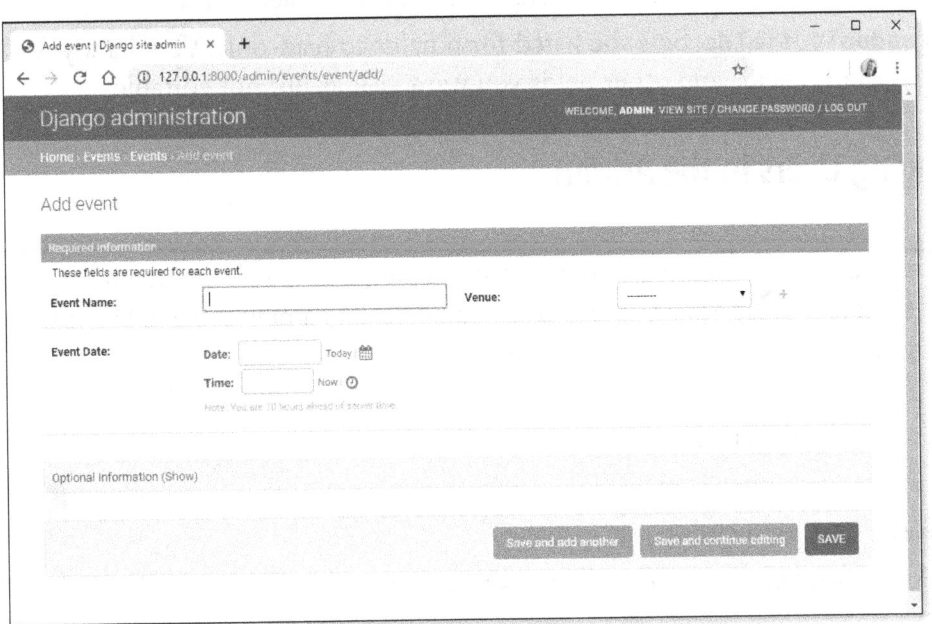

Figure 7-11. The event edit form with fieldset options set.

Grouping fields like this on such a simple form is arguably overkill, but it demonstrates how Django's highly configurable model admin can make managing form data easier.

I have only covered about half of the options and methods available for the `ModelAdmin` class in this chapter. If you want to explore the remaining options and methods for the class, the Django documentation[1] is a great reference.

Other admin options you want to check out are:

- **`date_hierarchy`**. Provides a date-based drilldown for the field.
- **`empty_value_display`**. Changes how empty values are displayed.
- **`exclude`**. Excludes a field or fields from the form
- **`filter_horizontal`**. Adds a JavaScript horizontal filter for many-to-many fields. If you want to see the horizontal filter in action, see user permissions and groups in the next section.
- **`list_editable`**. Makes the change list fields editable.
- **`readonly_fields`**. Sets the listed form fields to read-only. Very handy for timestamp fields and other fields you want visible, but not editable.

Managing Users in the Admin

If you remember from the beginning of the chapter, Django's built-in authentication system is added to the admin interface when you create a new project. With the admin you can:

- Add and delete users
- Edit existing users
- Reset user passwords
- Assign staff and/or superuser status to a user

1 https://docs.djangoproject.com/en/dev/ref/contrib/admin/#modeladmin-objects

- Add or remove user permissions
- Create user groups; and
- Add users to a group

The superuser we created earlier has full access to all models in the admin and can add, change, and delete any model record. In a real application, you will want to limit the number of users who have full access to your site.

Adding a new user is easy—go to the admin index page and click the green plus sign on the right of the **Users** entry on the admin home page. Enter a username and password and click save to add the new user.

Return to the admin home page and click **Users** to open the user change list (Figure 7-12). Click on the username to open the user edit screen.

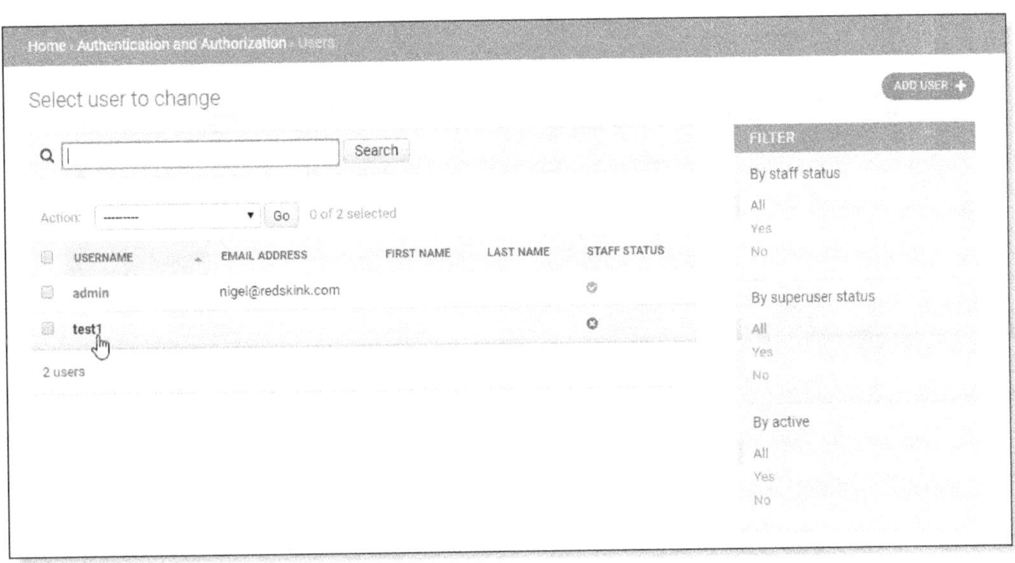

***Figure 7-12.** Select the new user from the user change list to edit the user's details.*

At the top of the user edit screen, you will see options to edit the user's password and personal info. Scroll down to the **Permissions** section and make sure "Staff status" is checked and "Superuser status" is unchecked (Figure 7-13).

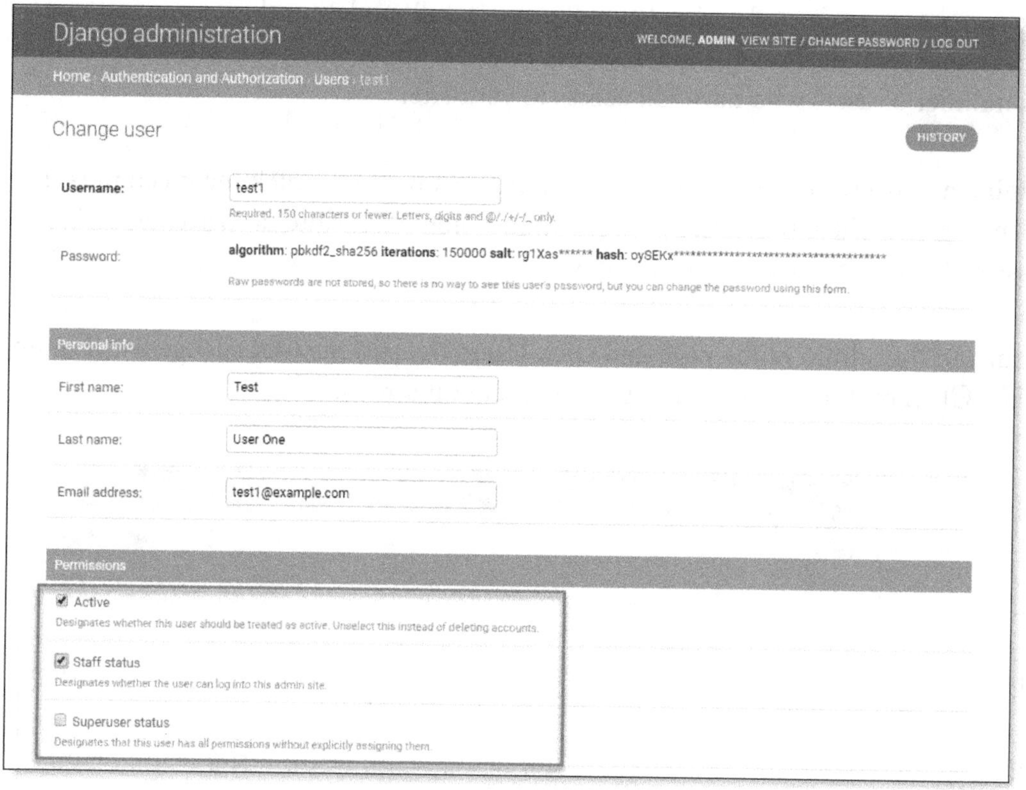

Figure 7-13. *Create a normal admin user (non-superuser) by making sure they are active and have staff status, but don't have superuser status.*

What we have created here is considered a normal admin user. Normal admin users (active, non-superuser staff members) are granted admin access through assigned permissions. Each object editable through the admin interface (e.g., events and venues) has four permissions: a create permission, a view permission, an edit permission, and a delete permission.

Assigning permissions to a user grants the user access to do what is described by those permissions. When you create a user, they have no permissions. It's up to you to give the user-specific permissions.

We will do that now—we will create a staff user who has permission to add and edit events, but not to delete them. Scroll down the edit page to the **User permissions** panel and add the following permissions using the horizontal filter (Figure 7-14):

```
events | event | Can add event
events | event | Can change event
```

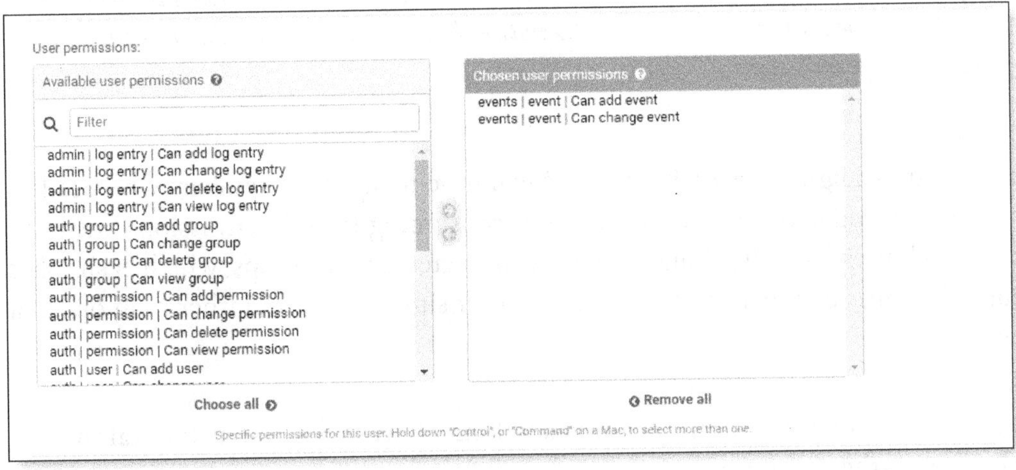

Figure 7-14. *Add permissions to the user by selecting in the horizontal filter and adding to the list. Make multiple selections by holding down the CTRL key (Command on a Mac).*

Once you have added the permissions, log out and log back in as the new user. The admin dashboard will now only show the `events` app, hiding all the other models that the user doesn't have permission to access (Figure 7-15).

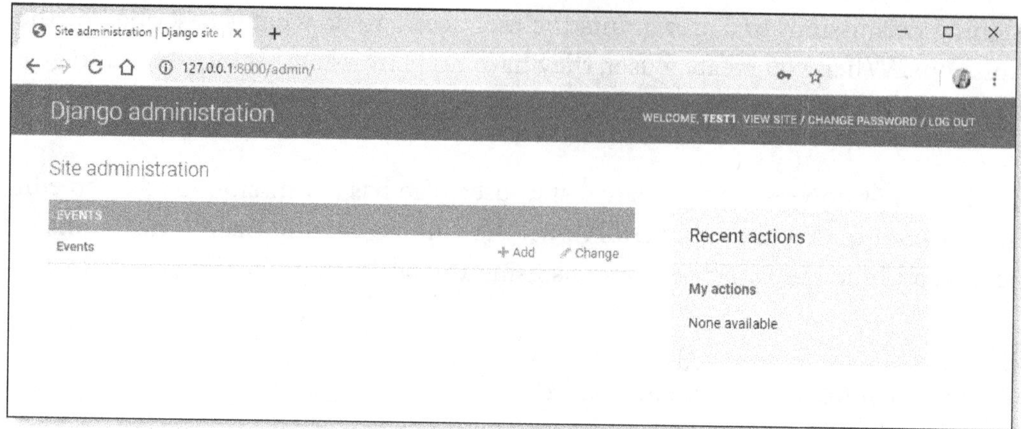

***Figure 7-15.** The new user's permission setting limits their admin access to the events app. If you open an event, you will also notice the delete button is hidden as they don't have delete permission.*

This is pretty straightforward, but what if you have many staff members who need permission to add and edit events? It's time-consuming to add permissions one at a time to each user. Luckily, Django allows you to create user groups, which is simply a group of permissions that can be added to a user simultaneously, rather than one at a time.

Let's create an "Event Admin" group. You will first have to log out as the staff user and log back in as the superuser.

Creating a group is like creating a user: go to the admin index page, click the green **Add** button to the right of the **Groups** listing, and name your new group "Event Admin". Then, add the permissions from the horizontal filter and save your new group (Figure 7-16).

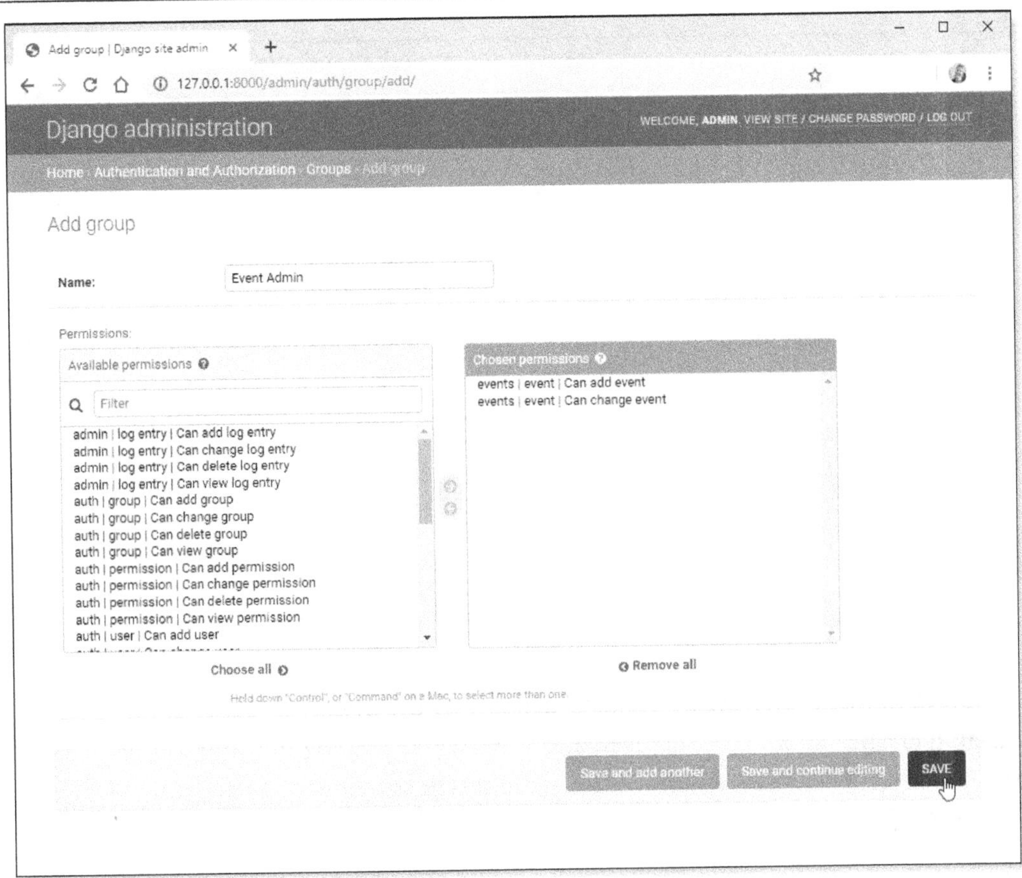

Figure 7-16. *Create a user group and add event add and change permissions to the group using the horizontal filter. Make multiple selections by holding down the CTRL key (Command key on a Mac).*

Once you have added the group, you can go back to the user and edit their permissions to add the new group (Figure 7-17).

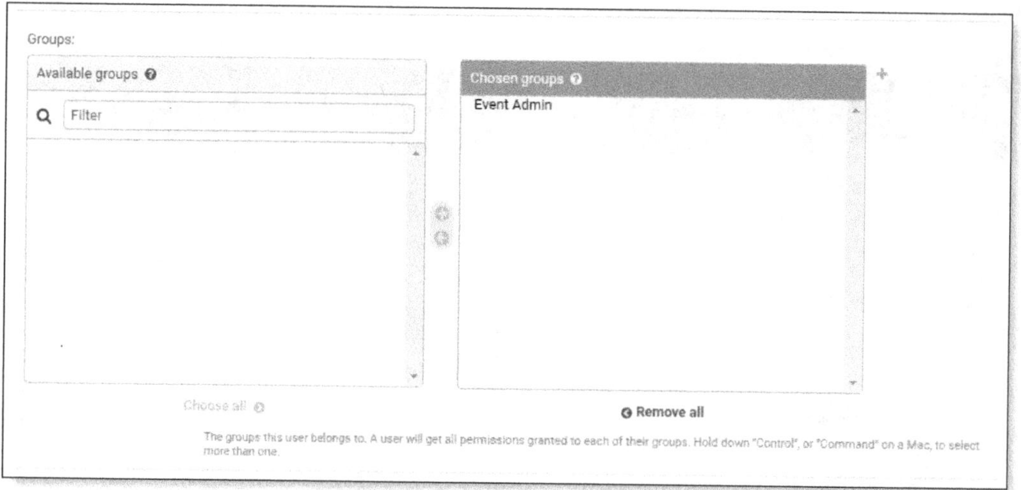

***Figure 7-17.** Adding a user to a group assigns all the group's permissions to the user.*

Don't forget to delete the permissions you assigned previously to prevent any permission clashes later. Save the user, and now, when you log out and log back in again as the staff user, they will have the same restricted view of the admin as we saw in Figure 7-15.

Changing Passwords

As a security measure, Django doesn't store raw passwords, so it's impossible to retrieve a password. A user can change their password, but they have to be logged in first.

So, how do you reset a password if the user has forgotten it?

The default admin configuration only allows an admin, or someone with permission to edit users, to reset a password by using the password reset form link on the user edit form (Figure 7-18).

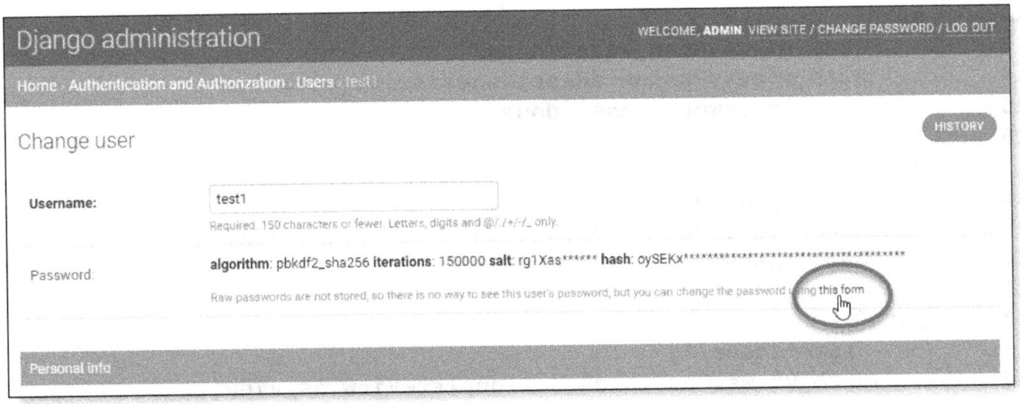

Figure 7-18. Default way to reset a user's password.

Obviously, we don't want to require an admin to log in and manually reset user passwords each time someone forgets their password.

Giving staff users permission to edit a user record is not practical either because giving anyone edit user permissions will allow them to edit all users (effectively turning them into a superuser).

Thankfully, Django has a password reset feature built in; we just have to turn it on. Make the following modifications to your site `urls.py` file (changes in bold):

```
# \myclub_root\myclub_site\urls.py

from django.contrib import admin
from django.urls import include, path
from django.contrib.auth import views as auth_views

urlpatterns = [
    path('admin/', admin.site.urls),
    path(
    'admin/password_reset/',
    auth_views.PasswordResetView.as_view(),
    name='admin_password_reset',
    ),
```

```
12      path(
13          'admin/password_reset/done/',
14          auth_views.PasswordResetDoneView.as_view(),
15          name='password_reset_done',
16      ),
17      path(
18          'reset/<uidb64>/<token>/',
19          auth_views.PasswordResetConfirmView.as_view(),
20          name='password_reset_confirm',
21      ),
22      path(
23          'reset/done/',
24          auth_views.PasswordResetCompleteView.as_view(),
25          name='password_reset_complete',
26      ),
27      path('', include('events.urls')),
28 ]
```

On **line 3**, we import the authentication views from `django.contrib.auth` and add four new path statements to our site URLs (**lines 7, 12, 17, and 22**). Once Django detects a URL named `admin_password_reset`, it will automatically add a password reset link to the login form (Figure 7-19).

Note we've only enabled the link, you would need to set up an email back end for the reset link to actually work.

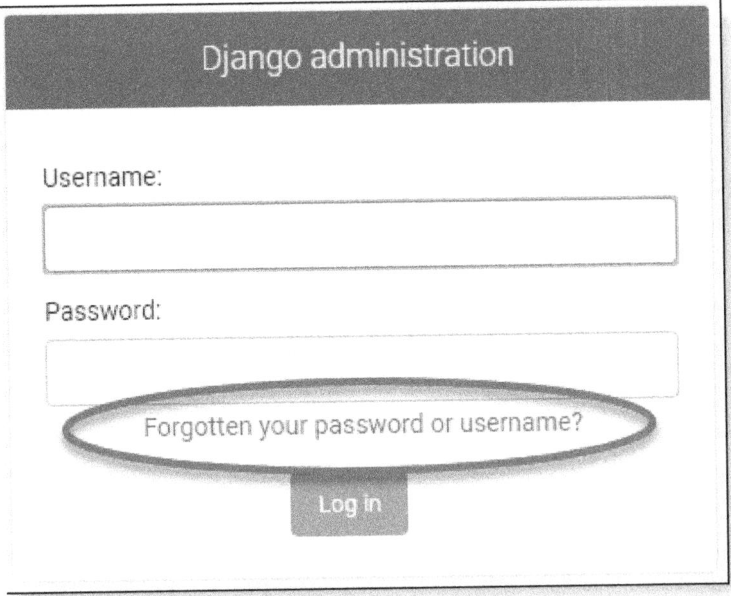

***Figure 7-19.** Adding the authentication views to your site URLs enables the password reset feature of the login form.*

Chapter Summary

In this chapter, we learned how to access the Django admin, register models with the admin, add and edit model records, customize the look of model change lists and edit forms in the admin, and how to manage users in the admin.

In the next chapter, we will learn the fundamentals of forms and form management in Django.

8

Django's Forms

HTML forms are a core component of modern websites. From Google's simple search box to large, multi-page submissions, HTML forms are the primary means of collecting information from website visitors and users.

The code for a basic HTML form is simple, for example:

```
<form>
    <p>First Name: <input type="text" name="firstname"></p>
    <p>Last Name: <input type="text" name="lastname"></p>
    <p><input type="submit" value="Submit"></p>
</form>
```

The `<form></form>` HTML tags define the form element, and each of the form fields are contained within the form element. In this form, I have defined two text fields and a submit button. In HTML5, there are many other field element types, including email fields, date and time fields, checkboxes, radio buttons and more.

I have rendered the form elements as paragraphs in this example, but it's also common to render forms as an ordered or unordered list, or as a table with the fields filling out the rows of the table. If you were to render this form in a web page, it would look like Figure 8-1.

First Name:

Last Name:

submit

Figure 8-1. *A simple HTML form.*

While creating a basic form is simple, things get more complicated once you need to use the form in a real-life situation. In a live website, you must validate the data submitted with the form. If the field is required, you must check that the field isn't blank. If the field isn't blank, you need to check if the data submitted is the valid data type. For example, if you are requesting an email address, you must check that a valid email address is entered.

You must also ensure your form deals with entered data safely. A common way hackers target a website is to submit malicious program code via forms to attempt to hack into the site.

To complicate matters further, website users expect feedback when they haven't filled out a form correctly. So, you must also have some way of displaying errors on the form for the user to correct before allowing them to submit the form.

Creating forms, validating data and providing feedback is a tedious process if you code it all by hand. Django is flexible in its approach to form creation and management—if you want to design your forms from scratch like this, Django doesn't do a lot to get in your way.

However, I don't recommend you do this. Unless you have a special application in mind, Django has many tools and libraries that make form building much easier. In particular, Django's `Form` class offers a very convenient set of class methods to take care of most of the form processing and validation for you.

With the `Form` class, you create a special class that looks a lot like a Django model. Form class fields have built-in validation, depending on the field type, and an associated HTML widget.

Let's explore the `Form` class further with the Django interactive shell. From within your virtual environment, run the command:

```
(env_myclub) ...\myclub_root> python manage.py shell
```

Once the shell is running, create your `SimpleForm` class:

```
1  >>> from django import forms
2  >>> class SimpleForm(forms.Form):
3  ...     firstname = forms.CharField(max_length=100)
4  ...     lastname = forms.CharField(max_length=100)
5  ...
6  >>>
```

Let's have a look at what we did here:

- **Line 1.** To use the `Form` class, we need to import the `forms` module from Django.
- **Line 2.** We create our `SimpleForm` class, which inherits from Django's `forms.Form` class.

- **Lines 3 and 4** are the firstname and lastname fields from our simple HTML form. Notice that the field declarations are almost identical to Django's model field declarations.

This is the first big plus for Django's Form class—you don't have to remember a new syntax for declaring form fields. But it gets better. Let's go back to the shell:

```
1  >>> f = SimpleForm()
2  >>> print(f.as_p())
<p><label for="id_firstname">Firstname:</label> <input type="text"
name="firstname" maxlength="100" required id="id_firstname"></p>
<p><label for="id_lastname">Lastname:</label> <input type="text"
name="lastname" maxlength="100" required id="id_lastname"></p>
>>>
```

Let's see what's happening here:

- **Line 1** should be easy enough to follow—we have created an instance of the SimpleForm class and named the instance f.
- **Line 2** is where the Django magic happens. as_p() is a class method that formats the form as paragraphs. You can see by the output that Django has created your form elements for you without you having to write a single HTML tag!

Django doesn't just output HTML paragraphs—you can also get Django to output HTML for displaying your form as a list or a table. Try these out for yourself:

```
>>> print(f.as_ul())
>>> print(f.as_table())
```

Note Django doesn't generate the <form></form> element for you, nor does it generate the <ul></ul> or <table></table> elements or the submit button. This is because they are structural elements on your page, so they should remain in the template.

Django's `Form` class also handles validation for you. Let's go back to the shell to try this out:

```
1 >>> f = SimpleForm({})
2 >>> f.is_valid()
3 False
4 >>> f.errors
{'firstname': ['This field is required.'], 'lastname': ['This field is required.']}
```

Reviewing what we did this time:

- **Line 1.** We created a new instance of the `SimpleForm` class and passed an empty dictionary (`{}`) to the form.
- **Line 2.** When Django created the `Form` class, it made `firstname` and `lastname` required by default, so when we run the `is_valid()` method on the empty form, it returns `False`.
- **Line 4.** Finally, if form validation fails, Django will create a dictionary of error messages. We can access this dictionary via the `errors` attribute of the `Form` class.

One other time-saving feature of the `Form` class is, when a form doesn't validate, Django re-renders the form with the error messages added. Let's try this out in the shell:

```
>>> print(f.as_p())
<ul class="errorlist"><li>This field is required.</li></ul>
<p><label for="id_firstname">Firstname:</label> <input type="text"
name="firstname" maxlength="100" required id="id_firstname"></p>
<ul class="errorlist"><li>This field is required.</li></ul>
<p><label for="id_lastname">Lastname:</label> <input type="text"
name="lastname" maxlength="100" required id="id_lastname"></p>
>>>
```

You can see Django added the errors to the form as unordered lists. If you were to render this form in your browser, it would look something like Figure 8-2.

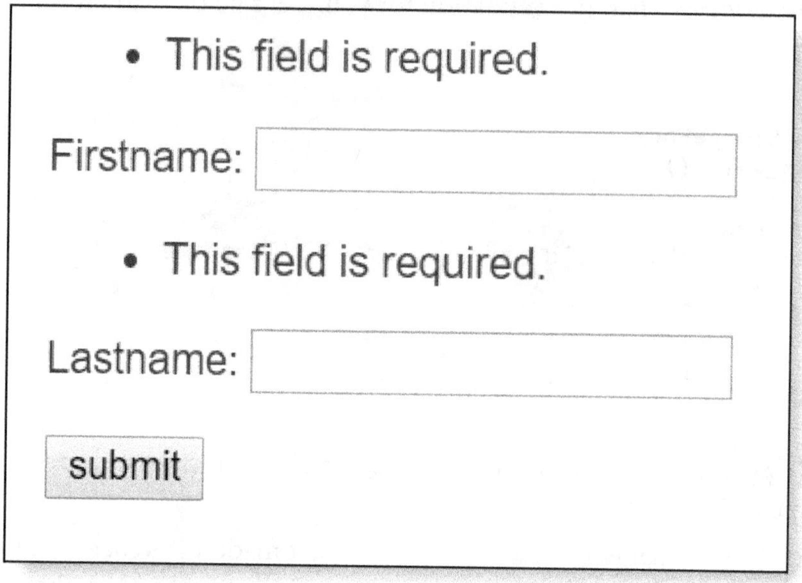

- This field is required.

Firstname:

- This field is required.

Lastname:

submit

Figure 8-2. *Django's* `Form` *class renders the error messages to the form automatically.*

Now we've had a look at how Django's `Form` class works, let's create our first form for the website. We will start with a simple form common to most websites—a contact form.

Creating a Contact Form

To create our `ContactForm` class, we first create a new file called `contact.py`. As the contact form is a part of the website, we will add it to the site app (new file):

```
# myclub_root\myclub_site\contact.py

from django import forms

class ContactForm(forms.Form):
    yourname = forms.CharField(max_length=100, label='Your Name')
    email = forms.EmailField(required=False, label='Your Email
```

```
Address')
6      subject = forms.CharField(max_length=100)
7      message = forms.CharField(widget=forms.Textarea)
```

This is like the `SimpleForm` class we created in the shell, with some differences:

- **Line 4.** If you don't specify the `label` attribute, Django uses the field name for the field label. We want the label for the `yourname` field to be more readable, so we set the label attribute to "Your Name".
- **Line 5.** We don't want the email address to be a required field, so we set the `required` attribute to `False`, so the person submitting the form can leave the email field blank. We are also changing the default label of the email field to "Your e-mail address".
- **Line 7.** The `message` field must allow the person submitting the form to enter a detailed message, so we are setting the field widget to a `Textarea`, replacing the default `TextInput` widget.

Now we have created our `ContactForm` class, we have a few tasks to complete to get it to render on our website:

1. Add our form to the site URLs.
2. Add navigation to our site template.
3. Create a template for the contact form; and
4. Create a new view to manage the contact form.

Add Contact Form URL to Site App

To show our contact form, we start by creating a URL for it. To do that, we need to modify our site's `urls.py` file (changes in bold):

```
# myclub_root\myclub_site\urls.py

from django.contrib import admin
from django.urls import include, path
```

```
3 from django.contrib.auth import views as auth_views
4 from . import contact
5
6 urlpatterns = [
7     path('admin/', admin.site.urls),
8     path('contact/', contact.contact, name='contact'),
      # ...
```

In **line 4** we've imported the contact module and in **line 8** we have added a URLconf that will direct the URL ending in "contact" to the new `contact` view we will write shortly.

Add Navigation to Site Template

We added a placeholder for the contact page in the top menu when we created the base template. Now we will turn the placeholder into a link for our contact form (changes in bold):

```
# myclub_site\templates\base.html

# ...

1 <header id="header">
2     <div id="logo"><img src="{% static 'logo.png' %}" alt="" /></div>
3     <div id="top_menu">
4       Home | Calendar | About |
5       <a href="/contact">Contact Us</a>
6     </div>
    # ...
```

I have made one change to the `base.html` template—in **line 5** we have turned the placeholder into a link to the contact page. I've also reformatted the code slightly.

Create the Contact Form Template

For our contact form to render, it needs a template. In your site templates folder, create a new folder called "contact". Inside the new folder, create a file called `contact.html` and enter the following template code (new file):

```
# \myclub_site\templates\contact\contact.html

1  {% extends "base.html" %}
2
3  {% block title %}Contact Us{% endblock title %}
4
5  {% block content %}
6  <h1>Contact us</h1>
7
8  {% if submitted %}
9    <p class="success">
10     Your message was submitted successfully. Thank you.
11   </p>
12
13 {% else %}
14   <form action="" method="post" novalidate>
15   <table>
16     {{ form.as_table }}
17     <tr>
18       <td> </td>
19       <td><input type="submit" value="Submit"></td>
20     </tr>
21   </table>
22   {% csrf_token %}
23   </form>
24 {% endif %}
25 {% endblock content %}
```

In the contact template, we are extending the base template, and replacing the title and content blocks with new content for our contact form. Some other things to note:

- **Line 8**. We are using the `{% if %}` template tag for the first time. `submitted` is a boolean value passed in from the view. The `{% if %}` / `{% else %}` / `{% endif %}` tags (**Lines 8, 13 and 24**) are creating a logical branch that is saying "if the form has been submitted, show the thank you message, otherwise show the blank form."

- **Line 14.** Is the start of our `POST` form. This is standard HTML. Note the `novalidate` attribute in the `<form>` tag. When using HTML5 in some of the latest browsers (notably Chrome), form fields will be automatically validated by the browser. As we want Django to handle form validation, the `novalidate` attribute tells the browser not to validate the form.
- **Line 16.** This is the line that renders the form fields. The `as_table` method will render the form fields as table rows. Django doesn't render the table tags or the submit button, so we are adding these on **line 15** and **lines 17 to 21**.
- **Line 22.** All `POST` forms targeted at internal URLs must use the `{% csrf_token %}` template tag. This is to protect against Cross-Site Request Forgeries (CSRF). A full explanation of CSRF is beyond the scope of this book; just rest assured that adding the `{% csrf_token %}` tag is a Good Thing.

Create the Contact Form View

Our last step is to create the new `contact` view. Open your `contact.py` file and add the contact view code (changes in bold):

```
# myclub_root\myclub_site\contact.py

from django import forms
from django.shortcuts import render
from django.http import HttpResponseRedirect


class ContactForm(forms.Form):
    yourname = forms.CharField(max_length=100, label='Your Name')
    email = forms.EmailField(required=False,label='Your e-mail address')
    subject = forms.CharField(max_length=100)
    message = forms.CharField(widget=forms.Textarea)


def contact(request):
    submitted = False
    if request.method == 'POST':
```

```
16         form = ContactForm(request.POST)
17         if form.is_valid():
18             cd = form.cleaned_data
19             # assert False
20             return HttpResponseRedirect('/contact?submitted=True')
21     else:
22         form = ContactForm()
23         if 'submitted' in request.GET:
24             submitted = True
25
26     return render(request,
27         'contact/contact.html',
28         {'form': form, 'submitted': submitted}
29         )
```

Let's step through the important bits of this code:

- **Line 2**. Import the `render()` shortcut function from `django.shortcuts`.
- **Line 3**. Import the `HttpResponseRedirect` class from `django.http`.
- **Line 13**. The beginning of our new `contact` view.
- **Line 15**. Check if the form was POSTed. If not, skip down to **line 22** and create a blank form.
- **Line 17**. Check to see if the form contains valid data. Notice there is no cruft for handling invalid form data. This is what's really cool about the `Form` class. If the form is invalid, the view drops right through to **line 26** and simply re-renders the form as Django has already automatically added the relevant error messages to the form.
- **Line 18**. If the form is valid, Django will *normalize* the data and save it to a dictionary accessible via the `cleaned_data` attribute of the `Form` class. In this context, normalizing means changing it to a consistent format. For example, regardless of what entry format you use, Django will always convert a date string to a Python `datetime.date` object.
- **Line 19**. We're not doing anything with the submitted form right now, so we put in an assertion error to test the form submission with Django's error page.
- **Line 20**. Once the form has been submitted successfully, we are using Django's `HttpResponseRedirect` class to redirect back to the contact view. We set the

`submitted` variable to `True`, so instead of rendering the form, the view will render the thank you message.

- **Line 26.** Renders the template and data back to the view.

To test the contact form, uncomment line 19, save the `contact.py` file and then navigate to `http://127.0.0.1:8000/contact` to see your new contact form. First, note there is a link to the contact form in the top menu.

Next, submit the empty form to make sure the form validation is working. Django should show the error messages (Figure 8-3).

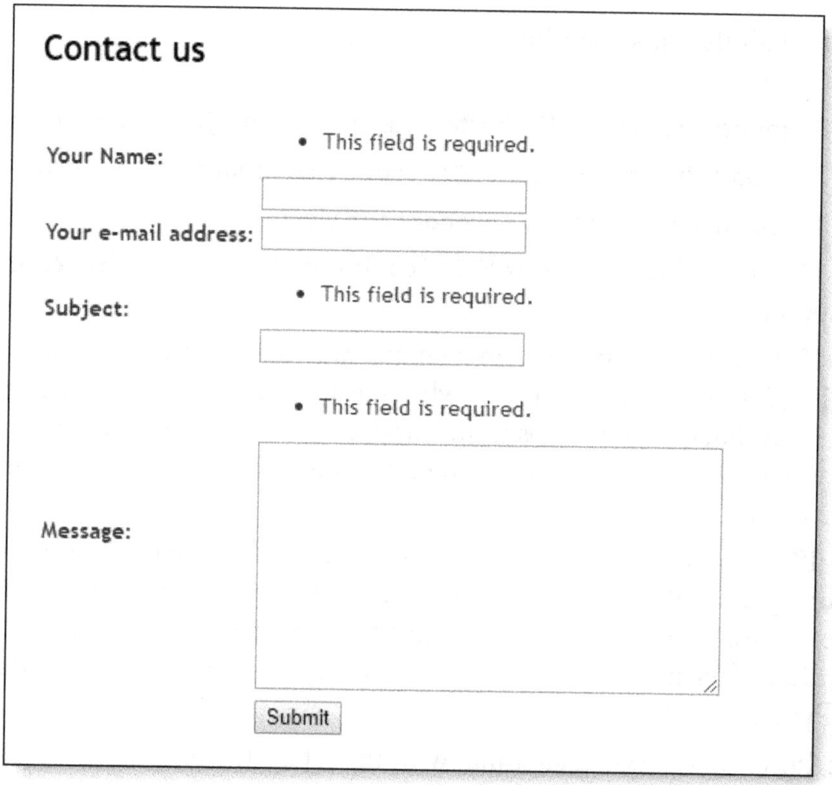

Figure 8-3. *The contact form showing errors for required fields.*

Now, fill out the form with valid data and submit it again. You should get an assertion error triggered by the `assert False` statement in the view (**line 19**). When we wrote our contact form view, we told Django to put the contents of the `cleaned_data` attribute into the variable `cd` (**line 18**).

With the `assert False` active in our view, we can check the contents of `cd` with the Django error page. Scroll down to the assertion error and open the **Local vars** panel. You should see the `cd` variable containing a dictionary of the complete form submission (Figure 8-4).

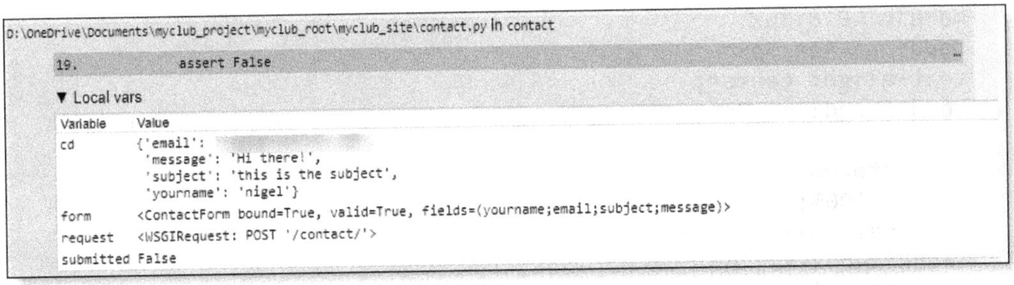

```
D:\OneDrive\Documents\myclub_project\myclub_root\myclub_site\contact.py in contact
19.         assert False
▼ Local vars
Variable   Value
cd         {'email':
            'message': 'Hi there!',
            'subject': 'this is the subject',
            'yourname': 'nigel'}
form       <ContactForm bound=True, valid=True, fields=(yourname;email;subject;message)>
request    <WSGIRequest: POST '/contact/'>
submitted  False
```

Figure 8-4. *Using the* `assert False` *statement allows us to check the contents of the submitted form.*

Once you have checked the submitted data is correct, click the back button in your browser and then click on the "Contact Us" link in the menu to take you back to the empty form.

Add Styles to the Contact Form

Our contact form is working great, but it still looks a bit plain—the fields don't line up well, and the error messages don't stand out. Let's make the form prettier with some CSS. Add the following to the end of your `main.css` file:

```
# \myclub_site\static\main.css

# ...

ul.errorlist {
    margin: 0;
    padding: 0;
}
.errorlist li {
    border: 1px solid red;
    color: red;
    background: rgba(255, 0, 0, 0.15);
    list-style-position: inside;
    display: block;
    font-size: 1.2em;
    margin: 0 0 3px;
    padding: 4px 5px;
    text-align: center;
    border-radius: 3px;
}
input, textarea {
    width: 100%;
    padding: 5px!important;
    -webkit-box-sizing: border-box;
    -moz-box-sizing: border-box;
    box-sizing: border-box;
    border-radius: 3px;
    border-style: solid;
    border-width: 1px;
    border-color: rgb(169,169,169)
}
input {
    height: 30px;
}
.success {
    background-color: rgba(0, 128, 0, 0.15);
    padding: 10px;
    text-align: center;
    color: green;
    border: 1px solid green;
    border-radius: 3px;
}
```

Once you have saved the changes to your CSS file, refresh the browser and submit the empty form. You may have to clear the browser cache to reload your CSS file. Not only should your form be better laid out, but showing pretty error messages too (Figure 8-5).

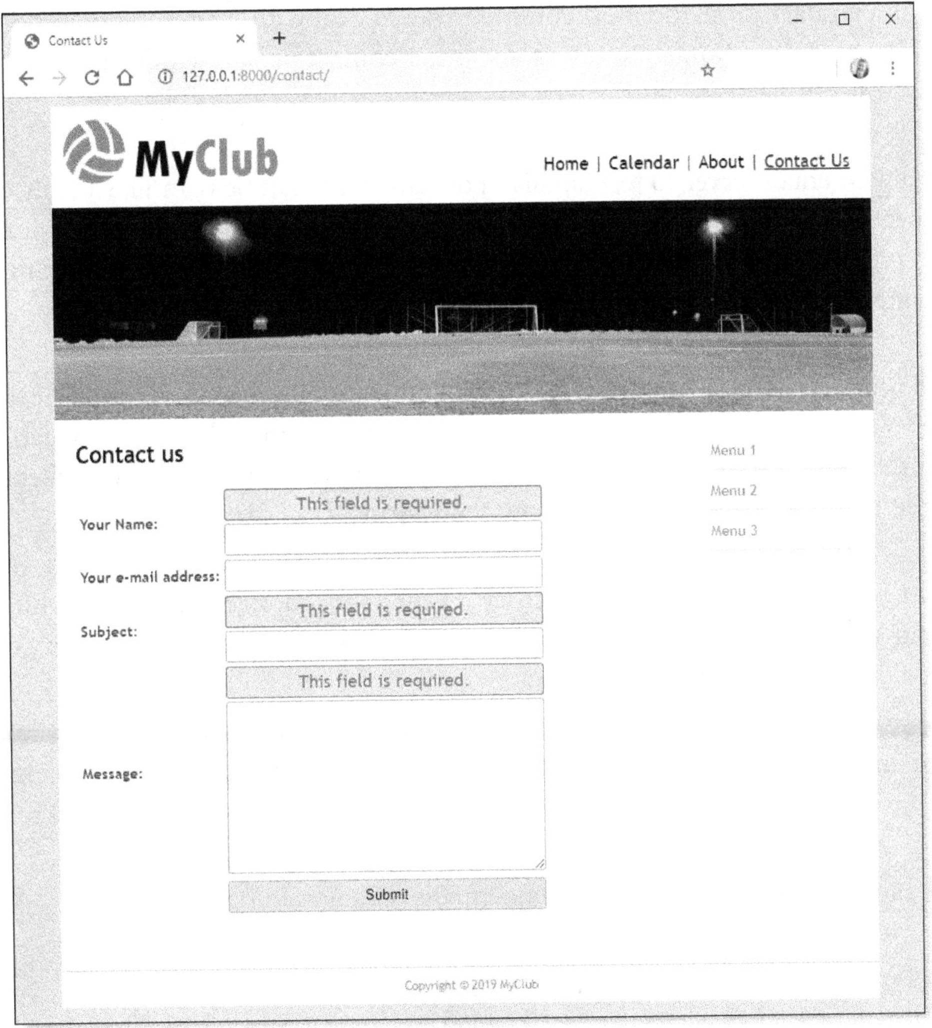

***Figure 8-5.** Adding some CSS changes our rather plain contact form into something to be proud of.*

Emailing the Form Data

Our contact form works well and looks good, but it's not much use right now because we aren't doing anything with the form data.

As this is a contact form, the most common way to deal with form submissions is to email them to a site administrator or some other contact person within the organization.

Setting up an email server to test emails in development can be painful. Luckily, this is another problem for which the Django developers have provided a handy solution. Django provides several email back ends, including a few designed for use during development.

We will use the `console` back end. This back end is useful in development as it doesn't require you to set up an email server while you are developing a Django application. The console back end sends email output to the terminal (console). You can check this in your terminal window after you submit your form.

There are other email back ends for testing: `filebased`, `locmem` and `dummy`, which send your emails to a file on your local system, save it in an attribute in memory or send to a dummy back end respectively.

You can find more information in the Django documentation under Email Back ends[1].

So, let's modify the `contact` view to send emails (changes in bold):

```
# myclub_root\myclub_site\contact.py

from django import forms
from django.shortcuts import render
from django.http import HttpResponseRedirect
```

1 https://docs.djangoproject.com/en/dev/topics/email/#topic-email-backends

```
4  from django.core.mail import send_mail, get_connection
5
6
7  class ContactForm(forms.Form):
8      yourname = forms.CharField(max_length=100, label='Your Name')
9      email = forms.EmailField(required=False,label='Your e-mail
address')
10     subject = forms.CharField(max_length=100)
11     message = forms.CharField(widget=forms.Textarea)
12
13
14 def contact(request):
15     submitted = False
16     if request.method == 'POST':
17         form = ContactForm(request.POST)
18         if form.is_valid():
19             cd = form.cleaned_data
20             # assert False
21             con = get_connection('django.core.mail.backends.console.
EmailBackend')
22             send_mail(
23                 cd['subject'],
24                 cd['message'],
25                 cd.get('email', 'noreply@example.com'),
26                 ['siteowner@example.com'],
27                 connection=con
28             )
29             return HttpResponseRedirect('/contact?submitted=True')
30     else:
31         form = ContactForm()
32         if 'submitted' in request.GET:
33             submitted = True
34
35     return render(request, 'contact/contact.html', {'form': form,
'submitted': submitted})
```

Let's have a look at the changes we've made:

- **Line 4.** Import the `send_mail()` and `get_connection()` functions from `django.core.mail`.
- **Line 20.** Comment out the `assert False` statement. If you don't do this, you will keep getting Django's error page.

- **Lines 21 to 28.** Open a connection to the email back end and use the `send_mail()` function to send the email.

This is all you need to send an email in Django. To switch to production, you only need to change the back end and add your email server settings to `settings.py`.

Test the view by filling out the form and submitting. If you look in the console window (PowerShell or command prompt) you will see the view sent the coded email straight to the console. For example, when I submitted the form, this was what Django output to PowerShell (I've shortened some of the longer lines):

```
Content-Type: text/plain; charset="utf-8"
MIME-Version: 1.0
Content-Transfer-Encoding: 7bit
Subject: this is the subject
From: nigel@masteringdjango.com
To: siteowner@example.com
Date: Fri, 22 May 2020 23:50:39 -0000
Message-ID: <...@DESKTOP.home>

This is the message
------------------------------------------
```

Now the form is complete, submit the form with valid data and the contact view will redirect to the contact page with "`submitted=True`" as a GET parameter—`http://127.0.0.1:8000/contact?submitted=True`. With `submitted` set to `True`, the `contact.html` template will execute the first `{% if %}` block and render the success message instead of the form (Figure 8-6).

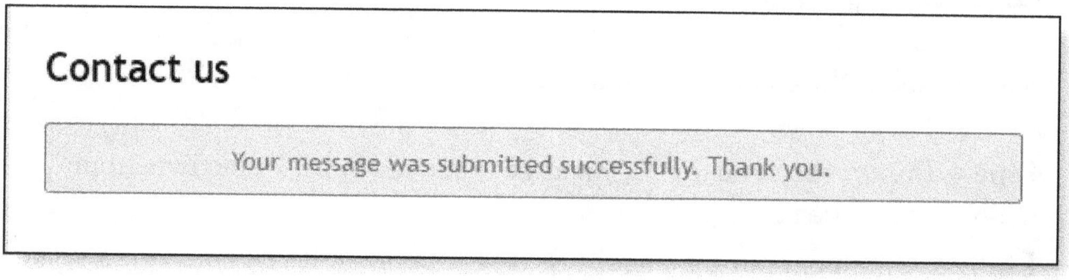

Contact us

Your message was submitted successfully. Thank you.

Figure 8-6. *Once a valid form has been submitted, the thank you message is shown instead of the form.*

Model Forms

The contact form is a common and simple use of a website form. Another common use for forms is to collect information from the user and save the information in the database. Examples include entering your personal information for a membership application, your name and address details for a sales order, and filling out a survey.

Using forms for collecting and saving data from users is so common, Django has a special form class to make creating forms from Django models much easier—*model forms*. With model forms, you create a Django model and then create a form that inherits from Django's `ModelForm` class. As always, the devil is in the detail, so let's create a form for our `Venue` model.

MyClub wants to allow venue managers to add their venue to the club database. We can't give venue managers admin access to the back end, so we will create a form they can fill out in the front end.

The process is as follows:

1. Create the `VenueForm` model form for collecting venue information from the user.
2. Add a new view to manage the form.
3. Create the form template; and
4. Add the new view and form to our `urls.py` file and update the site template to link to the venue form.

Create the Venue Form

Creating a form for the model is where the power of Django's `ModelForm` class really shines, as it's an almost trivial task. Create a new `forms.py` file in your `events` app and enter the following code (new file):

```
# \myclub_root\events\forms.py

1  from django import forms
2  from django.forms import ModelForm
3  from .models import Venue
4
5  class VenueForm(ModelForm):
6      required_css_class = 'required'
7      class Meta:
8          model = Venue
9          fields = '__all__'
```

That's it—a few lines of code is all Django needs to create a form for your model to show the necessary HTML on the page, validate your form fields, and pass form data to your view.

There are some things to note, however, so let's look at those now:

- **Line 2.** We import the `ModelForm` class, which does all the heavy lifting for us.
- **Line 3.** We import our `Venue` model.
- **Line 5.** Our `VenueForm` class inherits from `ModelForm`
- **Line 6.** `required_css_class` is a handy `ModelForm` class option that adds a CSS class to our required fields. We will use this class to add an asterisk (*) to the required fields in the form template.
- **Line 7.** The `ModelForm` class has an internal `Meta` class which we use to pass in the metadata options the `ModelForm` class needs to render our form:
    - **Line 8.** The model on which to base our form; and
    - **Line 9.** The model fields to render on the form. Here, we're using the special `__all__` value to tell Django to use all the form fields.

Add the Venue View

The view to add a venue builds on what we learned previously in the chapter. We will call the new view `add_venue`, so let's add the view code to the `views.py` file in our `events` app (changes in bold):

```
# \myclub_root\events\views.py

1  from django.shortcuts import render
2  from django.http import HttpResponse
3  from django.http import HttpResponseRedirect
4  from datetime import date
5  import calendar
6  from calendar import HTMLCalendar
7  from .models import Event
8  from .forms import VenueForm
9
10 # ...
11
12 def add_venue(request):
13     submitted = False
14     if request.method == 'POST':
15         form = VenueForm(request.POST)
16         if form.is_valid():
17             form.save()
18             return HttpResponseRedirect('/add_venue/?submitted=True')
19     else:
20         form = VenueForm()
21         if 'submitted' in request.GET:
22             submitted = True
23     return render(request,
24         'events/add_venue.html',
25         {'form': form, 'submitted': submitted}
26         )
```

At the top of the file, we're importing `HttpResponseRedirect` from `django.http` (**line 3**) and the form (`VenueForm`) from `forms.py` (**line 8**). This view is functionally identical to the view for our contact form, except we have removed the code for emailing the form data and replaced it with the `form.save()` method to save the form data to our database (**line 17**).

Create the Venue Form Template

Now, it's time to create the template for our form. We will inherit from the site's base template, so the form is similar to the contact form template. Create a new file called `add_venue.html` and add it to the `events` app's templates folder (new file):

```
# \events\templates\events\add_venue.html

{% extends "base.html" %}

{% block title %}Add Venue{% endblock title %}

{% block content %}
<h1>Add your venue to our database</h1>

{% if submitted %}
  <p class="success">
    Your venue was submitted successfully. Thank you.
  </p>
{% else %}
  <form action="" method="post" novalidate>
  <table>
    {{ form.as_table }}
    <tr>
      <td> </td>
      <td><input type="submit" value="Submit"></td>
    </tr>
  </table>
  {% csrf_token %}
  </form>
{% endif %}
{% endblock content %}
```

Except for some contextual changes to the display text, this template is identical to the contact form template, so I won't go over any details.

While we are working on the form template, we need to add a little tweak to the `main.css` file, so our required field labels will have an asterisk appended to the label:

```
# add to the end of \static\main.css

.required label:after {
    content: "*";
}
```

Link to the Add Venue Form

The last task to complete is to provide a new URL configuration for the `events` app and add an HTML anchor to the base template to link our website to the new add venue form.

First, let's add the URL configuration to the `events` app's `urls.py` file (changes in bold):

```
# \myclub_root\events\urls.py

1  from django.urls import path, re_path
2  from . import views
3
4  urlpatterns = [
5      path('', views.index, name='index'),
6      path('add_venue/', views.add_venue, name='add-venue'),
7      # ...
8  ]
```

One change here—I've added a new `path()` function on **line 6** which will redirect a URL ending with `add_venue/` to the `add_venue` view.

And now for the base template (change in bold):

```
# \myclub_site\templates\base.html

<aside id="rightsidebar">
  <nav id="nav">
    <ul>
      <li><a href="/add_venue">Add Your Venue</a></li>
      <li>Menu 2</li>
      <li>Menu 3</li>
    </ul>
  </nav>
</aside>
```

Here, in **line 4**, I've added a simple HTML anchor tag so the first menu item on the right sidebar links to our new add venue form.

Save all your files and fire up the development server. When you open your site, there should be a link to add a venue in the right sidebar. Click this link, and you should see your new add a venue form (Figure 8-7).

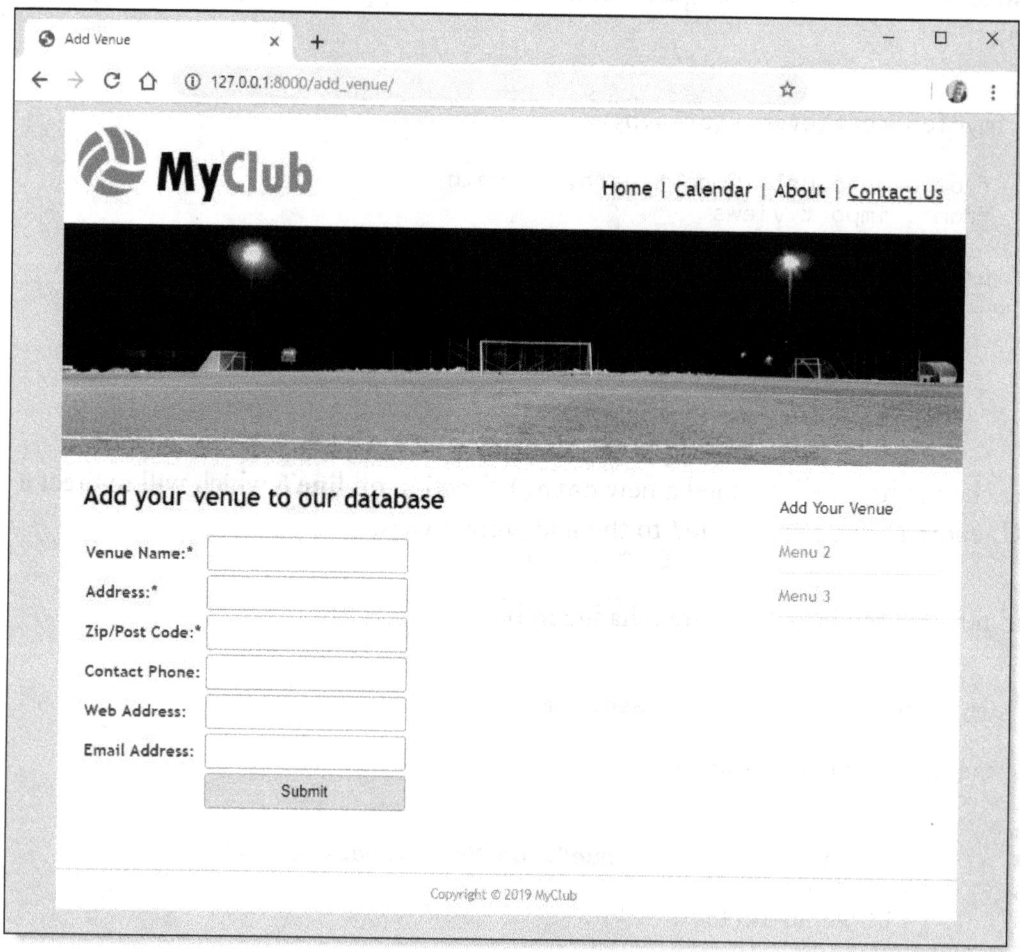

Figure 8-7. *The new form for adding a venue.*

Overriding Form Methods

While our new form for adding venues is functional, it has a problem—both contact phone and contact email address fields are optional. This was OK in the admin because a staff member would know that MyClub needs at least one form of contact in the database. User experience design best-practice says you should never assume site visitors know how to fill out a form correctly. So, we need to add custom validation to ensure the person filling out the form enters either a phone number or an email address.

As a part of the validation process, both regular forms and model forms run the `clean()` method. You can override this special method to provide custom validation. To override the `clean()` method in a `ModelForm` class, we add the override to the class (changes in bold):

```
# \myclub_root\events\forms.py

from django import forms
from django.forms import ModelForm
from .models import Venue

class VenueForm(ModelForm):
    required_css_class = 'required'
    class Meta:
        model = Venue
        fields = '__all__'

    def clean(self):
        cleaned_data = super().clean()
        phone = cleaned_data.get("phone")
        email_address = cleaned_data.get("email_address")
        if not (phone or email_address):
            raise forms.ValidationError(
                "You must enter either a phone number or an email, or both."
            )
```

Let's have a closer look at the new method we've added to the `VenueForm` class:

- **Line 12.** `super().clean()` maintains any validation logic from parent classes.
- **Lines 13 and 14.** We're retrieving the values for the venue phone number and email address from the dictionary saved in the `cleaned_data` attribute.
- **Line 15.** If both the phone number and email address are blank, a validation error is raised (**line 16**).

You can see how this new custom validation works in practice if you try to submit the form with both the phone number and email address fields blank (Figure 8-8).

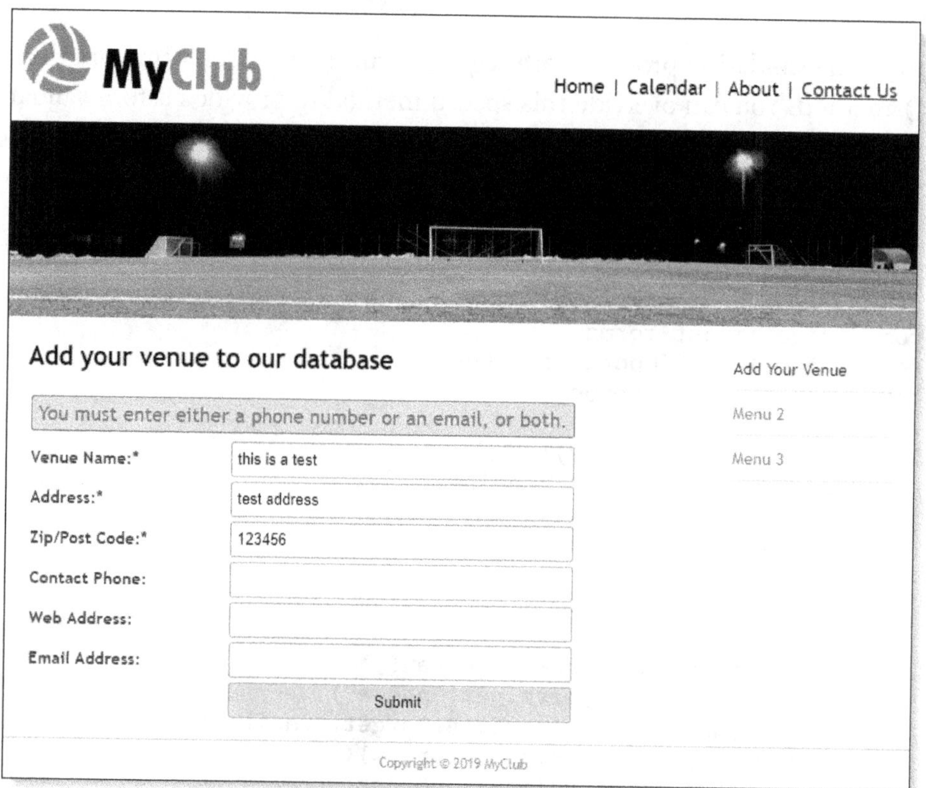

Figure 8-8. *Overriding the* `clean()` *method of the* `Form` *class provides a painless way to add custom validation to your form.*

Chapter Summary

In this chapter, we learned the fundamentals of how to create and manage forms in Django. We learned how to create a contact form for collecting feedback from site visitors, and how to create a form for a model, so users can submit data to the site database in the front end.

This chapter concludes Part 1 of the book. In the next chapter, we will move on from the fundamentals of Django to dig deeper into models, views, and templates, and cover more advanced topics on the Django admin, forms and user management.

Part 2

Django Essentials

9

Advanced Models

In this chapter, we'll dig much deeper into Django's models and comprehensively explore the essentials.

In the first section of the chapter, we'll explore the common data management functions built into Django. We'll cover common model methods that return QuerySets (and those that don't), model field lookups, aggregate functions, and building complex queries.

In later sections of the chapter, we'll cover adding and overriding model managers and model methods, and have a look at how model inheritance works in Django.

Working With Data

Django's QuerySet API provides a comprehensive array of methods and functions for working with data. In this section of the chapter, we will look at the common QuerySet methods, field lookups and aggregate functions, and how to build more complex queries with query expressions and `Q()` objects.

Methods That Return QuerySets

Table 9-1 lists all the built-in model methods that return QuerySets.

Method	Description
`filter()`	Filter by the given lookup parameters. Multiple parameters are joined by SQL `AND` statements (See Chapter 4)
`exclude()`	Filter by objects that don't match the given lookup parameters
`annotate()`	Annotate each object in the QuerySet. Annotations can be simple values, a field reference or an aggregate expression
`order_by()`	Change the default ordering of the QuerySet
`reverse()`	Reverse the default ordering of the QuerySet
`distinct()`	Perform an SQL `SELECT DISTINCT` query to eliminate duplicate rows
`values()`	Return dictionaries instead of model instances
`values_list()`	Return tuples instead of model instances
`dates()`	Return a QuerySet containing all available dates in the specified date range
`datetimes()`	Return a QuerySet containing all available dates in the specified date and time range
`none()`	Create an empty QuerySet
`all()`	Return a copy of the current QuerySet
`union()`	Use the SQL `UNION` operator to combine two or more QuerySets
`intersection()`	Use the SQL `INTERSECT` operator to return the shared elements of two or more QuerySets
`difference()`	Use the SQL `EXCEPT` operator to return elements in the first QuerySet that are not in the others
`select_related()`	Select all related data when executing the query (except many-to-many relationships)
`prefetch_related()`	Select all related data when executing the query (including many-to-many relationships)

Method	Description
`defer()`	Do not retrieve the named fields from the database. Used to improve query performance on complex datasets
`only()`	Opposite of `defer()`—return only the named fields
`using()`	Select which database the QuerySet will be evaluated against (when using multiple databases)
`select_for_update()`	Return a QuerySet and lock table rows until the end of the transaction
`raw()`	Execute a raw SQL statement
`AND (&)`	Combine two QuerySets with the SQL `AND` operator. Using `AND (&)` is functionally equivalent to using `filter()` with multiple parameters
`OR (|)`	Combine two QuerySets with the SQL `OR` operator

***Table 9-1.** Model methods that return QuerySets.*

Let's use the Django interactive shell to explore a few examples of the more common QuerySet methods not already covered in the book.

Modify the Filters To Suit Your Data

The examples in this chapter use data from my database. You will need to modify filters and search parameters to suit the data in your database. Date formats are also specific to your locale, so you may have to swap day and month parameters.

The data returned in the examples are illustrative. If you're paying attention, you will see the answers come from different datasets. This is because I have worked on many versions of this chapter over time. As your data will be different anyway, I have not changed all the examples to reflect a single dataset.

exclude()

`exclude()` will return a QuerySet of objects that don't match the given lookup parameters, for example:

```
>>> from events.models import Venue
>>> Venue.objects.exclude(name="South Stadium")
<QuerySet [<Venue: West Park>, <Venue: North Stadium>, <Venue: East
Park>]>
```

Using more than one lookup parameter will use an SQL `AND` operator under the hood:

```
>>> from events.models import Event
>>> from datetime import datetime, timezone
>>> venue1 = Venue.objects.get(name="East Park")
>>> Event.objects.exclude(venue=venue1,event_date=
datetime(2020,23,5,tzinfo=timezone.utc))
<QuerySet [<Event: Test Event>, <Event: Club Presentation - Juniors>,
<Event: Club Presentation - Seniors>, <Event: Gala Day>]>
```

The extra step in this example is because `Venue` is a foreign key to the `Event` model, so we first have to retrieve a `Venue` object.

annotate()

Annotations can be simple values, a field reference or an aggregate expression. For example, let's use Django's `Count` aggregate function to annotate our `Event` model with a total of all users attending each event:

```
>>> from events.models import Event
>>> from django.db.models import Count
>>> qry = Event.objects.annotate(total_attendees=Count('attendees'))
>>> for event in qry:
...     print(event.name, event.total_attendees)
...
```

```
Test Event 0
Gala Day 2
Club Presentation - Juniors 5
Club Presentation - Seniors 3
>>>
```

order_by() and reverse()

`order_by()` changes the default ordering of the QuerySet. Function parameters are the model fields to use to order the QuerySet. Ordering can be single level:

```
>>> from events.models import Event
>>> Event.objects.all().order_by('name')
<QuerySet [<Event: Club Presentation - Juniors>, <Event: Club
Presentation - Seniors>, <Event: Gala Day>, <Event: Test Event>]>
```

Or ordering can be multi-level. In the following example, the events are first ordered by event date and then by event name:

```
>>> Event.objects.all().order_by('event_date','name')
<QuerySet [<Event: Club Presentation - Juniors>, <Event: Club
Presentation - Seniors>, <Event: Gala Day>, <Event: Test Event>]>
```

By default, QuerySet fields are ordered in ascending order. To sort in descending order, use the - (minus) sign:

```
>>> Event.objects.all().order_by('-name')
<QuerySet [<Event: Test Event>, <Event: Gala Day>, <Event: Club
Presentation - Seniors>, <Event: Club Presentation - Juniors>]>
```

`reverse()` reverses the default ordering of the QuerySet:

```
>>> Event.objects.all().reverse()
<QuerySet [<Event: Test Event>, <Event: Club Presentation - Juniors>,
<Event: Club Presentation - Seniors>, <Event: Gala Day>]>
```

A model must have default ordering (by setting the `ordering` option of the model's `Meta` class) for `reverse()` to be useful. If the model is unordered, the sort order of the returned QuerySet will be meaningless.

Also, note both `order_by()` and `reverse()` are not free operations—they come at a time cost to your database and should be used sparingly on large datasets.

values() and values_list()

`values()` returns Python dictionaries, instead of a QuerySet object:

```
>>> Event.objects.values()
<QuerySet [{'id': 1, 'name': "Senior's Presentation Night", 'event_
date': datetime.datetime(2020, 5, 30, 18, 0, tzinfo=<UTC>), 'venue_
id': 2, 'manager_id': 1, 'description': 'Preso night'}, {'id': 2,
'name': "U15's Gala Day", 'event_date': datetime.datetime(2020, 5, 31,
12, 0, tzinfo=<UTC>), 'venue_id': 3, 'manager_id': 1, 'description':
"let's go!"}, {'id': 3, 'name': 'Test Event', 'event_date': datetime.
datetime(2020, 5, 23, 0, 28, 59, tzinfo=<UTC>), 'venue_id': 3,
'manager_id': None, 'description': ''}]>
```

You can also specify which fields you want returned:

```
>>> Event.objects.values('name','description')
<QuerySet [{'name': "Senior's Presentation Night", 'description':
'Preso night'}, {'name': "U15's Gala Day", 'description': "let's go!"},
{'name': 'Test Event', 'description': ''}]>
```

`values_list()` is the same as `values()`, except it returns tuples:

```
>>> Event.objects.values_list()
<QuerySet [(1, "Senior's Presentation Night", datetime.datetime(2020,
5, 30, 18, 0, tzinfo=<UTC>), 2, 1, 'Preso night'), (2, "U15's Gala
Day", datetime.datetime(2020, 5, 31, 12, 0, tzinfo=<UTC>), 3, 1, "let's
go!"), (3, 'Test Event', datetime.datetime(2020, 5, 23, 0, 28, 59,
tzinfo=<UTC>), 3, None, '')]>
```

You can also specify which fields to return:

```
>>> Event.objects.values_list('name')
<QuerySet [("Senior's Presentation Night",), ("U15's Gala Day",),
('Test Event',)]>
>>>
```

dates() and datetimes()

You use the `dates()` and `datetimes()` methods to return time-bounded records from the database (for example, all the events occurring in a particular month). For `dates()`, these time bounds are `year`, `month`, `week` and `day`. `datetimes()` adds `hour`, `minute` and `second` bounds. Some examples:

```
>>> from events.models import Event
>>> Event.objects.dates('event_date', 'year')
<QuerySet [datetime.date(2020, 1, 1)]>
>>> Event.objects.dates('event_date', 'month')
<QuerySet [datetime.date(2020, 5, 1)]>
>>> Event.objects.dates('event_date', 'week')
<QuerySet [datetime.date(2020, 5, 18), datetime.date(2020, 5, 25)]>
>>> Event.objects.dates('event_date', 'day')
<QuerySet [datetime.date(2020, 5, 23), datetime.date(2020, 5, 30),
datetime.date(2020, 5, 31)]>
>>>
```

select_related() and prefetch_related()

Selecting related information can be a database-intensive operation, as each foreign key relationship requires an additional database lookup. For example, each `Event` object in our database has a foreign key relationship with the `Venue` table:

```
>>> event1 = Event.objects.get(id=1)
>>> event1.venue # Foreign key retrieval causes additional database hit
<Venue: South Stadium>
```

For our simple example, this is not a problem, but in large databases with many foreign key relationships, the load on the database can be prohibitive.

You use `select_related()` to improve database performance by retrieving all related data the first time the database is hit:

```
>>> event2 = Event.objects.select_related('venue').get(id=2)
>>> event2.venue # venue has already been retrieved. Database is not
hit again.
<Venue: East Park>
>>>
```

`prefetch_related()` works the same way as `select_related()`, except it will work across many-to-many relationships.

Executing Raw SQL

While Django's developers provide the `raw()` query method for executing raw SQL, you are explicitly discouraged from doing so.

The Django ORM is very powerful. In the vast majority of cases where I have seen programmers resort to SQL it has been due to incomplete knowledge of Django's ORM on the programmers part, not a deficiency in the ORM.

If you find yourself in the situation where a query is so complex you can't find a way of completing the task with Django's ORM, it's likely you need to create a stored procedure or a new view within the database itself.

Methods That Don't Return QuerySets

Table 9-2 lists all the built-in model methods that don't return QuerySets.

Method	Description
`get()`	Return a single object. Throws an error if lookup returns multiple objects
`create()`	Shortcut method to create and save an object in one step
`get_or_create()`	Return a single object. If the object doesn't exist, it creates one
`update_or_create()`	Update a single object. If the object doesn't exist, it creates one
`bulk_create()`	Insert a list of objects in the database
`bulk_update()`	Update given fields in the listed model instances
`count()`	Count the number of objects in the returned QuerySet. Returns an integer
`in_bulk()`	Return a QuerySet containing all objects with the listed IDs
`iterator()`	Evaluate a QuerySet and return an iterator over the results. Can improve performance and memory use for queries that return a large number of objects
`latest()`	Return the latest object in the database table based on the given field(s)
`earliest()`	Return the earliest object in the database table based on the given field(s)
`first()`	Return the first object matched by the QuerySet
`last()`	Return the last object matched by the QuerySet
`aggregate()`	Return a dictionary of aggregate values calculated over the QuerySet
`exists()`	Return `True` if the QuerySet contains any results
`update()`	Perform an SQL `UPDATE` on the specified field(s)
`delete()`	Perform an SQL `DELETE` that deletes all rows in the QuerySet

Method	Description
`as_manager()`	Return a `Manager` class instance containing a copy of the QuerySet's methods
`explain()`	Return a string of the QuerySet's execution plan. Used for analyzing query performance

Table 9-2. *Model methods that don't return QuerySets.*

Let's return to the Django interactive shell to dig deeper into some common examples not already covered in the book.

get_or_create()

`get_or_create()` will attempt to retrieve a record matching the search fields. If a record doesn't exist, it will create one. The return value will be a tuple containing the created or retrieved object, and a boolean value that will be `True` if a new record was created:

```
>>> from events.models import MyClubUser
>>> usr, boolCreated = MyClubUser.objects.get_or_create(
first_name='John', last_name='Jones', email='johnj@example.com')
>>> usr
<MyClubUser: John Jones>
>>> boolCreated
True
```

If we try to create the object a second time, it will retrieve the new record from the database instead.

```
>>> usr, boolCreated = MyClubUser.objects.get_or_create(
...     first_name='John',
...     last_name='Jones',
...     email='johnj@example.com'
... )
>>> usr
```

```
<MyClubUser: John Jones>
>>> boolCreated
False
```

update_or_create()

`update_or_create()` works similar to `get_or_create()`, except you pass the search fields and a dictionary named `defaults` containing the fields to update. If the object doesn't exist, the method will create a new record in the database:

```
>>> usr, boolCreated = MyClubUser.objects.update_or_create(
first_name='Mary',  defaults={'email':'maryj@example.com'})
>>> usr
<MyClubUser: Mary Jones>
>>> boolCreated
True
```

If the record exists, Django will update all fields listed in the `defaults` dictionary:

```
>>> usr, boolCreated = MyClubUser.objects.update_or_create(
first_name='Mary', last_name='Jones', defaults={'email':'mary_j@
example.com'})
>>> usr
<MyClubUser: Mary Jones>
>>> usr.email
'mary_j@example.com'
>>> boolCreated
False
>>>
```

bulk_create() and bulk_update()

The `bulk_create()` method saves time by inserting multiple objects into the database at once, most often in a single query. The function has one required parameter—a list of objects:

```
>>> usrs = MyClubUser.objects.bulk_create(
...     [
...         MyClubUser(
...             first_name='Jane',
...             last_name='Smith',
...             email='janes@example.com'
...         ),
...         MyClubUser(
...             first_name='Steve',
...             last_name='Smith',
...             email='steves@example.com'
...         ),
...     ]
... )
>>> usrs
[<MyClubUser: Jane Smith>, <MyClubUser: Steve Smith>]
```

`bulk_update()`, on the other hand, takes a list of model objects and updates individual fields on selected model instances. For example, let's say the first two "Smiths" in the database were entered incorrectly. First, we retrieve all the "Smiths":

```
>>> usrs = MyClubUser.objects.filter(last_name='Smith')
>>> usrs
<QuerySet [<MyClubUser: Joe Smith>, <MyClubUser: Jane Smith>,
<MyClubUser: Steve Smith>]>
```

`bulk_update` will only work on a list of objects, so first, we must create a list of objects we want to update:

```
>>> update_list = [usrs[0], usrs[1]]
```

Then, we make the modifications to the objects in the list:

```
>>> update_list[0].last_name = 'Smythe'
>>> update_list[1].last_name = 'Smythe'
```

We can then use the `bulk_update` function to save the changes to the database in a single query:

```
>>> MyClubUser.objects.bulk_update(update_list, ['last_name'])
>>> MyClubUser.objects.all()
<QuerySet [<MyClubUser: Joe Smythe>, <MyClubUser: Jane Doe>,
<MyClubUser: John Jones>, <MyClubUser: Mary Jones>, <MyClubUser: Jane
Smythe>, <MyClubUser: Steve Smith>]>
>>>
```

count()

Counts the number of objects in the QuerySet. Can be used to count all objects in a database table:

```
>>> MyClubUser.objects.count()
9
```

Or used to count the number of objects returned by a query:

```
>>> MyClubUser.objects.filter(last_name='Smythe').count()
2
```

`count()` is functionally equivalent to using the `aggregate()` function, but `count()` has a cleaner syntax, and is likely to be faster on large datasets. For example:

```
>>> from django.db.models import Count
>>> MyClubUser.objects.all().aggregate(Count('id'))
{'id__count': 9}
```

in_bulk()

`in_bulk()` takes a list of id values and returns a dictionary mapping each id to an instance of the object with that id. If you don't pass a list to `in_bulk()`, all objects will be returned:

```
>>> usrs = MyClubUser.objects.in_bulk()
>>> usrs
{1: <MyClubUser: Joe Smythe>, 2: <MyClubUser: Jane Doe>, 3:
<MyClubUser: John Jones>}
```

Once retrieved, you can access each object by their key value:

```
>>> usrs[3]
<MyClubUser: John Jones>
>>> usrs[3].first_name
'John'
```

Any non-empty list will retrieve all records with the listed ids:

```
>>> MyClubUser.objects.in_bulk([1])
{1: <MyClubUser: Joe Smythe>}
```

List ids don't have to be sequential either:

```
>>> MyClubUser.objects.in_bulk([1, 3, 7])
{1: <MyClubUser: Joe Smythe>, 3: <MyClubUser: John Jones>, 7:
<MyClubUser: Mary Jones>}
```

latest() and earliest()

Return the latest or the earliest date in the database for the provided field(s):

```
>>> from events.models import Event
```

```
>>> Event.objects.latest('event_date')
<Event: Test Event>
>>> Event.objects.earliest('event_date')
<Event: Club Presentation - Juniors>
```

first() and last()

Returns the first or last object in the QuerySet:

```
>>> Event.objects.first()
<Event: Test Event>
>>> Event.objects.last()
<Event: Gala Day>
```

aggregate()

Returns a dictionary of aggregate values calculated over the QuerySet. For example:

```
>>> from django.db.models import Count
>>> Event.objects.aggregate(Count('attendees'))
{'attendees__count': 7}
>>>
```

For a list of all aggregate functions available in Django, see *Aggregate Functions* later in this chapter.

exists()

Returns `True` if the returned QuerySet contains one or more objects, `False` if the QuerySet is empty. There are two common use-cases—to check if an object is contained in another QuerySet:

```
>>> from events.models import MyClubUser

# Let's retrieve John Jones from the database
```

```
>>> usr = MyClubUser.objects.get(first_name='John', last_name='Jones')

# And check to make sure he is one of the Joneses
>>> joneses = MyClubUser.objects.filter(last_name='Jones')
>>> joneses.filter(pk=usr.pk).exists()
True
```

And to check if a query returns an object:

```
>>> joneses.filter(first_name='Mary').exists()
True
>>> joneses.filter(first_name='Peter').exists()
False
>>>
```

Field Lookups

Field lookups have a simple double-underscore syntax:

```
<searchfield>__<lookup>
```

For example:

```
>>> MyClubUser.objects.filter(first_name__exact="Sally")
<QuerySet [<MyClubUser: Sally Jones>]>
>>> MyClubUser.objects.filter(first_name__contains="Sally")
<QuerySet [<MyClubUser: Sally Jones>, <MyClubUser: Sally-Anne Jones>]>
```

A complete list of Django's field lookups is in Table 9-3.

Under the hood, Django creates SQL `WHERE` clauses to construct database queries from the applied lookups. Multiple lookups are allowed, and field lookups can also be chained (where logical):

```
>>> from events.models import Event

# Get all events in 2020 that occur before September
>>> Event.objects.filter(event_date__year=2020, event_date__month__
lt=9)
<QuerySet [<Event: Senior's Presentation Night>, <Event: U15's Gala
Day>, <Event: Test Event>]>
>>>

# Get all events occurring on or after the 10th of the month
>>> Event.objects.filter(event_date__day__gte=10)
<QuerySet [<Event: Senior's Presentation Night>, <Event: U15's Gala
Day>, <Event: Test Event>]>
>>>
```

Filter	Description
`exact/iexact`	Exact match. `iexact` is the case-insensitive version
`contains/icontains`	Field contains search text. `icontains` is the case-insensitive version
`in`	In a given iterable (list, tuple or QuerySet)
`gt/gte`	Greater than/greater than or equal
`lt/lte`	Less than/less than or equal
`startswith/istartswith`	Starts with search string. `istartswith` is the case-insensitive version
`endswith/iendswith`	Ends with search string. `iendswith` is the case-insensitive version
`range`	Range test. Range includes start and finish values
`date`	Casts the value as a date. Used for datetime field lookups
`year`	Searches for an exact year match
`iso_year`	Searches for an exact ISO 8601 year match
`month`	Searches for an exact month match

Filter	Description
`day`	Searches for an exact day match
`week`	Searches for an exact week match
`week_day`	Searches for an exact day of the week match
`quarter`	Searches for an exact quarter of the year match.
`time`	Casts the value as a time. Used for `datetime` field lookups
`hour/minute/second`	Searches for an exact hour, minute or second match
`isnull`	Checks if field is null. Returns `True` or `False`
`regex/iregex`	Regular expression match. `iregex` is the case-insensitive version

***Table 9-3.** Django's model field lookups.*

Aggregate Functions

Django includes seven aggregate functions:

- **`Avg`**. Returns the mean value of the expression.
- **`Count`**. Counts the number of returned objects.
- **`Max`**. Returns the maximum value of the expression.
- **`Min`**. Returns the minimum value of the expression.
- **`StdDev`**. Returns the population standard deviation of the data in the expression.
- **`Sum`**. Returns the sum of all values in the expression.
- **`Variance`**. Returns the population variance of the data in the expression.

They are translated to the equivalent SQL by Django's ORM.

Aggregate functions can either be used directly:

```
>>> from events.models import Event
>>> Event.objects.count()
4
```

Or with the `aggregate()` function:

```
>>> from django.db.models import Count
>>> Event.objects.aggregate(Count('id'))
{'id__count': 4}
>>>
```

More Complex Queries

Query Expressions

Query expressions describe a computation or value used as a part of another query. There are six built-in query expressions:

- **`F()`**. Represents the value of a model field or annotated column.
- **`Func()`**. Base type for database functions like `LOWER` and `SUM`.
- **`Aggregate()`**. All aggregate functions inherit from `Aggregate()`.
- **`Value()`**. Expression value. Not used directly.
- **`ExpressionWrapper()`**. Used to wrap expressions of different types.
- **`SubQuery()`**. Add a subquery to a QuerySet.

Django supports multiple arithmetic operators with query expressions, including:

- Addition and subtraction
- Multiplication and division
- Negation
- Modulo arithmetic
- The power operator

We have already covered aggregation in this chapter, so let's have a quick look at the other two commonly used query expressions: `F()` and `Func()`.

F() Expressions

The two primary uses for `F()` expressions is to move computational arithmetic from Python to the database, and to reference other fields in the model.

Let's start with a simple example: say we want to delay the first event in the event calendar by two weeks. A conventional approach would look like this:

```
>>> from events.models import Event
>>> import datetime
>>> e = Event.objects.get(id=1)
>>> e.event_date += datetime.timedelta(days=14)
>>> e.save()
```

In this example, Django retrieves information from the database into memory, uses Python to perform the computation—in this case, add 14 days to the event date—and then saves the record back to the database.

For this example, the overhead for using Python to perform the date arithmetic is not excessive. However, for more complex queries, there is a definite advantage to moving the computational load to the database.

Now let's see how we accomplish the same task with an `F()` expression:

```
>>> from django.db.models import F
>>> e = Event.objects.get(id=1)
>>> e.event_date = F('event_date') + datetime.timedelta(days=14)
>>> e.save()
```

We're not reducing the amount of code we need to write here, but by using the `F()` expression, Django creates an SQL query to perform the computational logic inside the database rather than in memory with Python.

While this takes a huge load off the Django application when executing complex computations, there is one drawback—because the calculations take place inside the database, Django is now out of sync with the updated state of the database. We can test this by looking at the `Event` object instance:

```
>>> e.event_date
<CombinedExpression: F(event_date) + DurationValue(14 days, 0:00:00)>
```

To retrieve the updated object from the database, we need to use the `refresh_from_db()` function:

```
>>> e.refresh_from_db()
>>> e.event_date
datetime.datetime(2020, 6, 27, 18, 0, tzinfo=datetime.timezone(
datetime.timedelta(0), '+0000'))
```

The second use for `F()` expressions—referencing other model fields—is straightforward. For example, you can check for users with the same first and last name:

```
>>> MyClubUser.objects.filter(first_name=F('last_name'))
<QuerySet [<MyClubUser: Don Don>]>
```

This simple syntax works with all of Django's field lookups and aggregate functions.

Func() Expressions

`Func()` expressions can be used to represent any function supported by the underlying database (e.g. `LOWER`, `UPPER`, `LEN`, `TRIM`, `CONCAT`, etc.). For example:

```
>>> from events.models import MyClubUser
>>> from django.db.models import F, Func
>>> usrs = MyClubUser.objects.all()
>>> qry = usrs.annotate(f_upper=Func(F('last_name'), function='UPPER'))
>>> for usr in qry:
...     print(usr.first_name, usr.f_upper)
...
Joe SMYTHE
Jane DOE
John JONES
Sally JONES
Sally-Anne JONES
Sarah JONES
Mary JONES
Jane SMYTHE
Steve SMITH
Don DON
>>>
```

Notice how we are using `F()` expressions again to reference another field in the `MyClubUser` model.

Q() Objects

Like `F()` expressions, a `Q()` object encapsulates an SQL expression inside a Python object. `Q()` objects are most often used to construct complex database queries by chaining together multiple expressions using `AND` (&) and `OR` (|) operators:

```
>>> from events.models import MyClubUser
>>> from django.db.models import Q
>>> Q1 = Q(first_name__startswith='J')
>>> Q2 = Q(first_name__endswith='e')
>>> MyClubUser.objects.filter(Q1 & Q2)
<QuerySet [<MyClubUser: Joe Smythe>, <MyClubUser: Jane Doe>,
<MyClubUser: Jane Smythe>]>
>>> MyClubUser.objects.filter(Q1 | Q2)
<QuerySet [<MyClubUser: Joe Smythe>, <MyClubUser: Jane Doe>,
<MyClubUser: John Jones>, <MyClubUser: Sally-Anne Jones>, <MyClubUser:
Jane Smythe>, <MyClubUser: Steve Smith>]>
>>>
```

You can also perform NOT queries using the negate (~) character:

```
>>> MyClubUser.objects.filter(~Q2)
<QuerySet [<MyClubUser: John Jones>, <MyClubUser: Sally Jones>,
<MyClubUser: Sarah Jones>, <MyClubUser: Mary Jones>, <MyClubUser: Don
Don>]>
>>> MyClubUser.objects.filter(Q1 & ~Q2)
<QuerySet [<MyClubUser: John Jones>]>
```

Model Managers

A `Manager` is a Django class that provides the interface between database query operations and a Django model. Each Django model is provided with a default `Manager` named `objects`. We used the default manager in Chapter 4 and again in this chapter every time we query the database, for example:

```
>>> newevent = Event.objects.get(name="Xmas Barbeque")

# and:

>>> joneses = MyClubUser.objects.filter(last_name='Jones')
```

In each example, `objects` is the default `Manager` for the model instance.

You can customize the default `Manager` class by extending the base `Manager` class for the model. The two most common use-cases for customizing the default manager are:

1. Adding extra manager methods; and
2. Modifying initial QuerySet results.

Adding Extra Manager Methods

Extra manager methods add table-level functionality to models. To add row-level functions, i.e., methods that act on single instances of the model, you use *model methods*, which we cover in the next section of the chapter.

Extra manager methods are created by inheriting the `Manager` base class and adding custom functions to the custom `Manager` class. For example, let's create an extra manager method for the `Event` model to retrieve the total number of events for a particular event type (changes in bold):

```
# \myclub_root\events\models.py

# ...

1  class EventManager(models.Manager):
2      def event_type_count(self, event_type):
3          return self.filter(name__icontains=event_type).count()
4
5
6  class Event(models.Model):
7      name = models.CharField('Event Name', max_length=120)
8      event_date = models.DateTimeField('Event Date')
9      venue = models.ForeignKey(Venue, blank=True, null=True,
on_delete=models.CASCADE)
10     manager = models.ForeignKey(User, blank=True, null=True,
on_delete=models.SET_NULL)
11     attendees = models.ManyToManyField(MyClubUser, blank=True)
12     description = models.TextField(blank=True)
13     objects = EventManager()
14
15     def __str__(self):
16         return self.name
```

Let's have a look at this partial listing from your `events` app's `models.py` file:

- In **line 1**, we've entered a new class called `EventManager` that inherits from Django's `models.Manager` base class.

- **Lines 2 and 3** define the `event_type_count()` custom manager method we're adding to the model. This new method returns the total number of the specified event type. Note we're using the `icontains` field lookup to return all events that have the key phrase in the title.
- In **line 13** we're replacing the default manager with our new `EventManager` class. Note that `EventManager` inherits from the `Manager` base class, so all the default manager methods like `all()` and `filter()` are included in the custom `EventManager()` class.

Once it has been created, you can use your new manager method just like any other model method:

```
# You must exit and restart the shell for this example to work.

>>> from events.models import Event
>>> Event.objects.event_type_count('Gala Day')
1
>>> Event.objects.event_type_count('Presentation')
2
```

The Shell and Changing Model Code

Any changes made to models are not applied unless you restart the shell, so this applies not only to this example but any other examples that modify model code.

Renaming the Default Model Manager

While the base manager for each model is named `objects` by default, you can change the name of the default manager in your class declaration. For example, to change the default manager name for our `Event` class from "objects" to "events", we just need to change **line 13** in the code above from:

```
13      objects = EventManager()
```

To:

```
    events = EventManager()
```

Now you can refer to the default manager like so:

```
>>> from events.models import Event
>>> Event.events.all()
<QuerySet [<Event: Test Event>, <Event: Club Presentation - Juniors>,
<Event: Club Presentation - Seniors>, <Event: Gala Day>]>
>>>
```

Overriding Initial Manager QuerySets

To change what is returned by the default manager QuerySet, you override the `Manager.get_queryset()` method. This is easiest to understand with an example. Let's say we regularly have to check what venues are listed in our local city. To cut down on the number of queries we have to write, we will create a custom manager for our `Venue` model (changes in bold):

```
# \myclub_root\events\models.py

from django.db import models
from django.contrib.auth.models import User


class VenueManager(models.Manager):
    def get_queryset(self):
        return super(VenueManager, self).get_queryset().filter(
zip_code='00000')


class Venue(models.Model):
    name = models.CharField('Venue Name', max_length=120)
    address = models.CharField(max_length=300)
    zip_code = models.CharField('Zip/Post Code', max_length=12)
    phone = models.CharField('Contact Phone', max_length=20,
blank=True)
    web = models.URLField('Web Address', blank=True)
    email_address = models.EmailField('Email Address',blank=True)

```

```
18      venues = models.Manager()
19      local_venues = VenueManager()
20
21      def __str__(self):
22          return self.name

# ...
```

Let's look at the changes:

- **Lines 5 to 7** define the new `VenueManager` class. The structure is the same as the `EventManager` class, except this time we're overriding the default `get_queryset()` method and returning a filtered list that only contains local venues. This assumes local venues have a "00000" zip code. In a real website, you would have a valid zip code here, or better still, a value for the local zip code saved in your settings file.
- In **line 18** we've renamed the default manager to `venues`.
- In **line 19** we're adding the custom model manager (`VenueManager`).

Note there is no limit to how many custom managers you can add to a Django model instance. This makes creating custom filters for common queries a breeze. Once you have saved the `models.py` file, you can use the custom methods in your code. For example, the default manager method has been renamed, so you can use the more intuitive `venues`, instead of `objects`:

```
>>> from events.models import Venue
>>> Venue.venues.all()
<QuerySet [<Venue: South Stadium>, <Venue: West Park>, <Venue: North
Stadium>, <Venue: East Park>]>
```

And our new custom manager is also easily accessible:

```
>>> Venue.local_venues.all()
<QuerySet [<Venue: West Park>]> # Assuming this venue has a local zip
code
>>>
```

Model Methods

Django's `Model` class comes with many built-in methods. We have already used some of them—`save()`, `delete()`, `__str__()` and others. Where manager methods add table-level functionality to Django's models, model methods add row-level functions that act on individual instances of the model.

There are two common cases where you want to play with model methods:

1. When you want to add business logic to the model by adding custom model methods; and
2. When you want to override the default behavior of a built-in model method.

Custom Model Methods

As always, it's far easier to understand how custom model methods work by writing a couple, so let's modify our `Event` class (changes in bold):

```
# myclub_root\events\models.py

# ...

class Event(models.Model):
    name = models.CharField('Event Name', max_length=120)
    event_date = models.DateTimeField('Event Date')
    venue = models.ForeignKey(Venue, blank=True, null=True, on_delete=models.CASCADE)
    manager = models.ForeignKey(User, blank=True, null=True, on_delete=models.SET_NULL)
    attendees = models.ManyToManyField(MyClubUser, blank=True)
    description = models.TextField(blank=True)
    events = EventManager()

    def event_timing(self, date):
        if self.event_date > date:
            return "Event is after this date"
        elif self.event_date == date:
```

```
14                return "Event is on the same day"
15            else:
16                return "Event is before this date"
17
18        @property
19        def name_slug(self):
20            return self.name.lower().replace(' ','-')
21
22        def __str__(self):
23            return self.name
```

Let's have a look at what's happening with this new code:

- In **line 10** I have added a new method called `event_timing`. This is a straightforward method that compares the event date to the date passed to the method. It returns a message stating whether the event occurs before, on or after the date.
- In **line 19** I have added another custom method that returns a slugified event name. The `@property` decorator on **line 18** allows us to access the method directly, like an attribute. Without the `@property`, you would have to use a method call (`name_slug()`).

Let's test these new methods out in the Django interactive interpreter. Don't forget to save the model before you start!

First, the `name_slug` method:

```
>>> from events.models import Event
>>> events = Event.events.all()
>>> for event in events:
...     print(event.name_slug)
...
test-event
club-presentation---juniors
club-presentation---seniors
gala-day
```

This should be easy to follow. Notice how the `@property` decorator allows us to access the method directly like it was an attribute. I.e., `event.name_slug` instead of `event.name_slug()`.

Now, to test the `event_timing` method (assuming you have an event named "Gala Day"):

```
>>> from datetime import datetime, timezone
>>> e = Event.events.get(name="Gala Day")
>>> e.event_timing(datetime.now(timezone.utc))
'Event is befor this date'
>>>
```

Too easy.

Date and Time in Django

Remember, Django uses timezone aware dates, so if you are making date comparisons like this in any of your code, not just in class methods, you can't use `datetime.now()` without timezone information as Django will throw a `TypeError: can't compare offset-naive and offset-aware datetimes`. To avoid this error, you must provide timezone information with your dates.

Overriding Default Model Methods

It's common to want to override built-in model methods like `save()` and `delete()` to add business logic to default database behavior.

To override a built-in model method, you define a new method with the same name. For example, let's override the `Event` model's default `save()` method to assign management of the event to a staff member (changes in bold):

```
# myclub_root\events\models.py

# ...
```

```
1  class Event(models.Model):
2      name = models.CharField('Event Name', max_length=120)
3      event_date = models.DateTimeField('Event Date')
4      venue = models.ForeignKey(Venue, blank=True, null=True,
on_delete=models.CASCADE)
5      manager = models.ForeignKey(User, blank=True, null=True,
on_delete=models.SET_NULL)
6      attendees = models.ManyToManyField(MyClubUser, blank=True)
7      description = models.TextField(blank=True)
8      events = EventManager()
9
10     def save(self, *args, **kwargs):
11         self.manager = User.objects.get(username='admin')
           # Note: User 'admin' must exist
12         super(Event, self).save(*args, **kwargs)

# ...
```

The new `save()` method starts on **line 10**. In the overridden `save()` method, we're first assigning the staff member with the username "admin" to the `manager` field of the model instance (**line 11**). This code assumes you have named your admin user "admin". If not, you will have to change this code.

Then we call the default `save()` method with the `super()` function to save the model instance to the database (**line 12**).

Once you save your `models.py` file, you can test out the overridden model method in the Django interactive shell (Remember, the username you entered on line 11 has to exist in the database for the test to work):

```
>>> from events.models import Event
>>> from events.models import Venue
>>> from datetime import datetime, timezone
>>> v = Venue.venues.get(id=1)
>>> e = Event.events.create(name='New Event', event_date=datetime.
now(timezone.utc), venue=v)
```

Once the new record is created, you can test to see if your override worked by checking the `manager` field of the `Event` object:

```
>>> e.manager
<User: admin>
>>>
```

Model Inheritance

Don't Build Custom User Models Like This!

The following examples are a convenient way to show you how multi-table inheritance and abstract base classes work without messing up the models in your database.

This is not how you would go about creating a custom user model as it's not connected to Django's authentication system. Also, Django's `User` class includes `first_name`, `last_name`, `email` and `date_joined` fields, so you need not create them yourself.

I will show you how to extend Django's `User` class in Chapter 14.

Models are Python classes, so inheritance works the same way as normal Python class inheritance. The two most common forms of model inheritance in Django are:

1. **Multi-table inheritance**, where each model has its own database table; and
2. **Abstract base classes**, where the parent model holds information common to all its child classes but doesn't have a database table.

You can also create *proxy models* to modify the Python-level behavior of a model without modifying the underlying model fields, however, we won't be covering them here. See the Django documentation for more information on proxy models[1].

1 https://docs.djangoproject.com/en/dev/topics/db/models/#proxy-models

Multi-table Inheritance

With multi-table inheritance, the parent class is a normal model, and the child inherits the parent by declaring the parent class in the child class declaration. For example:

```
# Example for illustration - don't add this to your code!

class MyClubUser(models.Model):
    first_name = models.CharField(max_length=30)
    last_name = models.CharField(max_length=30)
    email = models.EmailField('User Email')

    def __str__(self):
        return self.first_name + " " + self.last_name


class Subscriber(MyClubUser):
    date_joined = models.DateTimeField()
```

The parent model in the example is the `MyClubUser` model from our `events` app. The `Subscriber` model inherits from `MyClubUser` and adds an additional field (`date_joined`). As they are both standard Django model classes, a database table is created for each model. I've created these models in my database, so you can see the tables Django creates (Figure 9-1).

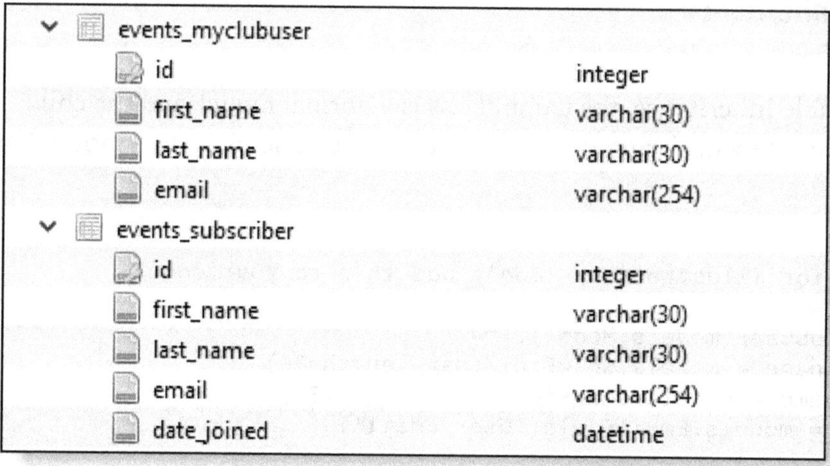

Figure 9-1. *Database tables are created for both the parent and the child model. You will only see these tables if you run the example code.*

Abstract Base Classes

Abstract base classes are handy when you want to put common information into other models without having to create a database table for the base class.

You create an abstract base class by adding the `abstract = True` class `Meta` option (**line 7** in this illustrative example):

```
# Example for illustration - don't add this to your code!

1  class UserBase(models.Model):
2      first_name = models.CharField(max_length=30)
3      last_name = models.CharField(max_length=30)
4      email = models.EmailField('User Email')
5
6      class Meta:
7          abstract = True
8          ordering = ['last_name']
9
10
11 class MyClubUser(UserBase):
```

```
12     def __str__(self):
13         return self.first_name + " " + self.last_name
14
15
16 class Subscriber(UserBase):
17     date_joined = models.DateTimeField()
```

Abstract base classes are also useful for declaring class `Meta` options that are inherited by all child models (**line 8**).

As the `MyClubUser` model from our `events` app now inherits the first name, last name and email fields from `UserBase`, it only needs to declare the `__str__()` function to behave the same way as the original `MyClubUser` model we created earlier.

This example is very similar to the example for multi-table inheritance in the previous section. If you saved and migrated these models, you would get the same result as Figure 9-1—Django would create the `events_myclubuser` and `events_subscriber` tables in your database, but because `UserBase` is an abstract model, it won't be added to the database as a table.

Chapter Summary

In this chapter, we dug much deeper into Django's models, exploring the essentials of Django's models.

We looked at the common data management functions built into Django. We also learned about the common model methods that return QuerySets and those that don't, model field lookups, aggregate functions, and building complex queries.

We also covered adding and overriding model managers and model methods, and had a look at how model inheritance works in Django.

In the next chapter, we will take a similar deep-dive into the inner workings of Django's views.

10

Advanced Views

In Chapter 5, we explored the basics of Django's views. In this chapter, we will dig much deeper into the inner workings of Django's views and have a comprehensive look at the more advanced view topics and tools that you will regularly need as a Django programmer.

We will look inside request and response objects, learn how to use Django's built-in middleware as well as build your own, and how to generate non-HTML content like PDF and CSV files. We'll also look at how to paginate data in views, and finish up with a simple technique for splitting your views into multiple files, so your `views.py` file doesn't get too complicated and unwieldy.

Request and Response Objects

Django's request and response objects are Python classes that pass information to and from the browser.

When Django receives a request, it creates an `HttpRequest` object that contains all the details of the request. Django then parses the URL and loads the view associated with that URL (set by a URLconf in your `urls.py` file). Django passes the `HttpRequest` instance to the view as the first argument to the view function.

Once the view processes the request, it must return an `HttpResponse` object. By the way, this is the easiest way to tell if a Django function is a view—if it doesn't return an `HttpResponse` object, it's not a view.

Request Objects

A request object is a Python class. You can create a request instance in the Django shell by importing the class from the `django.http` module:

```
>>> from django.http import HttpRequest
>>> r = HttpRequest()
>>> r.scheme
'http'
>>> r.META
{}
```

HttpRequest Attributes

Once you have created the `HttpRequest` instance, you can access any of the object attributes. In the above example, I have retrieved the values for the `scheme`, `method`, `encoding`, `content_type` and `META` attributes. A complete list of `HttpRequest` object attributes is in Table 10-1.

Request Attribute	Description
`scheme`	Scheme of the request. E.g., `HTTP` or `HTTPS`
`body`	Raw request body as a bytestring
`path`	Full path of the requested page, not including scheme or domain
`path_info`	Full path of the requested page, not including scheme, domain or script path
`method`	HTTP method. E.g., `GET` or `POST`

Request Attribute	Description
encoding	Current encoding of form submission data. Defaults to DEFAULT_CHARSET
content_type	MIME type of the request
content_params	Dictionary of parameters from the CONTENT_TYPE header
GET	QueryDict of HTTP GET parameters
POST	QueryDict of HTTP POST parameters
COOKIES	Dictionary of all cookies
FILES	A dictionary-like object containing all uploaded files
META	Dictionary containing all available HTTP headers
headers	Dictionary of all HTTP-prefixed headers
resolver_match	The resolved URL
current_app	Used by the url template tag as the current_app argument to reverse(). Set by application code
urlconf	Root URLconf for the request. Set by application code
session	Set by SessionMiddleware
site	Set by CurrentSiteMiddleware
user	Set by AuthenticationMiddleware

Table 10-1. *Django's* `HttpRequest` *class attributes.*

In the example on the previous page, the request object lacks context (i.e., it wasn't sent by a browser or as a part of an API access request), so most of the attribute values are empty.

This is not particularly useful, so let's switch to the development server and examine a complete request from our browser by using `assert False` to trigger Django's error page.

Before starting the development server, make the following change to your `index` view:

```
# myclub_root\events\views.py

# ...

def index(request, year=date.today().year, month=date.today().month):
    assert False
    year = int(year)
    month = int(month)
    # ...
```

Once you have saved your `views.py` file, fire up the server and the `assert False` should trigger the Django error page (Figure 10-1).

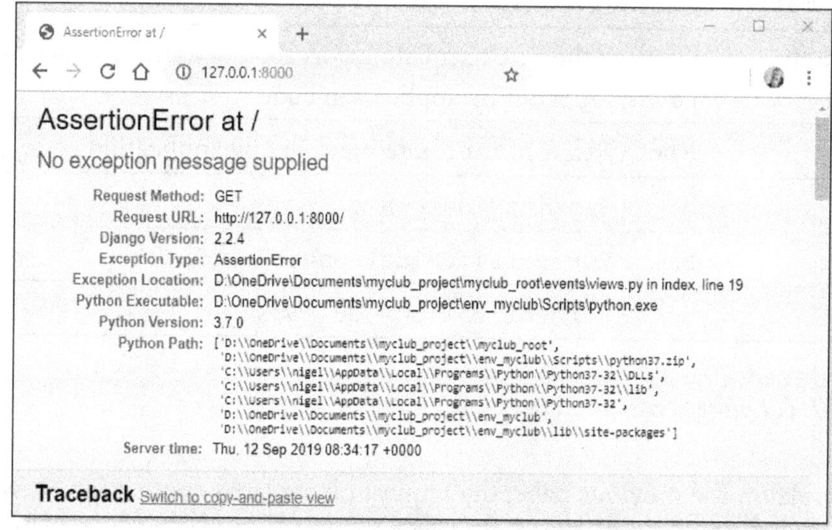

Figure 10-1. *The* `assert False` *statement triggers Django's error page so you can examine the request data.*

Once on the error page, scroll down to the **Request Information** panel to see the request information the browser passed to Django (Figure 10-2). I have cut the screenshot off after a few `META` variables—as you can see, it's a long list!

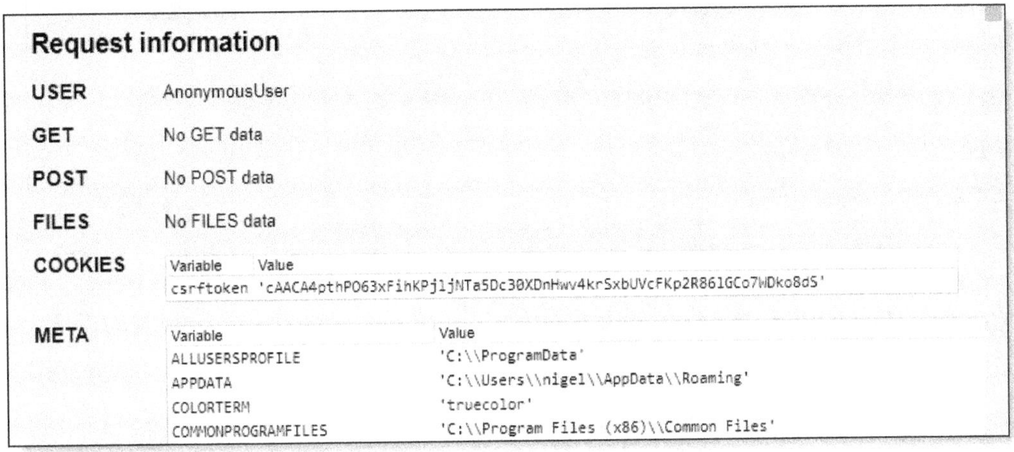

Figure 10-2. *All the request information is displayed on Django's error page.*

Once you have checked out all the variables added to the request, enter the following URL into the address bar and refresh your browser:

```
http://127.0.0.1:8000/?some_var=3
```

Now, your request information should look like Figure 10-3. Notice how the `GET` data dictionary is populated with the `some_var` variable.

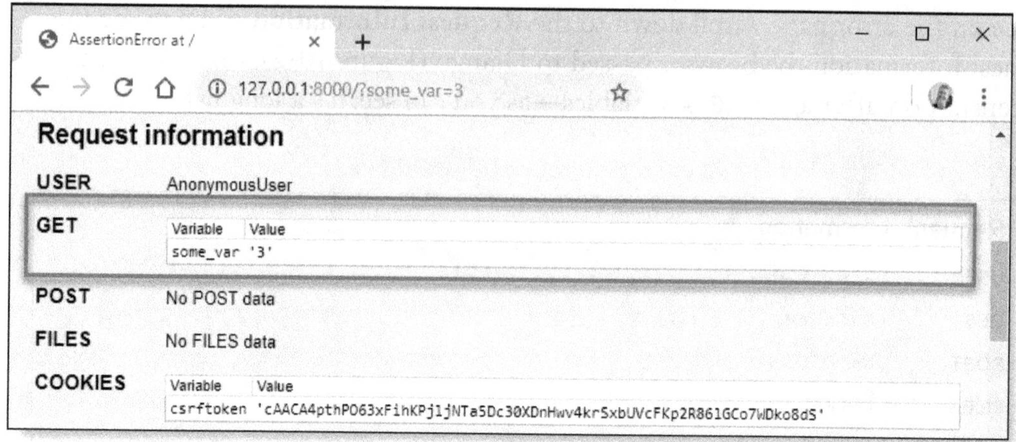

Figure 10-3. The `GET` *dictionary is populated with the query string from the URL.*

Exercise: Examining POST Data

You can complete this exercise to check out post data with the `add_venue` view. Just insert `assert False` on the line after the function declaration, and when you submit the venue form, the error page will trigger.

You can also see what the request looks like to an authenticated user by logging in to the admin and then clicking on **VIEW SITE** in the Django admin toolbar (Figure 10-4).

You can see that, not only has the `USER` variable been set, but Django has also created a cookie named `sessionid` to keep track of the authenticated session for the admin user.

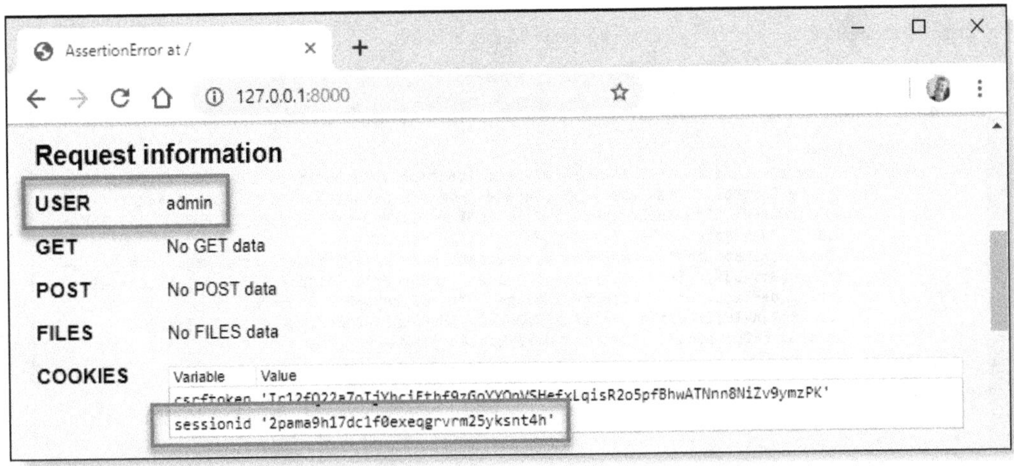

***Figure 10-4.** The authenticated user has been added to the request. Also, note Django has set the session cookie to track the authenticated session.*

All the `HttpRequest` attributes in Table 10-1 are accessible from inside your view code. Let's explore some of these attributes using our `index` view. Make the following changes, save your `views.py` file and reload your browser (changes in bold):

```
# myclub_root\events\views.py

# ...

def index(request, year=date.today().year, month=date.today().month):
    usr = request.user
    ses = request.session
    path = request.path
    path_info = request.path_info
    headers = request.headers
    assert False
    # ...
```

To view the values returned by each of these methods, scroll down to the last panel before **Request information** and open up the **Local vars** panel (Figure 10-5).

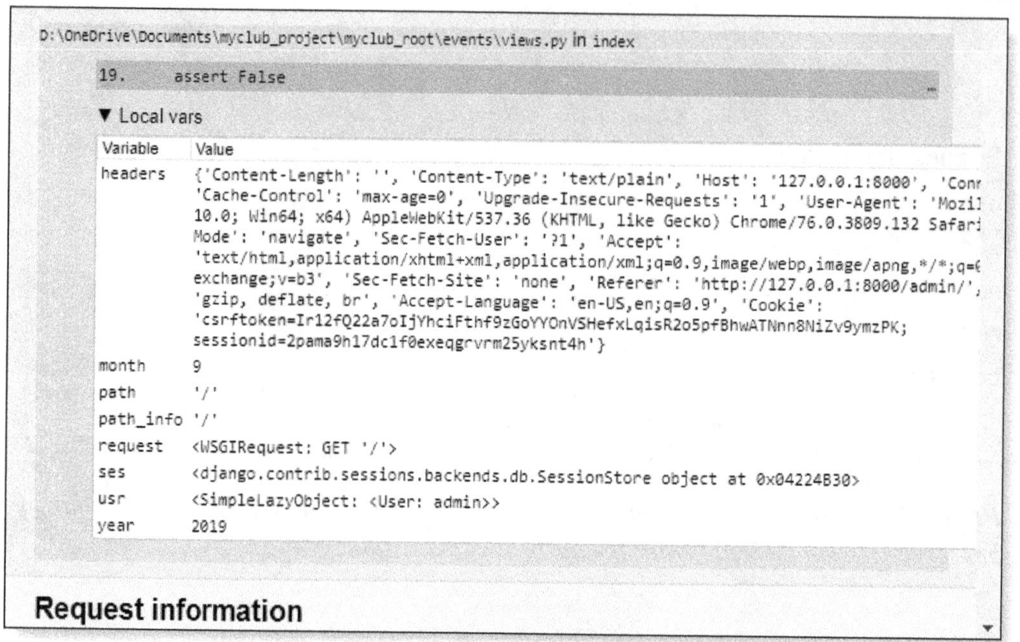

***Figure 10-5.** The "Local vars" panel showing the values returned from a few* `HttpRequest` *class methods.*

Some additional information to note with these examples:

- **`request.user`** and **`request.session`** give you direct access to the `user` and `session` objects from within your view code. This can be very useful when working with authenticated users and sessions.
- While they are the same in this example, **`request.path`** and **`request.path_info`** are subtly different. If your web server is using path aliases, `path` can return something like `/web/wsgiscripts/your_page`, whereas `path_info` will only return `/your_page` for the same page. `path_info` is considered more portable for this reason.
- **`request.headers`** is a convenient way to access all of the HTTP-prefixed headers, and the `Content-Length` and `Content-Type` headers.

Comment out the test values in your view before moving on.

HttpRequest Methods

The `HttpRequest` class also has several different methods you can use in your code (Table 10-2).

Request Method	Description
`get_host()`	Return the original host of the request. E.g., `127.0.0.1:8000`
`get_port()`	Return the originating port of the request
`get_full_path()`	Returns the `path` attribute and query string (if any)
`get_full_path_info()`	Same as `get_full_path()`, but uses `path_info` instead of path
`get_signed_cookie()`	Returns a cookie value for a signed cookie
`is_secure()`	Boolean. Returns `True` if the request is secure
`is_ajax()`	Boolean. Returns `True` if the request was made via `XMLHttpRequest`
`read()`, `readline()`, `readlines()`, `__iter__()`	Read from the request using a file-like interface. These functions behave the same way as the equivalent file functions.

Table 10-2. *Django's* `HttpRequest` *class methods.*

If you want a more detailed explanation of the `HttpRequest` methods, and some example use-cases, see the Django Documentation[1].

1 https://docs.djangoproject.com/en/dev/ref/request-response/#methods

Different Methods, Same Result!

You will notice that some of these attributes and methods will return the same value. For example:

```
request.get_host()
request.META['HTTP_HOST']
request.headers['Host']
```

If you try these out in your code, you will find they all return the same value.

In such cases, it doesn't matter which one you use—they're all easy to understand—just be consistent. Don't keep swapping from `request.headers` to `request.META` (for example).

Response Objects

While Django creates `HttpRequest` objects for you, it's up to you to create `HttpResponse` objects. Each view must create, populate and return a response.

Creating a response instance is easy—like the request, we're importing the class from `django.http`:

```
>>> from django.http import HttpResponse
>>> resp = HttpResponse("<h1>MyClub Events</h1>")
>>> resp.content
b'<h1>MyClub Events</h1>'
```

You can treat a response as a file-like object for adding content:

```
>>> resp.write("<p>Welcome to the events page!</p>")
>>> resp.content
b'<h1>MyClub Events</h1><p>Welcome to the events page!</p>'
>>>
```

You can also test the response from your views in the interactive shell by importing the view and passing an `HttpRequest` object:

```
>>> from django.http import HttpRequest
>>> from events.views import index
>>> r = HttpRequest()
>>> resp = index(r)
>>> resp
<HttpResponse status_code=200, "text/html; charset=utf-8">
>>> resp.content
b'\n<!doctype html>\n<html>\n\n<head> ...
```

`HttpRequest` has five attributes you can access:

- **`content`**. A bytestring representing the content.
- **`charset`**. The charset of the response. Defaults to `DEFAULT_CHARSET`.
- **`status_code`**. The `HTTP` status code. E.g., `200`.
- **`reason_phrase`**. The `HTTP` reason phrase. E.g., `'OK'`.
- **`closed`**. `True` if the response has been closed.

The `HttpResponse` class also has several methods you can use (Table 10-3).

As response objects are a critical part of every view you write, they're covered extensively throughout the book, so we won't go into any more detail here. If you want to dig deeper into each of the attributes and methods of the `HttpResponse` class, see the Django documentation[2].

2 https://docs.djangoproject.com/en/dev/ref/request-response/#id2

Method	Description
`__init__()`	Instantiate an `HttpResponse` object
`__setitem__(header, value)`	Set the given header
`__delitem__(header)`	Delete the given header
`__getitem__(header)`	Get the given header
`has_header(header)`	Returns `True` if the header exists
`set_default(header, value)`	If it hasn't already been created, set the given header
`getvalue()`	Returns the response content
`set_cookie(key)`	Sets a cookie
`set_signed_cookie(key, value)`	Sets a cryptographically signed cookie
`delete_cookie(key)`	Deletes the given cookie
`close()`	Closes the response. Called directly by the WSGI server
`write(), flush(), tell()`	Treats the response as a file-like object
`writelines()`	Writes a list of lines to the response

Table 10-3. *Django's* `HttpResponse` *class methods.*

Serving Files with FileResponse Objects

Serving Files—Caveats

While `FileResponse` provides a simple way to provide file downloads with your Django application, it's not recommended you do so unless you have a simple, low traffic website.

A more robust and just as simple solution is to save the file on Dropbox, or Google Drive or Amazon s3 and have a link to the file in your page HTML.

If you have a large site that must serve files, you will do well to heed the Django developers' advice on serving static files in production[3].

Django makes it easy to serve files from your views with the `FileResponse` class.

`FileResponse` is a subclass of `StreamingHttpResponse` that accepts binary data, and generates a response with the correct `Content-Type` and `Content-Disposition` headers, ready to send to the browser as a binary stream or as a file attachment.

To serve files from a view is as simple as importing the module:

```
from django.http import FileResponse
```

And then writing a view to send the file to the browser:

```
# Illustrative example. If you want to test this example,
# you need to create a '\myclub_root\downloads' folder in
# your project and add a file called "test.pdf".
# You will also need a URLconf to point to the view.

def get_file(request):
    return FileResponse(open('downloads/test.pdf', 'rb'))
```

3 https://docs.djangoproject.com/en/dev/howto/static-files/deployment/

In this example view, I am using Python's `open()` function to open a file from the filesystem. `FileResponse` accepts any file-like object, so you could just as easily provide it with a byte stream (e.g., `io.BytesIO`).

For a more comprehensive example of using `FileResponse`, see *Generating PDF Files* later in the chapter.

QueryDict Objects

A `QueryDict` is a dictionary-like class that has been customized to handle multiple values for the same key. This is necessary because some HTML form elements (e.g. `<select multiple>`) set multiple values for the same key.

When an `HttpRequest` object is passed to your view, the `GET` and `POST` attributes will be instances of `django.http.QueryDict`.

Let's check out how a `QueryDict` works by first creating a new `HttpRequest` object in the Django interactive shell:

```
>>> from django.http import HttpRequest, QueryDict
>>> r = HttpRequest()
>>> r.GET
<QueryDict: {}>
```

In this example, the `GET` attribute of the new `HttpRequest` instance is empty. We can populate the `GET` attribute by passing a querystring to the `QueryDict` class:

```
>>> r.GET = QueryDict('manager=bob&manager=dave&event=Presentation')
>>> r.GET
<QueryDict: {'manager': ['bob', 'dave'], 'event': ['Presentation']}>
```

It's important to note that once created, `GET` and `POST` data are immutable, so cannot be changed. For example:

```
>>> r.GET.update({'manager': 'ted'})
Traceback (most recent call last):
# ...
AttributeError: This QueryDict instance is immutable
```

To create a modifiable `QueryDict`, you must use the `copy()` method:

```
>>> r1 = r.GET.copy()
>>> r1
<QueryDict: {'manager': ['bob', 'dave'], 'event': ['Presentation']}>
>>> r1.update({'manager': 'ted'})
>>> r1
<QueryDict: {'manager': ['bob', 'dave', 'ted'], 'event':
['Presentation']}>
>>>
```

A complete list of available `QueryDict` methods is in Table 10-4.

Method	Description
`__init__()`	Instantiate a `QueryDict` object
`__getitem__(key)`	Get the value of the given key. Returns the last item if there are multiple values for the key
`__setitem__(key, value)`	Set the value of the given key
`__contains__(key)`	Returns `True` if the key exists
`get(key)`	Same as `__getitem__()`, but with a hook for returning a default value
`setdefault(key)`	Return the key value if it exists, otherwise set default value
`update()`	Appends to the current `QueryDict` items

Method	Description
`items()`	Same as Python `dict.items()`, but returns an iterator instead of a view object. Uses the same last-value logic as `__getitem__()`
`values()`	Same as Python `dict.values()`, but returns an iterator instead of a view object. Uses the same last-value logic as `__getitem__()`
`copy()`	Returns a copy of the object. Useful for creating mutable copies of the original `QueryDict` object
`getlist(key)`	Returns a list of data with the given key
`setlist(key, list)`	Sets the given key to list
`appendlist(key, item)`	Appends the item to the end of the list of items associated with the given key
`setlistdefault(key, list)`	Like `setdefault()`, but takes a list instead of a single value
`lists()`	Like `items()`, but includes all values, not just the last value
`pop(key)`	Returns the list of values for the key and removes it from the list
`popitem()`	Removes an arbitrary member of the `QueryDict` object
`dict()`	Returns a Python dictionary representation of the `QueryDict`
`urlencode()`	URL encode the `QueryDict` data

Table 10-4. *Django's* `QueryDict` *class methods.*

Note that the `items()`, `values()` and `lists()` methods return a generator, not a `QueryDict` object:

```
>>> r1.values()
<generator object MultiValueDict.values at 0x03DCD8B0>
```

So, to retrieve the key values, you must iterate the list. You can do this with Python's `list()` function:

```
>>> list(r1.values())
['ted', 'Presentation']
>>> list(r1.items())
[('manager', 'ted'), ('event', 'Presentation')]
```

Or create your own `for` loop iterator:

```
>>> for item in r1.lists():
...     print(item)
...
('manager', ['bob', 'dave', 'ted'])
('event', ['Presentation'])
>>>
```

TemplateResponse Objects

While the content of an `HttpResponse` object can be modified, its static, pre-rendered structure is difficult to modify. Once the `HttpResponse` is rendered, it also loses the template and context details provided to the view.

Sometimes, it's handy to be able to modify a response after it's been constructed by the view but before it's rendered. The two most common use-cases for this functionality are decorators and middleware that need to modify the response.

Django provides this functionality with the `TemplateResponse` object. `TemplateResponse` inherits from `SimpleTemplateResponse`, although you are unlikely to use `SimpleTemplateResponse` directly.

A `TemplateResponse` can be used anywhere you would use a regular `HttpResponse`. We can also use it in place of the `render()` shortcut function. Let's try that out now by changing the `index` view slightly (changes in bold):

```
# myclub_root\events\views.py

# Don't forget to add this import to the top of the file!
from django.template.response import TemplateResponse

def index(request, year=date.today().year, month=date.today().month):
    # ...
    return TemplateResponse(request,
        'events/calendar_base.html',
        {'title': title, 'cal': cal, 'announcements': announcements}
    )
```

Other than importing `TemplateResponse` from `django.template.response`, we've only changed one thing—we're returning a `TemplateResponse` instead of calling the `render()` shortcut to render and return an `HttpResponse`.

Once you have made the changes, switch over to the Django interactive shell to see the effect of the changes:

```
>>> from django.http import HttpRequest
>>> from events.views import index
>>> req = HttpRequest()
>>> resp = index(req)
>>> resp
<TemplateResponse status_code=200, "text/html; charset=utf-8">
>>>
```

You can see the response object is now a `TemplateResponse` instance, not an `HttpResponse` instance. We also have four new attributes that are not available for an `HttpResponse` object:

- **`template_name`**. The name of the template to be rendered.
- **`context_data`**. Context data to be used when rendering the template.

- **`rendered_content`**. The current rendered value of the response content.
- **`is_rendered`**. A boolean—`True` if the content has been rendered.

You can see the values of these attributes in the shell:

```
>>> resp.template_name
'events/calendar_base.html'
>>> resp.context_data
{'title': 'MyClub Event Calendar - May 2020', 'cal': # ...
>>> resp.rendered_content
'\n<!doctype html>\n<html>\n\n<head>\n    <meta charset="utf-8"> # ...
>>> resp.is_rendered
False
```

I have truncated the data output from `context_data` and `rendered_content` to simplify the example.

It's important to note the response is not yet rendered for display. You can check this out by trying to access the content, as you would with an `HttpResponse` instance:

```
>>> resp.content
Traceback (most recent call last):
# ...
django.template.response.ContentNotRenderedError: The response content
must be rendered before it can be accessed.
>>>
```

To render the content, you call the `render()` method of the `TemplateResponse` object:

```
>>> resp.render()
<TemplateResponse status_code=200, "text/html; charset=utf-8">
>>> resp.content
b'\n<!doctype html>\n<html>\n\n<head>\n    <meta charset="utf-8">\n # ...
>>> resp.is_rendered
True
```

If you look closely at your output, you will see that `resp.content` is the same as `resp.rendered_content`. Also, note that once the response is rendered, `is_rendered` is `True`.

This is where the advantage of a `TemplateResponse` shows. Now, you can modify the response. For example, you can change the context:

```
>>> resp.context_data = {'title': 'Changed', 'cal': 'Nothing to see here'}
>>> resp.rendered_content
# This will show the changed context data in the template
```

This is easy enough, but there is a trap you must be aware of—the content is only rendered once. As we have already called `render()` in the previous example, the content of the response remains the same:

```
>>> resp.content
# This is still the original content
```

Even calling `render()` again, will not change the content:

```
>>> resp.render()
<TemplateResponse status_code=200, "text/html; charset=utf-8">
>>> resp.content
# Still the same!
```

To force the content to re-render, you must explicitly assign `response.content`:

```
>>> resp.content = resp.rendered_content
>>> resp.content
# New content, finally!
```

This process works the same with `template_name`:

```
>>> resp.template_name
'events/calendar_base.html'
```

```
>>> resp.template_name = 'base.html'
>>> resp.rendered_content
# This is the new content rendered with the base.html template

>>> resp.content
# This is still the old content from the last example

>>> resp.content = resp.rendered_content
>>> resp.content
# After explicit assignment, this is now rendered with the new content
>>>
```

`TemplateResponse` inherits three methods from `SimpleTemplateResponse` that you can override to add more functionality to your responses:

- **`resolve_context`**. Preprocesses the context data.
- **`resolve_template`**. Resolves the template instance to use for rendering.
- **`add_post_render_callback`**. Adds a callback that will run after rendering.

For more information on these methods, and extra information on `TemplateResponse` and `SimpleTemplateResponse` objects, see the Django documentation[4].

Middleware

Middleware is a framework of hooks that sit between Django's request and response processes. Each middleware performs a specific function and must accept a request and return a response (just like a view). There are seven middleware installed by default when you run `startapp`. These default middleware are listed in your `settings.py` file under `MIDDLEWARE`:

```
# myclub_root\myclub_site\settings.py

# ...

MIDDLEWARE = [
```

4 https://docs.djangoproject.com/en/dev/ref/template-response/

```
        'django.middleware.security.SecurityMiddleware',
        'django.contrib.sessions.middleware.SessionMiddleware',
        'django.middleware.common.CommonMiddleware',
        'django.middleware.csrf.CsrfViewMiddleware',
        'django.contrib.auth.middleware.AuthenticationMiddleware',
        'django.contrib.messages.middleware.MessageMiddleware',
        'django.middleware.clickjacking.XFrameOptionsMiddleware',
]
# ...
```

The functions performed by each middleware is as follows:

- **SecurityMiddleware** provides security enhancements to the request/response cycle.
- **SessionMiddleware** enables session support.
- **CommonMiddleware** adds conveniences like rewriting URLs based on the `APPEND_SLASH` setting, forbids access to disallowed user-agents, and sets the `Content-Length` header.
- **CsrfViewMiddleware** adds protection against Cross-Site Request Forgeries.
- **AuthenticationMiddleware** adds the `user` attribute, and provides for utilization of web server provided authentication.
- **MessageMiddleware** enables cookie- and session-based message support.
- **XFrameOptionsMiddleware** provides clickjacking protection.

Each middleware is processed in the same order as they are listed in `settings.py`. In the request phase, middleware is applied from top to bottom. Each middleware either passes a response to the next middleware or short-circuits to the view.

In the response phase, middleware are processed in reverse order. If a middleware short-circuits to the view, the response will only pass through the same middleware called on the request cycle.

Some of the default middleware depend on other middleware, so the order of the middleware matters. For example, `AuthenticationMiddleware` and `MessageMiddleware` depend on `SessionMiddleware`, so `SessionMiddleware` must be listed before them in MIDDLEWARE. The Django documentation has some general advice on middleware ordering[5].

Writing Your Own Middleware

To create your own middleware, you need to create a callable that takes a get_response object and returns a middleware object. As I said earlier, middleware is a callable that takes a request and returns a response, just like a view.

As middleware can live anywhere on your Python path, we will create a new file to demonstrate how to write your own middleware (new file):

```
# myclub_root\myclub_site\mymiddleware.py

class MyMiddleware:
    def __init__(self, get_response):
        self.get_response = get_response

    def __call__(self, request):
        # This code is executed before before the
        # next middleware or view is called
        request.META['CUSTOM_KEY'] = "Nige was here"

        response = self.get_response(request)

        # This code is executed after the view is called
        # I.e. on the "return journey"
        assert False
        return response
```

I have created the middleware as a Python class, but you can also create a function that does the same thing:

```
def my_middleware(get_response):
    # Configuration and initialization
```

5 https://docs.djangoproject.com/en/dev/ref/middleware/#middleware-ordering

```
    def middleware(request):
        # This code is executed before the
        # next middleware or view is called
        request.META['CUSTOM_KEY'] = "Nige was here"

        response = get_response(request)

        # This code is executed after the view is called
        # I.e. on the "return journey"
        assert False
        return response

    return middleware
```

To add your custom middleware to your Django application, you just need to add it to `MIDDLEWARE` (change in bold):

```
# myclub_root\myclub_site\settings.py

# ...

MIDDLEWARE = [
    'myclub_site.mymiddleware.MyMiddleware',
    'django.middleware.security.SecurityMiddleware',
    # ...
]
# ...
```

I am using the class-based version of the middleware here. If you decide to use the function-based version, you need to change the class name to the function name.

Save your `settings.py` file, restart the development server and navigate to `http://127.0.0.1:8000/` and the `assert False` statement you inserted in the `MyMiddleware` class should trigger Django's error page.

If you scroll down to the response, you should see the custom `META` tag I added to the custom middleware (Figure 10-6).

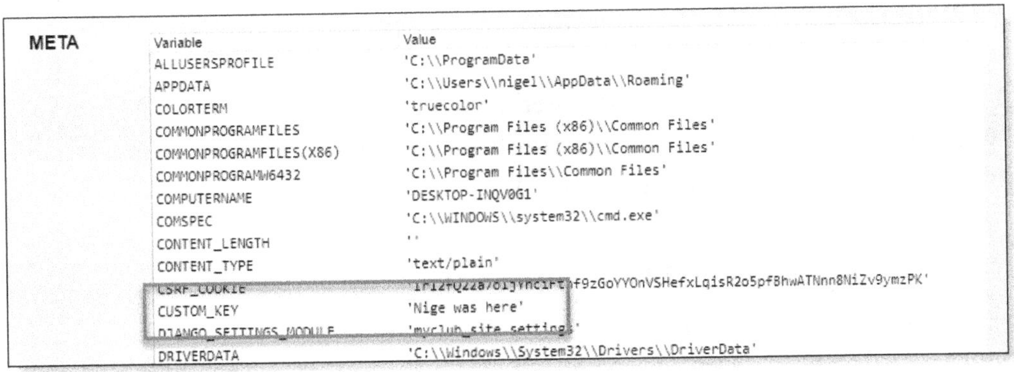

META

Variable	Value
ALLUSERSPROFILE	'C:\\ProgramData'
APPDATA	'C:\\Users\\nigel\\AppData\\Roaming'
COLORTERM	'truecolor'
COMMONPROGRAMFILES	'C:\\Program Files (x86)\\Common Files'
COMMONPROGRAMFILES(X86)	'C:\\Program Files (x86)\\Common Files'
COMMONPROGRAMW6432	'C:\\Program Files\\Common Files'
COMPUTERNAME	'DESKTOP-INQV0G1'
COMSPEC	'C:\\WINDOWS\\system32\\cmd.exe'
CONTENT_LENGTH	''
CONTENT_TYPE	'text/plain'
CSRF_COOKIE	'[illegible]f9zGoYYOnVSHefxLqisR2o5pf8hwATNnn8NiZv9ymzPK'
CUSTOM_KEY	'Nige was here'
DJANGO_SETTINGS_MODULE	'myclub_site.settings'
DRIVERDATA	'C:\\Windows\\System32\\Drivers\\DriverData'

Figure 10-6. *The new* `MyMiddleware` *class has added a custom* `META` *tag to your response.*

This is a very simple example; however, it provides a clear demonstration of how you can use middleware to modify Django's input and output during the request/response cycle.

Don't forget to comment out `MyMiddleware` in `MIDDLEWARE` before you move on. Otherwise, all your views will throw an assertion error!

Generating Non-HTML Content

The response from your views does not have to be HTML; Django can generate any text-based format you choose. You can also output binary data like PDF files and images.

Note we are talking about generating the files on the fly here. If you want to serve static files for download, you are better off using `FileResponse` (see earlier in the chapter).

Generating Text-based Files

A Django view can generate any text-based file by setting the correct MIME type and writing the content to the response. In the following code, I have added two new views to our `views.py` file (changes in bold):

```
# myclub_root\events\views.py

# Add this import to the top of your file
import csv
from .models import Event, Venue

def gen_text(request):
    response = HttpResponse(content_type='text/plain')
    response['Content-Disposition'] = 'attachment; filename="bart.txt"'
    lines = [
        "I will not expose the ignorance of the faculty.\n",
        "I will not conduct my own fire drills.\n",
        "I will not prescribe medication.\n",
    ]
    response.writelines(lines)
    return response


def gen_csv(request):
    response = HttpResponse(content_type='text/csv')
    response['Content-Disposition'] = 'attachment; filename="venues.csv"'
    writer = csv.writer(response)
    venues = Venue.venues.all()
    writer.writerow(['Venue Name', 'Address', 'Phone', 'Email'])
    for venue in venues:
        writer.writerow([venue.name, venue.address, venue.phone, venue.email_address])
    return response
```

Let's have a look at these two new functions:

- At the top of the file, I have added new imports for Python's `csv` library and our `Venue` model for the csv generator function.
- **Line 1** is the start of the plain-text generator function.
- **Lines 2 and 3** are where we set the MIME type (`content_type`) and `Content-Disposition` of the response. This tells your browser the content is a text file attachment.
- In **line 9** we're using the `HttpResponse.writelines()` method to write the lines of text to the response.
- **Line 13** is the start of the csv generator function.
- **Lines 14 and 15** are where we set the MIME type (`content_type`) and `Content-Disposition` of the response. This tells your browser that the content is a csv file attachment.
- In **line 16**, we're using Python's `csv` library to create a new `csv.writer` object.
- In **line 17**, we're retrieving all the venue records from the database.
- And in **lines 19 and 20**, we're writing all the venue records to the response using the `writerow()` function from the `csv` library.

To try these functions out in your browser, you will need to add two URLconf's to your `urls.py` file (changes in bold):

```
# myclub_root\events\urls.py

# ...

urlpatterns = [
path('', views.index, name='index'),
path('gentext/', views.gen_text, name='generate-text-file'),
path('gencsv/', views.gen_csv, name='generate-csv-file'),
# ...
```

Now, if you navigate to `http://127.0.0.1:8000/gentext` or `http://127.0.0.1:8000/gencsv`, your browser will prompt you to download a text file and csv file respectively.

Beware of Sending Large Files!

While this method works fine for small files, you can run into issues with timeouts or a load balancer dropping the connection with larger files.

When generating larger files, you should use Django's `StreamingHttpResponse` class. You will find more information on streaming large files in the Django Documentation[6].

Generating PDF Files

To generate PDF files dynamically in Django, you use the ReportLab PDF library for Python.

First, you must install the library into your virtual environment with `pip`:

```
(env_myclub) ...\myclub_root> pip install reportlab
Collecting reportlab
Downloading .../reportlab-3.5.23-cp37-cp37m-win32.whl (2.2MB)
    100% |################################| 2.2MB 3.8MB/s
Collecting pillow>=4.0.0 (from reportlab)
Downloading .../Pillow-6.1.0-cp37-cp37m-win32.whl (1.7MB)
    100% |################################| 1.8MB 3.6MB/s
Installing collected packages: pillow, reportlab
Successfully installed pillow-6.1.0 reportlab-3.5.23
(env_myclub) ...\myclub_root>
```

Once the ReportLab library is installed, you can use the library to generate PDF files on the fly. Let's add a new view to see how this works (all new code):

```
# myclub_root\events\views.py

# Add these imports to the top of your file
from django.http import FileResponse
import io
from reportlab.pdfgen import canvas
```

6 https://docs.djangoproject.com/en/dev/howto/outputting-csv/#streaming-large-csv-files

```
from reportlab.lib.units import inch
from reportlab.lib.pagesizes import letter

1  def gen_pdf(request):
2      buf = io.BytesIO()
3      c = canvas.Canvas(buf, pagesize=letter, bottomup=0)
4      textob = c.beginText()
5      textob.setTextOrigin(inch, inch)
6      textob.setFont("Helvetica-Oblique", 14)
7      lines = [
8          "I will not expose the ignorance of the faculty.",
9          "I will not conduct my own fire drills.",
10         "I will not prescribe medication.",
11     ]
12     for line in lines:
13         textob.textLine(line)
14     c.drawText(textob)
15     c.showPage()
16     c.save()
17     buf.seek(0)
18     return FileResponse(buf, as_attachment=True, filename='bart.pdf')
```

At the top of the `views.py` file, I've imported a few modules from the `reportlab` library, the `io` library from Python, and the `FileResponse` class from Django.

If you remember from earlier in the chapter, `FileResponse` is a subclass of `StreamingHttpResponse` that accepts binary data, and will generate a response with the correct `Content-Type` and `Content-Disposition` headers, ready to send to the browser as a binary stream or as a file attachment.

In the code above, we're using the `reportlab` library to generate the binary content for Django's `FileResponse` class. Let's have a closer look at the Django-specific parts of this code:

- **Line 2** creates a bytestream buffer to hold the content for the PDF file.
- **Lines 3 to 16** use ReportLab to create a simple PDF file and write it to the buffer `buf`.
- **Line 17** sets the buffer offset to the beginning of the file.

- **Line 18** uses `FileResponse` to send the PDF file to the browser as an attachment.

I've not gone into much detail about how ReportLab works here because I want to keep this book focused on Django. ReportLab is an enormous library with a vast array of useful functions. If you want to dig deeper into generating PDF's from Django, I encourage you to explore the ReportLab PDF Library User Guide[7].

To test this new view in your browser, first, add a new URLconf (change in bold):

```
# myclub_root\events\urls.py

# ...

urlpatterns = [
path('', views.index, name='index'),
path('gentext/', views.gen_text, name='generate-text-file'),
path('gencsv/', views.gen_csv, name='generate-csv-file'),
path('genpdf/', views.gen_pdf, name='generate-pdf-file'),
# ...
```

Once you save the files and run the development server, if you navigate to `http://127.0.0.1:8000/genpdf`, your browser will either show the PDF file or prompt you to download it.

Pagination

With modern data-driven websites, managing data split across many pages is a common task.

Django makes pagination in views easy with the `Paginator` class. The `Paginator` class has two required arguments:

1. **`object_list`**—A list, tuple, QuerySet or other sliceable object; and

7 https://www.reportlab.com/docs/reportlab-userguide.pdf

2. **per_page**—The maximum items to include on a page.

For example, we can instantiate a `Paginator` instance in the Django interactive shell like so:

```
>>> from django.core.paginator import Paginator
>>> from events.models import MyClubUser
>>> p = Paginator(MyClubUser.objects.all(), 3)
```

If you try this code out in your shell, you will get and `UnorderedObjectListWarning`. This is because we haven't set the ordering of the `MyClubUser` QuerySet. This is easy to fix with the `order_by()` filter:

```
>>> p = Paginator(MyClubUser.objects.all().order_by('last_name'), 3)
```

The `Paginator` class has two built-in methods:

1. `page(number)`
2. `get_page(number)`

For example:

```
>>> p1 = p.page(1)
>>> p1
<Page 1 of 4>
>>> p2 = p.get_page(2)
>>> p2
<Page 2 of 4>
```

While it might appear both methods perform the same function, `get_page()` provides a more robust handling of invalid data. For example:

```
>>> bad_p = p.page('x')
Traceback (most recent call last):
# ...
```

```
django.core.paginator.PageNotAnInteger: That page number is not an
integer
>>>
```

If the page number is not a number, `page()` will throw an error, whereas `get_page()` returns the first page:

```
>>> bad_p = p.get_page('x')
>>> bad_p
<Page 1 of 4>
>>>
```

Also, if the page number is out of range or negative, `get_page()` returns the last page:

```
# page() throws an error
>>> no_p = p.page(5)
Traceback (most recent call last):
django.core.paginator.EmptyPage: That page contains no results

# get_page() returns the last page
>>> no_p = p.get_page(5)
>>> no_p
<Page 4 of 4>
>>> no_p = p.get_page(-3)
>>> no_p
<Page 4 of 4>
```

The Paginator class also has three attributes:

- **`count`**. Total objects on all pages
- **`num_pages`**. Total number of pages
- **`page_range`**. An iterator of page numbers

For Example:

```
>>> p.count
10
>>> p.num_pages
```

```
4
>>> p.page_range
range(1, 5)
>>> for n in p.page_range:
...     print(n)
...
1
2
3
4
>>>
```

Page Objects

A `Page` object is created when you call `Paginator.page()`. The `Page` class has a few attributes and methods which are listed in Table 10-5.

Attribute/Method	Type	Description
`object_list`	Attribute	List of objects on the page
`number`	Attribute	Page number of the page
`paginator`	Attribute	The associated `Paginator` object
`has_next()`	Method	Boolean. Returns `True` if there's a next page
`has_previous()`	Method	Boolean. Returns `True` if there's a previous page
`has_other_pages()`	Method	Boolean. Returns `True` if there's a next or previous page
`next_page_number()`	Method	Returns the next page number. Raises `InvalidPage` if not
`previous_page_number()`	Method	Returns the previous page number. Raises `InvalidPage` if not
`start_index()`	Method	Returns the index of the first object on the page
`end_index()`	Method	Returns the index of the last object on the page

Table 10-5. *Django's* `Page` *class attributes and methods.*

Let's try a few of these attributes and methods with the Django interactive shell:

```
>>> p = Paginator(MyClubUser.objects.all().order_by('last_name'), 3)
>>> p1 = p.page(1)
>>> p1.object_list
<QuerySet [<MyClubUser: Jane Doe>, <MyClubUser: Don Don>, <MyClubUser:
John Jones>]>
>>> for usr in p1:
...     print(usr.first_name)
...
Jane
Don
John
>>> p1.has_next()
True
>>> p1.has_previous()
False
```

Pagination in Views

To display paginated data in your browser requires two things: 1) a view that creates a `Paginator` object, populates it with data, and sends it to a 2) template that parses the `Paginator` and displays the page data.

Let's start with the template. I am creating a new template called `subscribers.html` and storing it in the `\events\templates\events` folder (new file):

```
# \events\templates\events\subscribers.html

{% extends ‘base.html’ %}

{% block title %}MyClub Subscribers{% endblock title %}

{% block content %}
  <h1>MyClub Subscribers</h1>
  <table border=”1” width=100%>
    <tr style=”text-align: center”><th>Last Name</th><th>First Name</th></tr>
    {% for subscriber in subscribers %}
```

```
10       <tr>
11         <td style=”padding: 10px”>{{ subscriber.last_name|upper }}</td>
12         <td style=”padding: 10px”>{{ subscriber.first_name }}</td>
13       </tr>
14     {% endfor %}
15   </table>
16
17   <div style=”padding-top: 20px;”>
18     {% if subscribers.has_previous  %}
19       <a href=”?page=1”>&laquo; first</a>
20       <a href=”?page={{ subscribers.previous_page_number }}”>previous</a>
21     {% endif %}
22
23     Page {{ subscribers.number }} of {{ subscribers.paginator.num_pages }}
24
25     {% if subscribers.has_next %}
26       <a href=”?page={{ subscribers.next_page_number }}”>next</a>
27       <a href=”?page={{ subscribers.paginator.num_pages }}”>last &raquo;</a>
28     {% endif %}
29   </div>
30 {% endblock content %}
```

Most of this should be familiar by now. However, there are a few lines to note:

- **Lines 9 to 14.** We're iterating over the `subscribers` QuerySet and listing the subscribers' names in table rows. I have applied some minimal styles to make the table prettier; in a real website, you should use CSS classes to format the table.
- **Lines 18 to 28.** We're building a simple text-based navigation bar to display the selected page in the browser. Note how the `Paginator` class's methods and attributes are all available to the template:
    - **Line 18** checks if the page has a previous page with the `has_previous()` method. If it's true, the template displays the left navigation text. Note how we're using `href` attributes to pass `GET` parameters back to the view in **lines 19 and 20.** You will see how to handle this information when we create the view.

- ▷ **Line 23** uses the standard "Page x of y" format to display what page we are on.
- ▷ **Line 15** checks if the page has a next page with the `has_next()` method. If it's true, the template displays the right navigation text. Note how we're using `href` attributes again to pass `GET` parameters back to the view in **lines 26 and 27**.

Now, let's add the view to our `views.py` file (changes in bold):

```
# myclub_root\events\views.py

# Add these imports to the top of your file
from django.core.paginator import Paginator
from .models import Event, Venue, MyClubUser

# ...

1  def list_subscribers(request):
2      p = Paginator(MyClubUser.objects.all(), 3)
3      page = request.GET.get('page')
4      subscribers = p.get_page(page)
5      return render(request,
6          'events/subscribers.html',
7          {'subscribers': subscribers}
8          )
```

Let's have a look at what's going on here:

- At the top of the file, I have imported the `Paginator` class from `django.core.paginator`, and the `MyClubUser` model.
- In **line 2**, we're populating the paginator `p` with a QuerySet containing all users from the database.
- In **line 3**, we're retrieving the page number from the `GET` parameter in the request.
- And in **line 4**, we're setting the `subscribers` QuerySet to contain the subscriber objects from the selected page.

Now we've created the template and the view, we just need to add a URLconf to show the template in the browser (change in bold):

```
# myclub_root\events\urls.py

urlpatterns = [
    # ...
    path('getsubs/', views.list_subscribers, name='list-subscribers'),
    # ...
```

Once you have saved the files and started the development server, if you navigate to `http://127.0.0.1:8000/getsubs/` your browser should look like Figure 10-7.

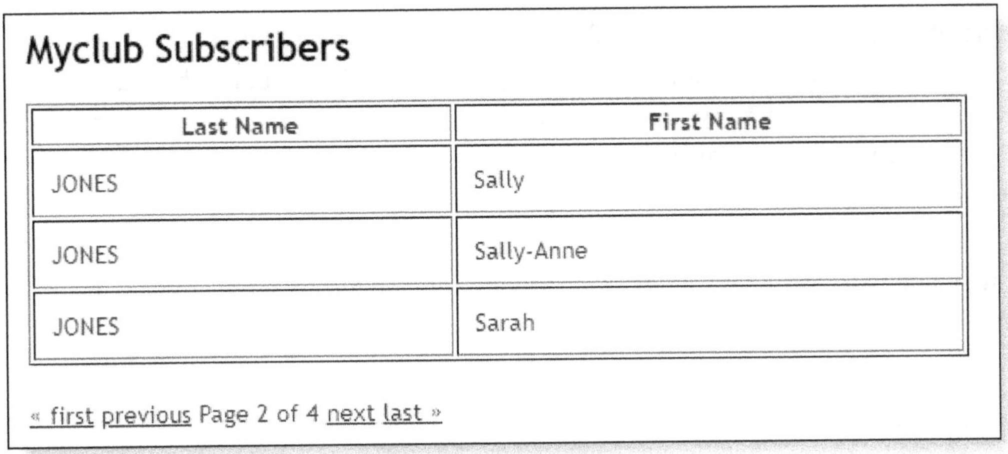

Myclub Subscribers

Last Name	First Name
JONES	Sally
JONES	Sally-Anne
JONES	Sarah

« first previous Page 2 of 4 next last »

Figure 10-7. *Your new view showing paginated data.*

Splitting Views Into Multiple Files

It's common for the size of your `views.py` file to get unwieldy as the complexity of your application grows.

The default advice is to split website functions into apps that each does one thing, but this is not always practical, and doesn't take into account the "one thing" can still get quite complex!

To simplify your app and keep your views module small, you can split your views into multiple files.

This is simpler to do than you might think if you take advantage of how Python's dot notation works. For example, let's look at how we usually access our `index` view:

```
views.index
```

Because everything in Python is an object, Python doesn't care whether `views` is a module (file with `.py` extension) or a package (folder). We can take advantage of this feature to turn our `views.py` file into a package and avoid having to mess with our URL structure while we're at it. This can be a huge timesaver if you have to refactor your code.

The first step is to add a new folder named views to the `events` app, and then add three new files to the folder:

1. `__init__.py`
2. `myclub_views.py`
3. `demo_views.py`

When you are done, your folder structure should look like this:

```
\events
# ...
    \views
        __init__.py
        demo_views.py
        myclub_views.py
    # ...
```

The most important file in this new structure is `__init__.py`. Not only does this file tell Python to treat the `\views` folder as a package, but it's where you tell Python where to find your views. We need to add two lines to this file:

```
# myclub_root\events\views\__init__.py

from .myclub_views import *
from .demo_views import *
```

These lines are simply saying "import all the views from `myclub_views` and `demo_views` modules (`myclub_views.py` and `demo_views.py`)".

Now we just need to split the view functions up into each file. First, the MyClub views:

```
# myclub_root\events\views\myclub_views.py

from django.shortcuts import render
from django.http import HttpResponseRedirect
from django.template.response import TemplateResponse
from django.core.paginator import Paginator
from datetime import date
import calendar
from calendar import HTMLCalendar
from events.models import Event, Venue, MyClubUser
from events.forms import VenueForm


def index(request, year=date.today().year, month=date.today().month):
    year = int(year)
    month = int(month)
    if year < 2000 or year > 2099: year = date.today().year
    month_name = calendar.month_name[month]
    title = "MyClub Event Calendar - %s %s" % (month_name,year)
    cal = HTMLCalendar().formatmonth(year, month)
    cal = HTMLCalendar().formatmonth(year, month)
    announcements = [
        {
            'date': '6-10-2020',
            'announcement': "Club Registrations Open"
        },
```

```
        {
            'date': '6-15-2020',
            'announcement': "Joe Smith Elected New Club President"
        }
    ]
    return TemplateResponse(request,
        'events/calendar_base.html',
        {'title': title, 'cal': cal, 'announcements': announcements}
    )


def all_events(request):
    # event_list = Event.objects.all()
    # Need to use this version after Chapter 9:
    event_list = Event.events.all()
    return render(request,
        'events/event_list.html',
        {'event_list': event_list}
    )


def add_venue(request):
    submitted = False
    if request.method == 'POST':
        form = VenueForm(request.POST)
        if form.is_valid():
            form.save()
            return HttpResponseRedirect('/add_venue/?submitted=True')
    else:
        form = VenueForm()
        if 'submitted' in request.GET:
            submitted = True
    return render(request,
        'events/add_venue.html',
        {'form': form, 'submitted': submitted}
        )


def list_subscribers(request):
    p = Paginator(MyClubUser.objects.all(), 3)
    page = request.GET.get('page')
    subscribers = p.get_page(page)
    return render(request,
        'events/subscribers.html',
        {'subscribers': subscribers}
        )
```

Then we need to add the views we've written to demonstrate the various functions in Django to the demo_views.py file:

```
# myclub_root\events\views\demo_views.py

from django.shortcuts import render
from django.http import HttpResponse
from django.http import FileResponse
import csv
import io
from reportlab.pdfgen import canvas
from reportlab.lib.units import inch
from reportlab.lib.pagesizes import letter
from events.models import Venue


def gen_text(request):
    response = HttpResponse(content_type='text/plain')
    response['Content-Disposition'] = 'attachment; filename="bart.txt"'
    lines = [
        "I will not expose the ignorance of the faculty.\n",
        "I will not conduct my own fire drills.\n",
        "I will not prescribe medication.\n",
    ]
    response.writelines(lines)
    return response


def gen_csv(request):
    response = HttpResponse(content_type='text/csv')
    response['Content-Disposition'] = 'attachment; filename="venues.
csv"'
    writer = csv.writer(response)
    venues = Venue.venues.all()
    writer.writerow(['Venue Name', 'Address', 'Phone', 'Email'])
    for venue in venues:
        writer.writerow([venue.name, venue.address, venue.phone, venue.
email_address])
    return response


def gen_pdf(request):
    buf = io.BytesIO()
    c = canvas.Canvas(buf, pagesize=letter, bottomup=0)
```

```
    textob = c.beginText()
    textob.setTextOrigin(inch, inch)
    textob.setFont("Helvetica-Oblique", 14)
    lines = [
        "I will not expose the ignorance of the faculty.",
        "I will not conduct my own fire drills.",
        "I will not prescribe medication.",
    ]
    for line in lines:
        textob.textLine(line)
    c.drawText(textob)
    c.showPage()
    c.save()
    buf.seek(0)
    return FileResponse(buf, as_attachment=True, filename='bart.pdf')
```

These two files contain the same content as the original `views.py` file, with some small changes:

1. Each new file only imports the packages and modules needed for the views it contains.
2. The internal imports have changed slightly because `views` is now a package:

    a. `from .models ...` is now `from events.models`; and

    b. `from .forms ...` is now `from events.forms`.

Save these files and rename the original `views.py` file to `views.py.old` (or delete it) and you should find the site behaves the same way it did when all your views were in one file.

Chapter Summary

In this chapter, we dug much deeper into the inner workings of Django's views and had a comprehensive look at the more advanced view topics and tools you will regularly use as a Django programmer.

We looked inside request and response objects, learned how to use Django's built-in middleware as well as build our own, and how to generate non-HTML content like PDF and CSV files. We also looked at how to paginate data in views, and finished up with a simple technique for splitting your views into multiple files, so your `views.py` file doesn't get too complicated and unwieldy.

In the next chapter, we will take a deep dive into another critical component of all Django applications—templates.

11

Advanced Templates

In Chapter 6, we covered the basics of how Django's templates work, how to pass information from a Django view to the browser, and how Django doesn't get in the way of you creating a professional, modern look for your website. I also introduced you to some of the more common Django template tags and filters.

In this chapter, we will dig much deeper into templates and cover the most common template tags and filters, complete with example implementations.

I will also show you how to create your own custom template filters and tags, how to work with `Context` and `RequestContext` objects, and context processors. We'll also have a look at how Django's template back ends and template loaders work.

Setting Up the Demo Files

To explore template tags and filters, I have created a demonstration template named `template_demo.html`, and a demonstration view called `template_demo` defined in your `demo_views.py` file (assuming you split the views in Chapter 10).

Using the Source Code

There is a listing of the complete demonstration template at the end of the chapter. However, the chapter is designed to be completed in order, so there are sections in the complete listing that rely on changes you make throughout the chapter.

If you try to run the complete source files in your browser now, they will not work.

If you are going to use the source, you must complete each section of the chapter in order and only copy the sections in the source code relevant to the section you are working on.

To work through the chapter, we first need to set up the basic framework for each of these files so we can work through the examples. First, the `template_demo.html` file (new file):

```
# \events\templates\events\template_demo.html

{% load static %}
<!doctype html>
<html>
<head>
    <meta charset="utf-8">
    <title>Testing out the Template System</title>
    <style>
    .row {
        background-color: lightskyblue;
    }
    .altrow {
        background-color: lightgray;
    }
    table td {
        text-align: center;
    }
    </style>
</head>
```

```
<body>
    <h1>Templates Demo File</h1>
</body>
</html>
```

This file forms the skeleton for our demonstration code. Save the file to your `events\templates\events` folder.

Next, we must add the `template_demo` view to `demo_views.py` (all new code):

```
# \events\views\demo_views.py

# Add these imports to the top of the file
from django.core import serializers
from datetime import datetime

# ...

def template_demo(request):
    empty_list = []
    color_list = ['red', 'green', 'blue', 'yellow']
    somevar = 5
    anothervar = 21
    today = datetime.now()
    past = datetime(1985, 11, 5)
    future = datetime(2035, 11, 5)
    best_bands = [
        {'name': 'The Angels', 'country': 'Australia'},
        {'name': 'AC/DC', 'country': 'Australia'},
        {'name': 'Nirvana', 'country': 'USA'},
        {'name': 'The Offspring', 'country': 'USA'},
        {'name': 'Iron Maiden', 'country': 'UK'},
        {'name': 'Rammstein', 'country': 'Germany'},
    ]
    aussie_bands = ['Australia', ['The Angels', 'AC/DC', 'The Living End']]
    venues_js = serializers.serialize('json', Venue.venues.all())
    return render(request,
        'events/template_demo.html',
        {
            'somevar': somevar,
            'anothervar': anothervar,
            'empty_list': empty_list,
```

```
            'color_list': color_list,
            'best_bands': best_bands,
            'today': today,
            'past': past,
            'future': future,
            'aussie_bands': aussie_bands,
            'venues': venues_js,
        }
    )
```

After adding the imports to the top of the file, you can add the `template_demo` view to the end of the file. The purpose of this view is to add several variables to the context for use in the demo template.

Finally, to show the demonstration template in your browser, you also need to add a new URLconf to your `urls.py` file (change in bold):

```
# myclub_root\events\urls.py

from django.urls import path, re_path
from . import views

urlpatterns = [
    path('', views.index, name='index'),
    path('tdemo/', views.template_demo, name='tdemo'),
    # ...
]
```

Once you have created and saved these files, run the development server and navigate to `http://127.0.0.1:8000/tdemo`. Your screen should look like Figure 11-1.

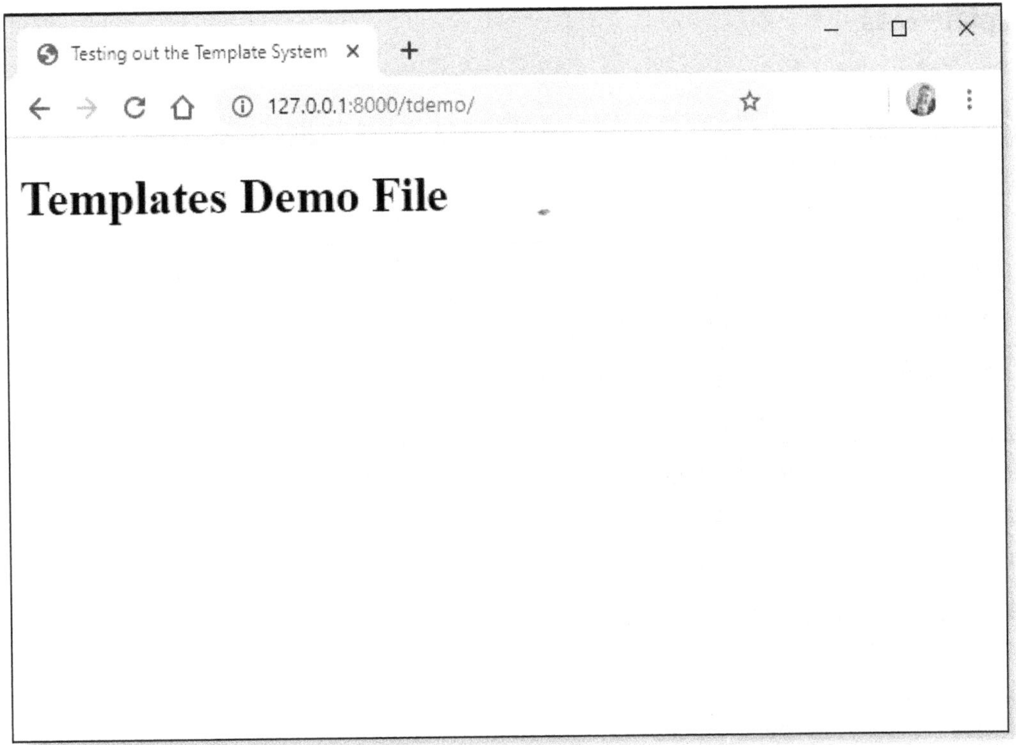

Figure 11-1. The blank demonstration template.

Django's Default Template Tags and Filters

Django has a variety of template tags and filters designed to make rendering content in your templates easier. A list of Django's template tags is in Table 11-1, and a list of Django's template filters is in Table 11-2.

Template Tags

Tag	Description
`autoescape`	Turns autoescape behavior on and off
`block`	Defines a block that can be overridden by child templates
`comment`	Used for documenting and commenting out code
`csrf_token`	To protect from Cross-Site Request Forgeries, you **must** use `{% csrf_token %}` on all POST forms that post to internal URLs
`cycle`, `resetcycle`	Cycles through the tag arguments each time the tag is encountered in code. `resetcycle` will reset the cycle back to the beginning
`debug`	Outputs debugging information into the template
`extends`	Lets Django know the template extends a parent template
`filter`	Filters the contents of the block through one or more filters
`firstof`	Outputs the first non-False argument
`for ... endfor`	Tags for a `for` loop
`empty`	Optional empty clause for use with `for` loop. The empty clause text is shown if the given iterable is empty or can't be found
`if ... endif`	Tags to perform an `if` evaluation
`ifchanged`	Checks if a value has changed from the last iteration of a loop
`include`	Loads a template and include it in the current template
`load`	Loads a custom template tag set
`lorem`	Displays random lorem ipsum text
`now`	Shows the current date and time
`regroup`	Regroups a list of objects by a common attribute

Tag	Description
`spaceless`	Removes whitespace between HTML template tags
`templatetag`	Outputs Django template syntax characters. E.g., `{% templatetag openbrace %}` will output {
`url`	Performs a URL reverse lookup to return an absolute path reference (without the domain name). Use this tag to avoid hard-coding URLs in the template
`verbatim`	Stops the template engine from rendering the contents of the block. Commonly used to prevent JavaScript template clashes with Django syntax
`widthratio`	Sets the width of an image as a ratio of a given maximum value
`with`	Use a simple name for a complex variable

Table 11-1. *Django's template tags.*

Let's have a closer look at a few of the more common tags in this table. To test the tags, add the snippets of source code to your `template_demo.html` file as you go. Make sure you add them between the `<body></body>` HTML tags.

The comment Tag

The `comment` tag stops the comment block from showing in your template. Add this snippet to your file:

```
<h2>Comment Tag</h2>
<!-- This is a normal HTML comment which shows in your browser
source-->
{% comment "this won't show at all in your browser source" %}
  <p>Three six nine, the goose drank wine</p>
{% endcomment %}
```

When you refresh your browser and look at the page source, you will see the regular HTML comment is rendered in the source but the Django comment block is not rendered at all.

The `comment` tag is useful when you want to hide a section of your template. For example, a section that is only shown in debug.

The cycle Tag

The `cycle` tag will cycle through all of its arguments. Cycle arguments can be literal strings or template variables:

```
# Example only - don't add to your file

{% cycle 'blue' 'brown' 'red' 'cyan' %}
{% cycle var1 var2 var3 %}
```

Try this snippet in the demo file:

```
{% for i in '12345' %}
<p style="color: {% cycle 'blue' 'brown' 'red' 'cyan' %};">
    Colored Text
</p>
{% endfor %}
```

If the loop counter is more than the number of items in its arguments list, `cycle` loops back to the beginning. In the above example, there are only four colors in this list, but the loop runs five times, so the last row of text will be blue (Figure 11-2).

Cycle is most commonly used to apply alternate row styling to a table:

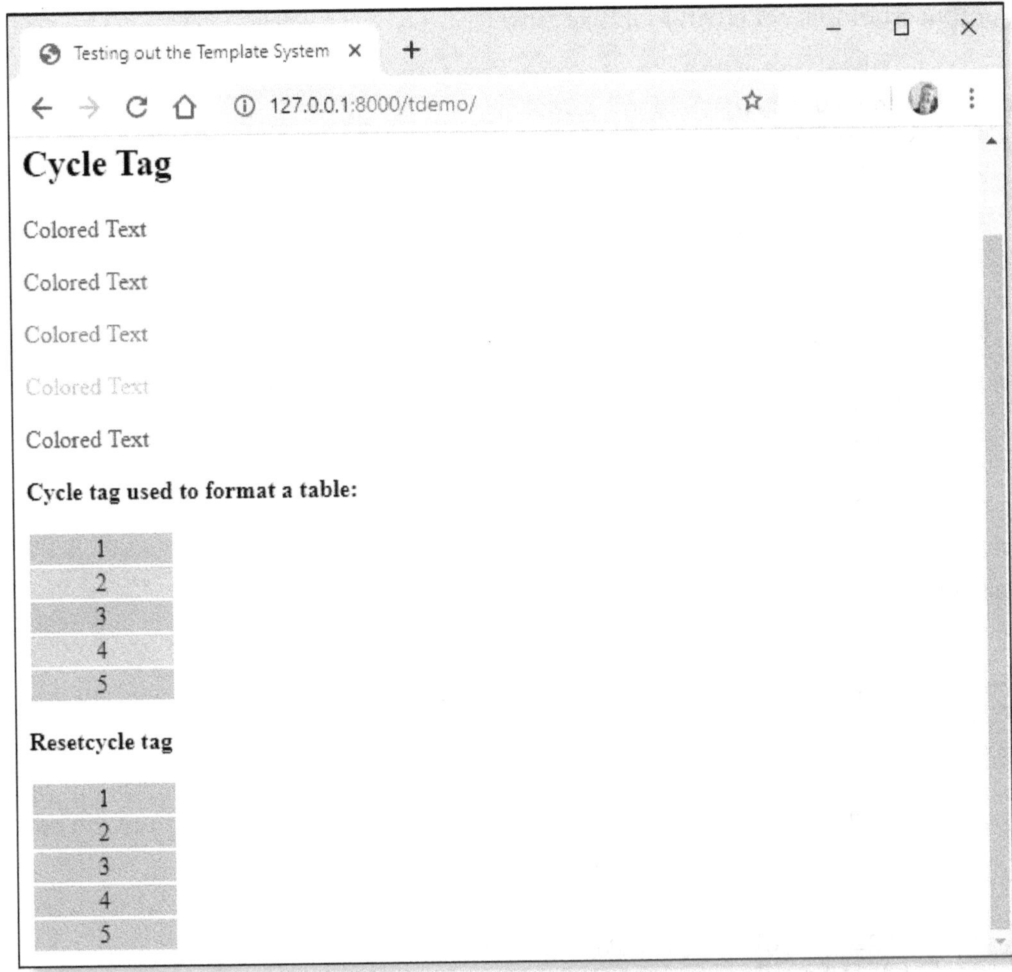

Figure 11-2. The `cycle` *tag output in the demo template. Paperback users refer to your browser to see the colors.*

```
<p><strong>Cycle tag used to format a table:</strong></p>
<table border=0 style="width: 100px">
    {% for i in '12345' %}
    <tr class="{% cycle 'row' 'altrow' %}">
        <td>{{ i }}</td>
    </tr>
    {% endfor %}
</table>
```

The output from this code will look like this:

```
<table border=0 style="width: 100px">
    <tr class="row">
        <td>1</td>
    </tr>
    <tr class="altrow">
        <td>2</td>
    </tr>
    <tr class="row">
        <td>3</td>
    </tr>
    <tr class="altrow">
        <td>4</td>
    </tr>
    <tr class="row">
        <td>5</td>
    </tr>
</table>
```

When you run this code in the browser, the table will display with alternate blue and gray rows (Figure 11-2).

Django also has a `resetcycle` tag to reset the cycle. This example will apply the `row` class to all rows as the cycle is reset on each loop:

```
<p><strong>Resetcycle tag:</strong></p>
<table border=0 style="width: 100px">
    {% for i in '12345' %}
    <tr class="{% cycle 'row' 'altrow' %}">
        <td>{{ i }}</td>
    </tr>
    {% resetcycle %}
    {% endfor %}
</table>
```

This code will output:

```
<table border=0 style="width: 100px">
    <tr class="row">
        <td>1</td>
    </tr>
    <tr class="row">
        <td>2</td>
    </tr>
    <tr class="row">
        <td>3</td>
    </tr>
    <tr class="row">
        <td>4</td>
    </tr>
    <tr class="row">
        <td>5</td>
    </tr>
</table>
```

As the cycle is reset on each loop, this table will display with all rows colored blue (Figure 11-2).

The filter Tag

The `filter` tag applies the selected filters to the text in the filter block:

```
<h2>Filter Tag</h2>
{% filter striptags|upper %}
<p>This text will be converted to uppercase and have the HTML tags
<em>removed</em>.</p>
{% endfilter %}
```

The firstof Tag

The `firstof` tag will output the first non-False argument:

```
<h2>Firstof Tag</h2>
<p>{% firstof None False '' empty_list 'This one!' 'Not this one' %}</p>
```

The for Tag

The `for` tag behaves the same way as a Python for loop and uses a simple "for object in list" format:

```
<h2>For Tag</h2>
<p><strong>List Colors:</strong></p>
<ul>
{% for item in color_list %}
<li>{{ item }}{{ forloop.counter }}</li>
{% endfor %}
</ul>
```

The for loop keeps track of a few variables for you to use in your template logic:

```
<p><strong>The for loop variables:</strong></p>
<table border=1>
<tr>
    <th>Item</th>
    <th>forloop.counter</th>
    <th>forloop.counter0</th>
    <th>forloop.revcounter</th>
    <th>forloop.revcounter0</th>
    <th>forloop.first</th>
    <th>forloop.last</th>
</tr>
{% for item in color_list %}
<tr>
    <td>{{ item }}</td>
    <td>{{ forloop.counter }}</td>
    <td>{{ forloop.counter0 }}</td>
    <td>{{ forloop.revcounter }}</td>
    <td>{{ forloop.revcounter0 }}</td>
    <td>{{ forloop.first }}</td>
    <td>{{ forloop.last }}</td>
</tr>
{% endfor %}
</table>
```

The `for` tag also has an optional `empty` tag that will show the empty clause if there are no items in the list:

```
<p><strong>For...empty Tag</strong></p>
<p><strong>The for...empty tag will show the empty clause if there are
no items in the list:</strong></p>
<p><strong>This list has items to show:</strong></p>
<ul>
{% for item in color_list %}
<li>{{ item }}</li>
{% empty %}
<li>Nothing in the list!</li>
{% endfor %}
</ul>
<p><strong>But this one doesn't:</strong></p>
<ul>
{% for item in empty_list %}
<li>{{ item }}</li>
{% empty %}
<li>Nothing in the list!</li>
{% endfor %}
</ul>
```

The if Tag

Django's `if` template tag uses the same syntax as Python's `if` statement:

```
# Python

    if x:
        # ...
    elif y:
        # ...
    else:
        # ...

# Django

    {% if x %}
        # ...
    {% elif y %}
```

```
        # ...
    {% else %}
        # ...
    {% endif %}
```

The exception is the `{% endif %}` tag, which Django requires. If you don't include the closing tag, Django will throw a `TemplateError`.

Here's some code to try out in your browser:

```
<h2>If Tag</h2>
{% if empty_list %}
This line won't show as list is empty.
{% elif color_list %}
color_list is not empty, so this line shows.
{% else %}
Optional else clause. This won't show in this example.
{% endif %}
```

Python's boolean operators work in `if` tags:

```
{% if somevar > 5 %}
somevar is greater than 5
{% else %}
somevar is less than 5
{% endif %}
<br />
{% if empty_list and color_list %}
Both lists have content
{% else%}
One list is empty
{% endif %}
<br />
{% if empty_list or color_list %}
At least one list has content
{% endif %}
<br />
{% if not empty_list %}
Negated an empty list, so this will print.
{% endif %}
```

```
<br />
{% if anothervar is True %}
This prints if and only if anothervar is True.
{% endif %}
<br />
{% if novar is None %}
This appears if novar is None, or if novar is not found in the context.
{% endif %}
<br />
{% if anothervar is True %}
This prints if and only if anothervar is True.
{% endif %}
<br />
{% if novar is None %}
This appears if novar is None, or if novar is not found in the context.
{% endif %}
```

These are only a few examples; the complete list of boolean operators are:

- `>`—Greater than
- `<`—Less than
- `>=`—Greater than or equal
- `<=`—Less than or equal
- `==`—Equal
- `!=`—Not equal
- **`is`**—Is a particular object
- **`is not`**—Is not a particular object
- **and**—Both expressions must be true
- **or**—Either expression can be true
- **not**—Negate the expression

The `in` operator is supported by the `if` tag:

```
{% if "dog" in "catdog" %}
The best half!
{% endif %}
```

```
<br />
{% if "orange" in color_list %}
Orange is in the list!
{% else %}
Orange is not in the list!
{% endif %}
```

You can also use filters with boolean operators and the `if` tag:

```
{% if color_list|length < 10 %}
List has less than 10 elements
{% endif %}
```

Operators can also be chained to create more complex expressions:

```
{% if somevar >= 5 and anothervar != 30 %}
Both comparisons are true, so this will print.
{% endif %}
```

A caveat: while Django supports complex expressions and nesting, using actual parentheses in the `if` tag is not supported and will throw an error.

The lorem Tag

The `lorem` tag outputs Lorem Ipsum sample text. The number of words an paragraphs output are set by the provided arguments:

```
<h2>Lorem Tag</h2>
<p><strong>This one will output a number of words:</strong></p>
{% lorem 5 w %}
<p><strong>This one outputs a number of HTML paragraphs:</strong></p>
{% lorem 2 p %}
<p><strong>This one outputs plain text paragraphs:</strong></p>
{% lorem 1 b %}
<p><strong>And finally, we can output a number of random words:</
strong></p>
{% lorem 10 w random %}
```

```
<p><strong>or random paragraphs:</strong></p>
{% lorem 3 p random %}
```

The now Tag

The `now` tag shows the current date and time formatted according to the supplied string:

```
<h2>Now Tag</h2>
{% now "m-d-Y H:i" %}
```

The `now` tag uses the same string formatting syntax as the `date` filter. For more information, see the Django documentation[1].

The regroup Tag

The `regroup` tag rearranges a list of objects by a common attribute:

```
<h2>Regroup Tag</h2>
{% regroup best_bands by country as band_list %}
<p>Best Bands:</p>
<ul>
  {% for band in band_list %}
  <li>
  {{ band.grouper }}
  <ul>
    {% for band in band.list %}
    <li>{{ band.name }}</li>
    {% endfor %}
  </ul>
  </li>
  {% endfor %}
</ul>
```

1 https://docs.djangoproject.com/en/dev/ref/templates/builtins/#date

The url Tag

The `url` tag avoids hard coding URLs in the template by doing a reverse lookup of the url name provided to the tag. For example, you can retrieve the url for this page by doing a reverse lookup for the url name `tdemo`:

```
<h2>Url Tag</h2>
{% url 'tdemo' %}
```

The widthratio Tag

The `widthratio` tag sets the width of an image proportional to a maximum width. Useful for bar charts and the like:

```
<h2>Widthratio Tag</h2>
<img src=" {% static 'redbar.png'%}" width="{% widthratio 33 100 200
%}">
<img src=" {% static 'bluebar.png'%}" height="200px" width="
{% widthratio 33 100 200 %}">
<img src=" {% static 'greenbar.png'%}" height="300px" width="
{% widthratio 33 100 200 %}">
```

You will need to copy the three image files from the `\static` directory in the source code to the `\static` directory in your project for this example to work.

The with Tag

The `with` tag creates an alias for a complex variable. Useful for reducing the overhead of methods that hit the database multiple times:

```
<h2>With Tag</h2>
{% with total_items=color_list|length %}
The list has {{ total_items }} item{{ total_items|pluralize }}
{% endwith %}
<hr />
```

Template Filters

Filter	Description
add	Adds the argument to the variable
addslashes	Adds slashes before quotes
capfirst, lower, upper, title	Capitalizes the first character, converts to lowercase, uppercase or title case of the value, respectively
center, ljust, rjust	Center, left justify or right justify the value in a field of a given width
cut	Removes all values of the argument from the given string
date, time	Formats a date or time according to the given format
default	Sets default for a value if it's empty or False
default_if_none	Sets default if value is None
dictsort, dictsortreversed	Sorts a list of dictionaries by key given in the argument. dictsortreversed provides reverse sort
divisibleby	True if the value is divisible by the argument
escape, force_escape	Escapes HTML in a string value. Use force_escape after you apply filters to already escaped results or when you need multiple escaping
escapejs	Escapes characters in a string for use in JavaScript strings
filesizeformat	Human readable filesize. E.g., "5 MB"
first, last	First/last item in a list
floatformat	Rounds a floating-point number
get_digit	Returns requested digit from given whole number
join	Joins a list with a string
json_script	Safely outputs an object as JSON

Filter	Description
`length`	Returns the length of the value
`length_is`	`True` if the value's length matches the argument
`linebreaks`	Replaces line breaks in plain text with ` ` or `<p></p>` HTML tags
`linebreaksbr`	Replaces newlines with ` ` HTML tags
`linenumbers`	Displays text with line numbers
`make_list`	Returns value turned into a list
`phone2numeric`	Converts a phone number with text to its numeric equivalent
`pluralize`	Pluralizes the suffix if value > 1
`random`	Returns a random item from a given list
`safe`	Marks a string as not requiring further HTML escaping
`safeseq`	Applies `safe` filter to each item in a sequence
`slice`	Slices a list
`slugify`	Slugifies a string
`stringformat`	Formats a value according to the argument. Uses `printf` style formatting
`striptags`	Strips all HTML tags
`timesince`, `timeuntil`	Formats a date as a time-since or time-until value
`truncatechars`, `truncatechars_html`	Truncates value to the specified number of characters. `truncatechars_html` is an HTML aware version
`truncatewords`, `truncatewords_html`	Truncates value to the specified number of words. `truncatewords_html` is an HTML aware version
`unordered_list`	Formats a list as an HTML unordered list. Works recursively to create nested lists

Filter	Description
`urlencode`, `iriencode`	Escapes a value for including in a URL. `iriencode` is the internationalized version and can encode non-ASCII and unicode characters
`urlize`, `urlizetrunc`	Converts a URL into a clickable link. `urlizetrunc` will truncate the URL if it's longer than the given length
`wordcount`	Returns the number of words in a string
`wordwrap`	Wraps words at the specified length
`yesno`	Maps values for `True`, `False` and `None`
Humanize Filters	
`apnumber`	Spells out the numbers 1-9 (Associated Press style)
`intcomma`	Adds commas to large numbers. It respects localization (e.g., use "." instead of "," for European locales)
`intword`	Uses words for numbers over 1 million
`naturalday`	Uses "yesterday", "today", and "tomorrow" as appropriate
`naturaltime`	Returns a string representation of time durations
`ordinal`	Converts an integer to an ordinal string

Table 11-2. *Django's template filters.*

Let's have a closer look at a few of the more common filters on this list. To test the filters, add the snippets of source code to your `template_demo.html` file as you go. Make sure you add them between the `<body></body>` HTML tags.

The add Filter

The `add` filter adds the argument to the value:

```
<h2>Add Filter</h2>
{{ somevar|add:'12' }}<br />
{{ somevar|add:anothervar }}<br />
```

The addslashes Filter

The `addslashes` filter adds slashes before quotes in the value:

```
<h2>Addslashes Filter</h2>
{{ "I'm not. She didn't."|addslashes }}<br />
{{ 'He said "NO!"'|addslashes }}
```

Sentence Casing Filters

Django's template language has four filters to change the casing of sentences:

1. `capfirst`
2. `lower`
3. `upper`
4. `title`

To see them in action, add the following snippet to your demo file:

```
<h2>Sentence Casing Filters</h2>
{{ "the 'capfirst' filter will capitalize the first word"|capfirst }}<br
/>
{{ "The 'lower' Filter will Convert the Sentence to LOWERCASE"|lower
}}<br />
{{ "the 'upper' filter will convert the sentence to uppercase"|upper }}<br
/>
{{ "and the 'title' filter will convert the sentence to title case"|title
}}
```

Field Alignment Filters

The field alignment filters `ljust`, `rjust` and `center` will align the value within a field of the specified number of characters:

```
<h2>Field Alignment Filters</h2>
<pre>|{{ "Left Justified"|ljust:"30" }}|</pre><br />
```

```
<pre>|{{ "Centered"|center:"30" }}|</pre><br />
<pre>|{{ "Right Justified"|rjust:"30" }}|</pre>
```

The cut Filter

The `cut` filter removes all values of the argument from the given string:

```
<h2>Cut Filter</h2>
{{ "I really don't like the letter 'e' for some reason"|cut:"e" }}
```

The date and time Filters

The `date` and `time` filters format the date or time according to the given format:

```
<h2>Formatting Dates and Times</h2>
{{ today|date:"l jS E Y" }}<br />
{{ today|time:"H:i" }}
```

Both the `date` and `time` filters use a string format syntax designed to be like PHP string formatting to make it easier for template designers to transition away from PHP.

It only works in Django's templates, lest the stink of PHP contaminates any other part of the Django codebase ;).

The available format strings can be found in Django's documentation[2].

The default and default_if_none Filters

The `default` filter will show the default value if the value is empty or `False`, the `default_if_none` filter will show the default value if the value is `None`:

2 https://docs.djangoproject.com/en/dev/ref/templates/builtins/#date

```
<h2>Showing Default Values</h2>
{{ empty_list|default:"Empty list" }}<br />
{{ empty_list|default_if_none:"This won't show as Empty != None" }}<br />
{{ None|default_if_none:"Obvious, but you get the idea" }}
```

The dictsort and dictsortreversed Filters

Sort a list of dictionaries by the given key with `dictsort`:

```
<h2>Sorting Dictionaries</h2>
{{ best_bands|dictsort:"name"}}
```

You can also sort in reverse with `dictsortreversed`:

```
{{ best_bands|dictsortreversed:"name"}}
```

The divisibleby Filter

The `divisibleby` filters tests if the value is divisible by the argument:

```
<h2>Divisibleby Filter</h2>
{{ anothervar|divisibleby:"4" }}<br />
{{ anothervar|divisibleby:"3" }}
```

The filesizeformat Filter

The `filesizeformat` filter formats the value as a human-readable file size:

```
<h2>Filesizeformat Filter</h2>
<p><strong></strong></p>
{{ 44040192|filesizeformat }}
```

The first and last Filters

Retrieve the first item with the `first` filter:

```
<h2>Retrieving the First and Last Items from a List</h2>
{{ color_list|first }}
```

Retrieve the last item with the `last` filter:

```
{{ color_list|last }}
```

The floatformat Filter

Floating point numbers can be rounded with the `floatformat` filter. By default it rounds to one decimal place:

```
<h2>Format Floating Point Numbers</h2>
{{ 3.14159265|floatformat }}
```

You can also specify the number of decimal places:

```
{{ 3.14159265|floatformat:4 }}
```

The get_digit Filter

The `get_digit` filter returns the requested digit from the given whole number. It will return the original value if it's not an integer or the argument is less than 1:

```
<h2>get_digit Filter</h2>
<p><strong></strong></p>
{{ anothervar|get_digit:1 }}<br />
{{ anothervar|get_digit:0 }}<br />
{{ "Hello"|get_digit:2 }}<br />
```

The join Filter

The `join` filter joins a list with the given string to create a single string:

```
<h2>Join Filter</h2>
<p><strong></strong></p>
{{ color_list|join:" and " }}
```

The json_script Filter

Add the following snippet to your demo file to check out the output of the `json_script` filter:

```
<h2>Output JSON</h2>
<p><strong>JSON can be output using the <code>json_script</code>
filter:</strong></p>
<p>(You will need to look in the page source to see this one)</p>
{{ best_bands|json_script:"best-bands" }}
{{ venues|json_script:"all-venues" }}
```

It's hard to see what the `json_script` filter does without digging into the page source, so I have reproduced it here. The `json_script` filter will output a Python object as a JSON script. For example:

```
{{ best_bands|json_script:"best-bands" }}
```

This filter will output the `best_bands` dictionary as a JSON object:

```
<script id="best-bands" type="application/json">
    [
        {"name": "The Angels", "country": "Australia"},
        {"name": "AC/DC", "country": "Australia"},
        {"name": "Nirvana", "country": "USA"},
        {"name": "The Offspring", "country": "USA"},
        {"name": "Iron Maiden", "country": "UK"},
        {"name": "Rammstein", "country": "Germany"}
    ]
</script>
```

Note how Django wraps the JSON in a `<script></script>` tag and the script id is set to the same value as the `json_script` argument.

Not all Django objects are serializable—a notable example being QuerySets. With QuerySets, you use `django.core.serializers` to serialize the QuerySet. For example, we can JSON serialize a QuerySet containing all our venues from the database (this code is already in your `demo_views.py` file):

```
from django.core import serializers
from events.models import Venue

# ...

venues_js = serializers.serialize('json', Venue.venues.all())
```

Once you pass `venues_js` back to the view in the context, it can be added to the template with:

```
{{ venues|json_script:"all-venues" }}
```

I haven't reproduced the output here; check your browser page source to see the serialized venues.

The length_is Filter

The `length_is` filter will output a boolean value depending on whether the value does or does not match the argument:

```
<h2>Length_is Filter</h2>
{{ color_list|length_is:"4" }}<br />
{{ empty_list|length_is:"2" }}<br />
{{ "Hello"|length_is:"5" }}
```

The make_list Filter

The `make_list` filter turns the given value into a list. Numbers will be cast to strings before converting to a list:

```
<h2>Make_list Filter</h2>
{{ "Hello"|make_list }}<br />
{{ "12345"|make_list }}<br />
{{ anothervar|make_list }}<br />
{{ 3.14159265|make_list }}
```

The phone2numeric Filter

The `phone2numeric` filter converts an alphanumeric phone number to a numeric phone number:

```
<h2>Phone2numeric Filter</h2>
{{ "1800 BITE ME"|phone2numeric }}
```

The random Filter

The `random` filter returns a random item from the given list:

```
<h2>Random Filter</h2>
<p>(This list will change every time you refresh the browser)</p>
{{ color_list|random }}<br />
{{ color_list|random }}<br />
{{ color_list|random }}
```

The slice Filter

The `slice` filter slices a list using Python's list slicing syntax:

```
<h2>Slice Filter</h2>
{{ color_list|slice:":3" }}<br />
```

```
{{ color_list|slice:"2:" }}<br />
{{ color_list|slice:":-1" }}<br />
{{ color_list|slice:"1:2" }}
```

The slugify Filter

The `slugify` filter will slugify the given string:

```
<h2>Slugify Filter</h2>
{{ "Number of the Beast"|slugify }}
```

`slugify` will also strip out everything that isn't an alphanumeric character, underscore or hyphen:

```
{{ "slugify won't use these: /\$#^&"|slugify }}
```

The string_format Filter

The `string_format` filter uses Python's old-style `printf` formatting syntax to format numbers and numeric strings:

```
<h2>Stringformat Filter</h2>
{{ 314159265|stringformat:"E" }}<br />
{{ 3.14159265|stringformat:".2f" }}
```

For a complete reference to all formatting options, see Python's printf-style string formatting documentation[3].

The striptags Filter

The `striptags` filter strips all HTML tags from the value:

3 https://docs.python.org/3/library/stdtypes.html#old-string-formatting

```
<h2>Striptags Filter</h2>
{{ "<h1>The Title</h1>"|striptags }}
```

This is a straightforward filter to use; however, it comes with a big caveat. See the warning below.

Striptags is Not Guaranteed to be HTML Safe!

The `striptags` filter is not guaranteed to output HTML-safe text when provided with non-valid HTML input. Never apply the safe filter to striptags output. For a more robust solution, Use the `clean()` method of the bleach library[4].

The timesince and timeuntil Filters

Use the `timesince` and `timeuntil` filters to compare the difference between a date value and a given past or future date (similar to Python's `timedelta` function).

To calculate time to a future date, use the `timesince` filter:

```
<h2>Calculating the Difference Between Dates</h2>
{{ today|timesince:future }}
```

To calculate time to a past date, use the `timeuntil` filter:

```
{{ today|timeuntil:past }}
```

These filters can seem counter-intuitive when you first use them as the filter argument is the reference date. This leads to a situation that looks backwards when you first encounter these tags:

4 https://bleach.readthedocs.io/en/latest/clean.html

- If you want to calculate the time to a future date, you use the `timesince` filter. The output of this filter is the time that has passed *since* your date value and the future date value.
- If you want to calculate the time from a past date, you use the `timeuntil` filter. The output of this filter is the time that has passed *until* the past date reaches your date value.

If you get these the wrong way around, your output will be "0 minutes".

Truncating Strings

It's common to need to truncate a sentence or string for display in a web page. For example, teaser text from the beginning of an article. Django provides four filter tags for accomplishing this task—`truncatechars`, `truncatewords`, and their HTML-aware versions `truncatechars_html` and `truncatewords_html`.

For example, you can truncate a string to a certain number of characters with `truncatechars`:

```
<h2>Truncating Strings</h2>
{{ "The Title"|truncatechars:7 }}<br />
```

This won't work if there are HTML tags in the string. This is because `truncatechars` will treat HTML tags as regular text.

To fix this issue, use `truncatechars_html` which ignores HTML tags:

```
{{ "<em>The Title</em>"|truncatechars_html:7 }}<br />
```

In each case, Django appends an ellipsis (…) to the end of the truncated string.

Truncating words works the same way:

```
{{ "The Title"|truncatewords:1 }}<br />
<p><strong>HTML aware version:</strong></p>
{{ "<em>The Title</em>"|truncatewords_html:1 }}
```

The unordered_list Filter

The `unordered_list` filter recursively show a nested list:

```
<h2>Unordered Lists</h2>
<ul>
  {{ aussie_bands|unordered_list }}
</ul>
```

Note, you must supply the HTML `<ul></ul>` tags yourself.

The urlencode Filter

The `urlencode` filter formats a string so it can be included in a URL:

```
<h2>Encoding URLs</h2>
{{ "https://bestbands.example.com/bands?album=Master of
Puppets&rating=awesome"|urlencode }}
```

If you need to encode non-ASCII characters, use the internationalized version `iriencode`.

The urlize Filter

Create hyperlinks with the `urlize` filter:

```
<h2>Creating Hyperlinks</h2>
<p><strong></strong></p>
{{ "The djangobook.com website is awesome!"|urlize }}<br />
```

The filter automatically detects URLs in the provided string and converts them to a hyperlink.

You can use the `urlizetrunc` filter to truncate long URLs:

```
{{ "The djangobook.com website is awesome!"|urlizetrunc:11 }}
```

The wordcount Filter

The `wordcount` filter counts the number of words in a string:

```
<h2>Wordcount Filter</h2>
{{ "The djangobook.com website is awesome!"|wordcount }}
```

The wordwrap Filter

The `wordwrap` filter wraps the string at the specified number of characters:

```
<h2>Wordwrap Filter</h2>
<pre>{{ "Now I lay me down to sleep"|wordwrap:4 }}</pre>
```

The yesno Filter

The `yesno` filter maps `True`, `False` and `None` values to strings. You can use the default values:

```
<h2>Yesno Filter</h2>
{{ True|yesno }}<br />
{{ False|yesno }}<br />
{{ None|yesno }}<br />
```

Or you can create your own custom mapping:

```
{{ True|yesno:"yeah baby,heck no,meh" }}<br />
{{ False|yesno:"yeah baby,heck no,meh" }}<br />
{{ None|yesno:"yeah baby,heck no,meh" }}
```

The Humanize Filters

For the humanize filters to work in your demo file, you must load the `humanize` app in your `INSTALLED_APPS` (change in bold):

```
# myclub_root\myclub_site\settings.py

INSTALLED_APPS = [
    # ...
    'django.contrib.staticfiles',
    'django.contrib.humanize',
]
```

And you need to load the `humanize` library in any template you wish to use the humanize filters (change in bold):

```
# \events\templates\events\template_demo.html

{% load static humanize %}
# ...
```

The humanize filters add a "human touch" to numbers and dates. Each filter also respects the user's locale and language settings.

The `apnumber` filter spells out the numbers 1-9 Associated Press style:

```
<h2>The Humanize Filters</h2>
{{ 1|apnumber }}, {{ 5|apnumber }}, {{ 12|apnumber }}<br />
```

The `intcomma` adds commas to large numbers. It respects localization (e.g., uses "." instead of "," for European locales):

```
{{ 4500|intcomma }}; {{ 42123456.78|intcomma }}<br />
```

The `intword` uses words for numbers over 1 million:

```
{{ 4000000|intword }}; {{ 42000000000|intword }}<br />
```

The `naturalday` uses "yesterday", "today", and "tomorrow" as appropriate:

```
{{ today|naturalday }}<br />
```

The `naturaltime` filter returns a string representation of time durations:

```
{{ today|naturaltime }}; {{ past|naturaltime }}; {{ future|naturaltime
}}<br />
```

And the `ordinal` filter converts an integer to an ordinal string:

```
{{ 1|ordinal }}, {{ 2|ordinal }}, {{ 3|ordinal }}, {{ 20|ordinal }}
```

How Invalid Variables are Handled

Django's template system fails silently if an invalid variable is encountered. The rationale behind this is you don't want the whole template to break if a bad variable is passed.

The default behavior is to interpret the invalid variable as an empty string (`''`). Filters applied in this case are ignored.

The exceptions are the `if`, `for` and `regroup` template tags where the invalid variable is interpreted as `None`. Filters *are* applied in these cases.

You can override this default behavior by setting the `string_if_invalid` configuration option. A handy trick if you are debugging a troublesome template is to set `string_if_invalid` to `'%s'`, which will replace the invalid variable with the name of the variable.

If you set `string_if_invalid` to anything other than an empty string, filters will be applied.

Debug Only!

As many of Django's templates rely on invalid variables failing silently, changing the value of `string_if_invalid` should only be done in rare cases where other debugging techniques (e.g., Django's error page) are not successful in identifying the problem with the template.

Even in these rare cases, `string_if_invalid` should only be changed temporarily and should never be used as a development default.

Custom Tags and Filters

You can create custom template tags and filters with the DTL by defining them in Python and then loading them in a template with the `{% load %}` tag.

To create custom template tags and filters, you must first create a Python package named `templatetags` that contains the tag and filter definitions. This package must live inside an app that is included in your `INSTALLED_APPS` list.

We will create some custom tags and filters inside our `events` app, so first, create a new folder and files inside your `events` app:

```
\events
    # ...
    \templatetags
        __init__.py
        event_custom_tags.py
    # ...
```

\templatetags is a new folder, and the empty __init__.py file tells Python that the templatetags folder is a package. The file event_custom_tags.py is where we will store the custom filter and tag definitions.

Custom Filters

Let's start by creating a custom filter that reverses a string:

```
# myclub_root\events\templatetags\event_custom_tags.py

1  from django import template
2
3  register = template.Library()
4
5  @register.filter(name='reverse')
6  def reverse(value):
7      return value[::-1]
```

Let's have a closer look at this code:

- In **line 1**, we're importing Django's template library.
- In **line 3**, we're adding a module-level variable called register. This variable must be present for the module to be a valid tag library.
- **Line 5** uses the register.filter() decorator to register our custom filter with Django.
- **Line 6** defines our simple filter.
- **Line 7** uses a Python string slice trick to return the string in reverse order.

To use this filter in a template, you must first load the custom tag library into the template with the {% load %} tag (change in bold):

```
# \events\templates\events\template_demo.html

{% load static humanize event_custom_tags %}
# ...
```

Once the custom tag library is loaded, you can use your new custom filter in the template:

```
<h2>Custom Tags and Filters</h2>
{{ "James is in rehab again"|reverse }}<br />
```

This example will output "niaga baher ni si semaJ".

NOTE: If you are following along and building the `template_demo.html` file and module code as you go, restart the development server for Django to load the new package.

There is a problem with this filter, however. As it expects a string, if you pass a number to the filter, you will get an error. For example, if you pass an integer to the filter:

```
{{ 100|reverse }}
```

Django will throw a `TypeError`:

```
TypeError at /tdemo/
'int' object is not subscriptable
```

As you will most often be working with strings in templates, Django provides a handy decorator you can use in such situations (changes in bold):

```
# myclub_root\events\templatetags\event_custom_tags.py

from django import template
from django.template.defaultfilters import stringfilter

register = template.Library()

@register.filter(name='reverse')
@stringfilter
def reverse(value):
    return value[::-1]
```

Once you have imported the `stringfilter` function (**line 2**), and added the `@stringfilter` decorator (**line 7**), any numbers passed to the filter will be converted to their string representation before the filter is applied.

Now, when you pass a number to the filter, it will output a reversed string. In our above example, the modified filter will now output "`001`" instead of throwing an error.

Filters and Autoescaping

When writing a custom filter, you need to consider how it will interact with Django's auto-escaping behavior.

There are a few caveats and ways to approach autoescaping depending on the data you are trying to filter. For up-to-date information on how to manage auto-escaping of custom filters, see Django's documentation[5].

Custom Tags

Custom tags come in two different flavors:

1. **Simple Tags** take zero or more arguments and returns a result.
2. **Inclusion Tags** display data by rendering another template.

Simple Tags

Simple tags are useful for returning snippets of text that are repeated often throughout your templates. By creating a tag, you don't have to repeat the same information in each template. For example, let's say you want to add a "date created" entry at the bottom of each page on a website. Rather than type the statement out after every piece of content, we can use a custom tag to generate the content. Let's start with adding a new tag definition to `event_custom_tags.py` (changes in bold):

5 https://docs.djangoproject.com/en/dev/howto/custom-template-tags/#filters-and-auto-escaping

```
# myclub_root\events\templatetags\event_custom_tags.py

1  from django import template
2  from django.template.defaultfilters import stringfilter
3  from datetime import datetime
4  
5  register = template.Library()
6  
7  # ...
8  
9  @register.simple_tag
10 def create_date(date_val):
11     return "This content was created on %s" % date_val.strftime('%A %B %d, %Y')
```

Let's have a look at what's going on here:

- **Line 3.** I have imported the `datetime` module from Python.
- **Line 9.** We're registering the tag with the `@register.simple_tag` decorator.
- **Line 10.** The `create_date` tag definition.
- **Line 11.** We're returning a simple text snippet containing a message and the value of `date_val` formatted using Python's `datetime.strftime` function.

To display the output for this tag, you add it to a template and pass it a date value:

```
# Example only. Don't add to your demo file

{% create_date date_val %}
```

For example, let's add the simple tag to our template with `today` as the date value:

```
{% create_date today %}
```

When you reload the demo template, it should output "This content was created on" with today's date appended in long date format.

Inclusion Tags

Inclusion tags are more complicated than simple tags because you must tell Django what template you want to use with the inclusion tag, and you must return a dictionary which Django will use as a context for the specified template. Let me show you how this works with an example (new code):

```
# myclub_root\events\templatetags\event_custom_tags.py

# ...

1  @register.inclusion_tag('events/announcements.html')
2  def announcements():
3      announcements = [
4          {
5              'date': '6-10-2020',
6              'announcement': "Club Registrations Open"
7          },
8          {
9              'date': '6-15-2020',
10             'announcement': "Joe Smith Elected New Club President"
11         }
12     ]
13     return {'announcements': announcements}
```

Remember our announcements template include from Chapter 6? This is an implementation of the same function using a custom include tag. In **line 1**, I am using the `@register.inclusion_tag()` decorator to register the tag and passing it the `announcements.html` template to use with the tag.

In **lines 3 to 12**, I am recreating the same announcements list we used in Chapter 6, and in **line 13**, I am returning a context dictionary containing the announcements list.

Now, all you need to do to show the announcements list in the template is to add the custom tag to your template:

```
{% announcements %}
```

If you load `template_demo.html` into your browser, you will see the announcements at the bottom of the page. You could also experiment with the inclusion tag yourself and add it to the event calendar in place of the template include.

More Advanced Template Tags

Django provides full access to all the internals of the DTL, so it's possible to build more advanced custom template tags. However, this is a specialized need outside of the scope of this book. If you are curious, you can check out advanced custom template tags in the Django documentation[6].

Context, RequestContext and Context Processors

So far, we have only viewed the context as a simple Python dictionary passed to the `render()` shortcut method, but there is more to it. Under the hood, the `render()` method is creating an instance of a `RequestContext` class, which is a subclass of the `Context` class. Both classes live in the `django.template` library.

The Context Class

The `Context` class is a dictionary-like object that can be instantiated directly in code:

```
>>> from django.template import Context
>>> con = Context()
>>> con
[{'True': True, 'False': False, 'None': None}]
```

As you can see, an empty context is a simple object with only a single dictionary of built-ins for representing `True`, `False` and `None` in the context. You can instantiate a populated context by passing it a dictionary:

6 https://docs.djangoproject.com/en/dev/howto/custom-template-tags/#advanced-custom-template-tags

```
>>> con = Context({"fn":"Bruce", "ln":"Bruce"})
```

As the context is a dictionary-like object, you can access and change key values like an ordinary dictionary:

```
>>> con['ln']
'Bruce'
>>> con['ln'] = "Dickinson"
>>> con['ln']
'Dickinson'
>>> con.get('fn')
'Bruce'
```

Setting Default Values

The `Context` class also has a `setdefault()` method that will add a new `key:value` pair if the key doesn't exist, and return the value:

```
>>> con.setdefault('band', 'Iron Maiden')
'Iron Maiden'
>>> con
[{'True': True, 'False': False, 'None': None}, {'fn': 'Bruce', 'ln':
'Dickinson', 'band': 'Iron Maiden'}]
```

If the key exists, `setdefault()` will return its value:

```
>>> con.setdefault('band', 'Samson')
'Iron Maiden'
```

Updating the Context

New data can be added to the context with the `update()` method, however, it operates differently than the regular dictionary `update()` method:

```
>>> con.update({'fn': 'James', 'ln': 'Hetfield', 'band': 'Metallica'})
{'fn': 'James', 'ln': 'Hetfield', 'band': 'Metallica'}
```

```
>>> con
[{'True': True, 'False': False, 'None': None}, {'fn': 'Bruce', 'ln':
'Dickinson', 'band': 'Iron Maiden'}, {'fn': 'James', 'ln': 'Hetfield',
'band': 'Metallica'}]
```

A Context object is a stack, so update() adds a new dictionary to the context; it doesn't update the existing.

Converting the Context to a Single Dictionary

To get the whole context as a single dictionary, you use the flatten() method:

```
>>> con
[{'True': True, 'False': False, 'None': None}, {'fn': 'Bruce', 'ln':
'Dickinson', 'band': 'Iron Maiden'}, {'fn': 'James', 'ln': 'Hetfield',
'band': 'Metallica'}]
>>> con.flatten()
{'True': True, 'False': False, 'None': None, 'fn': 'James', 'ln':
'Hetfield', 'band': 'Metallica'}
```

You need to be careful with this method because if there are duplicate keys in the stack, the flattened key value will be set to the last value on the stack, and this may not be what you want.

Using the Context as a Stack

As the Context object is a stack, you can push() and pop() like a regular Python stack:

```
>>> con = Context()
>>> con.push(fn="Bruce", ln="Dickinson", band="Iron Maiden")
{'fn': 'Bruce', 'ln': 'Dickinson', 'band': 'Iron Maiden'}
>>> con.push(fn="James", ln="Hetfield", band="Metallica")
{'fn': 'James', 'ln': 'Hetfield', 'band': 'Metallica'}
>>> con
[{'True': True, 'False': False, 'None': None}, {'fn': 'Bruce', 'ln':
'Dickinson', 'band': 'Iron Maiden'}, {'fn': 'James', 'ln': 'Hetfield',
```

```
'band': 'Metallica'}]
>>> con.pop()
{'fn': 'James', 'ln': 'Hetfield', 'band': 'Metallica'}
>>> con.pop()
{'fn': 'Bruce', 'ln': 'Dickinson', 'band': 'Iron Maiden'}
```

If you pop() an empty stack, Django will raise an exception:

```
>>> con.pop()
Traceback (most recent call last):
# ...
    raise ContextPopException
django.template.context.ContextPopException
>>>
```

RequestContext and Context Processors

RequestContext is a subclass of Context that differs in two significant ways:

1. RequestContext takes an HttpRequest object as its first argument; and
2. RequestContext populates the context dictionary with variables according to the context_processors configuration option.

In most applications, you will use RequestContext far more often than Context. The render() shortcut method uses RequestContext by default, so when we pass a simple dictionary to render(), Django creates a RequestContext object for us.

context_processors is a list of callables defined in TEMPLATES in your settings.py file:

```
# myclub_root\myclub_site\settings.py

# ...

TEMPLATES = [
    {
```

```
        'BACKEND': 'django.template.backends.django.DjangoTemplates',
        'DIRS': [os.path.join(BASE_DIR, 'myclub_site/templates')],
        'APP_DIRS': True,
        'OPTIONS': {
            'context_processors': [
                'django.template.context_processors.debug',
                'django.template.context_processors.request',
                'django.contrib.auth.context_processors.auth',
                'django.contrib.messages.context_processors.messages',
            ],
        },
    },
]
```

There are four default context processors—`debug`, `request`, `auth` and `messages`. Each of these context processors will merge additional variables into the context:

- **`django.template.context_processors.debug`**:
  - `debug`—Set to `True` if in `DEBUG` mode.
  - `sql_queries`—A list of dictionaries representing all SQL queries executed so far in the request.
- **`django.template.context_processors.request`**:
  - `request`—The current `HttpRequest` object.
- **`django.contrib.auth.context_processors.auth`**:
  - `user`—An `auth.user` instance representing the currently logged in user.
  - `perms`—An object representing the current users' permissions.
- **`django.contrib.messages.context_processors.messages`**:
  - `messages`—A list of messages as strings.
  - `DEFAULT_MESSAGE_LEVELS`—A mapping of message level names to their numeric value.

We can test out how these extra variables are added to the context with a simple example. Add the `context_demo` view to your `demo_views.py` file (new code):

```
# myclub_root\events\views\demo_views.py

# Add these import to the top of your file
from django.template import RequestContext, Template

# ...

1  def context_demo(request):
2      template = Template('{{ user }}<br>{{ perms }}<br>{{ request
}}<br>{{ messages }}')
3      con = RequestContext(request)
4      return HttpResponse(template.render(con))
```

You can see in **line 2,** I am creating a simple text template that renders some of the added context variables, and in **line 3,** I am instantiating a new `RequestContext` object.

You will also need to add a URLconf to navigate to the view (change in bold):

```
# myclub_root\events\urls.py

urlpatterns = [
    path('', views.index, name='index'),
    path('condemo/', views.context_demo, name='condemo'),
    # ...
]
```

Now, if you navigate to `http://127.0.0.1:8000/condemo/`, your browser should look like Figure 11-3.

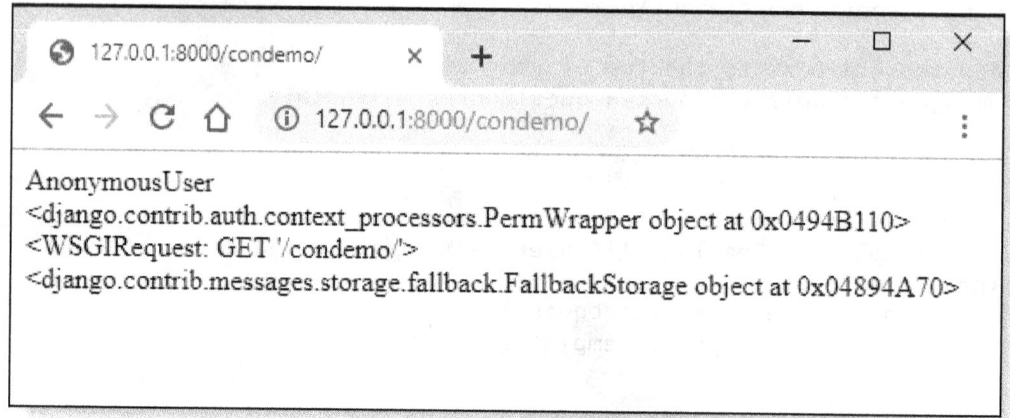

***Figure 11-3.** Django's default context processors have added a few variables to the context.*

Django includes five other built-in template context processors which, if enabled, add more variables to the context that can be accessed in the template:

- **`django.template.context_processors.i18n`**:
  - `LANGUAGES`—Adds the value of the `LANGUAGES` setting. This is a lengthy list of tuples in the format `('language code', 'language')`.
  - `LANGUAGE_BIDI`—`False` if language is a left-to-right language, `True` if it's a right-to-left language.
  - `LANGUAGE_CODE`—The language code of the request, e.g., `'en-us'`.
- **`django.template.context_processors.media`**:
  - `MEDIA_URL`—The value of the `MEDIA_URL` setting.
- **`django.template.context_processors.static`**:
  - `STATIC_URL`—The value of the `STATIC_URL` setting.
- **`django.template.context_processors.csrf`**:

    - Adds a token for the `csrf_token` template tag. Rarely used because CSRF middleware is enabled by default, so `{% csrf_token %}` already works without needing to load this processor.

- **`django.template.context_processors.tz`**:
    - `TIME_ZONE`—A variable containing the active time zone.

Adding one of the built-in context processors is simple, you just add the processor call to the `context_processors` list (change in bold):

```
# myclub_root\myclub_site\settings.py

# ...

'context_processors': [
    'django.template.context_processors.debug',
    'django.template.context_processors.request',
    'django.contrib.auth.context_processors.auth',
    'django.contrib.messages.context_processors.messages',
    'django.template.context_processors.i18n',
],
```

In this example, I have added the `i18n` context processor. We can test this out in the browser with a small change to our `context_demo()` view (change in bold):

```
# myclub_root\events\views\demo_views.py

# ...

1  def context_demo(request):
2      template = Template('{{ LANGUAGE_CODE }}<br>{{ LANGUAGE_BIDI }}')
3      con = RequestContext(request)
4      return HttpResponse(template.render(con))
```

I have simply changed **line 2** to render two new variables provided by the `i18n` context processor to the context.

Now, if you navigate to `http://127.0.0.1:8000/condemo/`, your browser should look like Figure 11-4.

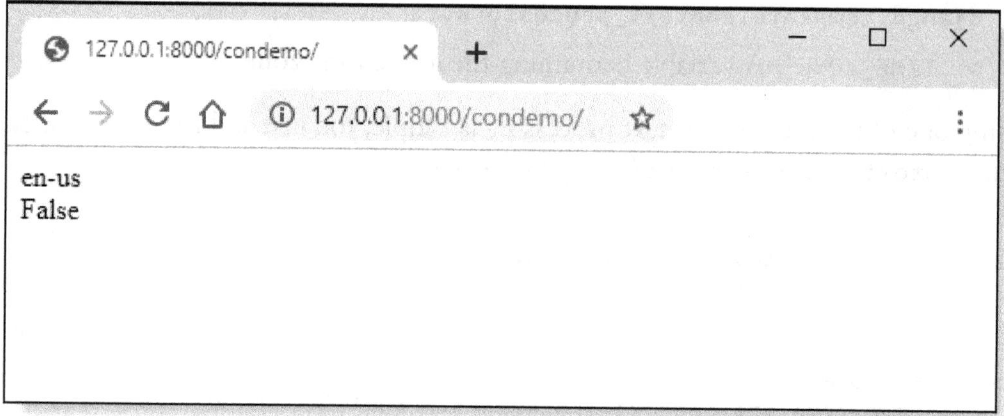

Figure 11-4. *Django's* `i18n` *context processor has added more variables to the context.*

Writing Custom Context Processors

A context processor is a simple object that takes a request and returns a dictionary to add to the context. This makes them handy for adding common variables to the context without having to add the variable to each view, thus breaking the DRY principle.

This is an example of a simple context processor:

```
# myclub_root\events\views\demo_views.py

# ...

def my_processor(request):
    return {
        'foo': 'foo',
        'bar': 'bar',
        'baz': 'baz',
    }
```

Make sure you add `my_processor` before the `context_demo` view in your code.

You can load this custom processor by making a small change to the view (changes in bold):

```
# myclub_root\events\views\demo_views.py

# ...

1  def context_demo(request):
2      template = Template('{{ foo }}<br>{{ bar }}<br>{{ baz }}')
3      con = RequestContext(request, processors=[my_processor])
4      return HttpResponse(template.render(con))
```

I've changed the template code in **line 2**, but the important change here is **line 3** where I have added the `processors` option. `processors` is a list of additional processors to pass to `RequestContext`.

Now, if you navigate to `http://127.0.0.1:8000/condemo/`, your browser should look like Figure 11-5.

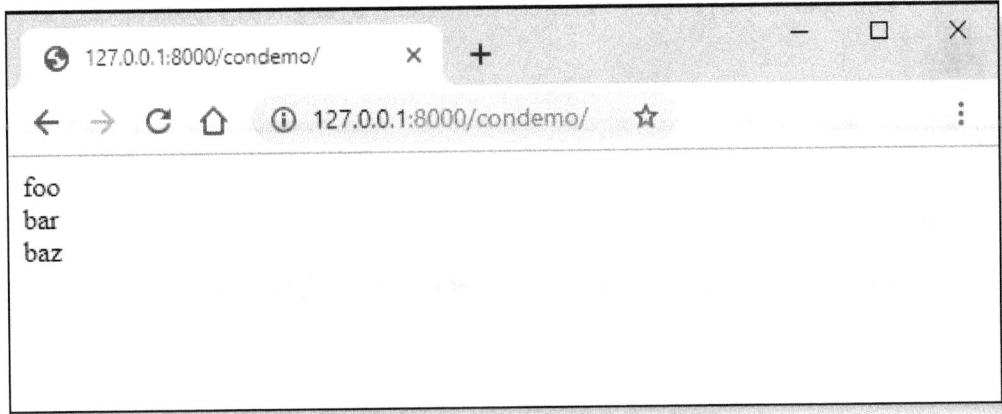

Figure 11-5. *Adding a custom context processor to your app to add additional context variables to your views.*

This is a simple example. If you have more complex needs and want to apply a custom context processor, you can create a module for your context processor (`.py` file) and load it in your settings just like the built-in context processors. Your custom processor module can live anywhere on your Python path; just make sure its location is logical. If it's specific to an app, save it in the app directory, otherwise, if it's site-wide, save it in your Django website app (`myclub_site` in our case).

Template Back Ends and Loaders

Django comes with two built-in template back ends—the Django Template Language (DTL) back end and the Jinja2[7] back end.

The DTL back end is the most common back end by a significant margin, so it's enabled by default when you create an app with `startapp`. If you want to use the Jinja2 engine, you must change your TEMPLATE settings to use the Jinja2 engine:

```
# myclub_root\myclub_site\settings.py

TEMPLATES = [
    {
        'BACKEND': 'django.template.backends.django.DjangoTemplates',
        # ...
```

Change to:

```
TEMPLATES = [
    {
        'BACKEND': ' django.template.backends.jinja2.Jinja2.',
        # ...
```

7 http://jinja.pocoo.org/

When Should I Use the Jinja2 Template Engine?

Good question, and one I don't have a definitive answer for.

I've always been pragmatic with my approach to programming, so I don't get hung up on what tool to use, no matter how new and bright and shiny it is.

If Jinja2 solves a problem for you that the DTL doesn't, use it. If you don't have a particular reason to use Jinja2, stick with the DTL.

Personally, I have never had a problem I couldn't solve with the DTL, so I haven't used Jinja2.

Template Loaders

Django's template loaders find and load templates. Like the template engine, the most common template loaders are enabled by default.

`django.template.loaders.filesystem.Loader` loads templates from the filesystem as listed in the `DIRS` setting. We have already added one search path to `DIRS` in Chapter 6: `os.path.join(BASE_DIR, 'myclub_site/templates')`. To provide additional search paths, you just add them to the `DIRS` list.

`django.template.loaders.app_directories.Loader` is also enabled by default and, if `APP_DIRS` is `True`, it will search each app in your project for templates, in the order listed in the `INSTALLED_APPS` setting.

If your app overrides an admin template, it *must* be listed before `django.contrib.admin` in your `INSTALLED_APPS`; otherwise, the default admin templates will override your custom templates.

The Order of `INSTALLED_APPS` Matters!

As Django uses short-circuit logic when searching for templates, the order of `INSTALLED_APPS` matters. We have already discussed this when I explained the importance of namespacing templates, but it's also important if you want to override Django's default templates, for example, admin templates.

Django comes with two other built-in loaders that you can use—`django.template.loaders.cached.Loader` is useful for when you want to speed up template rendering by caching template instances, and `django.template.loaders.locmem.Loader` which loads templates from a Python dictionary and is useful for testing.

You can also create your own custom loaders, but this is a rare case, so I won't cover custom loaders in this book. If you want more information on creating your own loaders, see the Django documentation[8].

Code Listings

The following are the code listings for the demo views and HTML template used in this chapter. File paths are at the top of each listing.

demo_views.py (partial listing)

I have omitted most of the code from previous chapters from this listing so you can see what's been added.

```
# myclub_root\events\views\demo_views.py

from django.shortcuts import render
from django.http import HttpResponse
from django.http import FileResponse
from django.core import serializers
from django.template import RequestContext, Template
```

8 https://docs.djangoproject.com/en/dev/ref/templates/api/#custom-loaders

```
from datetime import datetime
import csv
import io
from reportlab.pdfgen import canvas
from reportlab.lib.units import inch
from reportlab.lib.pagesizes import letter
from events.models import Venue

# ...

def template_demo(request):
    empty_list = []
    color_list = ['red', 'green', 'blue', 'yellow']
    somevar = 5
    anothervar = 21
    today = datetime.now()
    past = datetime(1985, 11, 5)
    future = datetime(2035, 11, 5)
    best_bands = [
        {'name': 'The Angels', 'country': 'Australia'},
        {'name': 'AC/DC', 'country': 'Australia'},
        {'name': 'Nirvana', 'country': 'USA'},
        {'name': 'The Offspring', 'country': 'USA'},
        {'name': 'Iron Maiden', 'country': 'UK'},
        {'name': 'Rammstein', 'country': 'Germany'},
    ]
    aussie_bands = ['Australia', ['The Angels', 'AC/DC', 'The Living End']]
    venues_js = serializers.serialize('json', Venue.venues.all())
    return render(request,
        'events/template_demo.html',
        {
            'somevar': somevar,
            'anothervar': anothervar,
            'empty_list': empty_list,
            'color_list': color_list,
            'best_bands': best_bands,
            'today': today,
            'past': past,
            'future': future,
            'aussie_bands': aussie_bands,
            'venues': venues_js,
        }
    )
```

```
def my_processor(request):
    return {
        'foo': 'foo',
        'bar': 'bar',
        'baz': 'baz',
    }


def context_demo(request):
    # template = Template('{{ user }}<br>{{ perms }}<br>{{ request }}<br>{{ messages }}')
    # template = Template('{{ LANGUAGE_CODE }}<br>{{ LANGUAGE_BIDI }}')
    template = Template('{{ foo }}<br>{{ bar }}<br>{{ baz }}')
    con = RequestContext(request, processors=[my_processor])
    return HttpResponse(template.render(con))
```

template_demo.html (complete listing)

```
# myclub_root\events\templates\events\template_demo.html

{% load static humanize event_custom_tags %}
<!doctype html>
<html>
  <head>
    <meta charset="utf-8">
    <title>Testing out the Template System</title>
    <style>
      .row {
        background-color: lightskyblue;
      }
      .altrow {
        background-color: lightgray;
      }
      table td {
        text-align: center;
      }
    </style>
  </head>
  <body>
    <h2>Comment Tag</h2>
    <!-- This is a normal HTML comment which does show in your browser-->
```

```
    {% comment "this won't show at all in your browser" %}
      <p>Three six nine, the goose drank wine</p>
    {% endcomment %}

    <h2>Cycle Tag</h2>
    {% for i in '12345' %}
      <p style="color: {% cycle 'blue' 'brown' 'red' 'cyan' %};">
        Colored Text
      </p>
    {% endfor %}

    <p><strong>Cycle tag used to format a table:</strong></p>
    <table border=0 style="width: 100px">
      {% for i in '12345' %}
      <tr class="{% cycle 'row' 'altrow' %}">
        <td>{{ i }}</td>
      </tr>
      {% endfor %}
    </table>

    <p><strong>Resetcycle tag:</strong></p>
    <table border=0 style="width: 100px">
      {% for i in '12345' %}
      <tr class="{% cycle 'row' 'altrow' %}">
        <td>{{ i }}</td>
      </tr>
      {% resetcycle %}
      {% endfor %}
    </table>

    <h2>Filter Tag</h2>
    {% filter striptags|upper %}
    <p>This text will be converted to uppercase and have the HTML tags <em>removed</em>.</p>
    {% endfilter %}

    <h2>Firstof Tag</h2>
    <p>{% firstof None False '' empty_list 'This one!' 'Not this one' %}</p>

    <h2>For Tag</h2>
    <p><strong>List Colors:</strong></p>
    <ul>
    {% for item in color_list %}
    <li>{{ item }}{{ forloop.counter }}</li>
    {% endfor %}
```

```
    </ul>
    <p><strong>The for loop variables:</strong></p>
    <table border=1>
    <tr>
        <th>Item</th>
        <th>forloop.counter</th>
        <th>forloop.counter0</th>
        <th>forloop.revcounter</th>
        <th>forloop.revcounter0</th>
        <th>forloop.first</th>
        <th>forloop.last</th>
    </tr>
    {% for item in color_list %}
    <tr>
        <td>{{ item }}</td>
        <td>{{ forloop.counter }}</td>
        <td>{{ forloop.counter0 }}</td>
        <td>{{ forloop.revcounter }}</td>
        <td>{{ forloop.revcounter0 }}</td>
        <td>{{ forloop.first }}</td>
        <td>{{ forloop.last }}</td>
    </tr>
    {% endfor %}
    </table>
    <p><strong>For...empty Tag</strong></p>
    <p><strong>This list has items to show:</strong></p>
    <ul>
    {% for item in color_list %}
    <li>{{ item }}</li>
    {% empty %}
    <li>Nothing in the list!</li>
    {% endfor %}
    </ul>
    <p><strong>But this one doesn't:</strong></p>
    <ul>
    {% for item in empty_list %}
    <li>{{ item }}</li>
    {% empty %}
    <li>Nothing in the list!</li>
    {% endfor %}
    </ul>

    <h2>If Tag</h2>
    {% if empty_list %}
    This line won't show as list is empty.
    {% elif color_list %}
```

```
color_list is not empty, so this line shows.
{% else %}
Optional else clause. This won't show in this example.
{% endif %}
<br />
{% if somevar > 5 %}
somevar is greater than 5
{% else %}
somevar is less than 5
{% endif %}
<br />
{% if empty_list and color_list %}
Both lists have content
{% else%}
One list is empty
{% endif %}
<br />
{% if empty_list or color_list %}
At least one list has content
{% endif %}
<br />
{% if not empty_list %}
Negated an empty list, so this will print.
{% endif %}
<br />
{% if anothervar is True %}
This prints if and only if anothervar is True.
{% endif %}
<br />
{% if novar is None %}
This appears if novar is None, or if novar is not found in the context.
{% endif %}
<br />
{% if anothervar is True %}
This prints if and only if anothervar is True.
{% endif %}
<br />
{% if novar is None %}
This appears if novar is None, or if novar is not found in the context.
{% endif %}
<br />
{% if "dog" in "catdog" %}
The best half!
{% endif %}
```

```
<br />
{% if "orange" in color_list %}
Orange is in the list!
{% else %}
Orange is not in the list!
{% endif %}
<br />
{% if color_list|length < 10 %}
List has less than 10 elements
{% endif %}
<br />
{% if somevar >= 5 and anothervar != 30 %}
Both comparisons are true, so this will print.
{% endif %}

<h2>Lorem Tag</h2>
<p><strong>This one will output a number of words:</strong></p>
{% lorem 5 w %}
<p><strong>This one outputs a number of HTML paragraphs:</strong></p>
{% lorem 2 p %}
<p><strong>This one outputs plain text paragraphs:</strong></p>
{% lorem 1 b %}
<p><strong>And finally, we can output a number of random words:</strong></p>
{% lorem 10 w random %}
<p><strong>or random paragraphs:</strong></p>
{% lorem 3 p random %}

<h2>Now Tag</h2>
{% now "m-d-Y H:i" %}

<h2>Regroup Tag</h2>
{% regroup best_bands by country as band_list %}
<p>Best Bands:</p>
<ul>
  {% for band in band_list %}
  <li>
  {{ band.grouper }}
  <ul>
    {% for band in band.list %}
    <li>{{ band.name }}</li>
    {% endfor %}
  </ul>
  </li>
  {% endfor %}
</ul>
```

```
    <h2>Url Tag</h2>
    {% url 'tdemo' %}

    <h2>Widthratio Tag</h2>
    <img src=" {% static 'redbar.png'%}" width="{% widthratio 33 100 200 %}">
    <img src=" {% static 'bluebar.png'%}" height="200px" width="{% widthratio 33 100 200 %}">
    <img src=" {% static 'greenbar.png'%}" height="300px" width="{% widthratio 33 100 200 %}">

    <h2>With Tag</h2>
    {% with total_items=color_list|length %}
    The list has {{ total_items }} item{{ total_items|pluralize }}
    {% endwith %}
    <hr />

  <h1>Template Filters</h1>

    <h2>Add Filter</h2>
    {{ somevar|add:'12' }}<br />
    {{ somevar|add:anothervar }}<br />

    <h2>Addslashes Filter</h2>
    {{ "I'm not. She didn't."|addslashes }}<br />
    {{ 'He said "NO!"'|addslashes }}

    <h2>Sentence Casing Filters</h2>
    {{ "the 'capfirst' filter will capitalize the first word"|capfirst }}<br />
    {{ "The 'lower' Filter will Convert the Sentence to LOWERCASE"|lower }}<br />
    {{ "the 'upper' filter will convert the sentence to uppercase"|upper }}<br />
    {{ "and the 'title' filter will convert the sentence to title case"|title }}

    <h2>Field Alignment Filters</h2>
    <pre>|{{ "Left Justified"|ljust:"30" }}|</pre><br />
    <pre>|{{ "Centered"|center:"30" }}|</pre><br />
    <pre>|{{ "Right Justified"|rjust:"30" }}|</pre>

    <h2>Cut Filter</h2>
    {{ "I really don't like the letter 'e' for some reason"|cut:"e" }}

```

```
    <h2>Formatting Dates and Times</h2>
    {{ today|date:"l jS E Y" }}<br />
    {{ today|time:"H:i" }}

    <h2>Showing Default Values</h2>
    {{ empty_list|default:"Empty list" }}<br />
    {{ empty_list|default_if_none:"This won't show as Empty != None" }}<br />
    {{ None|default_if_none:"Obvious, but you get the idea" }}

    <h2>Sorting Dictionaries</h2>
    {{ best_bands|dictsort:"name"}}
    {{ best_bands|dictsortreversed:"name"}}

    <h2>Divisibleby Filter</h2>
    {{ anothervar|divisibleby:"4" }}<br />
    {{ anothervar|divisibleby:"3" }}

    <h2>Filesizeformat Filter</h2>
    <p><strong></strong></p>
    {{ 44040192|filesizeformat }}

    <h2>Retrieving the First and Last Items from a List</h2>
    {{ color_list|first }}
    {{ color_list|last }}

    <h2>Format Floating Point Numbers</h2>
    {{ 3.14159265|floatformat }}
    {{ 3.14159265|floatformat:4 }}

    <h2>get_digit Filter</h2>
    <p><strong></strong></p>
    {{ anothervar|get_digit:1 }}<br />
    {{ anothervar|get_digit:0 }}<br />
    {{ "Hello"|get_digit:2 }}<br />

    <h2>Join Filter</h2>
    <p><strong></strong></p>
    {{ color_list|join:" and " }}

    <h2>Output JSON</h2>
    <p><strong>JSON can be output using the <code>json_script</code> filter:</strong></p>
    <p>(You will need to look in the page source to see this one)</p>
    {{ best_bands|json_script:"best-bands" }}
```

```
{{ venues|json_script:"all-venues" }}

<h2>Length_is Filter</h2>
{{ color_list|length_is:"4" }}<br />
{{ empty_list|length_is:"2" }}<br />
{{ "Hello"|length_is:"5" }}

<h2>Make_list Filter</h2>
{{ "Hello"|make_list }}<br />
{{ "12345"|make_list }}<br />
{{ anothervar|make_list }}<br />
{{ 3.14159265|make_list }}

<h2>Phone2numeric Filter</h2>
{{ "1800 BITE ME"|phone2numeric }}

<h2>Random Filter</h2>
<p>(This list will change every time you refresh the browser)</p>
{{ color_list|random }}<br />
{{ color_list|random }}<br />
{{ color_list|random }}

<h2>Slice Filter</h2>
{{ color_list|slice:":3" }}<br />
{{ color_list|slice:"2:" }}<br />
{{ color_list|slice:":-1" }}<br />
{{ color_list|slice:"1:2" }}

<h2>Slugify Filter</h2>
{{ "Number of the Beast"|slugify }}
{{ "slugify won't use these: /\$#^&"|slugify }}

<h2>Stringformat Filter</h2>
{{ 314159265|stringformat:"E" }}<br />
{{ 3.14159265|stringformat:".2f" }}

<h2>Striptags Filter</h2>
{{ "<h1>The Title</h1>"|striptags }}

<h2>Calculating the Difference Between Dates</h2>
{{ today|timesince:future }}
{{ today|timeuntil:past }}

<h2>Truncating Strings</h2>
{{ "The Title"|truncatechars:7 }}<br />
```

```
    {{ "<em>The Title</em>"|truncatechars_html:7 }}<br />
    {{ "The Title"|truncatewords:1 }}<br />
    <p><strong>HTML aware version:</strong></p>
    {{ "<em>The Title</em>"|truncatewords_html:1 }}

    <h2>Unordered Lists</h2>
    <ul>
      {{ aussie_bands|unordered_list }}
    </ul>

    <h2>Encoding URLs</h2>
    {{ "https://bestbands.example.com/bands?album=Master of Puppets&rating=awesome"|urlencode }}

    <h2>Creating Hyperlinks</h2>
    <p><strong></strong></p>
    {{ "The djangobook.com website is awesome!"|urlize }}<br />
    {{ "The djangobook.com website is awesome!"|urlizetrunc:11 }}

    <h2>Wordwrap Filter</h2>
    <pre>{{ "Now I lay me down to sleep"|wordwrap:4 }}</pre>

    <h2>Yesno Filter</h2>
    {{ True|yesno }}<br />
    {{ False|yesno }}<br />
    {{ None|yesno }}<br />
    {{ True|yesno:"yeah baby,heck no,meh" }}<br />
    {{ False|yesno:"yeah baby,heck no,meh" }}<br />
    {{ None|yesno:"yeah baby,heck no,meh" }}

    <h2>The Humanize Filters</h2>
    {{ 1|apnumber }}, {{ 5|apnumber }}, {{ 12|apnumber }}<br />
    {{ 4500|intcomma }}; {{ 42123456.78|intcomma }}<br />
    {{ 4000000|intword }}; {{ 42000000000|intword }}<br />
    {{ today|naturalday }}<br />
    {{ today|naturaltime }}; {{ past|naturaltime }}; {{ future|naturaltime }}<br />
    {{ 1|ordinal }}, {{ 2|ordinal }}, {{ 3|ordinal }}, {{ 20|ordinal }}

    <h2>Custom Tags and Filters</h2>
    {{ "James is in rehab again"|reverse }}<br />
    {{ 100|reverse }}<br />
    {% create_date today %}
    {% announcements %}
  </body>
</html>
```

event_custom_tags.py (complete listing)

```
# myclub_root\events\templatetags\event_custom_tags.py

from django import template
from django.template.defaultfilters import stringfilter
from datetime import datetime

register = template.Library()

@register.filter(name='reverse')
@stringfilter
def reverse(value):
    return value[::-1]

@register.simple_tag
def create_date(date_val):
    return "This content was created on %s" % date_val.strftime('%A %B %d, %Y')

@register.inclusion_tag('events/announcements.html')
def announcements():
    announcements = [
        {
            'date': '6-10-2020',
            'announcement': "Club Registrations Open"
        },
        {
            'date': '6-15-2020',
            'announcement': "Joe Smith Elected New Club President"
        }
    ]
    return {'announcements': announcements}
```

Chapter Summary

In this chapter, we dug much deeper into templates and covered the most common template tags and filters, complete with example implementations.

I also showed you how to create your own custom template filters and tags, how to work with `Context` and `RequestContext` objects and context processors, and how Django's template back ends and template loaders work.

In the next chapter, we will take a deep dive into advanced Django admin topics.

12

Advanced Django Admin

In this chapter, we'll take a deep dive into advanced Django admin topics.

We will start with customizing the admin—changing the site text, style sheets, replacing the default admin, creating custom admin apps, and customizing Django's admin templates.

In the latter part of the chapter, we'll dig into the `ModelAdmin` class and write our own admin actions, and learn how to add a WYSIWYG editor to the admin.

Customizing the Admin

Django's admin is designed to be highly customizable, but it can be difficult to get your head around at first. In this section, I will lead you through your options for customizing the admin, starting with the simplest customizations and building on that knowledge, so it's easier to grasp the more complex options.

Changing Admin Site Text

The easiest customizations to make in the Django admin is to replace the generic Django admin text in the HTML title, the admin homepage and the login page. The default text can be replaced by setting a value for the `site_title`, `site_header` and `index_title` attributes of your `admin.site` class (changes in bold):

```
# myclub_root\myclub_site\urls.py

# ...

admin.site.site_header = 'MyClub Administration'
admin.site.site_title = 'MyClub Site Admin'
admin.site.index_title = 'MyClub Site Admin Home'

urlpatterns = [
# ...
```

If you make these three changes to your `urls.py` file, your admin should look like Figure 12-1.

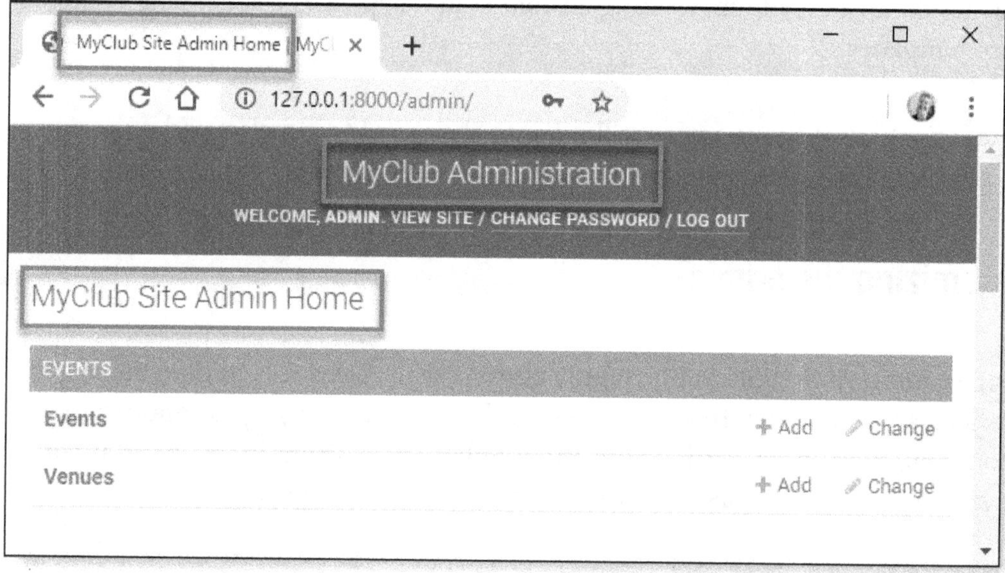

Figure 12-1. *Changing the admin site text is one of the easiest customizations you can make on the Django admin.*

Customizing Admin Styles

Django's admin uses about a dozen CSS files for styling the admin. To override the default styles, you need to create your own style sheets and save them in a place where Django can find them.

As we discussed earlier in the book, Django uses short circuit logic when looking for templates and media files. So for Django to use your custom CSS files, they must be lower in the search hierarchy than the `admin` app. The best place to put them is in your site `\static\` folder.

While you can customize all the admin CSS files, I will work with the largest and most important—`base.css`. Rather than create a new file from scratch, we will copy Django's version of this file and modify it.

The file is buried quite deep in your virtual environment's folders, so I have broken the structure up below to make it easier to find:

```
...\env_myclub
    \Lib
        \site-packages
            \django
                \contrib
                    \admin
                        \static\admin\css\base.css
```

If you're on a Mac, there is an extra folder for your Python version under the `/lib` folder (i.e., `/lib/python3.x/site-packages`).

I've deliberately left the rest of the compound path together on the last line. For Django to find your modified `base.css` file, the folder structure must be the same as the default.

Now, go to your Django project and recreate the folder structure:

```
myclub_root
    \myclub_site
        \static
            \admin\css\ # New Folders
                base.css # Paste base.css to css folder
```

Create an `\admin` folder in the existing `\static` folder, create a `\css` folder inside the `\admin` folder, and then paste the `base.css` file into the `\css` folder. Make sure the folder structure looks like the one above before you continue.

Once the `base.css` file is copied to your project, any modification you make to the file will be applied to the admin. I will not go through examples on how to modify the CSS for the admin site, as I want to focus on teaching you Django, not CSS, but feel free to experiment. If you copy the `base.css` file from the source code[1], your admin will look like Figure 12-2, with the admin colors now matching the MyClub site branding.

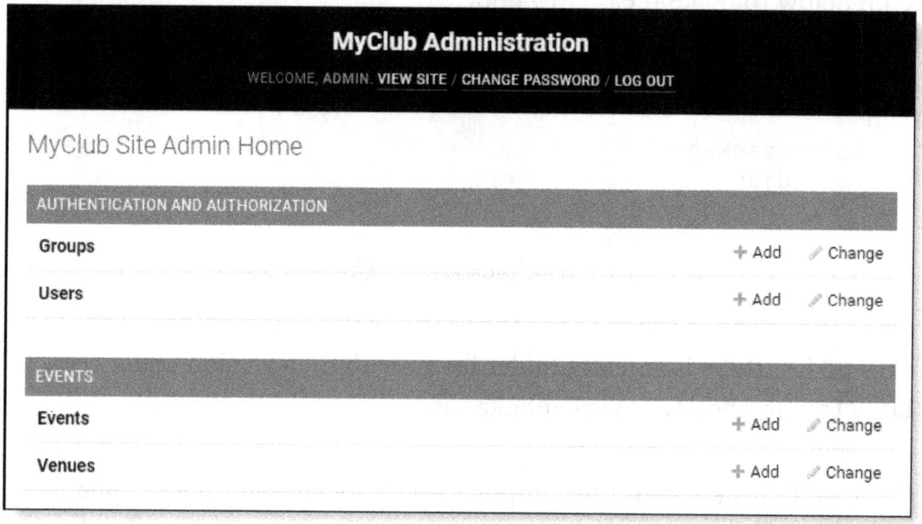

Figure 12-2. *By modifying the admin* `base.css` *file, the admin colors match the MyClub site branding.*

1 https://djangobook.com/mastering-django-source/

NOTE: If you are using the printed book, you won't see much change in the image as it's black and white, but trust me, the admin is now dark blue and green instead of pastel blue and yellow!

We will dig into customizing the admin templates later in the chapter, but first, let's have a look at some of the customizations we can make to the admin site.

Customizing the Default Admin Site

The default admin app (`django.contrib.admin.site`) is an instance of `django.contrib.admin.sites.AdminSite`. The attributes and methods of the `AdminSite` class are listed in Table 12-1.

Attribute/Method	Type	Description
`site_header`	attribute	Admin site header. Default is "Django administration"
`site_title`	attribute	Admin site title. Default is "Django site admin"
`site_url`	attribute	URL for "View site" link. Set to `None` to remove the link
`index_title`	attribute	Title of admin index page. Default is "Site administration"
`index_template`	attribute	Path to a custom template that will be used by the admin site main index view
`app_index_template`	attribute	Path to a custom template that will be used by the admin site app index view
`empty_value_display`	attribute	Global display value for empty fields. Default is a dash (-). Override at `ModelAdmin` level with the `ModelAdmin.empty_value_display` attribute

Attribute/Method	Type	Description
`login_template`	attribute	Path to a custom template that will be used by the admin site login view.
`login_form`	attribute	Subclass of `AuthenticationForm` that will be used by the admin site login view
`logout_template`	attribute	Path to a custom template that will be used by the admin site logout view
`password_change_template`	attribute	Path to a custom template that will be used by the admin site password change view
`password_change_done_template`	attribute	Path to a custom template that will be used by the admin site password change done view
`each_context()`	method	A dictionary of variables added to the context for every admin page. Override to add custom variables to the context
`has_permission()`	method	Returns `True` if the current user has permission to view the admin, i.e., is an active staff member
`register()`	method	Registers a `ModelAdmin` class with the admin application

Table 12-1. *Django's* `AdminSite` *class attributes and methods*

To customize the admin, you subclass `AdminSite` and override existing methods and attributes, as well as add your own.

There are two ways to customize the admin site:

1. Override the default admin; or
2. Create a new custom instance of the admin and register your models with that instance.

As you will see in a moment, it's also possible to do both.

Choosing which is the best approach for your project depends on your requirements:

- If the customizations apply to all apps and models in the project, override the default admin.
- If the customizations apply to certain apps and models in the project, create a custom instance of the admin.

As Django is designed to be flexible, there are no hard and fast rules, so your implementation should reflect the logic of your project.

Overriding the Default Admin

To override the default admin, you must create a custom admin module (`admin.py` file), and a custom configuration for your website app (`myclub_site`) that sets the `default_site` attribute to your custom admin class.

Let's create the custom admin class first (new file):

```
# myclub_root\myclub_site\admin.py

from django.contrib.admin import AdminSite


class MyClubAdmin(AdminSite):
    site_header = 'Custom Administration'
    site_title = 'Custom Site Admin'
    index_title = 'Custom Site Admin Home'
```

You can see the new `MyClubAdmin` class subclasses `AdminSite`, and sets the same three admin site text variables we set earlier on in the chapter.

To make Django use our custom admin as the default, we need to create a configuration file for the class and set the `default_site` attribute of the admin app (new file):

```
# myclub_root\myclub_site\apps.py

from django.contrib.admin.apps import AdminConfig


class MyClubAdminConfig(AdminConfig):
    default_site = 'myclub_site.admin.MyClubAdmin'
```

In this simple configuration class, we're subclassing the `AdminConfig` class and setting `default_site` to point to our custom admin class. Now the class creation and configuration modules are done, we must tell Django to use the custom admin instead of the default admin by changing our settings (changes in bold):

```
# myclub_root\myclub_site\settings.py

# ...

INSTALLED_APPS = [
    'events.apps.EventsConfig',
    # 'django.contrib.admin',
    'myclub_site.apps.MyClubAdminConfig',
    'django.contrib.auth',
    # ...
```

A simple change here—we've replaced the default Django admin (`django.contrib.admin`) with our new custom admin. Before we fire up the development server, there's one more thing to do. As we set the `site_header`, `site_title` and `index_title` options in our `urls.py` file, these values will override our new admin site class, so we need to remove them from the file. I'm just going to comment them out, which has the same effect (changes in bold):

```
# myclub_root\myclub_site\urls.py

# ...
# admin.site.site_header = 'MyClub Administration'
# admin.site.site_title = 'MyClub Site Admin'
# admin.site.index_title = 'MyClub Site Admin Home'

urlpatterns = [
# ...
```

Now, if you run the development server and navigate to `http://127.0.0.1:8000/admin/`, your admin will look like Figure 12-3.

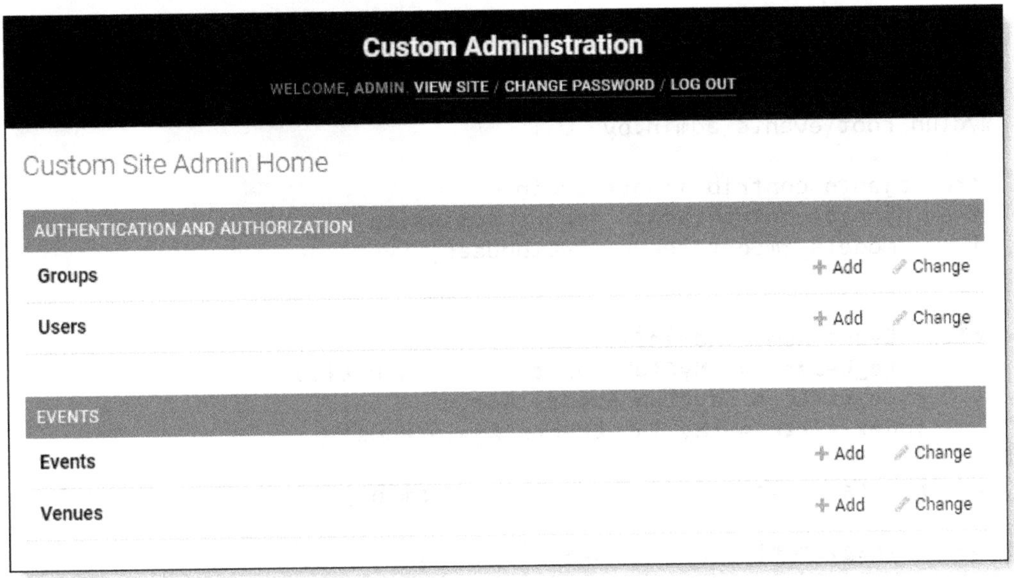

Figure 12-3. *Overriding the default admin allows you to create a customized admin for your entire project.*

Creating a Custom Admin Site

Keeping in mind that the Django admin is just another app, you can create your own version of the admin by creating a custom instance of the `AdminSite` class.

The `AdminSite` class is identical to the last example, but the implementation is different. Instead of creating the class and telling Django to use the custom admin class as the default, we create the class and register each of our models with the custom admin class.

The custom class can exist anywhere in your project tree, but I will create it inside the `events` app because it's convenient, and I will register the `events` app's models with the custom app.

Let's start with the custom admin class (changes in bold):

```
# myclub_root\events\admin.py

1  from django.contrib import admin
2  from django.contrib.admin import AdminSite
3  from .models import Venue, MyClubUser, Event
4
5
6  class EventsAdmin(AdminSite):
7      site_header = 'MyClub Events Administration'
8      site_title = 'MyClub Events Admin'
9      index_title = 'MyClub Events Admin Home'
10
11 admin_site = EventsAdmin(name='eventsadmin')
12
13 @admin.register(Venue, site=admin_site)
14 class VenueAdmin(admin.ModelAdmin):
15     # ...
16
17
18 @admin.register(Event, site=admin_site)
19 class EventAdmin(admin.ModelAdmin):
20     # ...
```

Let's have a look at what's going on here (I've removed the class code to keep the listing short):

- **Line 2.** I've imported the `AdminSite` class from `django.contrib.admin`.
- **Lines 6 to 9.** This is the custom admin class. You can see its structure is identical to our earlier example.
- **Line 11.** This is our custom `AdminSite` instance.
- **Line 13.** I'm registering the `Venue` model with the custom admin.
- **Line 18.** I'm registering the `Event` model with the custom admin.

Now we have created the custom admin instance and registered our models with it, we need to create a new URLconf to point to the custom admin (changes in bold):

```
# myclub_root\myclub_site\urls.py

# Add this import to the top of your file
from events.admin import admin_site


urlpatterns = [
    path('admin/', admin.site.urls),
    path('eventsadmin/', admin_site.urls),
    # ...
```

Two small changes here: we've added an import for the `admin_site` class instance, and set up a new URLconf so `eventsadmin/` points to our custom admin class. Notice I haven't changed the URLconf for the default admin site. This is how you can create a Django project with multiple custom admin interfaces.

To test the custom admin, fire up the development server and navigate to `http://127.0.0.1:8000/eventsadmin/`. Your custom admin site should look like Figure 12-4.

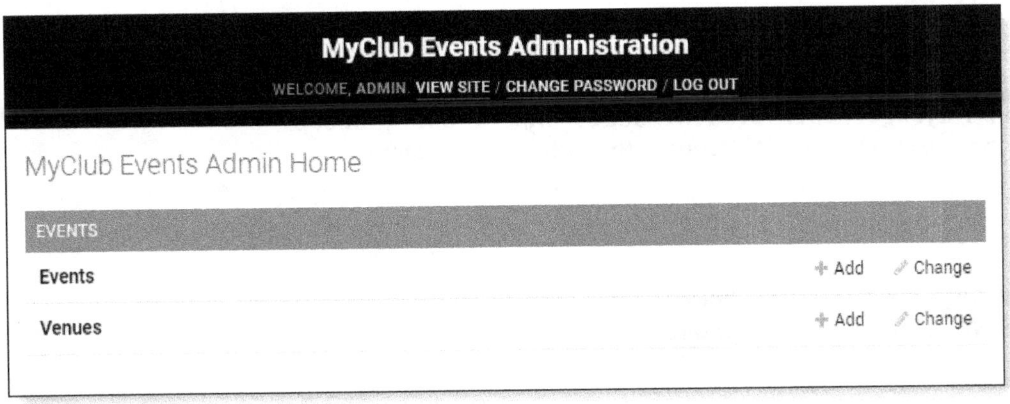

Figure 12-4. *We've created a custom admin for our* `events` *app's models.*

These are simple examples; we are only setting the admin text for our custom admin instances. For your projects, remember all the methods and attributes in Table 12.1 can be overridden in the same way as the examples, giving you significant flexibility for adding custom behaviors to your admin sites.

Before we move on, did you notice something about our custom events admin? If you look closely, you will see that the **Authentication and Authorization** admin group is not shown.

This is because when Django creates the default admin site (`admin.site`), it registers these models with the admin for us. This makes sense because one of the primary uses for the default admin is to manage users, groups and permissions.

It should also make sense that when we create a custom admin, Django doesn't make this assumption—it leaves it up to us to decide whether a custom admin interface includes access to users and groups.

If you want users and groups in your custom admin, registering them is easy (changes in bold):

```
# myclub_root\events\admin.py

from django.contrib import admin
from django.contrib.admin import AdminSite
from django.contrib.auth.models import User, Group
from .models import Venue, MyClubUser, Event


# ...

admin_site.register(User)
admin_site.register(Group)
```

At the top of the file, we import the `User` and `Group` models from `django.contrib.auth.models`, and at the end of the file, we register them with our custom admin app.

Now, if you navigate to `http://127.0.0.1:8000/eventsadmin/`, your admin will look like Figure 12-5.

Figure 12-5. *Register user and group models with the custom admin app.*

Customizing Admin Templates

The Django admin has 24 templates in total (not including templates for special functions like user registration and authorization): 13 HTML page templates for constructing admin pages, and 11 templates for admin template tags.

The default templates are located in your virtual environment folder under `\Lib\site-packages\django\contrib\admin\templates\admin`, or for Mac users it's `/lib/python3.x/site-packages/` and then the rest of the path.

The HTML templates are in Table 12-2.

Template	Cust?	Parent
`404.html`	N	`base_site.html`
`500.html`	N	`base_site.html`
`app_index.html`	Y	`index.html`
`base.html`	N	Root HTML page
`base_site.html`	N	`base.html`
`change_form.html`	Y	`base_site.html`
`change_list.html`	Y	`base_site.html`
`delete_confirmation.html`	Y	`base_site.html`
`delete_selected_confirmation.html`	N	`base_site.html`
`index.html`	N	`base_site.html`
`invalid_setup.html`	N	`base_site.html`
`login.html`	N	`base_site.html`
`object_history.html`	Y	`base_site.html`

Table 12-2. *Django's admin HTML page templates.*

All HTML templates except `app_index.html` are children of `base_site.html`, which itself is a child of `base.html`. `app_index.html` adds one more step to the hierarchy, inheriting from `index.html`.

The "Cust?" column indicates if the template can be customized at app and model levels. An "N" in this column means the template can only be customized at project level. I will explain the difference shortly.

The remainder of the admin templates are used when rendering admin template tags. These templates are listed in Table 12-3. The "Tag" column lists the admin template tag associated with the template and the "Used in" column shows which admin template the admin tag is used in. The "Ovr?" column indicates whether the template can be overridden by you apps and models.

Template	Ovr?	Tag	Used in
actions.html	Y	admin_actions	change_list.html
change_form_object_tools.html	Y	change_form_object_tools	change_form.html
change_list_object_tools.html	Y	change_list_object_tools	change_list.html
change_list_results.html	Y	result_list	change_list.html
date_hierarchy.html	Y	date_hierarchy	change_list.html
filter.html	N	admin_list_filter	change_list.html
pagination.html	Y	pagination	change_list.html
popup_response.html	Y	N/A	added to the response when there's a popup
prepopulated_fields_js.html	Y	prepopulated_fields_js	change_form.html
search_form.html	Y	search_form	change_list.html
submit_line.html	Y	submit_row	change_form.html

Table 12-3. *Django's admin template tag templates.*

How to Override a Template

Overriding an admin template is a similar process to overriding admin style sheets, except you are adding an `\admin` folder to your website app's `\templates` folder:

```
\myclub_root
    \myclub_site
        \templates
            \admin # New folder
```

There are three scopes, or levels, of template customization available:

1. **Project level**. Template is overridden for the whole project.
2. **App level**. Template is overridden for a specific app.
3. **Model level**. Template is overridden for a specific model.

The scope of the customization is set by creating a folder hierarchy in your `\templates\admin` folder:

```
\admin
# Project scope
    \app_name
    # App scope
        \model_name
        # Model scope
```

This is easier to understand with an example, so let's create the following folder and file structure for our MyClub project. Copy the template files from Django's admin:

```
\admin
    index.html # Copy from Django admin
    \events
        change_list.html # Copy from Django admin
        \venue
            search_form.html # Copy from Django admin
```

Let's start with a project-level customization. Open your `index.html` file and make the following change (in bold):

```
# myclub_root\myclub_site\templates\admin\index.html

    {% endfor %}
{% else %}
    <p>{% trans "You don't have permission to view or edit anything."
%}</p>
{% endif %}
<p>Customized at project level.</p>
</div>
{% endblock %}
```

I've only reproduced a snippet of the file here to show you where to add the extra paragraph to the HTML. The snippet is from a bit past the middle of the file—line 53 in my version of Django.

If you run the development server and go to the events admin home page (`http://127.0.0.1:8000/eventsadmin/`), it should now look like Figure 12-6.

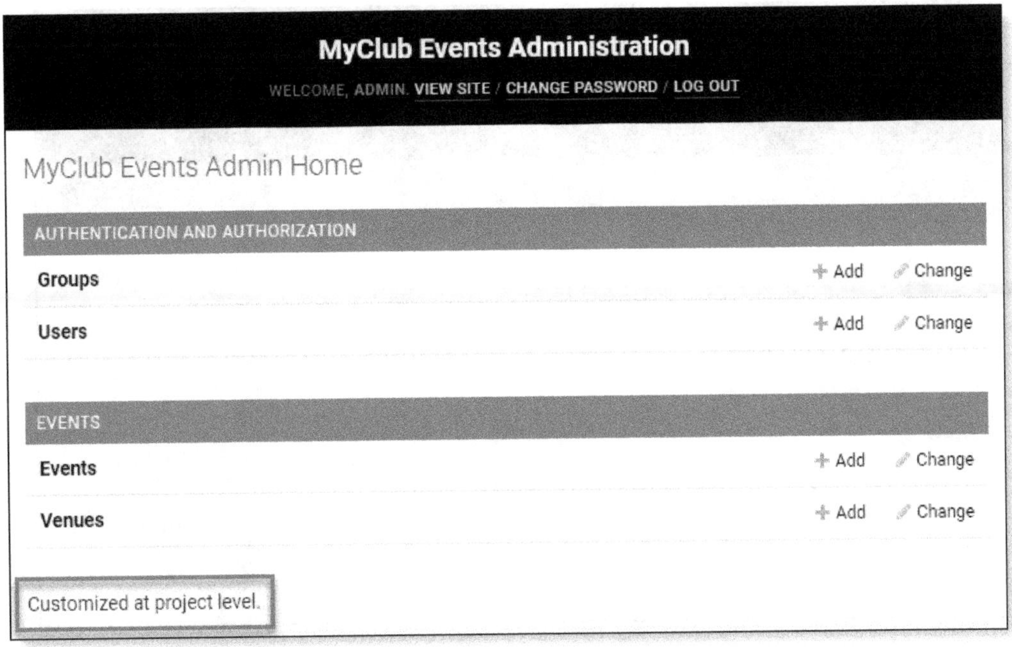

Figure 12-6. Project-level template customization in the Django admin.

Now, let's change the `change_list.html` file to apply an app-level customization (change in bold):

```
# ...\templates\admin\events\change_list.html

{% block content %}
<div id="content-main">
    <p>Customized at App level</p>
    {% block object-tools %}
        <ul class="object-tools">
        {% block object-tools-items %}
            {% change_list_object_tools %}
```

This snippet is around the middle of the file—line 42 in the version I have. After saving the file and refreshing the events admin, both the `Events` and `Venues` models change lists will show the customization (Figure 12-7).

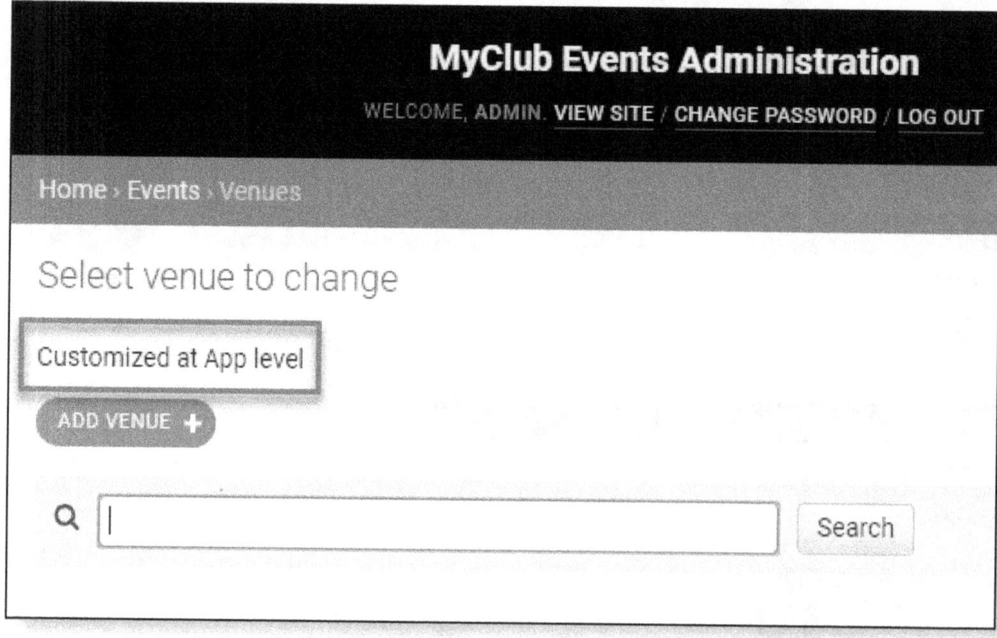

Figure 12-7. *App-level template customization in the Django admin.*

Finally, let's have a look at an example of overriding an admin template at the model level. Add the following code to your `search_form.html` file (change in bold):

```
# ...\templates\admin\events\venue\search_form.html

{% endfor %}
</div>
</form><p>Customized at model level</p></div>
{% endif %}
```

This snippet is at the end of the file. Save the file, run the development server and navigate to your venue admin and your venue admin will look like Figure 12-8.

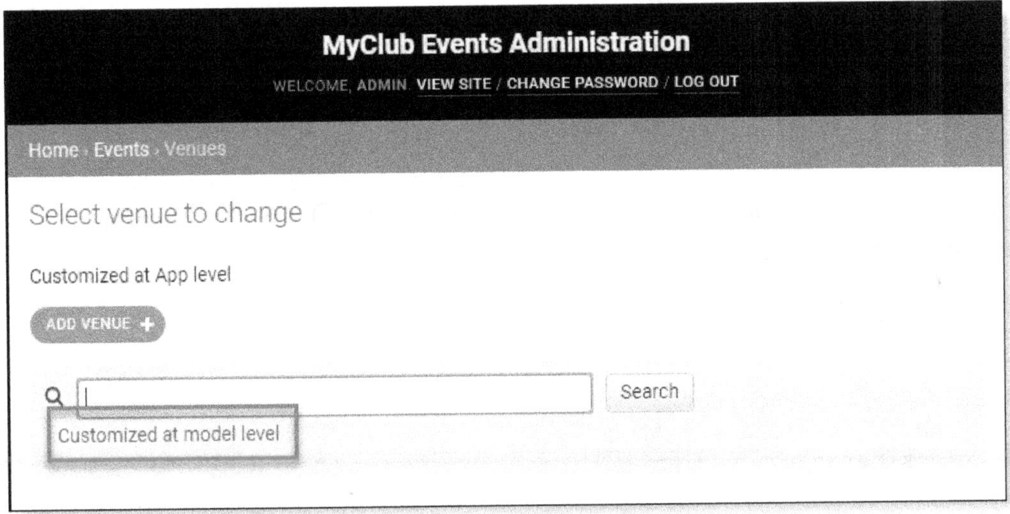

***Figure 12-8.** Model-level template customization in the Django admin.*

These are simple examples, but it shows you just how easy it is to customize the Django admin templates to suit your project.

All Django's admin templates can be overridden and customized in this way. The only restriction is that not all templates can be overridden at app and model level. Refer back to Table 12-2 and Table 12-3 for details on which templates can be overridden by your apps and models.

Admin Template Best Practice

While I am replacing the entire template in these examples, best practice is to only replace the parts of the template you are modifying.

Django's admin templates use blocks extensively, and you should take advantage of this. Only add the blocks you are overriding to your custom templates.

This not only reduces unnecessary repetition of code, but adds a degree of future-proofing to your code when Django's developers change admin templates.

Custom Validation in the Admin

Django's admin uses the `django.forms` library for constructing each of the admin forms, so we can add custom form validation to the admin in the same way we added validation to the venue form in Chapter 8.

The `ModelForm` class is identical to the one we created in Chapter 8. To refresh your memory, here's the `VenueForm` class:

```
# myclub_root\events\forms.py

class VenueForm(ModelForm):
    required_css_class = 'required'
    class Meta:
        model = Venue
        fields = '__all__'

    def clean(self):
        cleaned_data = super().clean()
        phone = cleaned_data.get("phone")
        email_address = cleaned_data.get("email_address")
        if not (phone or email_address):
            raise forms.ValidationError(
                "You must enter either a phone number or an email, or
                 both."
            )
```

The custom `clean()` method of the `VenueForm` class will raise a `ValidationError` if neither phone number nor email address are provided.

Rather than repeat ourselves, we will use this class in our `VenueAdmin` class (changes in bold):

```
# myclub_root\events\admin.py

# Add this import to the top of your file
1  from events.forms import VenueForm
2
3  # ...
4
5  @admin.register(Venue, site=admin_site)
6  class VenueAdmin(admin.ModelAdmin):
7      form = VenueForm
8      list_display = ('name', 'address', 'phone')
        # ...
```

The key changes to this file are:

- **Line 1.** I've imported the `VenueForm` class from `events.forms`.
- **Line 7.** I've set the form for the class to use `VenueForm`.

This is all you need to do to add custom validation to an admin form. If you now try to add a venue to the admin without a phone number or an email address, you will get the custom validation error (Figure 12-9).

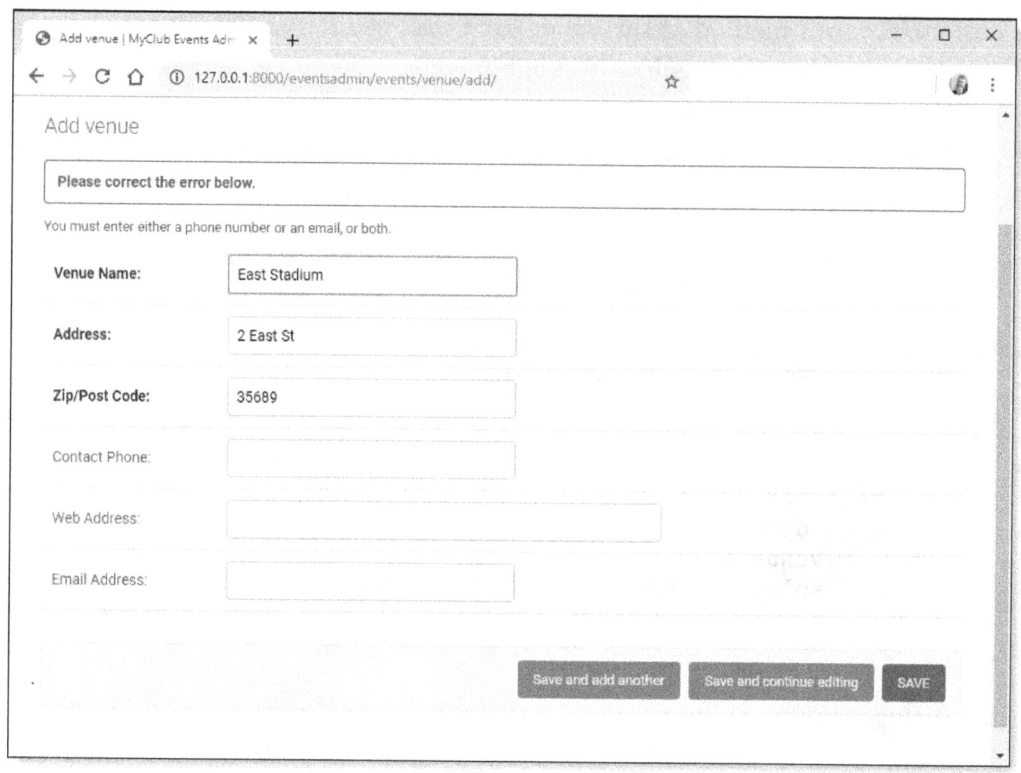

***Figure 12-9.** Adding custom validation to the admin is as simple as creating a* `ModelForm` *class to provide the custom validation.*

Add Your Own Custom Forms to the Admin

The `form` option is not only useful for providing custom validation—it can also be used to add your own custom forms to the admin. The form option is available for `ModelAdmin` and `InlineModelAdmin` which, along with the `InlineModelAdmin.formset` option, provide all the flexibility you will ever need for creating advanced custom forms for the admin.

More information can be found in the Django documentation[2].

2 https://docs.djangoproject.com/en/dev/ref/contrib/admin/#django.contrib.admin.ModelAdmin.form

The ModelAdmin Class

Each model in your project is represented in the admin as an instance of the `ModelAdmin` class. We have already covered some of the `ModelAdmin` class methods and options in Chapter 7. Table 12-4 lists common `ModelAdmin` options, and Table 12-5 lists common `ModelAdmin` methods.

ModelAdmin Options

Option	Description
`actions`	A list of available actions for the change list page
`actions_on_top`, `actions_on_bottom`	Set where the actions bar appears. Defaults to top
`actions_selection_counter`	Controls if a selection counter is shown next to action dropdown. Default is `True`
`date_hierarchy`	Set to a `DateField` or `DateTimeField` and the change list page will include a date-drilldown filter
`empty_value_display`	Display value for empty fields. Default is a dash (-)
`exclude`	A list of field names to exclude from the admin form
`fields`	Hide/show fields and change form layout
`fieldsets`	Arrange admin form fields in groups
`filter_horizontal`, `filter_vertical`	Add a JavaScript filter to `ManyToMany` fields
`form`	Specify a custom form for the model admin
`formfield_overrides`	Override field options for use in the admin
`inlines`	Add `InlineModelAdmin` objects to the model

Option	Description
list_display	Control which fields are shown on the change list page
list_display_links	Set which fields on the change list page should link to the edit page
list_editable	Make listed fields editable on the change list page
list_filter	Activate filters on the right sidebar of the change list page
list_max_show_all	Set maximum items to show on "Show All"
list_per_page	Control how many items show on each page of the change list
list_select_related	Select related (foreign key) objects when retrieving model objects. Saves on database queries
ordering	Specify how listed objects should be ordered
paginator	Set a custom paginator for the change list page
prepopulated_fields	Prepopulate admin form fields with data
preserve_filters	Preserve filters after an object has been changed. Default is True
radio_fields	Use radio fields instead of checkboxes for fields where choices has been set
autocomplete_fields	Change ForeignKey and ManyToManyField fields to searchable autocomplete inputs
raw_id_fields	Display only ID field for ForeignKey fields. Saves overhead of retrieving all related objects
readonly_fields	Set fields to read-only
save_as	Set to True to change "Save and add another" to "Save as new"
save_as_continue	Set to False to redirect to change list view after save

Option	Description
`save_on_top`	Set location of save buttons. Default is `False` (save buttons on bottom only). Set to `True` to add save buttons to the top and bottom of the form
`search_fields`	Enable a search box on the change list page
`show_full_result_count`	Display full count of filtered objects. Default is `True`
`sortable_by`	Set which columns are sortable. Set to an empty collection to disable sort
`view_on_site`	Controls whether "View on site" link is displayed. Default is `True`

***Table 12-4.** Django's* `ModelAdmin` *class options.*

Most of the common `ModelAdmin` class options are covered in various parts of this book. For the options that need additional explanation, I have included notes below.

The inlines Option

The `inlines` option allows an admin user to edit child models on the same page as the parent model. Inlines are instances of the `InlineModelAdmin` class, which contains most of the same methods and options as a regular `ModelAdmin` class.

You don't use the `InlineModelAdmin` class directly; you use the `TabularInline` or `StackedInline` subclasses to produce a tabbed or stacked inline formset.

Inlines are best demonstrated with an example. Let's create a `TabularInline` instance in our events admin (changes in bold):

```
# myclub_root\events\admin.py

# ...

1   class EventInline(admin.TabularInline):
2       model = Event
3       fields = ('name', 'event_date')
4       extra = 1
5
6
7   @admin.register(Venue, site=admin_site)
8   class VenueAdmin(admin.ModelAdmin):
9       form = VenueForm
10      list_display = ('name', 'address', 'phone')
11      ordering = ('name',)
12      search_fields = ('name', 'address')
13      inlines = [
14          EventInline,
15      ]
```

The key changes to the file are:

- **Line 1** is the class declaration for our new inline. It inherits from `admin.TabularInline`.
- **Line 2** sets the `model` option to inline. This is the child model to be shown on our admin form.
- **Line 3** sets the fields to display on the inline form. This behaves the same way as a regular `ModelAdmin` object.
- **Line 4** sets the `extra` option. This governs how many extra blank inline forms will be shown.
- **Lines 13 to 15** set the `inlines` option to include our `EventInline` class instance.

Save the file, run the development server, and open an event from the event change list. Remember, we're still using the custom events admin we created earlier, so you need to navigate to `http://127.0.0.1:8000/eventsadmin/`.

Your event edit form should look like Figure 12-10. The form will be a bit longer than this; I have trimmed some of the fields, so the screen capture isn't too long.

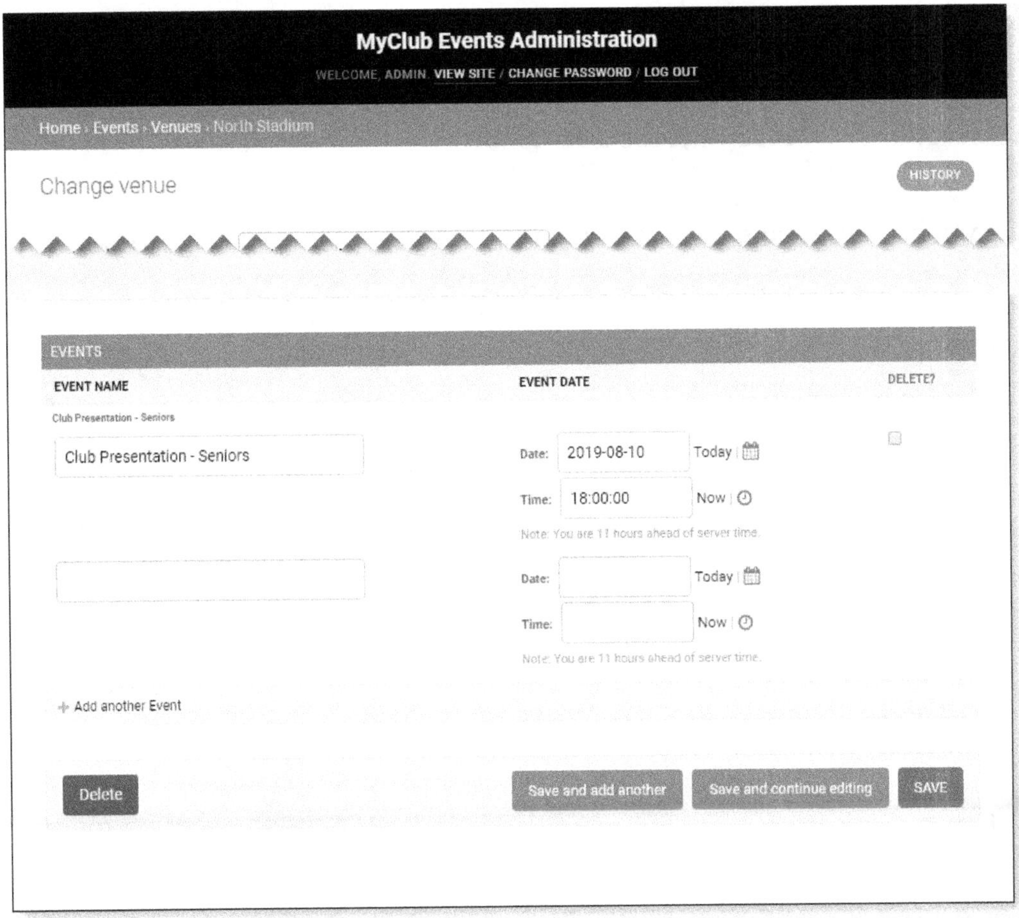

Figure 12-10. *Adding an inline class allows you to edit child models from inside the parent.*

To show the inline as a stacked form, change:

```
class EventInline(admin.TabularInline):
```

To:

```
class EventInline(admin.StackedInline):
```

Once you have re-saved the file, your inline form will look like Figure 12-11.

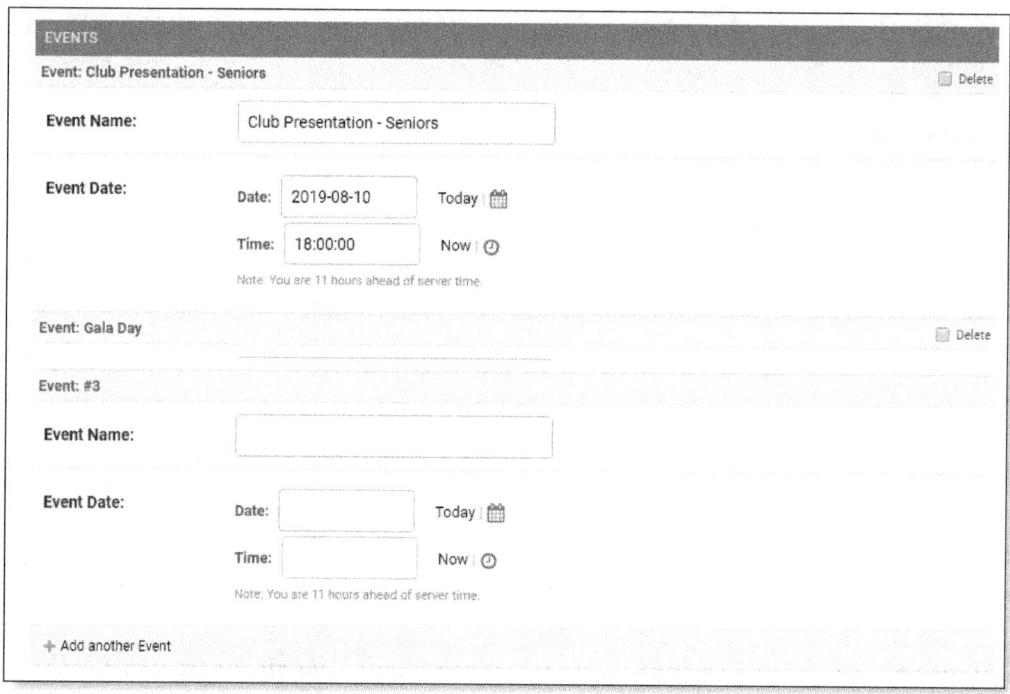

Figure 12-11. *The* `InlineStacked` *class will stack the inline form fields instead side-by-side in a tabular format.*

If you want to inline a model across a many-to-many relationship, things are a little more complicated because of the way Django uses intermediate models to represent many-to-many relationships. For example, if we wanted to inline the attendees to an event, we would have to do things slightly different. Let's see how this is done by adding another inline class to our events admin (changes in bold):

```
# myclub_root\events\admin.py

1  class AttendeeInline(admin.TabularInline):
2      model = Event.attendees.through
3      verbose_name = 'Attendee'
4      verbose_name_plural = 'Attendees'
5
6
7  @admin.register(Event, site=admin_site)
8  class EventAdmin(admin.ModelAdmin):
9      # ...
10     inlines = [
11         AttendeeInline,
12     ]
```

The inlines option we've added to the `EventAdmin` class (**Lines 10 to 12**) is identical to the previous example, however, the inline class declaration has some differences:

- **Line 2.** The `through` attribute references the intermediate model that manages the many-to-many relationship. If you look at your database with DB Browser for SQLite, you can see the table for this automatically created model (`events_event_attendees`).
- **Line 3.** Sets the `verbose_name` attribute. If you don't set this, your inline form will show the object name in your admin, which isn't very user-friendly.
- **Line 4.** Sets the `verbose_name_plural` attribute. This will be used as the title for your inline forms, rather than the object name.

Once you save the file, if you edit an event, you will see Django added the attendees for the event inline to the event edit form (Figure 12-12).

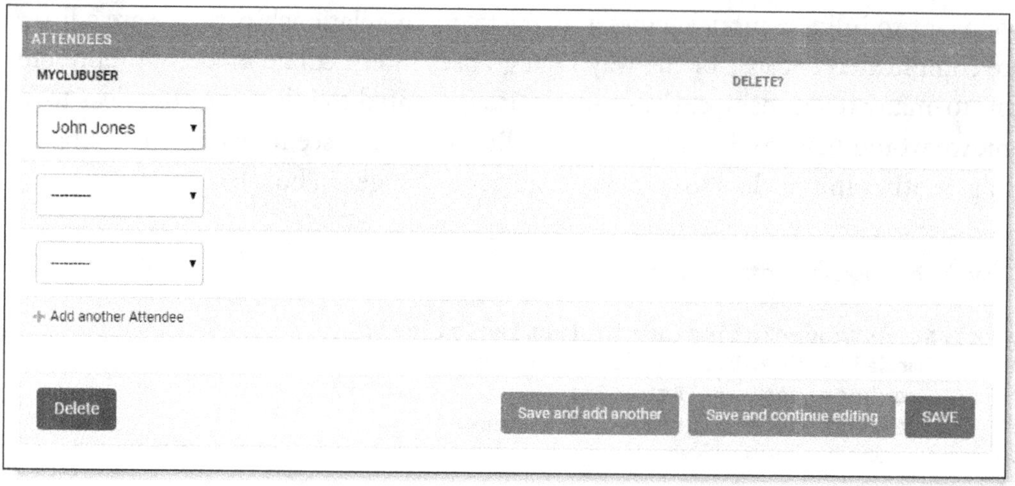

***Figure 12-12.** Adding inline forms for many-to-many relationships take a little more work, but are still quite simple to implement.*

The `InlineModelAdmin` class has many more features than the basics I have covered here. If you want to dig deeper into the class, including how to customize inline forms, see the Django documentation[3].

The list_display_links Option

In the admin change list, the first column fields link to the object change page by default. You can change this behavior by setting `list_display_links` to a tuple containing the fields to link to the change page. For example (change in bold):

```
# myclub_root\events\admin.py

# ...

@admin.register(Venue, site=admin_site)
class VenueAdmin(admin.ModelAdmin):
    list_display = ('name', 'address', 'phone')
    list_display_links = ('name', 'address')
    #...
```

3 https://docs.djangoproject.com/en/dev/ref/contrib/admin/#inlinemodeladmin-objects

After making the change, when you open the venue change list, the venue address is now linked to the change page (Figure 12-13).

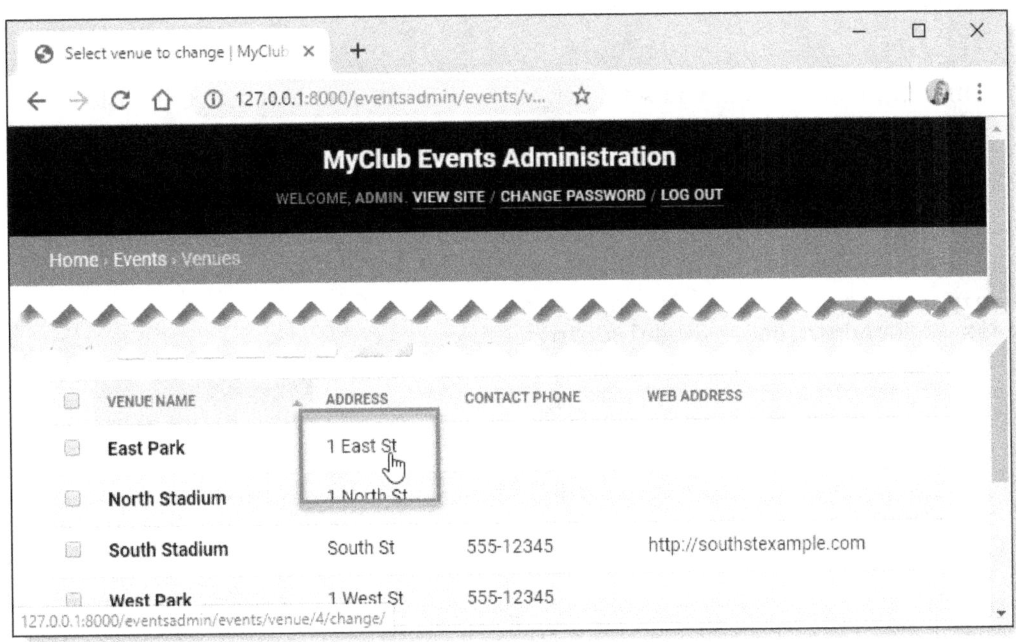

Figure 12-13. *Setting the* `list_display_links` *option allows you to link multiple fields in the change list to the object change page.*

If you want to make the change list read-only, you can set `list_display_links` to `None`.

There is a caveat with `list_display_links`—for it to work, you must also set the `list_display` option.

The list_editable Option

Use the `list_editable` option to make fields on the change list page editable. This is a handy feature for updating fields that change often.

There are two ways to implement `list_editable`:

1. Maintain a link to the change page, but make a field or fields editable; or
2. Make the whole change list editable

In the first implementation, you set `list_editable` to a tuple (change in bold):

```
# myclub_root\events\admin.py

# ...

@admin.register(Venue, site=admin_site)
class VenueAdmin(admin.ModelAdmin):
    list_display = ('name', 'address', 'phone')
    list_display_links = ('name', 'address')
    list_editable = ('phone',)
    ordering = ('name',)
    search_fields = ('name', 'address')
    inlines = [
        EventInline,
    ]
```

By setting `list_editable` to a tuple containing the phone model field, that field is now editable in the change list (Figure 12-14).

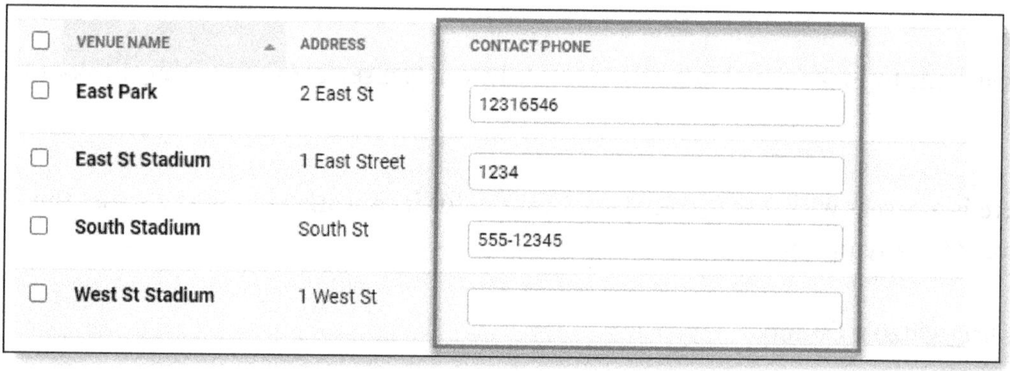

Figure 12-14. *By setting the* `list_editable` *option, you can make fields editable in the change list. Click "Save" to save any changes.*

In the second implementation, you can turn the entire change list into an editable formset by setting `list_editable = list_display`. You must also set `list_display_links` to `None` in this implementation as editable fields can't also be links (changes in bold):

```
# myclub_root\events\admin.py

# ...

@admin.register(Venue, site=admin_site)
class VenueAdmin(admin.ModelAdmin):
    list_display = ('name', 'address', 'phone')
    list_editable = list_display
    list_display_links = None
    ordering = ('name',)
    search_fields = ('name', 'address')
    inlines = [
        EventInline,
    ]
```

Once you have made the highlighted changes, the venue admin change list will look like Figure 12-15.

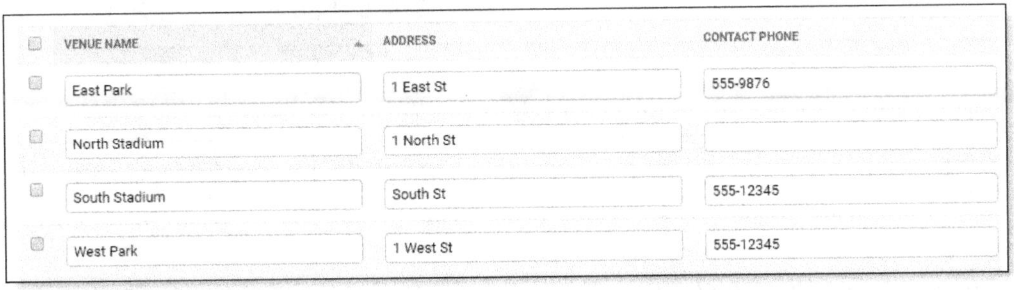

VENUE NAME	ADDRESS	CONTACT PHONE
East Park	1 East St	555-9876
North Stadium	1 North St	
South Stadium	South St	555-12345
West Park	1 West St	555-12345

Figure 12-15. *The venue change list is now an editable formset. Click "Save" to save any changes.*

The save_as option

By default, the Django admin doesn't have an option to duplicate a record. To enable saving an object as a new object, you set the `save_as` option to `True` (change in bold):

```
# myclub_root\events\admin.py

# ...

@admin.register(Event, site=admin_site)
class EventAdmin(admin.ModelAdmin):
    list_display = ('name', 'event_date', 'venue')
    list_filter = ('event_date', 'venue')
    ordering = ('-event_date',)
    save_as = True
    fieldsets = (

    # ...
```

Once you have set the `save_as` option, you will have a new "Save as new" button on the change page (Figure 12-16).

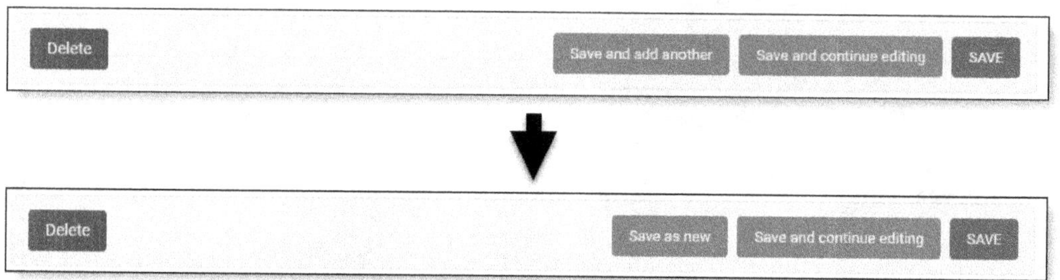

Figure 12-16. *Allow duplication of records by setting the* `save_as` *option to change the "Save and add another" button to "Save as new".*

ModelAdmin Methods

Django's `ModelAdmin` class provides a sizeable list of built-in methods that provide an easy interface for working with the current instance (Table 12-5). All `ModelAdmin` methods can be overridden, which makes `ModelAdmin` objects highly customizable.

Method	Description
`save_model()`	Override to conduct pre- and/or post-save operations
`delete_model()`	Override to conduct pre- and/or post-delete operations
`delete_queryset()`	Override to customize the deletion process for the "delete selected objects" action
`save_formset()`	Override to modify a formset before it's saved
`get_ordering()`, `get_autocomplete_fields()`, `get_readonly_fields()`, `get_prepopulated_fields()`, `get_list_display()`, `get_list_display_links()`, `get_exclude()`, `get_fields()`, `get_fieldsets()`, `get_list_filter()`, `get_list_select_related()`, `get_search_fields()`, `get_sortable_by()`, `get_inline_instances()`, `get_form()`, `get_formsets_with_inlines()`, `get_paginator()`	Use to interrogate the current `ModelAdmin` instance. Each of these methods returns the current value of the corresponding option. For example, `get_fields()` will return a list of the fields from the admin form. Override any of these methods to customize the behavior of the `ModelAdmin` instance
`get_search_results()`	Modify the change list page search results. Most often used to either return a custom QuerySet or to use an external tool (e.g., Haystack)

Method	Description
`save_related()`	Override to conduct pre- and/or post-save operations for related objects
`get_urls()`	Return the URLs for the `ModelAdmin` instance. Add custom URLs by overriding the method
`formfield_for_foreignkey()`, `formfield_for_manytomany()`, `formfield_for_choice_field()`	Override the default formfield for `ForeignKey` fields, `ManyToMany` fields, and for any field that has `choices` set
`get_changelist()`	Return a `ChangeList` class. Inherit from this class to change the behavior of the change list
`get_changelist_form()`	Override to return a custom `ModelForm` class to use in the changelist page formset
`get_changelist_formset()`	Return a custom formset to use on the change list page. Only works if `list_editable` is `True`
`lookup_allowed()`	Override to customize permitted lookups
`has_view_permission()`, `has_add_permission()`, `has_delete_permission()`, `has_module_permission()`	Return a boolean based on what actions are permitted on the `ModelAdmin` instance
`get_queryset()`	Return a QuerySet of all model instances that can be edited by the admin.
`message_user()`	Send a message to the user
`response_add()`	Called after admin form is submitted. Override to change default behavior after object has been created

Method	Description
`response_change()`	Called after admin form and related objects have been saved. Override to change default behavior after object has been changed
`response_delete()`	Called after the object has been deleted. Override to change default behavior after the object has been deleted
`get_changeform_initial_data()`	A hook to retrieve the initial data from an admin change form
`get_deleted_objects()`	Return all objects that were deleted. Used for customizing the deletion process for the `delete_view()` method

***Table 12-5.** Django's* `ModelAdmin` *class methods.*

Each of the `ModelAdmin` methods can be overridden by defining a custom method in your app's `ModelAdmin` classes. For example (changes in bold):

```
# myclub_root\events\admin.py

@admin.register(Venue, site=admin_site)
class VenueAdmin(admin.ModelAdmin):
    form = VenueForm
    list_display = ('name', 'address', 'phone')
    # list_display_links = ('name', 'address')
    # list_editable = ('phone',)
    # list_editable = list_display
    # list_display_links = None
    ordering = ('name',)
    search_fields = ('name', 'address')
    # inlines = [
    #     EventInline,
    # ]

    def get_list_display(self, request):
        return ('name', 'address', 'phone', 'web')
```

You can see in **lines 15 and 16**, I have added a new get_list_display() method that overrides the default method and adds the web column to the change list table. You will also need to comment out the list_display and list_editable options, and the inlines to set the change list back to the default. If you save this file and open your admin, the venues change list will look like Figure 12-17.

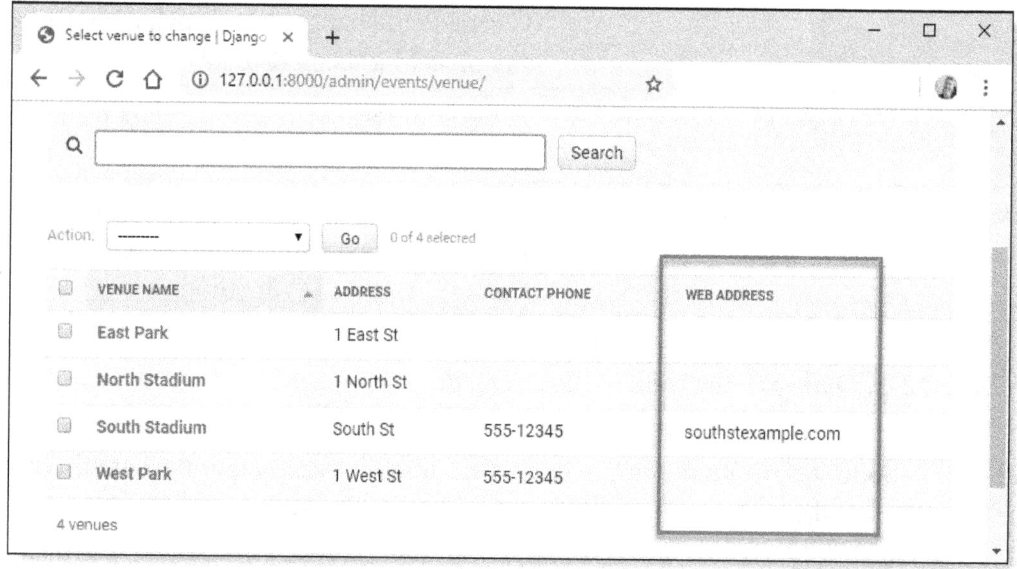

Figure 12-17. *Overriding a* ModelAdmin *method allows us to customize the behavior of the class instance.*

This is a simple example, but it illustrates how easy it is to hook into the ModelAdmin object and create customizable admin lists and forms for your models. Each method is constructed similarly, however, there are two caveats.

First, while most get_<option>() methods must return a list or a tuple, some (e.g., get_prepopulated_fields()) must return a dictionary, and some (e.g., get_form()) must return an object.

Second, save_model() and delete_model() are only for extra operations; you must save or delete the object in your code with a call to super(). For example:

```
# Example code only. Don't add to your file

class MyModelAdmin(admin.ModelAdmin):

    # ...

    def save_model(self, request, obj, form, change):
        # do something before save
        super().save_model(request, obj, form, change)
```

For more information on ModelAdmin methods, and sample implementations, see the Django documentation[4].

Admin Actions

Selecting one or more records and performing bulk actions on the selected records is a familiar task for most of us—whether it selecting online banking transactions for printout, or managing pages in a content management system.

Django provides the same functionality with *admin actions.*

The admin actions sit above all change lists in the admin. In Figure 12-18, we're looking at the admin actions for the events change list.

4 https://docs.djangoproject.com/en/dev/ref/contrib/admin/#modeladmin-methods

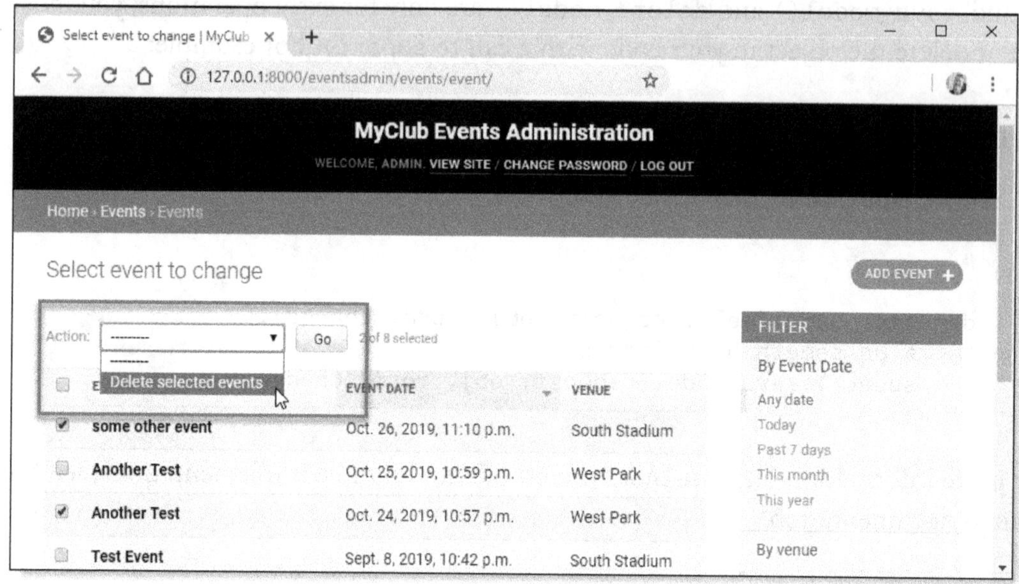

Figure 12-18. *The default admin action for all change lists.*

Django has one built-in admin action for deleting the selected objects from the database. In our case, we're deleting the selected events. If you went to the venues page, the action would be to delete the selected venues.

Adding your own admin actions is simple. An action is a regular Python function that takes three arguments:

1. The current `ModelAdmin` instance.
2. The current request; and
3. A QuerySet containing the selected objects.

As always, this is much easier to understand with an example.

Say we want to give an admin user the ability to set themselves as the person managing one or more events. To achieve this, we will create a "Manage selected events" admin action.

Let's start with the action function (changes in bold):

```
# myclub_root\events\admin.py

# ...

1  def set_manager(modeladmin, request, queryset):
2      queryset.update(manager=request.user)
3  set_manager.short_description = "Manage selected events"
4
5
6  @admin.register(Event, site=admin_site)
7  class EventAdmin(admin.ModelAdmin):
8      list_display = ('name', 'event_date', 'venue', 'manager')
9      list_filter = ('event_date', 'venue')
10     ordering = ('-event_date',)
11     actions = [set_manager]
12     fieldsets = (
13         # ...
```

The action function is simple:

- In **line 1**, we declare the function with the three required arguments.
- In **line 2**, we're setting the manager field for all records in the QuerySet to the current user.
- In **line 3**, we set the short description for the action function. This is the short description that will show in the dropdown on the change list page.
- In **line 8**, we've added the manager field to `list_display` so we can see the manager column in the change list.
- In **line 11**, `actions` is a list of action functions to add to the model admin. To add the action to our event model, we need to set this option.

Save the changes, reload your events change list, and you should see the new action in the dropdown, and a new "MANAGER" column has been added to the change list (Figure 12-19).

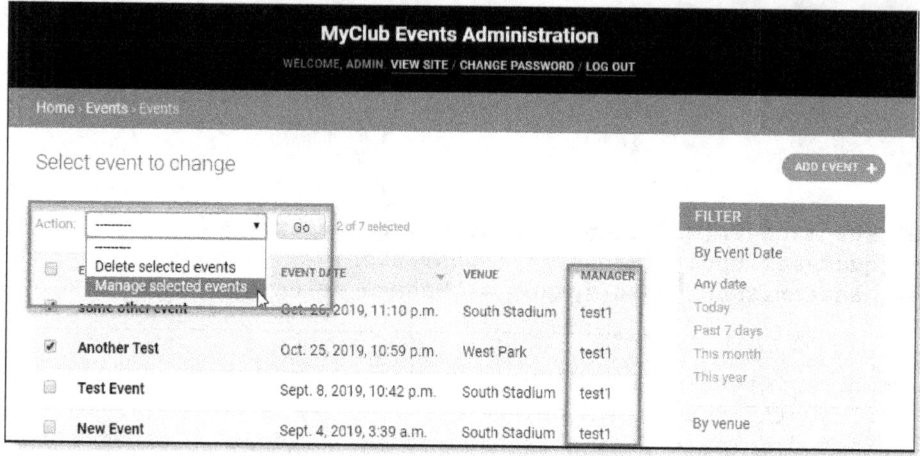

Figure 12-19. *The events change list page with the new action added. Also, note the new "MANAGER" column.*

I have selected the first two records as a demonstration. Once you have selected the records, click "Go" and the person managing the events will change to the current user (Figure 12-20).

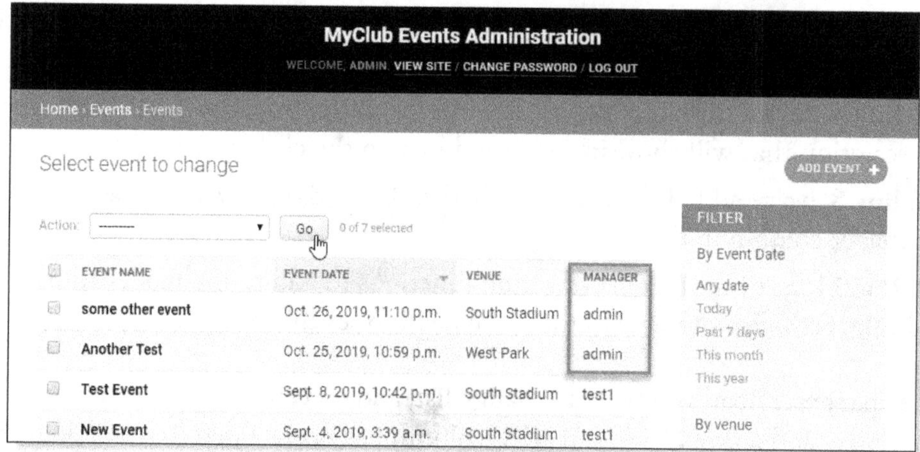

Figure 12-20. *With the new admin action, changing the manager on multiple events is easy.*

Modifying multiple records at once is one common application for admin actions. Another is exporting data from database tables and saving it in a comma-delimited file, so it can be opened in spreadsheet programs like Microsoft Excel.

Writing a csv export admin action is more complex than updating records, but the underlying principle is the same.

Let's add a new action to the events admin (changes in bold):

```
# myclub_root\events\admin.py

# Add the following to your imports at the top of the file
from django.http import HttpResponse
import csv

# ...

def venue_csv(modeladmin, request, queryset):
    response = HttpResponse(content_type='text/csv')
    response['Content-Disposition'] = 'attachment; filename="venue_export.csv"'
    writer = csv.writer(response)
    writer.writerow(['name', 'event_date', 'venue', 'description'])
    for record in queryset:
        rec_list = []
        rec_list.append(record.name)
        rec_list.append(record.event_date.strftime("%m/%d/%Y, %H:%M"))
        rec_list.append(record.venue.name)
        rec_list.append(record.description)
        writer.writerow(rec_list)
    return response
venue_csv.short_description = "Export Selected Venues to CSV"


@admin.register(Event, site=admin_site)
class EventAdmin(admin.ModelAdmin):
    list_display = ('name', 'event_date', 'venue', 'manager')
    list_filter = ('event_date', 'venue')
    ordering = ('-event_date',)
    actions = [set_manager, venue_csv]
    # ...
```

The export csv admin action is not much different than the csv file export view we created in Chapter 10.

Make sure you import Python's `csv` library with the other imports at the top of your `admin.py` file before writing the action function.

Let's step through the `venue_csv()` function in a little more detail:

- **Lines 2 and 3**. Set the `content_type` and `Content-Disposition` header so Django knows to treat the response as a file.
- **Line 4**. Create the `writer` object and send its output to the response.
- **Line 5**. Write the header row to the csv file.
- **Lines 6 to 12**. Add each record to the csv file and write it to the response.
- **Line 14**. Set the action short description for the change list dropdown.
- **Line 22**. Add the new action to the events change list.

Save the file and when you refresh the admin in your browser, the new action will appear in the dropdown (Figure 12-21).

If you select some or all of the records, when you click "Go", a csv file named `venue_export.csv` will download in your browser.

The same basic process can be applied to just about anything you might want to perform on or with multiple records in the admin. If you want to dig deeper into more advanced admin action topics—like creating actions as `ModelAdmin` methods, and writing actions that provide intermediate pages—see the Django documentation[5].

5 https://docs.djangoproject.com/en/dev/ref/contrib/admin/actions/

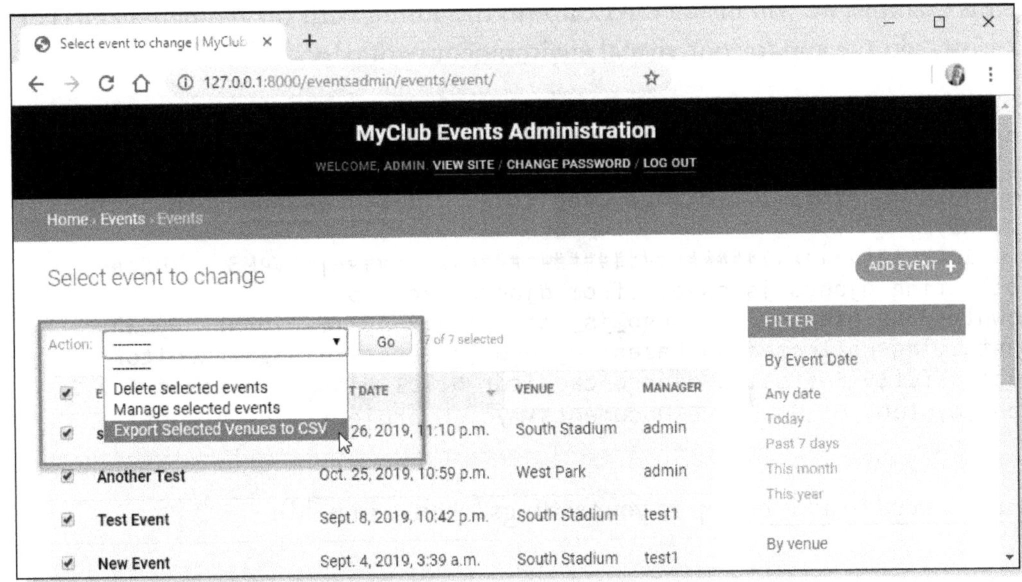

Figure 12-21. *The events change list page with the export csv action added.*

WYSIWYG Editor in the Admin

There are no Django-native implementations of a What You See, Is What You Get (WYSIWYG) editor in the admin.

This is deliberate—with the almost ubiquity of JavaScript text editors like CKEditor and TinyMCE, Django's creators saw no need to reinvent the wheel.

While it is possible to integrate a WYSIWYG editor yourself, the work has already been done by other Django developers. For a complete list of third-party apps that integrate various WYSIWYG editors with Django, go to the WYSIWYG Editors page on Django Packages[6].

6 https://djangopackages.org/grids/g/wysiwyg/

For this example, we will install CKEditor in the admin with the `django-ckeditor` app. First, add the app to your virtual environment with `pip`:

```
(env_myclub) ...\myclub_root> pip install django-ckeditor
Collecting django-ckeditor
Downloading https:.../django_ckeditor-5.7.1-py2.py3-none-any.whl
(2.4MB)
    100% |########################################| 2.4MB 4.7MB/s
Collecting django-js-asset (from django-ckeditor)
Downloading https:.../django_js_asset-1.2.2-py2.py3-none-any.whl
Installing collected packages: django-js-asset, django-ckeditor
Successfully installed django-ckeditor-5.7.1 django-js-asset-1.2.2
(env_myclub) D:\OneDrive\Documents\myclub_project\myclub_root>
```

Then, you need to add the app to your settings (change in bold):

```
# myclub_root\myclub_site\settings.py

# ...

INSTALLED_APPS = [
    'ckeditor',
    'events.apps.EventsConfig',
    # ...
]
```

Once the app has been installed, it's as simple as creating a custom form for the admin that uses the CKEditor widget (changes in bold):

```
# myclub_root\events\admin.py

# Add these imports to the top of the file
from django import forms
from ckeditor.widgets import CKEditorWidget

# ...

class EventAdminForm(forms.ModelForm):
    description = forms.CharField(widget=CKEditorWidget())
    class Meta:
```

```
4          model = Event
5          fields = '__all__'
6
7
8   @admin.register(Event, site=admin_site)
9   class EventAdmin(admin.ModelAdmin):
10      form = EventAdminForm
        # ...
```

Once we have added imports for `django.forms` and the `CKEditorWidget` at the top of the file, we need to create a custom form for the event admin. Let's have a quick look at the custom form class:

- **Line 1.** The custom admin form class inherits from `forms.ModelForm`.
- **Line 2.** We've added the `CKEditorWidget` custom widget to the description field.
- **Line 10.** We've told the `EventAdmin` class to use our custom admin form.

Save the file. Now, when you edit an event in the admin, the description field has a rich-text editor attached to it (Figure 12-22).

This is the minimal installation for the `django-ckeditor` app. There are many customizations available as well as configuration options that allow for file uploads. If you want to check out the customization options available, see the Django CKEditor page on GitHub[7].

7 https://github.com/django-ckeditor/django-ckeditor

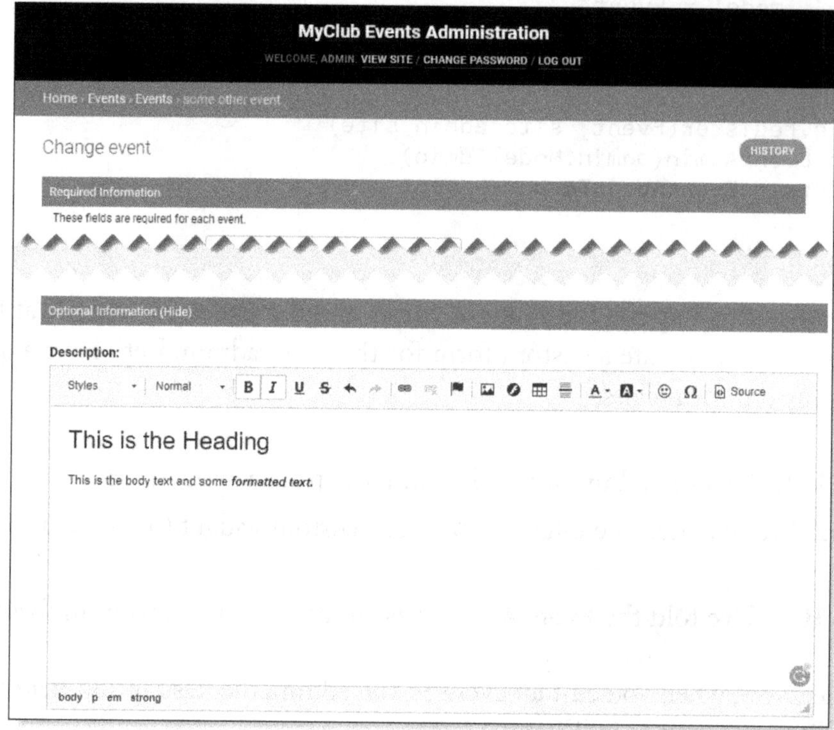

***Figure 12-22.** Adding a WYSIWYG editor to the admin with the* `django-ckeditor` *third-party app.*

Chapter Summary

In this chapter, we took a deep dive into advanced Django admin topics.

We started with customizing the admin—changing the site text, style sheets, replacing the default admin, creating custom admin apps, and customizing Django's admin templates. In the latter part of the chapter, we dug into the `ModelAdmin` class and wrote our own admin actions, and learned how to add a WYSIWYG editor to the admin.

In the next chapter, we will explore Django's class-based views.

13

Class Based Views

At the fundamental level, a view is a piece of code that accepts a request and returns a response. While all the views we have created so far have been function-based views, Django also has class-based views.

When Django was first created, there were only function-based views included with Django. As Django grew, it was clear that, while function-based views covered simple cases well, extending and customizing them was difficult.

Class-based views provide an alternative way to implement views in Django. Note the use of the word alternative—there is nothing in Django stopping you from using function-based views if you want to.

Django's class-based views are not designed to replace function-based views, but to provide the advantages of using classes in views. Advantages of class-based views include:

- The ability to implement HTTP methods like GET and POST as class methods, instead of conditional branching in code.
- You can extend and add functionality to basic classes with inheritance.
- Allows the use of mixins and other object-oriented techniques.
- Abstracting common idioms and patterns into generic views makes view development easier for common cases.

In this chapter, I will pull apart Django's class-based views and show you that, while they may seem complex, they're actually constructed from simple building blocks.

I will show you how these simple building blocks are put together to create powerful generic views for automating the grunt work of building views to display list and detail data, edit and update forms, and to show date filtered data.

I will finish the chapter with working examples of the most common class-based generic views built into Django.

Comprehensive, Not Complex

Understanding how Django's class-based views work has been described as being like wading through spaghetti. I can see how this opinion might be justified, especially given how much the class-based view codebase has changed since class-based views were introduced in Django 1.3.

However, I believe this perception of complexity has far more to do with a mismatch between programmers' expectations of how a class-based view should behave and how the Django developers implemented them.

From my perspective, Django's class-based views result from taking the Don't Repeat Yourself (DRY) Principle and code factoring to their logical limit.

In keeping with Django's general philosophy of providing all the building materials, rather than a complete house, Django's class-based views provide the programmer with a toolkit of building blocks.

Django's developers then combined these basic blocks into class-based generic views for common tasks like list and detail views of objects, views for creating, updating and deleting objects, and views for filtering objects based on date ranges. All generic views are designed to save you time by seeking to eliminate repetition and minimizing the amount of code you have to write.

I believe Django's class-based views are comprehensive, not complex. Where the perceived complexity comes in is when programmers try to take it all in in one go. So in the next section, I will take it one step at a time and show you how each block fits together to create a comprehensive, powerful and flexible toolkit for building class-based views.

The Basics—View, RedirectView and TemplateView

The underlying philosophy that governs the structure of Django's class-based views, and the many generic views built upon them, is based on two simple rules:

1. Attributes are objects; and
2. Each class should have only one parent; all other attributes and methods must come from mixins.

The first rule encapsulates Python's "everything is an object" philosophy, and means that most attributes have a corresponding `get_<attribute>()` method. In most cases, the `get_<attribute>()` method returns the attribute by default.

For simple classes, this adds complexity. However, for more complex classes, this means that attributes are callables you can override and customize in your code.

For example, the `queryset` attribute has a `get_queryset()` method that returns the default `queryset`. But by overriding the `get_queryset()` method, you can now customize the data returned from the database.

Think about that for a moment. *Everything* can be made into a callable (within some logical limits). As long as your `get_<attribute>()` method returns the same datatype, your custom class-based views can override any attribute or method in the class.

If that hasn't got your creative wheels turning, I don't know what will!

The second rule, where each class must have only one parent, with all other functionality coming from mixins, we'll explore as I show you how each class builds on previous classes to complete Django's class-based views toolkit.

The View Class

The `View` class is the base class for all other views—both function- and class-based views. For this reason, you can import it from either `django.views.generic.base` or `django.views`.

Django's `View` class is simple by design—it provides an entry point for the request-response cycle and implements a dispatch-by-method interface for each of the `HTTP` methods (`GET`, `POST`, `PUT`, `PATCH`, `DELETE`, `HEAD`, `OPTIONS` and `TRACE`).

Django's URL resolver passes the request and associated arguments to a callable function. The view class provides all generic views with an `as_view()` class method that returns a function when a request arrives with a matching URL. The initialization process is:

1. `as_view()` conducts some error checks, and if they pass, it creates an instance of the class.
2. It then calls the `setup()` method to initialize the class attributes.
3. Finally, it calls it's `dispatch()` method which looks at the `HTTP` request method to see if a matching class method exists. If it does, it executes the method, otherwise, it calls `http_method_not_allowed()`.

   `dispatch()` will also call `http_method_not_allowed()` if the `HTTP` request method is not in `http_method_names`. `http_method_not_allowed()` adds a warning to the error log and returns a `HttpResponseNotAllowed` (`405` status code).

Both `setup()` and `dispatch()` can be overridden with custom class methods. `setup()` is useful for adding custom attributes to a class. `dispatch()` you need to be more careful with, as many of the generic views override this method.

For example, some of the generic authentication views add the `login_required` decorator to `dispatch()`. You definitely don't want to replace this!

We'll talk about when and where to override class-based view methods later in the chapter.

The view class has one attribute—`http_method_names`. Its default value is a list of all available `HTTP` methods:

```
http_method_names = ['get', 'post', 'put', 'patch', 'delete', 'head',
'options', 'trace']
```

You can override this when you create your own class instance. For example, to limit a view to the `GET` and `HEAD` methods, set `http_method_names` to include only these two methods:

```
    http_method_names = ['get', 'head']
```

You will rarely use the `View` class on its own, as every generic view in Django descends from this class. You are better off looking for a more feature-rich descendant to customize, rather than build your own.

The RedirectView Class

The `RedirectView` class is the simplest of the `View` class' descendants—it adds no mixins and only one additional class method (`get_redirect_url`). `RedirectView` also adds four attributes:

- **url**. The URL to direct to.
- **pattern_name**. The name of the URL pattern to redirect to. Use to perform reverse lookups, rather than hard-coding URLs with `url`.
- **permanent**. Default is `False` (`302` status code). Change to `True` to perform a permanent redirect (`301` status code).
- **query_string**. Boolean on whether to pass the `GET` query string (if any). Default is `False`.

`RedirectView` also provides implementations for all HTTP methods (except for `TRACE`):

- **get()**. A simple method that will return either a temporary (`302`) redirect, or permanent (`301`) redirect, based on the value of the `permanent` attribute.
- **options()**. `RedirectView` overrides this method to call `get()`, instead of returning a `response` object.
- **delete(), head(), patch(), post(), put()**. The remaining HTTP methods call `get()`.

If you are finding this hard to follow, I have reproduced the `RedirectView` class structure in Figure 13-1.

Stay Sane—Use the Django CBV Inspector

Grasping the overall structure of Django's class-based views can be tough, especially when you are working with the more advanced generic views and trying to decipher the method resolution order (MRO) so you can work out what methods to override and in what class.

Thankfully, there is an awesome tool that makes this process substantially easier—the Django CBV Inspector[1].

The Django CBV Inspector is your number one resource for working out which class overrides what method, and the MRO of each class, so you know where in the hierarchy you need to add your own overridden methods.

1 http://ccbv.co.uk/

	RedirectView
A	pattern_name
A	permanent
A	query_string
A	url
M	get_redirect_url()
M	get()
M	delete() - calls get()
M	head() - calls get()
M	patch() - calls get()
M	post() - calls get()
M	put() - calls get()

	View (parent)
A	http_method_names
M	as_view()
M	dispatch()
M	http_method_not_allowed()
M	options() - overridden by RedirectView
M	setup()

Figure 13-1. *The* `RedirectView` *class structure showing all publicly accessible attributes and methods of the class.*

The TemplateView Class

You can see in Figure 13-2, the `TemplateView` class itself is simple. It has no attributes of its own and only implements one HTTP method—`get()`. It gets most of its functionality from the addition of two mixins: `TemplateResponseMixin` and `ContextMixin`.

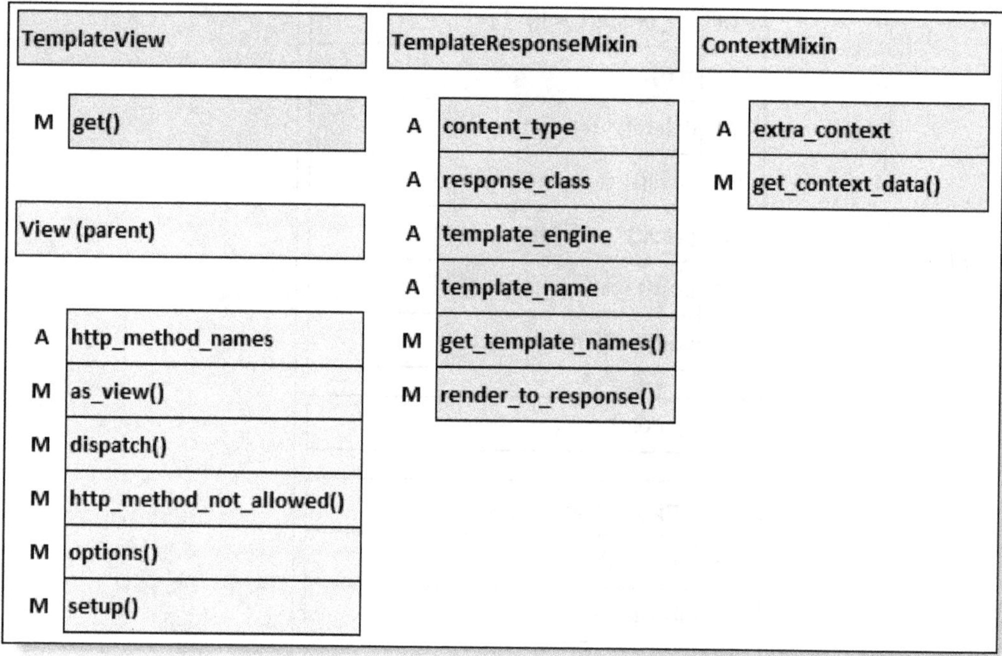

Figure 13-2. *The* `TemplateView` *class structure showing all publicly accessible attributes and methods of the class.*

The structure of the `TemplateView` class is where you can see the philosophy behind Django's class-based views. For example, `ContextMixin` is a very simple class—in the codebase it's only 7 lines—it has one attribute (`extra_context`) and one method (`get_context_data()`).

You could argue that it would be easier to add the attribute and method to the `TemplateView` class. But if you think about it, you should see a problem—many of the built-in generic views use context data, so without creating a mixin, Django's developers would have had to repeat the same code dozens of times.

Adding functionality to classes with mixins adhered to the DRY principle and allowed the Django developers to create a powerful and flexible class-based view library while minimizing code repetition.

This comes at the price of added complexity, but now you understand the basic philosophy, and have a tool like the Django CBV Inspector on hand, creating custom class-based views should be much easier.

Before we move on, let's have a closer look at the attributes and methods of the complete `TemplateView` class. First, the attributes:

- **`content_type`**. Response content type. Defaults to `None`, which means Django will use `DEFAULT_CONTENT_TYPE`.
- **`response_class`**. The class to be returned by `render_to_response()`. Default is `TemplateResponse`.
- **`template_engine`**. Name of the template engine to use when loading the template. Default is `None` (use configured engine).
- **`template_name`**. Full name of the template as a string.
- **`extra_context`**. A dictionary to include in the context.

And the methods:

- **`get()`**. Calls `get_context_data()` to retrieve the context, and then calls `render_to_response()` to render the template.
- **`get_template_names()`**. Returns the value of `template_name`.
- **`render_to_response()`**. Returns a response class. Default is `TemplateResponse`.
- **`get_context_data()`**. Returns the context. `extra_context` is appended if set.

I'll give you some practical examples of both `TemplateView` and `RedirectView` shortly.

From Little Things, Big Things Grow

This "one parent, zero or more mixins" structure is the foundation of all Django's class-based views. Advanced views are created by layering additional classes on simpler views (multi-level inheritance).

To see this in action, let's have a look at `MonthArchiveView`—one of the more complex views with no less than nine ancestors!

I won't explain each attribute and method in this example, just the overall structure, so you can see how a detailed generic view is constructed. To explore the attributes and methods of `MonthArchiveView`, refer to the Django documentation[2] and the Django CBV Inspector[3].

Let's start with a high-level view of the `MonthArchiveView` class:

```
1. MonthArchiveView
    1.1. MultipleObjectTemplateResponseMixin
        1.1.1. TemplateResponseMixin
2. BaseMonthArchiveView
    2.1. YearMixin
    2.2. MonthMixin
3. BaseDateListView
    3.1. MultipleObjectMixin
        3.1.1. ContextMixin
    3.2 DateMixin
4. View
```

2 https://docs.djangoproject.com/en/dev/ref/class-based-views/generic-date-based/#montharchiveview

3 https://ccbv.co.uk/projects/Django/3.0/django.views.generic.dates/MonthArchiveView/

At the first level, we have the generic view classes. Each class inherits from the one below it—`MonthArchiveView` inherits from `BaseMonthArchiveView`, which inherits from `BaseDateListView`, which inherits from `View`.

As each class-based view can only have one parent class, all classes at level 2 and 3 are mixins. You will notice two of the mixin classes (`MultipleObjectTemplateResponseMixin` and `MultipleObjectMixin`) are subclasses of simpler mixins (`TemplateResponseMixin` and `ContextMixin`).

While the multiple layers of a detailed generic view like `MonthArchiveView` can seem convoluted, it has a distinct advantage over inheriting from multiple classes (multiple inheritance). With multi-layer inheritance, the Method Resolution Order (MRO) is unambiguous and avoids the *diamond problem*[4], which can be a problem with multiple inheritance.

With multi-layer inheritance, the top-to-bottom structure of the generic view class and the MRO are the same—making it easier for you to identify where a particular method sits in the order of execution. We'll discuss MRO and overriding methods in the next section of the chapter.

Now, let's dig deeper into the `MonthArchiveView` class, starting with `BaseDateListView` (Figure 13-3).

4 https://en.wikipedia.org/wiki/Multiple_inheritance

BaseDateListView (parent of BaseMonthArchiveView)	
A	allow_empty
A	date_list_period overridden by BaseMonthArchiveView
M	get()
M	get_dated_items() overridden by BaseMonthArchiveView
M	get_dated_queryset()
M	get_date_list()
M	get_date_list_period()
M	get_ordering()

View (parent)	
A	http_method_names
M	as_view()
M	dispatch()
M	http_method_not_allowed()
M	options()
M	setup()

MultipleObjectMixin	
A	allow_empty overridden by BaseDateListView
A	context_object_name
A	model
A	ordering
A	page_kwarg
A	paginate_by
A	paginate_orphans
A	paginator_class
A	queryset
M	get_allow_empty()
M	get_context_data()
M	get_context_object_name()
M	get_ordering() overridden by BaseDateListView
M	get_paginate_by()
M	get_paginate_orphans()
M	get_paginator()
M	get_queryset()
M	paginate_queryset()

ContextMixin (parent of MultipleObjectMixin)	
A	extra_context
M	get_context_data() overridden by MultipleObjectMixin

DateMixin	
A	allow_future
A	date_field
A	uses_datetime_field
M	get_allow_future()
M	get_date_field()

Figure 13-3. *The* `BaseDateListView` *class structure.*

At the bottom of the inheritance chain is the `View` class. We won't go over this class again, as we covered it earlier in the chapter. `BaseDateListView` inherits from `View` and adds the features you would expect from a date list—attributes for the date period and whether the list can be empty, and methods that retrieve information like the list of dates, the QuerySet returned by the list of dates, and ordering information.

Two mixins provide additional functionality to `BaseDateListView`:

1. **`DateMixin`**. A simple mixin for working with date objects; and
2. **`MultipleObjectMixin`**. A more detailed mixin that adds attributes and methods for working with lists and paginated data.

Note also `MultipleObjectMixin` is a child class of `ContextMixin`, which provides the context for the class.

At the next level of inheritance is the `BaseMonthArchiveView` class (Figure 13-4).

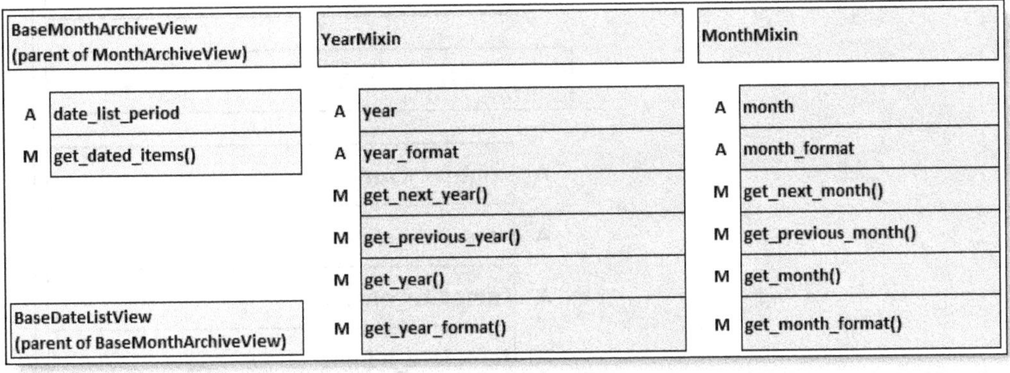

Figure 13-4. *The* `BaseMonthArchiveView` *class structure.*

`BaseMonthArchiveView` inherits from `BaseDateListView` and overrides the `date_list_period` attribute and the `get_dated_items()` method from the parent class.

If you dig into the code, you will find `get_dated_items()` in `BaseDateListView` is a stub that throws a `NotImplementedError` if it isn't overridden in a child class. This is a useful feature of Django's generic class-based views. When you're messing with classes and don't override a method you should have, Django will throw a `NotImplementedError` to warn you.

`BaseMonthArchiveView` also adds two mixins—`YearMixin` and `MonthMixin`—that help with filtering dates by year and month.

Finally, we have the `MonthArchiveView` class (Figure 13-5).

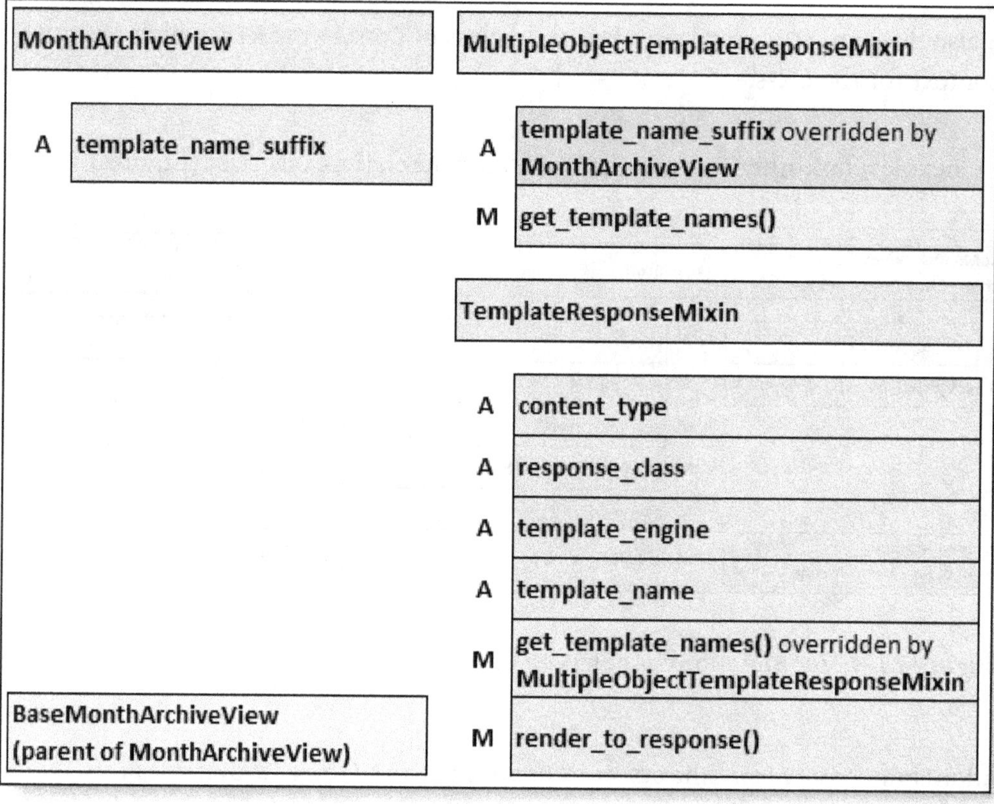

Figure 13-5. *The* `MonthArchiveView` *class structure.*

At the top of the class structure, all there is left to add is template information and a method for rendering the month archive to a response.

For this reason, `MonthArchiveView` is simple—it overrides a single attribute it gets from `MultipleObjectTemplateResponseMixin`. This mixin inherits from `TemplateResponseMixin` which provides template attributes and a `render_to_response()` method.

All Django's generic class-based views are constructed in the same multi-layered fashion. Once you understand how they are constructed, leveraging the power of Django's generic views becomes a far less daunting task.

While I could pick apart each generic view and show you how they work, I encourage you to conduct your own exploration of these classes and mixins to give yourself a better understanding of how you can use them in your own code.

Customizing Generic View Classes and Methods

A complete tutorial on how Django's class-based views can be customized and extended to suit your applications would take another book in its entirety. Because class-based views are so flexible, I will only discuss some general concepts and ideas in this section.

The first concept to grasp is Django does not limit you to the high-level generic views when deciding which class to customize. In the `MonthArchiveView` example from the last section, there are four classes you could inherit from when creating a custom generic view—`View`, `BaseDateListView`, `BaseMonthArchiveView` and `MonthArchiveView`.

`View` is too basic to be much use in a custom class, but `BaseDateListView` could be useful for a class that retrieves records based on a custom date range. If you created a custom class that inherited from `BaseDateListView`, you would automatically get attributes and methods for working with dated QuerySets and paginated data.

As another example, say you wanted to send monthly archive data to a file, or expose the data as an API. Here, you wouldn't need a template or a response object, so your custom class could superclass `BaseMonthArchiveView`.

As the date-based generic views (`YearAchiveView`, `MonthArchiveView`, `WeekArchiveView`, etc.) are all constructed in the same way, this last example could be used to create custom output for a variety of date ranges with minimal code modification.

The second concept is because the multi-layer approach exposes all attributes and methods in the parent, you don't have to fiddle around with intermediate classes when overriding methods and attributes.

For example, to create a custom month archive:

```
class MyCustMonthArchive(MonthArchiveView):
    # add custom attribs and methods
    # or override existing
```

If you have any experience with object-oriented programming, this is basic stuff. Still, I point it out because overriding attributes at the top of the MRO is a common source of bugs and therefore comes with some caveats.

There are two ways to override a method:

1. Replace the parent method with your own; or
2. Call the parent method with `super()`

With large generic view classes like `MonthArchiveView`, replacing the parent method is fraught because you can break modifications made to class objects further down the MRO (nine ancestors remember!).

Unless you are overriding a method that is not implemented in any other class, or you know for sure there are no consequences for replacing a method with your own, the second option is preferable.

`super()` can be used in two ways:

1. Call the parent method and return an object of the same datatype; or
2. Return an object that calls the parent with customized parameters.

If you want to study either of these implementations, the source code for Django's generic views is the best place to start. Examples of both can be found in `django.views.generic.list`:

```
# \env_myclub\Lib\site-packages\django\views\generic\list.py

# ...

class MultipleObjectTemplateResponseMixin(TemplateResponseMixin):
    """Mixin for responding with a template and list of objects."""
    template_name_suffix = '_list'

    def get_template_names(self):
        """
        Return a list of template names to be used for the request.
        Must return a list. May not be called if render_to_response
        is overridden.
        """
        try:
            names = super().get_template_names()
            # ...
            # Django appends some data to the names list
        return names
```

In this first snippet, Django is calling `get_template_names()` from `TemplateResponseMixin` with `super()` and appending additional data before returning the `names` list. Now, let's have a look at an example of the second way `super()` is implemented:

```
# ...
class MultipleObjectMixin(ContextMixin):
    """A mixin for views manipulating multiple objects."""
    # ...

    def get_context_data(self, *, object_list=None, **kwargs):
        """Get the context for this view."""
        # Django adds some extra context variables
        return super().get_context_data(**context)
```

This is a snippet of the `get_context_data()` method from `MultipleObjectMixin`. It overrides the same method from `ContextMixin`; in this case, additional context data is passed to the parent in `**kwargs`.

You will see a few more examples of both these implementations later in the chapter. I also encourage you to explore the Django source in more detail to get ideas on how you can customize the class-based views for your applications.

Using Django's Class-based Generic Views

Now you understand how Django's class-based views work, let's take a few of the most common class-based generic views for a test drive.

The following examples are to illustrate how each of these generic views is implemented in your code.

In a real website, you would put a lot more effort into page layout and formatting, but this is HTML and CSS, not Python or Django, so I have left out the extra cruft of building workflows and adding pretty styles so you can concentrate on the code.

Django provides three so-called base views—`View`, `TemplateView` and `RedirectView`.

We will not cover `View` here as it's rare to see this class used on its own.

TemplateView

The basic implementation of `TemplateView` is simple—pass a template name to the `as_view()` method. For example (changes in bold):

```
# myclub_root\myclub_site\urls.py

# Add this import to the top of your file
from django.views.generic.base import TemplateView

urlpatterns = [
    path('cbvdemo/', TemplateView.as_view(template_name='events/cbv_
demo.html')),
    # ...
```

I have made two minor changes to the site `urls.py` file:

1. I've imported `TemplateView` from `django.views.generic.base`; and
2. I've added a URLconf for the generic view.

To test this out in your browser, you need to create the template (new file):

```
# \events\templates\events\cbv_demo.html

{% extends "base.html" %}

{% block title %}{{ title|default:"Untitled Page" }}{% endblock title
%}

{% block content %}
{% if title %}
    <h1>{{ title }}</h1>
{% else %}
    <p>Nothing to see here</p>
{% endif %}
{% endblock content %}
```

There's nothing new in this simple template, so you should find it easy to follow.

Once you save the template and fire up the development server, navigate to `http://127.0.0.1:8000/cbvdemo`, and your browser should look like Figure 13-6.

Figure 13-6. *The* `TemplateView` *generic view makes it easy to show a template in your apps.*

You will notice the web page is missing data for the page title and content. This is because we have not passed a value to the `title` template variable.

We could fix this issue by adding a context and title variable to the URLconf, but let's not do that. Instead, I will use this as an example of how easy it is to create a custom class-based view to solve the problem.

First, we need to add a new view to the `demo_views.py` file (new code):

```
# myclub_root\events\views\demo_views.py

    # Add this import to the top of your file
    from django.views.generic.base import TemplateView

# ...

1   class TemplateViewDemo(TemplateView):
2
3       template_name = "events/cbv_demo.html"
4
5       def get_context_data(self, **kwargs):
6           context = super().get_context_data(**kwargs)
7           context['title'] = "Testing The TemplateView CBV"
8           return context
```

After importing `TemplateView` from `django.views.generic.base`, I've added a new custom class to the end of the file. Let's have a closer look at this new class:

- **Line 1** is the class declaration. Note how `TemplateViewDemo` inherits from `TemplateView`.
- In **line 3**, I set the `template_name` attribute to the same value as the first example.
- In **line 5**, I've overridden the `get_context_data()` method and added a value for title to the context.

Also, note the call to `super()` in **line 6**. Getting into the habit of calling `super()` every time you override `get_context_data()` is a Good Thing as several of Django's middleware applications work with context data, and you don't want to overwrite this information by arbitrarily setting the context.

Once we have created the custom class, we can simplify the URLconf (changes in bold):

```
# myclub_root\myclub_site\urls.py

# Add this import to the top of your file
from events.views import TemplateViewDemo
```

```
# ...

urlpatterns = [
    path('cbvdemo/', TemplateViewDemo.as_view()),
    # ...
```

Once you have made the changes, your browser should now look like Figure 13-7.

Figure 13-7. *Adding a custom class that inherits from* `TemplateView` *allows you to set the template in the class and add data to the context.*

RedirectView

`RedirectView` provides a class with hooks for managing redirects. The simplest implementation of `RedirectView` uses a URLconf (changes in bold):

```
# myclub_root\myclub_site\urls.py

# Add this import to the top of your file
from django.views.generic.base import RedirectView

urlpatterns = [
    path('home/', RedirectView.as_view(url='/')),
    # ...
```

This will redirect `http://127.0.0.1:8000/home/` to `http://127.0.0.1:8000/`.

By default, the redirect is temporary (`302` redirect). To change the redirect type, set the `permanent` attribute to `True` (change in bold):

```
urlpatterns = [
    path('home/', RedirectView.as_view(url='/', permanent=True)),
    # ...
```

`RedirectView` can also be used for more sophisticated view management. For example, it can be used to create URL aliases that redirect to other system resources, but that's deeper than I want to go with this overview.

Check out the Django documentation[5] or type "Django RedirectView" into your favorite browser to get some ideas on different implementations of `RedirectView`.

ListView and DetailView

Displaying a list of database records and opening a detail view when a record is selected is a common idiom in data management.

With Django's `ListView` and `DetailView` class-based generic views, creating basic list/detail views is an almost trivial task.

5 https://docs.djangoproject.com/en/dev/ref/class-based-views/base/#redirectview

To create list and detail views of your models only requires a model name and a template. Let's start by creating the views (changes in bold):

```
# myclub_root\events\views\demo_views.py

# Add these imports to the top of your file
from django.views.generic.list import ListView
from django.views.generic.detail import DetailView
from events.models import Venue, MyClubUser, Event
# ...

1  class ListViewDemo(ListView):
2      model = Event
3      context_object_name = 'all_events'
4
5
6  class DetailViewDemo(DetailView):
7      model = Event
8      context_object_name = 'event'
```

After importing the `ListView` and `DetailView` classes, we create two custom classes that inherit from them—`ListViewDemo` (**line 1**) and `DetailViewDemo` (**line 6**).

The only information Django requires to create these views is the model name. In this example, I am using the `Event` model (**lines 2 and 7**). The `context_object_name` attribute is not required; however, it's helpful to provide meaningful names to use in your templates.

When creating templates for `ListView` and `DetailView`, it's handy to use Django's file naming shortcut. If you don't specify a name for the template, Django will look for a template using the following naming convention:

- For a list view, Django will look for a template named "<model name>_list.html".
- For a detail view, Django will look for a template named "<model name>_detail.html".

Let's see this in action. First, the list view template. We will update the file we created in Chapter 6 (change in bold):

```
# \events\templates\events\event_list.html

1  {% extends "base.html" %}
2
3  {% block title %}ListView Demo{% endblock title %}
4
5  {% block content %}
6    <h1>All Events</h1>
7    <ul>
8      {% for event in all_events %}
9        <li>{{ event.name }}</li>
10     {% endfor %}
11   </ul>
12 {% endblock content %}
```

This should be easy to follow—I've just changed the page title and the page heading (**lines 3 and 6**) and changed the QuerySet name (**line 8**).

To see how this looks in the browser, we need a URLconf (changes in bold):

```
# myclub_root\events\urls.py

from django.urls import path, re_path
from . import views
from .views import ListViewDemo


urlpatterns = [
    path('', views.index, name='index'),
    # path('events/', views.all_events, name='show-events'), # This is from Ch6
    path('events/', ListViewDemo.as_view(), name='show-events'),
    # ...
```

Once you save the file and fire up the development server, navigate to `http://127.0.0.1:8000/events`, and your browser should look like Figure 13-8.

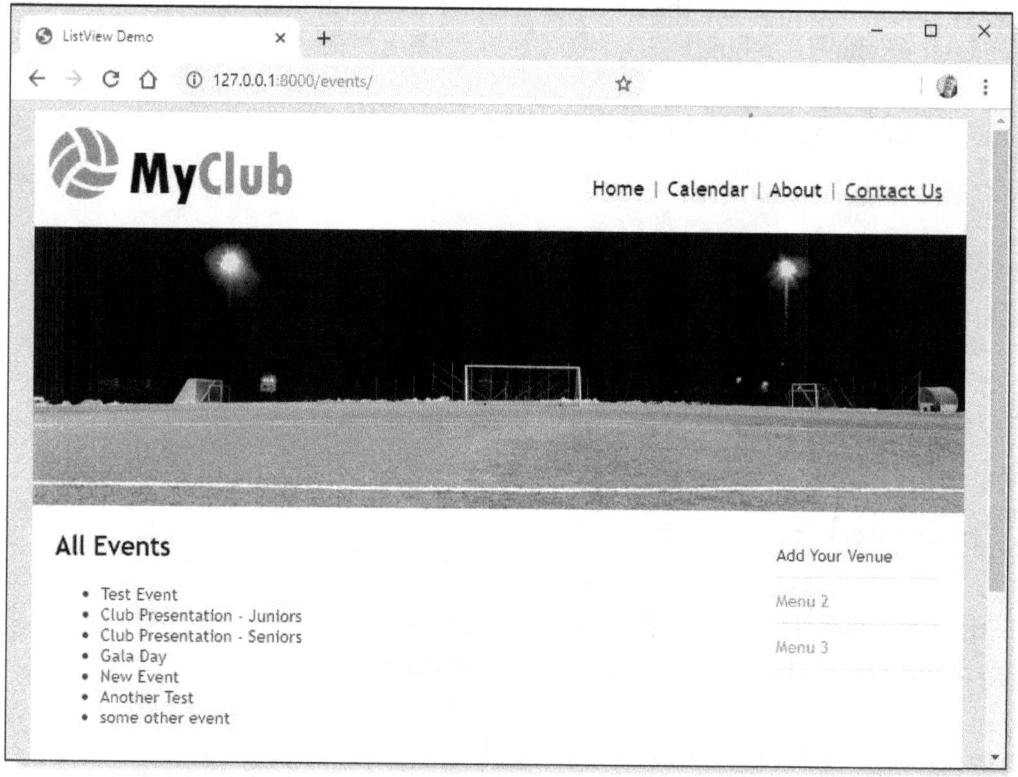

Figure 13-8. *Django's* `ListView` *class does all the heavy lifting to make it easy for you to create list views for your models.*

The template for the detail view is a little more involved because we have to write code for each of the model fields we want to show (new file):

```
# \events\templates\events\event_detail.html

{% extends "base.html" %}

{% block title %}DetailView Demo{% endblock title %}

{% block content %}
  <h1>Event: {{ event.name }}</h1>
  <table>
```

```
    <tr>
      <td><strong>Event Date:</strong></td><td>{{ event.event_date }}</td>
    </tr>
    <tr>
      <td><strong>Venue:</strong></td><td>{{ event.venue }}</td>
    </tr>
    <tr>
      <td><strong>Description:</strong></td><td>{{ event.description }}</td>
    </tr>
  </table>
{% endblock content %}
```

This time, the template displays the event name in the title and uses an HTML table to show the model fields.

To see how this looks in the browser, we need to add another URLconf (changes in bold):

```
# myclub_root\events\urls.py

from django.urls import path, re_path
from . import views
from .views import ListViewDemo, DetailViewDemo


urlpatterns = [
    path('', views.index, name='index'),
    path('events/', ListViewDemo.as_view(), name='show-events'),
    path('event/<int:pk>', DetailViewDemo.as_view(), name='event-detail'),
    # ...
```

The pattern to match is the interesting part. Another shortcut with Django's `DetailView` class is it expects you to pass the primary key for your model record in a `GET` parameter named `pk`. The capturing group `<int:pk>` does just that—passing whatever number follows the `event/` path to the view.

For example, when you navigate to `http://127.0.0.1:8000/event/1`, Django will attempt to retrieve the event record with the primary key equal to 1.

Assuming the record exists, your browser should look like Figure 13-9.

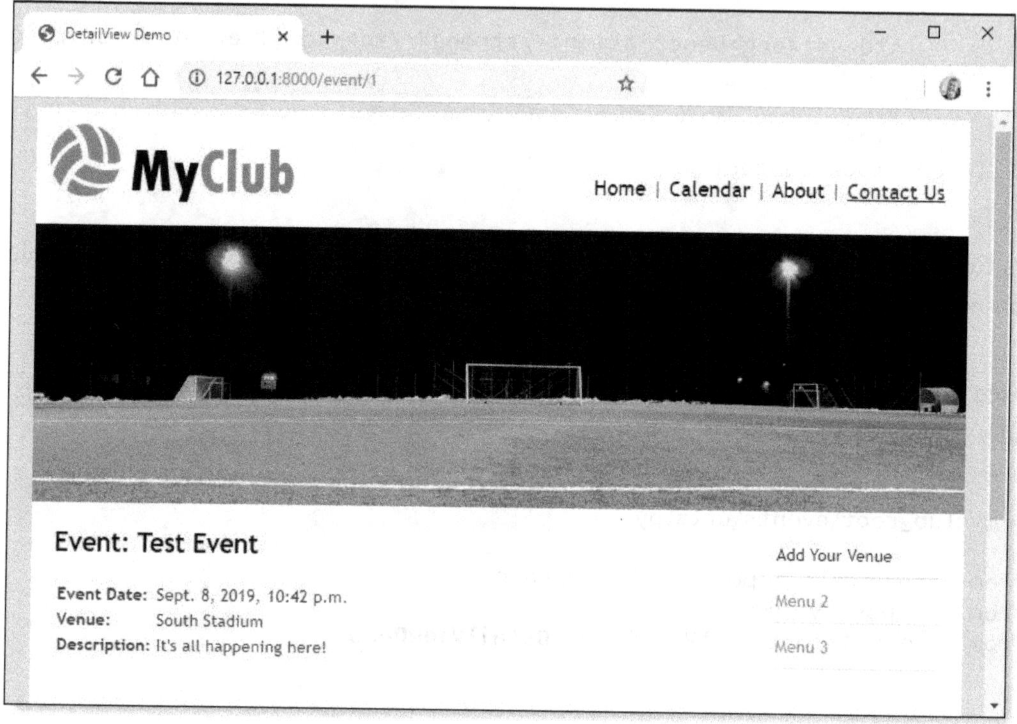

Figure 13-9. *Retrieving individual records with the* `DetailView` *class.*

Using the list and detail views together only needs a simple tweak to the list view template to turn the listings into hyperlinks (change in bold):

```
# \events\templates\events\event_list.html

{% extends "base.html" %}

{% block title %}ListView Demo{% endblock title %}
```

```
{% block content %}
<h1>All Events</h1>
<ul>
    {% for event in all_events %}
    <li><a href="/event/{{ event.id }}">{{ event.name }}</a></li>
    {% endfor %}
</ul>
{% endblock content %}
```

All I have done here is turn the event name into an anchor that links to `/event/<event.id>`. When you navigate to `http://127.0.0.1:8000/events` now, your browser should look like Figure 13-10. The URLconf for the detail view will match the `/event/<event.id>` pattern and show the corresponding event record when the link is clicked.

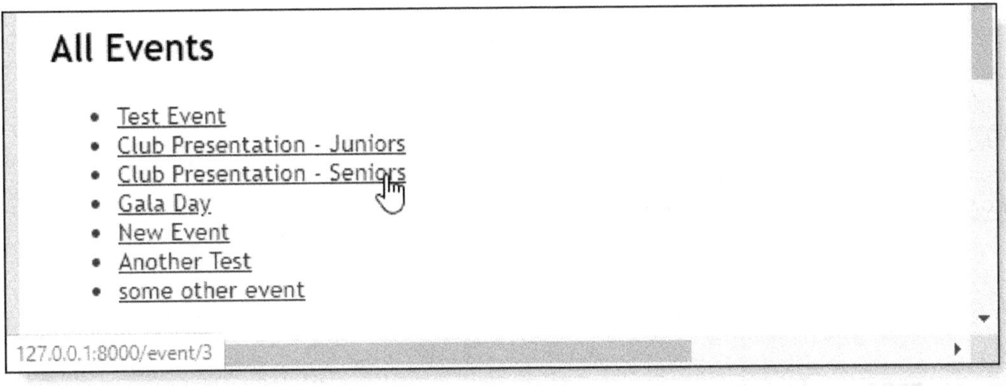

Figure 13-10. *Turning the event list into hyperlinks to the detail records links the event list to individual event records.*

Generic Editing Views

Django also provides class-based generic views for create, retrieve, update and delete (CRUD) database operations.

You already know how to retrieve database records with a generic view—we covered that when we looked at the `DetailView` class. The remaining operations—create, update, and delete—are provided by the conveniently named `CreateView`, `UpdateView` and `DeleteView` classes.

CreateView

We're going to stick with the `Event` model for the following examples.

With just a few lines of code, `CreateView` will display a form containing the model fields you specify, validate the input, save the information to the database and redirect to another view after successfully saving the record.

Let's start with the new view (new code):

```
# myclub_root\events\views\demo_views.py

# Add these imports to the top of your file
from django.views.generic.edit import CreateView
from django.urls import reverse_lazy

# ...

1  class CreateViewDemo(CreateView):
2
3      model = Event
4      fields = ['name', 'event_date', 'description']
5      success_url = reverse_lazy('show-events')
```

The class structure is like the generic views we have looked at previously in the chapter—we import `CreateView` at the top of the file, create a custom class that inherits from `CreateView` (**line 1**), and specify the model to use (**line 3**). We also need to tell Django which fields to show on the form (**line 4**).

I have introduced a new function in this class—`reverse_lazy()` (**line 5**). In keeping with the Don't Repeat Yourself (DRY) principle, it's always advisable to avoid hard-coding URLs. Django makes this task easy by providing the functions `reverse()` and `reverse_lazy()` for reversing URLs.

In other words, if you provide either `reverse()` or `reverse_lazy()` with the name of the URL, it will look up the URL name and replace it with the corresponding absolute URL.

We have been preparing to use reversible URLs ahead of time by naming our URLs. For example, with the URLconf:

```
path('events/', ListViewDemo.as_view(), name='show-events')
```

If we were to call `reverse('show-events')` at runtime, it would return the `URL` `http://127.0.0.1:8000/events/` (assuming the code was still running on Django's development server).

This allows for flexible and dynamic URL generation, however, it has a drawback—when a class or a function is compiled, Django doesn't know what the absolute URL is as it's not available until runtime.

Python solves this problem quite neatly with *lazy evaluation*. Put simply, lazy evaluation will only compute the value (in this case, the URL) when needed.

In our `CreateViewDemo` class, Django's `reverse_lazy()` function implements Python's lazy evaluation to wait until runtime to calculate the URL for `success_url`. In this example, `CreateViewDemo` will redirect back to the event listing page once a new event has been added to the database.

To turn this into a practical example, we will add the ability to add a new event record to the event listing page.

First, let's make a minor change to the event list template (change in bold):

```
# \events\templates\events\event_list.html

{% extends "base.html" %}

{% block title %}ListView Demo{% endblock title %}

{% block content %}
  <h1>All Events</h1>
  <ul>
    {% for event in all_events %}
      <li><a href="/event/{{ event.id }}">{{ event.name }}</a></li>
    {% endfor %}
  </ul>
  <p><a href="/event/add/">Add Event</a></p>
{% endblock content %}
```

Here, I've added a hyperlink to the bottom of the template. If you fire up the development server and navigate to `http://127.0.0.1:8000/events/`, your browser will look like Figure 13-11.

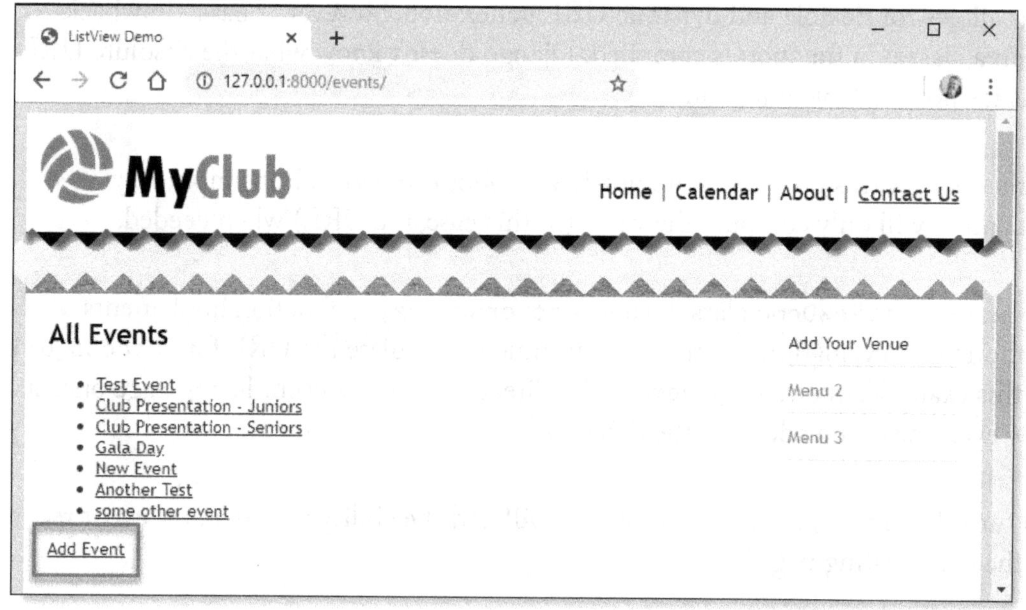

Figure 13-11. *Adding the "Add Event" link to your event list template.*

For this new link to work, we need to add a template for the blank form, and a URLconf that maps `/event/add/` to the `CreateViewDemo` view.

First, the template. Django's naming shortcut expects the `CreateView` template to be named `<model>_form.html`. So let's create the template (new file):

```
# \events\templates\events\event_form.html

1  {% extends "base.html" %}
2
3  {% block title %}CreateView Demo{% endblock title %}
4
5  {% block content %}
6    <h1>Add Event</h1>
7    <form method="post">{% csrf_token %}
8    <table>
9      {{ form.as_table }}
10     <tr>
11       <td><a href="/events/">Cancel</a></td>
12       <td><input type="submit" value="Add"></td>
13     </tr>
14   </table>
15   </form>
16 {% endblock content %}
```

We covered form creating in templates in Chapter 8, but for a refresher, let's have a quick look at what's going on:

- **Line 7.** The `csrf_token` tag must be added to all `POST` forms to prevent Cross-Site Request Forgeries.
- **Line 9.** I'm displaying the blank form in table format. Remember, Django doesn't generate the HTML table tags for you, so you must add them to the template (**lines 8 and 14**).

Now for the URLconf (changes in bold):

```
# myclub_root\events\urls.py

from django.urls import path, re_path
from . import views
from .views import ListViewDemo, DetailViewDemo
from .views import CreateViewDemo


urlpatterns = [
    path('', views.index, name='index'),
    path('events/', ListViewDemo.as_view(), name='show-events'),
    path('event/<int:pk>', DetailViewDemo.as_view(), name='event-detail'),
    path('event/add/', CreateViewDemo.as_view(), name='add-event'),
    # ...
```

Once you have added the URLconf and saved the files, you can click on "Add Event" on the events list page, and it will open a blank form for adding a new event (Figure 13-12).

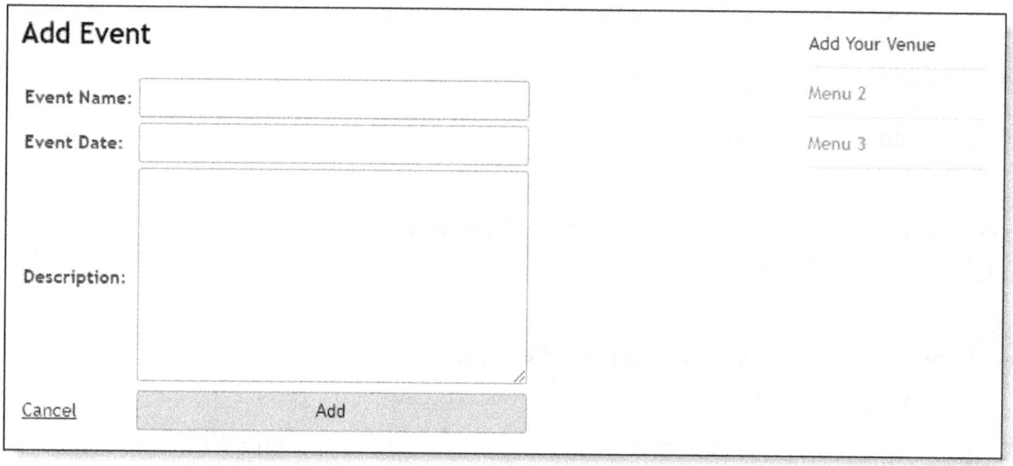

Figure 13-12. *Using the* `CreateView` *class-based generic view to create forms for adding records to your database.*

UpdateView

`UpdateView` has almost the same implementation as `CreateView`, with some minor changes because we're working with an existing record.

Let's start with the custom class (changes in bold):

```
# myclub_root\events\views\demo_views.py

# Add this import to the top of your file
from django.views.generic.edit import CreateView, UpdateView

# ...

1  class UpdateViewDemo(UpdateView):
2
3      model = Event
4      fields = ['name', 'event_date', 'description']
5      template_name_suffix = '_update_form'
6      success_url = reverse_lazy('show-events')
```

The only difference between this class and the `CreateView` class is **line 5**. By default, Django will look for a template named `<model>_form.html` when looking for a template for the update view. Unfortunately, this is the same as for a create view, so if you want to show a different form for your update view, you need to change the template name suffix so Django can find the correct template for your update view.

With the change to the `template_name_suffix` attribute, Django will now look for a template named `event_update_form.html`.

Now we have that problem sorted, let's create the template (new file):

```
# \events\templates\events\event_update_form.html

{% extends "base.html" %}

{% block title %}UpdateView Demo{% endblock title %}
```

```
{% block content %}
<h1>Update Event</h1>
<form method="post">{% csrf_token %}
<table>
    {{ form.as_table }}
    <tr><td> </td><td><input type="submit" value="Update"></td>
</table>
</form>
{% endblock content %}
```

The differences between this template and the template for the create view are simple contextual differences (e.g., I changed the button text from "Add" to "Update"), so I won't go over the details again.

To give the user the ability to update an event record, let's add an update link to the detail view (changes in bold):

```
# \events\templates\events\event_detail.html

{% extends "base.html" %}

{% block title %}DetailView Demo{% endblock title %}

{% block content %}
  # ...
  <tr>
  <td><a href="/event/update/{{ event.id }}">Update</a></td><td> </td>
  </tr>
</table>

{% endblock content %}
```

I haven't reproduced the template in its entirety here, just the end of the file to show you where I have added a new HTML table row and a hyperlink that appends the event id (primary key) to the end of a URL.

Now, all we need to do is add the URLconf (changes in bold):

```
# myclub_root\events\urls.py

from django.urls import path, re_path
from . import views
from .views import ListViewDemo, DetailViewDemo
from .views import CreateViewDemo, UpdateViewDemo


urlpatterns = [
    # ...
    path('event/update/<int:pk>', UpdateViewDemo.as_view(), name='update-
event'),
    # ...
```

Note the capturing group in this URL. Django will pass the event id to the view in the context variable `pk`, so your app can retrieve the correct database record.

Once all the files are saved, if you navigate to `http://127.0.0.1:8000/events/` and select one event, you will notice that an "Update" link has been added to the detail view. Click on this link, and you can edit the event record (Figure 13-13).

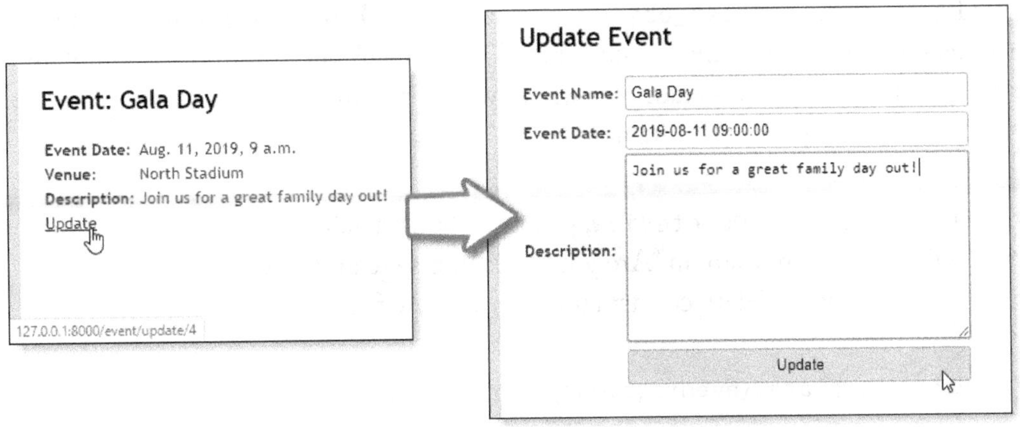

Figure 13-13. *Using the* `UpdateView` *class-based generic view to create forms for editing records to your database.*

DeleteView

`DeleteView` provides a simple class-based interface for deleting an object from the database. Like the other CRUD views, `DeleteView`'s minimal implementation is very simple. Let's start with a new custom class that inherits from `DeleteView` (changes in bold):

```
# myclub_root\events\views\demo_views.py

# Add this import to the top of your file
from django.views.generic.edit import CreateView, UpdateView, DeleteView

# ...

1  class DeleteViewDemo(DeleteView):
2
3      model = Event
4      context_object_name = 'event'
5      success_url = reverse_lazy('show-events')
```

The `DeleteViewDemo` class has only one difference from the classes we have created so far: I have set the `context_object_name` attribute (**Line 4**). If I didn't set the attribute, the object would be named "object", which isn't very useful for a template designer, so like all previous examples where we are passing objects to a template, I'm giving the object a meaningful name.

To delete an object with `DeleteView`, you must `POST` a valid form to the view. The form need not be more than an "Are you sure?" message and a submit button. For example, here's a basic delete confirmation form (new file):

```
# \events\templates\events\event_confirm_delete.html

{% extends "base.html" %}

{% block title %}DeleteView Demo{% endblock title %}

{% block content %}
<h1>Delete Event</h1>
```

```
<form method="post">{% csrf_token %}
    <table>
    <tr><td colspan=2>Are you sure you want to delete "{{ event }}"?</
td></tr>
    <tr><td><a href="/events/">Cancel</a></td><td><input type="submit"
value="Delete"></td>
    </table>
</form>
{% endblock content %}
```

Note the name of the template—the default template suffix for a delete form is "_confirm_delete", so I have named the template event_confirm_delete.html.

To implement our new delete form with the other editing views, we just need to add the delete link to the event detail template and add a URLconf. First, the template (change in bold):

```
# \events\templates\events\event_detail.html

# ...
    <td><a href="/event/update/{{ event.id }}">Update</a></td>
    <td><a href="/event/delete/{{ event.id }}">Delete Event</a></td>
    </tr>
</table>

{% endblock content %}
```

I've only reproduced a small snippet of the template here so you can see where the link is added. Like the event update link, I am passing the event id (primary key) to the view.

Now, all we need is a new URLconf (changes in bold):

```
# myclub_root\events\urls.py

from django.urls import path, re_path
from . import views
from .views import ListViewDemo, DetailViewDemo
```

```
from .views import CreateViewDemo, UpdateViewDemo, DeleteViewDemo


urlpatterns = [
    # ...
    path('event/update/<int:pk>', UpdateViewDemo.as_view(), name='update-
event'),
    path('event/delete/<int:pk>', DeleteViewDemo.as_view(), name='delete-
event'),
    # ...
```

Once all the files are saved, if you navigate to `http://127.0.0.1:8000/events/` and select one event, you will notice that a "Delete Event" link has been added to the detail view. Click on this link and you can edit the event record (Figure 13-14).

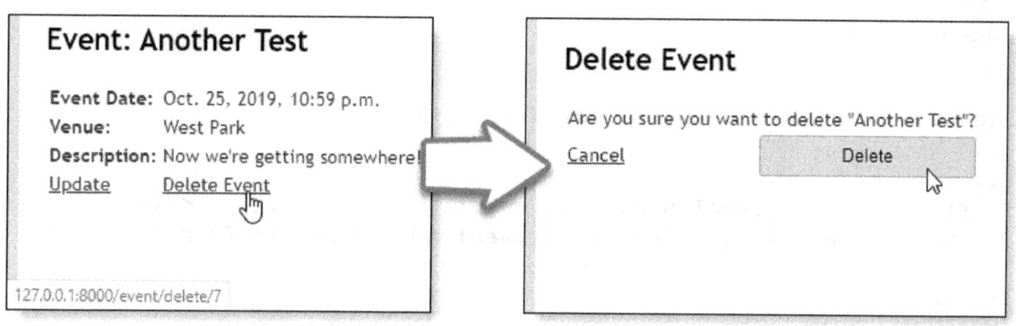

Figure 13-14. *Using the* `DeleteView` *class-based generic view to delete records from your database.*

FormView

There's one more generic editing view we need to look at—`FormView`.

If you remember from Chapter 8, we created the `contact()` function-based view to show a contact form that we created using Django's `form` class.

`FormView` provides a class-based implementation of a view to show a form. `FormView` can render any kind of HTML form, not just instances of the Django form class. Although, as I recommended in Chapter 8, the built-in `form` class is so useful, you will rarely need to resort to manually creating HTML forms.

Since we've already created the contact form, let's go ahead and re-create the `contact()` view as a class-based view using `FormView`.

First, let's add the new class-based view to our `contact.py` file (new code):

```
# myclub_root\myclub_site\contact.py

# Add the import to the top of your file:
from django.views.generic.edit import FormView

# ...

class ContactUs(FormView):
    template_name = 'contact/contact.html'
    form_class = ContactForm
    success_url = '/contact?submitted=True'

    def get(self, request, *args, **kwargs):
        context = self.get_context_data(**kwargs)
        if 'submitted' in request.GET:
            context['submitted'] = request.GET['submitted']
        return self.render_to_response(context)

    def form_valid(self, form):
        cd = form.cleaned_data
        con = get_connection('django.core.mail.backends.console.EmailBackend')
        send_mail(
            cd['subject'],
            cd['message'],
            cd.get('email', 'noreply@example.com'),
            ['siteowner@example.com'],
            connection=con
        )
        return super().form_valid(form)
```

At the top of the file, I have imported the `FormView` class from `django.views.generic.edit` (**line 2**). The new `ContactUs()` class-based view starts on **line 6**.

The first thing you will notice about this class is that the branching logic has been replaced by two class methods—`form_valid()` (**line 17**) and `get()` (**line 11**).

`form_valid()` is only called when the form has been successfully POSTed, so you need not do any error checking on the form, nor do you need to create a `post()` method as `FormView` provides a default implementation for you.

If an invalid form is submitted, `FormView` will reload the form and display any error messages. If the form submitted is valid, `form_valid()` emails the form data.

I won't explain the `send_mail()` code again here as it's identical to the example in Chapter 8. If you want a refresher on how this code works, see page 180.

The `get()` method is called in one of three circumstances:

1. When the form is first shown,
2. When an invalid form is submitted; or
3. After the form is successfully submitted.

The first two instances should be self-explanatory—the view will show either a blank form or a form displaying the validation errors.

In a `FormView` class, the redirect URL for a successful form submission is saved in the `success_url` attribute (**line 9**). As our `success_url` contains a `GET` attribute, the `get()` method adds the `submitted` attribute to the context and sets its value to `True` (**line 14**).

If you remember from the example in Chapter 8, the `contact.html` template shows a success message instead of the form if `submitted=True`.

That's all we need to do—no modifications to the `ContactForm()` class or `contact.html` template are required. To show our new class-based contact form, we just need to point a new URLconf at it (changes in bold):

```
# myclub_root\myclub_site\urls.py

# ...

urlpatterns = [
    # ...
    # path('contact/', contact.contact, name='contact'),
    path('contact/', contact.ContactUs.as_view(), name='contact'),
    # ...
]
```

Don't forget to comment out the old URLconf! If you navigate to `http://127.0.0.1:8000/contact/`, your contact form should work just as it did in Chapter 8, except it's now a class-based view.

So, Should I Use Class- or Function-based Views?

Easy answer: whichever one you are most comfortable with.

If you look at the class-based and function-based versions of the contact form view, they're nearly the same number of lines and perform the same function. You didn't even have to change the form or the template to switch from the function-based to the class-based view.

Personally, I believe that class-based have the edge over function-based views because encapsulating logic inside class methods is easier to follow and less error-prone than complex branching. Plus, with classes, you get to build complexity with inheritance, which is the awesome-sauce that makes classes so tasty.

But you are you, and I am me, so best you don't go down that rabbit hole; nothing but flame wars, stress and confusion there.

Do what works for you. And maybe your employer...

Generic Date Views

Django has seven class-based generic views for displaying date-based data:

- **`ArchiveIndexView`**. Show all database objects.
- **`YearArchiveView`**. Group database objects by year.
- **`MonthArchiveView`**. Group database objects by month.
- **`WeekArchiveView`**. Group database objects by week.
- **`DayArchiveView`**. Group database objects by day.
- **`TodayArchiveView`**. Show objects created today.
- **`DateDetailView`**. Show an individual record.

These generic date views make it simpler to display object indexes (e.g., a blog archive), and various views for showing records filtered by year, month, week and day.

Let's have a look at a few of these in more detail.

ArchiveIndexView

`ArchiveIndexView` provides a view that lists all objects in the database for a particular model. In its simplest form, `ArchiveIndexView` only requires a template and a URLconf.

For example, let's create a view that shows all the events in our database. Starting with the template (new file):

```
# \events\templates\events\event_archive.html

{% extends "base.html" %}

{% block title %}ArchiveIndexView Demo{% endblock title %}

{% block content %}
  <h1>Event Index</h1>
```

```
7     <ul>
8       {% for event in latest %}
9         <li>{{ event.event_date }}: {{ event.name }}</li>
10      {% endfor %}
11    </ul>
12
13 {% endblock content %}
```

Like all the generic views, `ArchiveIndexView` has a default suffix ("`_archive`"), so we're naming the file `event_archive.html`.

The template should be easy to follow. In **lines 8 to 10**, we're using the `{% for %}` template tag to build a list of events showing the event date and event name.

Now for the URLconf (changes in bold):

```
# myclub_root\events\urls.py

# Add the following imports to the top of your file
from django.views.generic.dates import ArchiveIndexView
from .models import Event


1  urlpatterns = [
2      path('', views.index, name='index'),
3      path('eventarchive/', ArchiveIndexView.as_view(model=Event,
date_field="event_date")),
4      # ...
```

Once you import `ArchiveIndexView` from `django.views.generic.dates`, the URLconf (**line 3**) does all the work. To show a list of objects from the database, all you have to pass to the view is a model name and the date field to filter by.

Save the files, fire up the development server, and navigate to `http://127.0.0.1:8000/eventarchive/` and your browser should look like Figure 13-15.

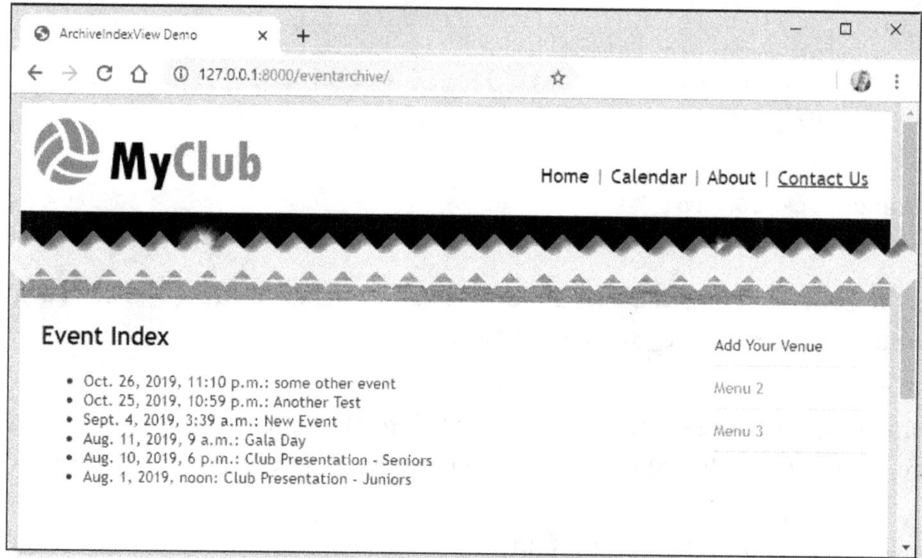

Figure 13-15. `ArchiveIndexView` *will show a list of date-filtered objects from your database.*

When I first wrote this section, it was mid-November 2019—notice how no events after October 2019 are listed? This is because the `allow_future` attribute defaults to `False` (this is the same for all of the date-based generic views). We need to change this attribute to `True` if we want to see future events in the list.

We could do this in the URLconf, but it's always best to keep your URLconfs as simple as possible, so I will create a custom class that inherits from `ArchiveIndexView`. Let's start with the class (new code):

```
# myclub_root\events\views\demo_views.py

# Add the import to the top of your file
from django.views.generic.dates import ArchiveIndexView

# ...

class ArchiveIndexViewDemo(ArchiveIndexView):
    model=Event
    date_field="event_date"
    allow_future = True
```

This code should be familiar, as it has a very similar structure to the generic editing views we covered earlier. Note how I am now setting the `model` and `date_field` attributes in the custom class, and I have set the `allow_future` attribute to `True`.

Now we have a custom class, the URLconf can be simplified (changes in bold):

```
# myclub_root\events\urls.py

# Add the import to the top of your file
from .views import ArchiveIndexViewDemo

urlpatterns = [
    path('', views.index, name='index'),
    path('eventarchive/', ArchiveIndexViewDemo.as_view(), name='event-
index'),
    # ...
```

After making the changes, refresh your browser and events with future dates will show in the index (Figure 13-16).

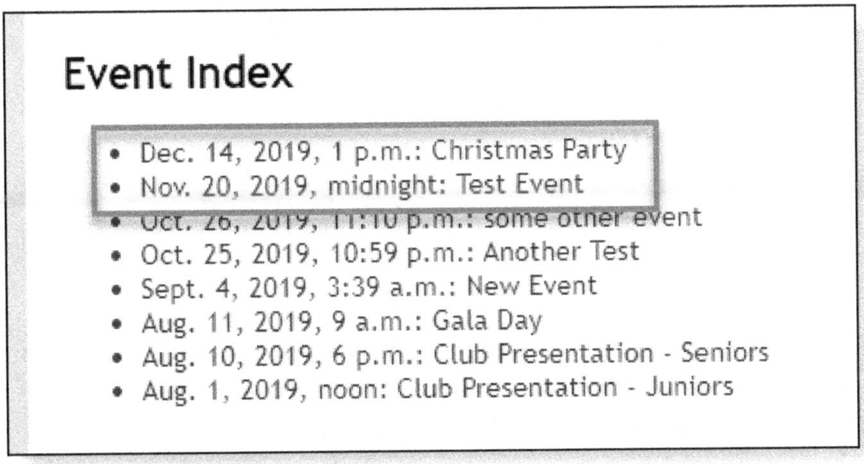

Event Index

- Dec. 14, 2019, 1 p.m.: Christmas Party
- Nov. 20, 2019, midnight: Test Event
- Oct. 26, 2019, 11:10 p.m.: some other event
- Oct. 25, 2019, 10:59 p.m.: Another Test
- Sept. 4, 2019, 3:39 a.m.: New Event
- Aug. 11, 2019, 9 a.m.: Gala Day
- Aug. 10, 2019, 6 p.m.: Club Presentation - Seniors
- Aug. 1, 2019, noon: Club Presentation - Juniors

Figure 13-16. *Setting the* `allow_future` *attribute to* `True` *allows future-dated records to show in the index.*

The Date Archive Views

The date archive views—`YearArchiveView`, `MonthArchiveView`, `WeekArchiveView`, `DayArchiveView` and `TodayArchiveView`—provide generic views for showing database objects filtered by year, month, week, day and today respectively.

The implementation for each view is identical, so I will not give you examples for all of them, just an example of the `MonthArchiveView` class we pulled apart earlier in the chapter.

As with all class-based generic views, we need a custom class, a template, and a URLconf. Starting with the custom class (changes in bold):

```
# myclub_root\events\views\demo_views.py

# Add the import to the top of your file
from django.views.generic.dates import ArchiveIndexView, MonthArchiveView

# ...

1  class MonthArchiveViewDemo(MonthArchiveView):
2      queryset = Event.events.all()
3      date_field="event_date"
4      context_object_name = 'event_list'
5      allow_future = True
6      month_format = '%m'
```

Two points to note:

- **Line 2**. We're setting the QuerySet for the class to contain all event records from the database. Remember, we renamed the model manager in Chapter 9, so it's `Event.events.all()`, not `Event.objects.all()`.
- **Line 6**. Set the month format to a zero-padded integer for parsing the month from the URL. Default is `%b` (e.g., `'Jan'`). `month_format` uses Python strftime format[6].

6 https://docs.python.org/3/library/datetime.html#strftime-and-strptime-format-codes

Now, let's create the template. The template name suffix for `MonthArchiveView` is "`_archive_month`" (new file):

```
# \events\templates\events\event_archive_month.html

{% extends "base.html" %}

{% block title %}MonthArchiveView Demo{% endblock title %}

{% block content %}
  <h1>Events in {{ month|date:"F Y" }}</h1>
<ul>
  {% for event in event_list %}
    <li>{{ event.event_date|date:"F j, Y" }}: {{ event.name }}</li>
  {% endfor %}
</ul>

<p>
  {% if previous_month %}
    <a href="/{{ previous_month|date:"Y/m/" }}">Previous Month</a>
       
  {% endif %}
  {% if next_month %}
    <a href="/{{ next_month|date:"Y/m/" }}">Next Month</a>
  {% endif %}
</p>

{% endblock content %}
```

The first half of this template is no different than what we've created before—I'm listing all of the events for the month, and applying date formatting filters to the dates passed to the class.

What's new is the second half of the template. If there are records in the database for the previous and/or next month to the month being filtered, Django will set the `previous_month` and/or `next_month` attributes.

Line 14 and **line 18** check for these variables. If they exist, the template shows hyperlinks to the previous and next month's records. In **line 15** and **line 19**, I am using Django's template filters to build a URL in `/Y/m` format.

Now, all we need is a URLconf (changes in bold):

```
# myclub_root\events\urls.py

# Add the import to the top of your file
from .views import ArchiveIndexViewDemo, MonthArchiveViewDemo

urlpatterns = [
    # ...
    path('<int:year>/<int:month>/', MonthArchiveViewDemo.as_view(),
name='event-montharchive'),
    # ...
```

I've created a capturing group that parses the year and month from the URL. For example, if the URL is `/2020/05`, then `year=2020` and `month=05`.

Save the files and fire up the development server. You must use a URL that is valid for a date in your database. I am working on this example in May 2020, so I will use May 2020 as a start and navigate to `http://127.0.0.1:8000/2020/05/`. Your dates and records will be different, but your browser should look like Figure 13-17.

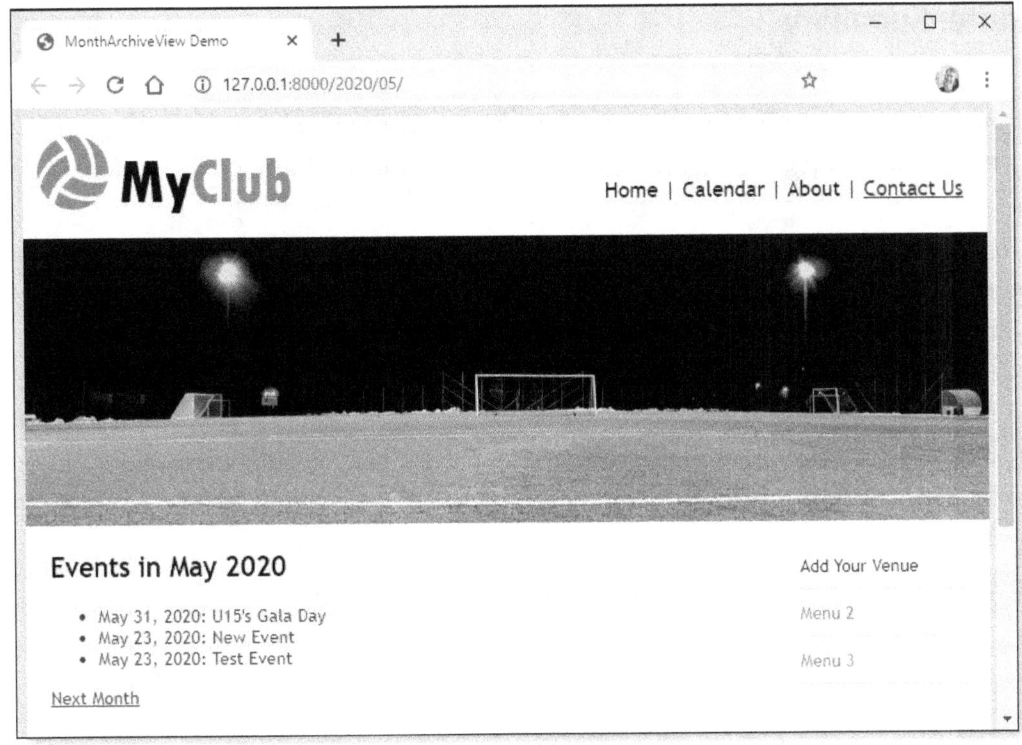

Figure 13-17. Using `MonthArchiveView` *to filter records by month.*

DateDetailView

`DateDetailView` is identical to `DetailView` in operation (See page 411). The difference between the two views is `DateDetailView` adds date-aware URL handling, e.g., `/2020/05/17/<id>`.

Chapter Summary

In this chapter, I pulled apart Django's class-based views and showed you that, while they may seem complex, they're constructed from simple building blocks.

I also showed you how these simple building blocks are put together to create powerful generic views. With these generic views we can automate the grunt work of building views that display list/detail data, edit and update forms, and date filtered data.

I finished the chapter with working examples of the most common class-based generic views built into Django.

In the next chapter, we will dig into advanced user management.

14

Advanced User Management

In this chapter, we will dig deeper into user management in Django. We'll start by exploring the `User` model class and creating users in code.

I'll then show you how to extend the `User` model and design a custom `User` model from scratch to do cool things like using an email address instead of a username to log in to Django.

Finally, I will close the chapter with techniques and code for managing users in the front end, hiding content, and restricting access to add and edit forms for your models' views.

Before We Start—Revert to Default Admin

We will be working with the admin in the next few chapters, so to avoid confusion, we will set the site back to using the default admin configuration, with custom header and titles.

First step is the easiest—delete or rename the site-level `admin.py` file (`myclub_root\myclub_site\admin.py`). If you have downloaded the source, you will see that I have renamed this file to `admin_deleted.py`.

Next is to make a few modifications to your site `urls.py` file (changes in bold):

```
# myclub_root\myclub_site\urls.py

1  from django.contrib import admin
2  from django.urls import include, path
3  from django.contrib.auth import views as auth_views
4  from . import contact
5  # from events.admin import admin_site
6  from django.views.generic.base import RedirectView
7  from events.views import TemplateViewDemo
8
9  admin.site.site_header = 'MyClub Administration'
10 admin.site.site_title = 'MyClub Site Admin'
11 admin.site.index_title = 'MyClub Site Admin Home'
12
13 urlpatterns = [
14     path('home/', RedirectView.as_view(url='/', permanent=True)),
15     path('cbvdemo/', TemplateViewDemo.as_view()),
16     path('admin/', admin.site.urls),
17     # path('eventsadmin/', admin_site.urls),
18     # ...
```

The changes here are straightforward—I've commented out the custom event admin class (**lines 5 and 17**), and added the site header and site and index titles (**lines 9 to 11**).

Now, we need to disable the custom admin in your settings file (changes in bold):

```
# myclub_root\myclub_site\settings.py

# ...

INSTALLED_APPS = [
    'ckeditor',
    'events.apps.EventsConfig',
    'django.contrib.admin',
    # 'myclub_site.apps.MyClubAdminConfig',
    # ...
```

A simple change—comment or delete the setting for `MyClubAdminConfig` and replace it with the default `django.contrib.admin`.

Finally, remove the custom events admin from the events app's `admin.py` file (changes in bold):

```
# myclub_root\events\admin.py

# ...

# class EventsAdmin(AdminSite):
#     site_header = 'MyClub Events Administration'
#     site_title = 'MyClub Events Admin'
#     index_title = 'MyClub Events Admin Home'

# admin_site = EventsAdmin(name='eventsadmin')

# ...

# @admin.register(Venue, site=admin_site)
@admin.register(Venue)
class VenueAdmin(admin.ModelAdmin):
    # ...

# ...

# @admin.register(Event, site=admin_site)
@admin.register(Event)
class EventAdmin(admin.ModelAdmin):
    # ...

# ...

# admin_site.register(Venue, VenueAdmin)
# admin.site.register(MyClubUser)
# admin_site.register(Event, EventAdmin)
# admin_site.register(User)
# admin_site.register(Group)
```

The changes should be easy to follow: I've commented out the custom admin class at the top of the file and all the admin registrations at the bottom of the file, and I have registered the `Event` and `Venue` models with the default admin. I've left the custom admin decorators in the file for your reference, but it's safe to delete them.

Once you have made the changes and saved the files, your admin should look like Figure 14-1. If you have difficulty making the correct changes or something is not working, you can compare your code to the source code[1].

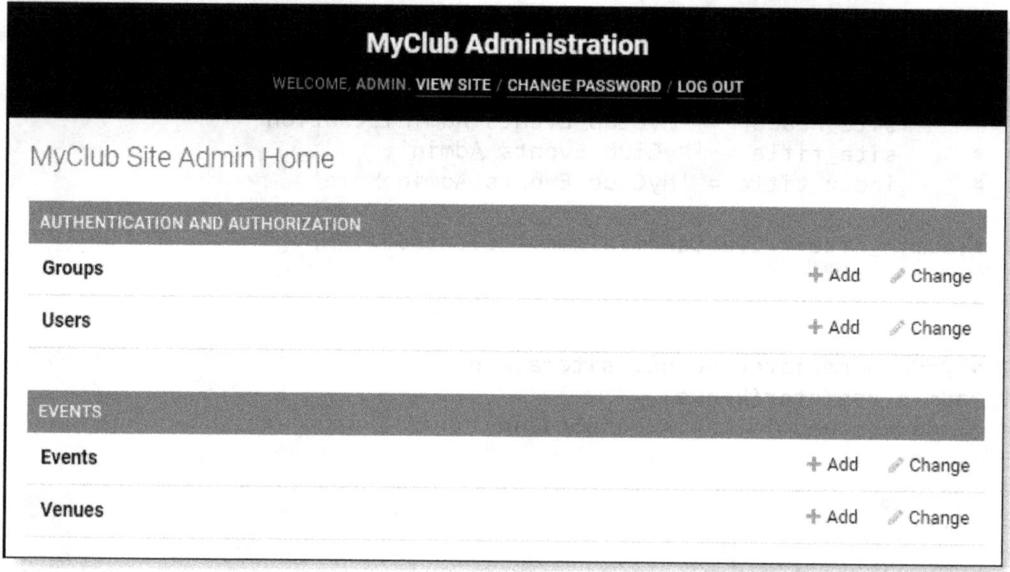

Figure 14-1. *The Django admin returned to the default configuration (with custom titles).*

The User Model Class

The `User` model class is core to Django's authentication system. The `User` model's fields, attributes and methods are in Table 14-1.

1 https://djangobook.com/mastering-django-source/

Name	Type	Description
`username`	Field	Unique alphanumeric username. Can also contain `_`, `@`, `+` and `.` . Maximum length is 150 characters
`first_name`	Field	Optional first name field
`last_name`	Field	Optional last name field
`email`	Field	Optional email address
`password`	Field	Required. Stored as a hash as Django doesn't store the raw password
`groups`	Field	Groups user is a member of
`user_permissions`	Field	Permissions granted to user
`is_staff`	Field	Boolean. `True` if user is a staff member
`is_active`	Field	Boolean. `True` if user is active
`is_superuser`	Field	Boolean. `True` if user is a superuser
`last_login`	Field	Date of last login
`date_joined`	Field	Date user was added to the database
`is_authenticated`	Attribute	Always `True` for current logged in user
`is_anonymous`	Attribute	Always `False`. Use `is_authenticated` instead
`get_username()`	Model Method	Returns the username for the user
`get_full_name()`	Model Method	Returns `first_name` and `last_name` separated by a space
`get_short_name()`	Model Method	Returns `first_name`
`set_password()`	Model Method	Set the user password

Name	Type	Description
check_password()	Model Method	Returns True if raw string matches the saved hash for the user
set_unusable_password()	Model Method	Marks the user as having no password set. Used for external authentication
has_usable_password()	Model Method	Normally True unless set_unusable_password() has been called
get_group_permissions()	Model Method	Returns a set of group permissions for the user
get_all_permissions()	Model Method	Returns all permissions for the user
has_perm()	Model Method	Checks if the user has a permission
has_perms()	Model Method	Checks if the user has the listed permissions
has_module_perms()	Model Method	Checks if the user has any permissions in the current package
email_user()	Model Method	Sends an email to the user
create_user()	Manager Method	Creates a regular user
create_superuser()	Manager Method	Creates a superuser
with_perm()	Manager Method	Returns all users with the given permission (Django 3 only)

Table 14-1. User *model class fields, attributes and methods.*

Creating Users

There are three ways to create a user in Django:

1. Create a user in the admin.
2. Let users sign up in the front end; and
3. Add a user in program code.

The first option we covered in Chapter 7 and the second option we'll look at shortly. So, let's start with the third option: creating a user in program code.

To create a user in code, you use the `create_user()` manager method:

```
>>> from django.contrib.auth.models import User
>>> user = User.objects.create_user('dennism', 'dennis@example.
com','den123')
```

When you create a user in code, you can supply a username, email address and password as positional arguments. Only a username is required.

Once the user is created, you can access the fields of the user instance. For example:

```
>>> user
<User: dennism>
>>> user.username
'dennis'
>>> user.email
'dennis@example.com'
>>> user.is_superuser
False
>>> user.is_active
True
>>> user.is_staff
False
>>> user.date_joined
datetime.datetime(2020, 5, 29, 5, 1, 11, 241616, tzinfo=<UTC>)
```

You can assign field values:

```
>>> user.last_name = 'mathis'
>>> user.first_name = 'dennis'
```

This will only change the field values in the current instance. To save the user, you must call the `save()` method:

```
>>> user.save()
```

Passwords are saved as a hash:

```
>>> user.password
# Outputs the password hash
```

To change a password in code, use the `set_password()` method:

```
>>> user.set_password('den456')
>>> user.password
# Outputs a hash for the new password
>>>
```

User model methods are also easy to use in code:

```
>>>user.get_full_name()
'dennis mathis'
>>>user.get_short_name()
'dennis'
```

Adding a permission is more complex than changing user object fields because Django's permissions are instances of the `Permission` class. When a user is first created, they have no permissions set:

```
>>> user.get_all_permissions()
set()
```

To create an instance of the `Permission` class, you must obtain the content-type of the Django model and the name of the permission you wish to add. For example:

```
>>> from django.contrib.auth.models import Permission
>>> from django.contrib.contenttypes.models import ContentType
>>> from events.models import Event
>>> content_type = ContentType.objects.get_for_model(Event)
```

In this first bit of code, we've retrieved the content-type for the `Event` model. Now, we need to add the permission to the current user instance:

```
>>> perm = Permission.objects.get(content_type=content_type,
codename='add_event')
>>> user.user_permissions.add(perm)
```

Once the permission has been added, you can see the permissions set now contains the `add_event` permission:

```
# You must retrieve a new instance of the user to see the updated
permissions
>>> user = User.objects.get(username='dennism')
>>> user.get_all_permissions()
{'events.add_event'}
>>>
```

Extending the User Model

There are two methods for extending the `User` model in Django:

1. Create a proxy model based on `User`; or
2. Use a `OneToOneField` to link to a model containing additional fields.

Option 1 is useful if you only want to add behaviors to the `User` model. As we usually extend the `User` model to add extra information to a user record, proxy models for `User` are not as useful, and won't be covered here. If you want more information on creating proxy models for `User`, see the Django documentation[2].

We will make some significant changes to the `MyClubUser` model in this chapter, so before we start, we will empty the `MyClubUser` table. If you tried out the abstract base classes in Chapter 9, you will also need to empty the `Subscriber` database table. This ensures that Django doesn't complain about data integrity when we change the table fields and relationships.

To delete all records in the tables, open the Django interactive shell and execute the following code:

```
>>> from events.models import MyClubUser
>>> MyClubUser.objects.all().delete()
(13, {'events.Event_attendees': 3, 'events.MyClubUser': 10})

# If you created the Subscriber model in Chapter 9, execute:

>>> from events.models import Subscriber
>>> Subscriber.objects.all().delete()
(1, {'events.Subscriber': 1})
>>>
```

Now the tables are empty, it's time to extend the `User` model. There are two common use-cases we will explore:

1. Extending the existing `User` model; and
2. Creating a new model that extends the `User` model.

In the first use-case, fields are added to the existing `User` model in the database. In the second use-case, a new model is added to the admin that extends the `User` model.

2 https://docs.djangoproject.com/en/dev/topics/db/models/#proxy-models

To demonstrate each of these use-cases, we will modify the `MyClubUser` model class we created in Chapter 4, and add a `Subscriber` class.

NOTE: If you played with the abstract base classes in Chapter 9, you need to be careful any code you left in your `models.py` file is commented out. If you are unsure, compare your code with the source code[3].

Here are the updates for your `models.py` file (changes in bold):

```
# myclub_root\events\models.py

class MyClubUser(models.Model):
    # first_name = models.CharField(max_length=30)
    # last_name = models.CharField(max_length=30)
    # email = models.EmailField('User Email')
    user = models.OneToOneField(User, blank=True, null=True, on_delete=models.SET_NULL)
    address = models.CharField(blank=True, max_length=100)
    phone = models.CharField(blank=True, max_length=30)
    volunteer = models.BooleanField(default=False)

    def __str__(self):
        # return self.first_name + " " + self.last_name
        return ''


MEMBER_CHOICES = [
    ('A', 'Adult'),
    ('J', 'Junior'),
    ('C', 'Concession'),
]


class Subscriber(models.Model):
    user = models.OneToOneField(User, blank=True, null=True, on_delete=models.SET_NULL)
    member_level = models.CharField(max_length=1, choices=MEMBER_CHOICES, default='A')
```

3 https://djangobook.com/mastering-django-source/

Let's have a closer look at the changes:

- **Lines 2 to 4.** I've commented out the name and email fields from the model, as they're already in the `User` model. You could also delete these lines as we won't be using them again.
- **Line 5.** This is the `OneToOneField` that connects `MyClubUser` to the `User` model.
- **Lines 6 to 8.** I have added address and phone information to the model, and a boolean field to indicate if the user is a club volunteer.
- **Line 10.** We will be inlining the `MyClubUser` class in the admin, so setting the `__str__()` function to an empty string will stop the object title from showing in the admin form. Make sure **line 11** is commented out or removed—leaving it in will throw an error as the class no longer defines first or last name fields.
- **Lines 15 to 19.** Provide a list of choices to add to the `choices` field I've added to the `Subscriber` class.
- **Line 22.** Is the class declaration for our new `Subscriber` class.
- **Line 23.** This is the `OneToOneField` that connects `Subscriber` to the `User` model.
- **Line 24.** I've added `member_level`, a `CharField` that will show a list of choices in admin forms and model forms in the front end. The list of choices are provided by the `MEMBER_CHOICES` list.

At first glance, `OneToOneField` doesn't look a whole lot different than `ForeignKey`. However, there is one major difference: the reverse relationship of a `OneToOneField` can only return a single object. This makes sense when you think about it. For example, the `manager` field in the `Event` class is a `ForeignKey` field as a single user can manage multiple events.

As the `user` field in the `MyClubUser` class is a `OneToOneField`, each user can only have one set of address and phone information. If you try to return more than one record, you get an error.

Once you have updated and saved the new classes, you need to update the database. Run the following commands from inside your virtual environment:

```
(env_myclub) ...\myclub_root> python manage.py makemigrations
(env_myclub) ...\myclub_root> python manage.py migrate
```

Once the migrations have been applied, it's time to update the `admin.py` file to show the new classes in the admin (changes in bold):

```
# myclub_root\events\admin.py

# Add these imports to the top of the file:
from django.contrib.auth.admin import UserAdmin
from .models import Venue, MyClubUser, Event, Subscriber

# ...

1  class MyClubUserInline(admin.StackedInline):
2      model = MyClubUser
3      can_delete = False
4      verbose_name = "Address and Phone"
5      verbose_name_plural = "Additional Info"
6
7
8  class MyClubUserAdmin(UserAdmin):
9      inlines = (MyClubUserInline,)
10
11
12 @admin.register(Subscriber)
13 class SubscriberAdmin(admin.ModelAdmin):
14     list_display = ('user', 'member_level')
15     list_filter = ('member_level',)
16
17
18 admin.site.unregister(User)
19 admin.site.register(User, MyClubUserAdmin)
```

We've covered most of this, so you should be able to follow the code changes; however, there are two lines we haven't covered before. The `can_delete` attribute (**line 3**) prevents a staff member from deleting the inline object. As we have a one-to-one relationship between the `User` model and `MyClubUser`, we don't want someone to delete the related record.

And in **line 18**, we're unregistering the `User` model before registering our custom `MyClubUserAdmin` model (**line 19**). The `django.contrib.admin` app automatically registers a default `User` model with the admin, so we have to unregister it before we can add our custom version.

Once you have saved the file, fire up the development server and navigate to `http://127.0.0.1:8000/admin/` and open a user record. Notice how an inline form has been added to the bottom of the user form (Figure 14-2).

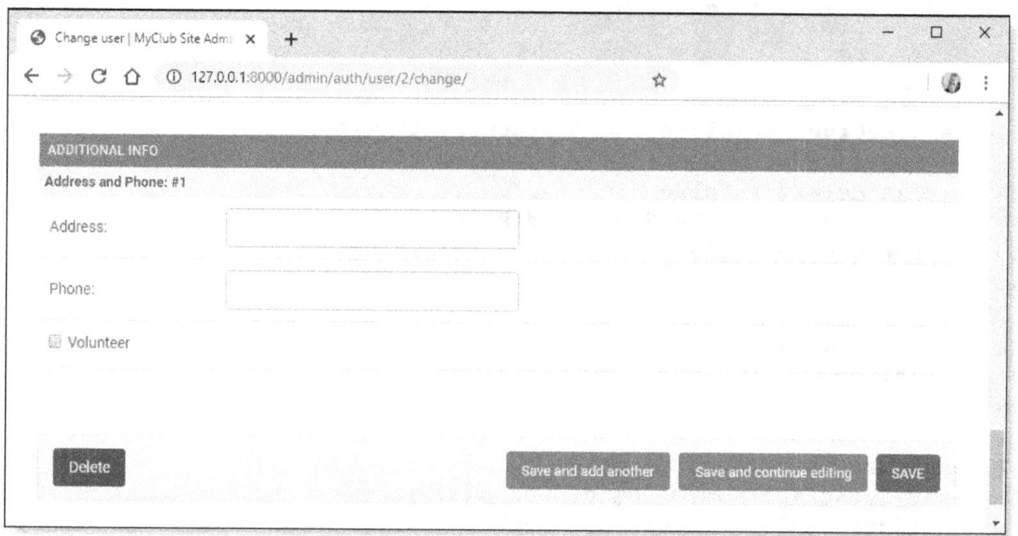

***Figure 14-2.** Additional user information has been added to the user form by creating a custom inline class that extends the* `User` *model.*

Navigating back to the admin homepage, you will also see that a **Subscribers** entry has been added to the **Events** group. Click on "Add", and you can add a new subscriber (Figure 14-3).

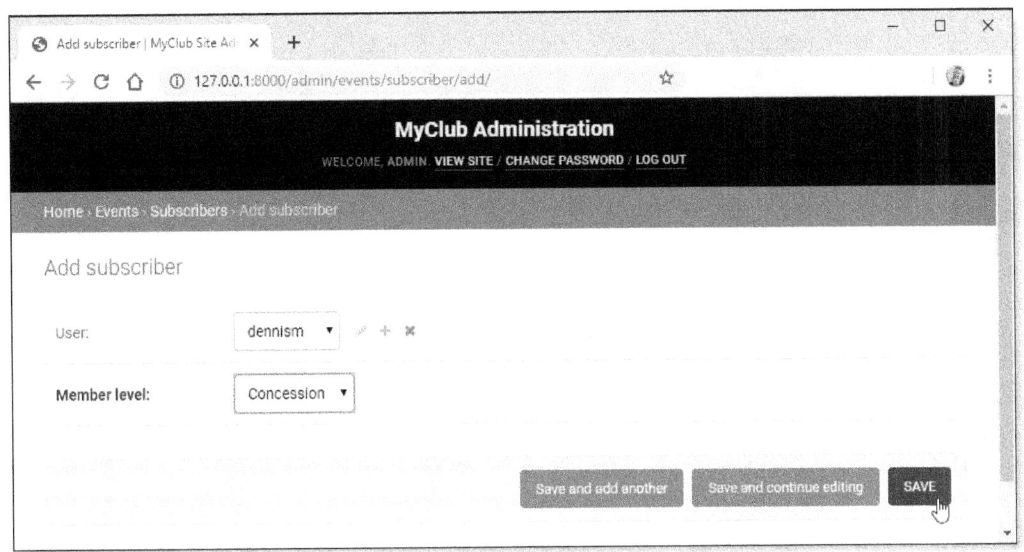

Figure 14-3. *The* `Subscriber` *model extends the* `User` *model by adding the* `member_level` *field.*

And finally, on the subscriber list page, you can see how the `list_display` and `list_filter` settings have laid out the page with columns for username and membership level and added a filter on the right so users can be filtered by their membership type (Figure 14-4).

We've only created simple models to extend the `User` model in these examples. This is to allow you to see how they're constructed without confusing you with complex models. When you build your own custom models to extend the `User` model, you repeat this same simple process to add extra fields to the model.

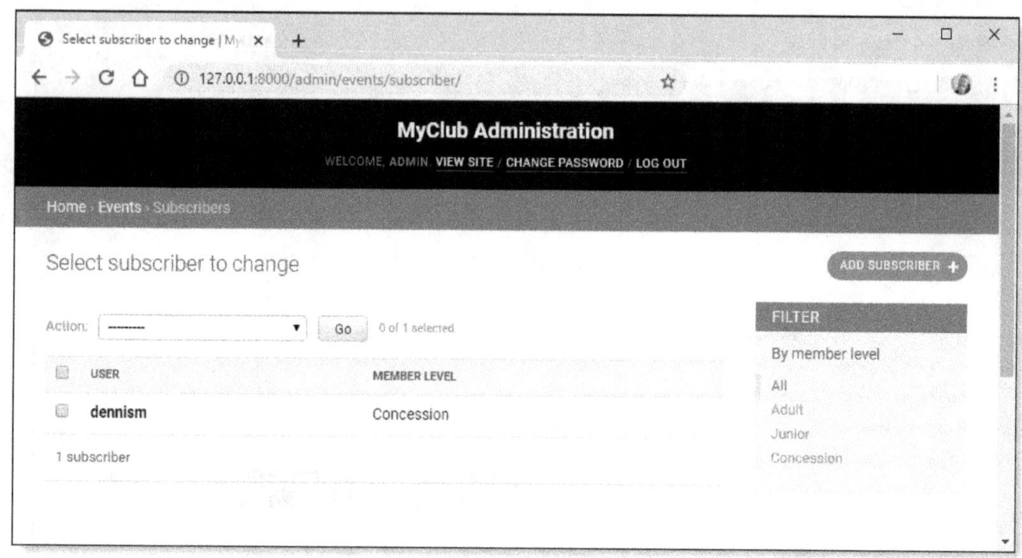

Figure 14-4. *Custom configuration options format the subscriber list page in the admin.*

Creating a Custom User Model

It's also possible to create a custom `User` model in Django. Custom `User` models are useful when you want to add fields or methods to the `User` model, or for changing the way users are authenticated (e.g., logging in with an email address instead of a username).

There are two caveats to creating a custom `User` model:

1. Don't create a custom `User` model for reusable apps. You can't have more than one custom `User` model in a project; and
2. The custom `User` model should only be created when starting a project.

Note the "should" in caveat 2. It is possible to change to a custom `User` model after a project has been created, but unless you have no other choice, it's not worth the trouble. To make the change, you have to manually fix your database schema and make database changes that require an in-depth understanding of Django's ORM.

If you do find yourself in the situation where you must consider adding a custom `User` model to an existing project, there is more information in the Django documentation[4].

As we have been working with a project that didn't have a custom `User` model defined from the start, we will create a new example project for this section of the chapter. Starting from the `\myclub_project` folder, create a new project called `cust_user_demo` and add an app called `users`. To refresh your memory, here are the commands to complete these tasks:

```
(env_myclub) ...\myclub_project> django-admin startproject cust_user_
demo
(env_myclub) ...\myclub_project> cd cust_user_demo
(env_myclub) ...\myclub_project\cust_user_demo> python manage.py
startapp users
```

Make Sure You're Running the Correct App!

In the following examples, we're running the new custom user app, not the MyClub app, so make sure you change the correct files!

Next, we need to add the `users` app to the project settings (changes in bold):

```
# cust_user_demo\cust_user_demo\settings.py

AUTH_USER_MODEL = 'users.User'

INSTALLED_APPS = [
    'users.apps.UsersConfig',
    'django.contrib.admin',
    # ...
]
```

4 https://code.djangoproject.com/ticket/25313

Only two changes here: we've added the `users` app to `INSTALLED_APPS`, and we've told Django to use a custom `User` model by assigning a value to the `AUTH_USER_MODEL` setting.

Now, we need to create the custom `User` model. Open up your `models.py` file and add a new class to the empty file:

```
# cust_user_demo\users\models.py

from django.db import models
from django.contrib.auth.models import AbstractUser

class User(AbstractUser):
    pass
```

When creating a custom `User` model, you can inherit from either `AbstractUser` or `AbstractBaseUser`. `AbstractUser` subclasses `AbstractBaseUser`, adding the default user fields and some additional methods. In practical terms, this means that:

- If you inherit from `AbstractBaseUser` you must add all the fields to the `User` model.
- If you inherit from `AbstractUser`, Django adds the default user fields for you (`username`, `email`, `is_staff`, etc.).

If you use `AbstractBaseUser`, you also lose the `get_full_name()`, `get_short_name()` and `email_user()` methods, so if you want any of these methods in your custom `User` model, you will need to write your own.

Since it makes the custom `User` model easier to implement, I have used `AbstractUser` in this example.

The custom `User` model doesn't do anything right now, but this is OK. This basic implementation has the advantage of giving you the flexibility to add to the `User` model later, without adding a lot of programming overhead.

Now the custom User model has been created, it's time to set up the database. First, check that you've entered everything correctly with the check command:

```
(env_myclub) ...\cust_user_demo> python manage.py check
System check identified no issues (0 silenced).
```

If there are issues, the check command will output detailed trace information for you to track down what's causing problems.

If you get no issues, you can run the migrations:

```
(env_myclub) ...\cust_user_demo> python manage.py makemigrations
Migrations for 'users':
users\migrations\0001_initial.py
    - Create model User
(env_myclub) ...\cust_user_demo> python manage.py migrate
Operations to perform:
Running migrations:
# Lots of migrations...
Applying sessions.0001_initial... OK
```

Once the database has been created, we need to add a superuser account:

```
(env_myclub) ...\cust_user_demo> python manage.py createsuperuser
Username: admin
Email address: admin@example.com
Password:
Password (again):
Superuser created successfully.
```

And add the custom User model to the admin:

```
# cust_user_demo\users\admin.py

from django.contrib import admin
from django.contrib.auth.admin import UserAdmin
from .models import User

admin.site.register(User, UserAdmin)
```

Save the file, run the development server and navigate to `http://127.0.0.1:8000/admin/` in your browser. Once you log in, you will see that the admin homepage has changed: the custom `User` model is listed in its own group instead of under the **Authentication and Authorization** group (Figure 14-5).

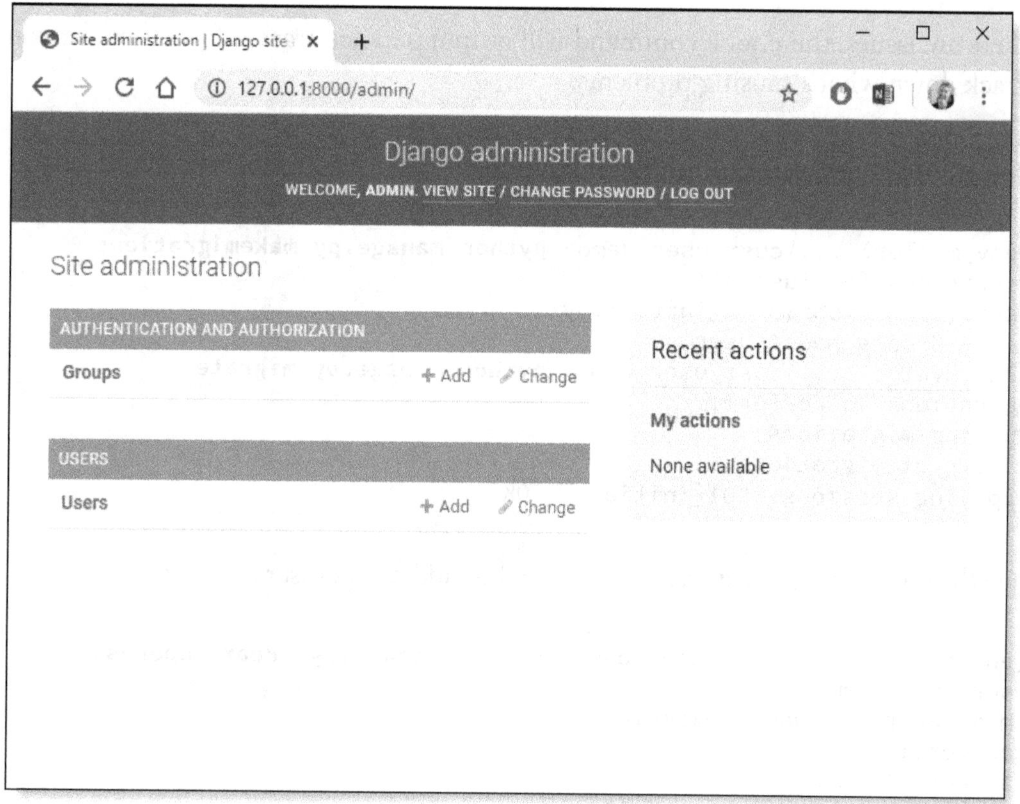

Figure 14-5. *The custom* `User` *model is added to its own group on the admin homepage.*

Other than the slightly different view on the homepage, the custom `User` model behaves like the default `User` model.

Given the simple implementation, Django's developers recommend you start all new projects with a custom `User` model, so if you ever need to extend or change the authentication system, you have the flexibility to do so.

While I agree with the reasoning, it's easy to extend the default `User` model as we have seen in previous examples. I believe there is another, stronger reason for implementing a custom `User` model from the beginning: when you want to use an email instead of a username for logging in.

Login With an Email Address

Using an email address and password to log in to a website is a common programming task. To use an email instead of a username to log in to Django, you *must* create a custom `User` model.

To use an email address instead of a username to log in to a website, we have two tasks to complete:

1. Create a custom `User` model with the `email` field as the login field; and
2. Create a custom model manager that uses the `email` field instead of the `username` field when creating new users.

The new user manager class and modified custom `User` class are listed below:

```
# cust_user_demo\users\models.py

from django.db import models
from django.contrib.auth.models import AbstractUser
from django.contrib.auth.base_user import BaseUserManager


class CustUserManager(BaseUserManager):

    def _create_user(self, email, password, is_staff, is_superuser,
**extra_fields):
        if not email:
```

```
            raise ValueError('Email address is required')
        email = self.normalize_email(email)
        user = self.model(
            email=email,
            is_active=True,
            is_staff=is_staff,
            is_superuser=is_superuser,
            **extra_fields
        )
        user.set_password(password)
        user.save()
        return user

    def create_user(self, email, password, **extra_fields):
        return self._create_user(email, password, False, False, **extra_fields)

    def create_superuser(self, email, password, **extra_fields):
        return self._create_user(email, password, True, True, **extra_fields)


class User(AbstractUser):
    email = models.EmailField(max_length=254, unique=True)
    username = models.CharField(max_length=150, blank=True, unique=False)
    address = models.CharField(blank=True, max_length=100)
    phone = models.CharField(blank=True, max_length=30)
    volunteer = models.BooleanField(default=False)

    USERNAME_FIELD = 'email'
    EMAIL_FIELD = 'email'
    REQUIRED_FIELDS = []

    objects = CustUserManager()

    def __str__(self):
        return self.email
```

This is almost all new code, so I have reproduced the entire listing here.

The default `create_user()` and `create_superuser()` class methods require a username. However, when you use an email as the login, a username is not required.

To solve this problem, we need to create a custom user manager that overrides these methods. `CustUserManager()` (**lines 6 to 27**) is our custom user manager.

After importing `BaseUserManager` from `django.contrib.auth.base_user` (**line 3**), `CustUserManager()` subclasses `BaseUserManager` (**line 6**) and implements three methods:

- **Line 8.** `_create_user()` (internal method)
- **Line 23.** `create_user()`
- **Line 26.** `create_superuser()`

When creating a new user, the only difference between a regular user and a superuser is the value of the `is_staff` and `is_superuser` fields. To avoid duplicating code, I've created the internal method `_create_user()` to do the work of creating and saving the new user. `_create_user()` accepts an email address, a password, and values for `is_staff` and `is_superuser`. `**extra_fields` allows you to add additional fields to the class if you override the class later.

`create_user()` and `create_superuser()` call `_create_user()` and set the `is_staff` and `is_superuser` fields accordingly:

- **`create_user()`**: `is_staff=False`, `is_superuser=False`
- **`create_superuser()`**: `is_staff=True`, `is_superuser=True`

The new custom `User` model declaration is on **line 30**. As we will use an email address instead of a username to log in, we need to change these fields from the default (**lines 31 and 32**). `email` has `unique` set to `True` as it's now being used to log a user in and must be unique in the database. We're not using the `username` field in our custom `User` model, so I've set `unique` to `False` and `blank` to `True`.

This might seem to break the rules a bit—defining a field we will not use—but the alternative is to subclass `AbstractBaseUser` and define *all* the model fields.

Remember the Zen of Python[5]—simple is better than complex. Plus, you may decide to implement a username at a later date.

In **lines 33, 34** and **35**, I've added the same `address`, `phone` and `volunteer` fields we added in the earlier example where we extended the `User` model.

Line 37 tells Django to use the `email` field as the username field (`USERNAME_FIELD`), and **line 38** sets the `email` field as the default `MailTo:` address for the class (`EMAIL_FIELD`).

Line 39 sets `REQUIRED_FIELDS` to an empty list. `REQUIRED_FIELDS` works at the model level—it has no relationship with the required fields in the database. In the default `User` model, `username` is a required field, so we set `REQUIRED_FIELDS` to an empty list to negate this rule.

Finally, **line 41** sets `CustUserManager()` as the custom user manager for our custom `User` class.

After saving your files, migrate the changes to the database:

```
(env_myclub) ...\cust_user_demo> python manage.py makemigrations
Migrations for 'users':
# ... new migrations
(env_myclub) ...\cust_user_demo> python manage.py migrate
```

Then, run the development server and navigate to `http://127.0.0.1:8000/admin/`. You will see the login form now asks for an email address and password, rather than a username and password (Figure 14-6).

We're still missing something—if you open one of your user accounts, the extra fields (`address`, `phone` and `volunteer`) are not on the form. This is because the default admin form for the model doesn't know about our new fields.

5 https://www.python.org/dev/peps/pep-0020/

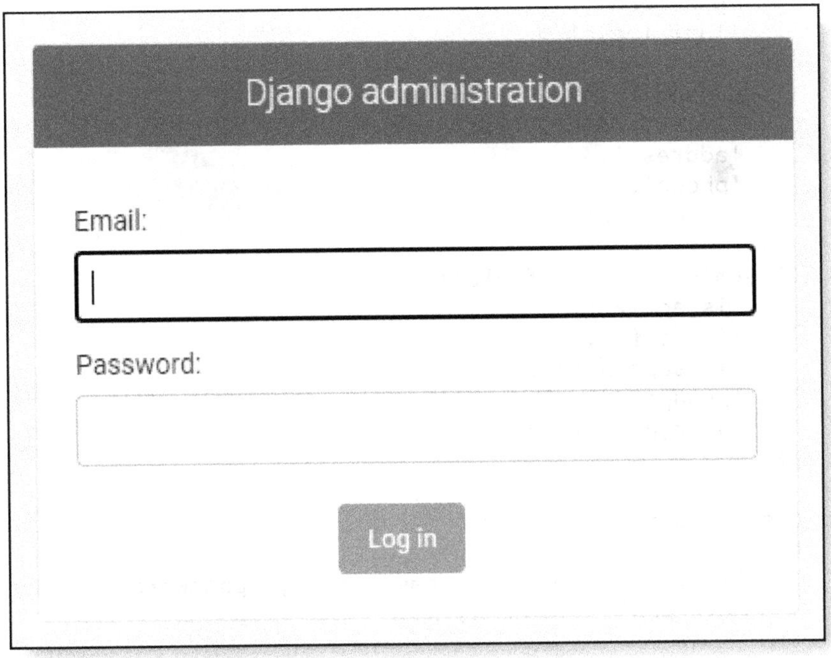

Figure 14-6. *With a custom* `User` *model, users can log in with an email address instead of the default username.*

This is an easy fix—we customize the admin form the same way we did in Chapters 7 and 12. Here's our custom admin class (new code):

```
# cust_user_demo\users\admin.py

from django.contrib import admin
from django.contrib.auth.admin import UserAdmin
from .models import User


@admin.register(User)
class CustomUserAdmin(UserAdmin):
    model = User
    fieldsets = (
        (None, {'fields': (
            'email',
```

```
12              'password',
13              'last_login'
14          )}),
15          ('Additional Info', {'fields': (
16              ('first_name', 'last_name'),
17              'address',
18              'phone',
19              'volunteer'
20          )}),
21          ('Permissions', {'fields': (
22              'is_active',
23              'is_staff',
24              'is_superuser',
25              'groups',
26              'user_permissions',
27          )}),
28      )
29      add_fieldsets = (
30          (None, {
31              'fields': ('email', 'password1', 'password2'),
32              'classes': ('wide',)
33          }),
34      )
35      list_display = ('email', 'is_staff', 'is_superuser', 'last_
login')
36      list_filter = ('is_staff', 'is_active')
37      search_fields = ('email',)
38      ordering = ('email',)
39      filter_horizontal = ('groups', 'user_permissions')
40      readonly_fields = ('last_login',)
41
42 # admin.site.register(User, UserAdmin)
```

The custom admin class is all new code, so I haven't highlighted the new code. Make sure you comment out the original model registration in **line 42**.

We covered customizing the admin in Chapter 7, but there are two sections of code I want to draw your attention to:

- **Lines 15 to 20**. I've added the three extra fields–`address`, `phone` and `volunteer`—to a group called **Additional Info**. The default `first_name` and `last_name` fields are also in this group.

- **Lines 29 to 34**. `add_fieldsets` is an attribute we've not covered before. It has the same syntax as `fieldsets`, but it's for specifying the fields and layout for the add user form. As we're using the user's email address instead of their username, the default add user form is no longer useful, so we specify a custom form with `add_fieldsets`.

Now, if you open a user record (refresh the admin), the custom form will show, complete with the three additional fields (Figure 14-7).

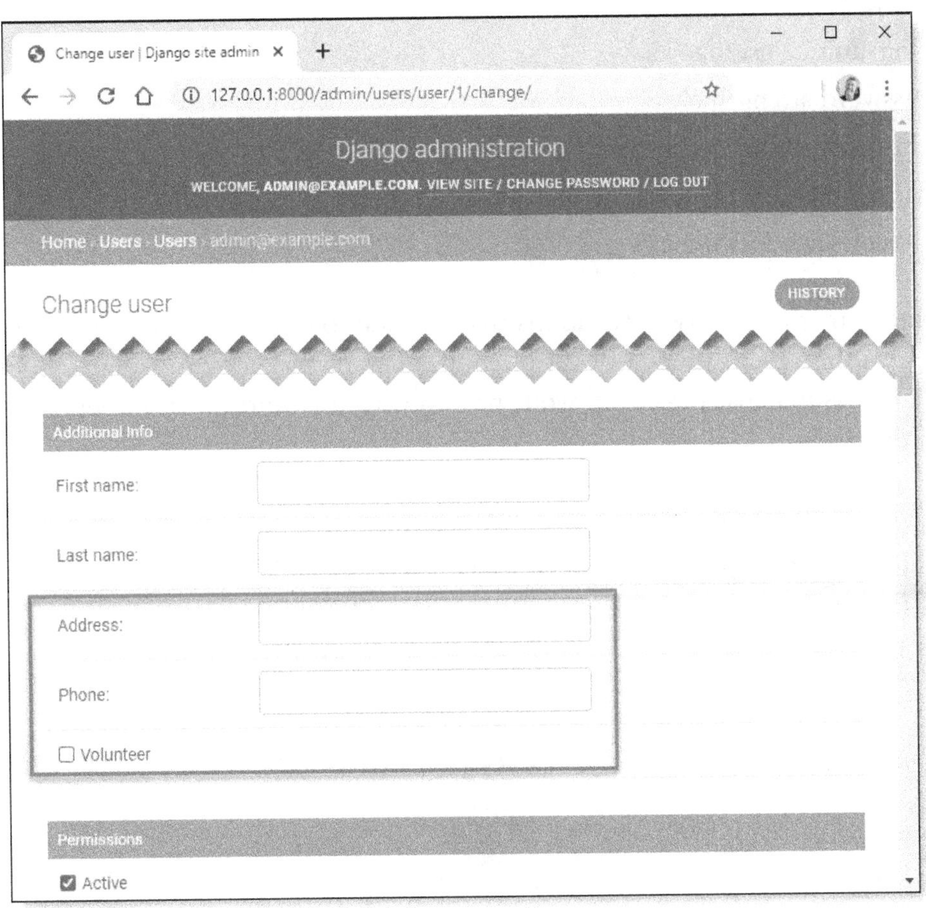

***Figure 14-7.** The custom admin form shows the default fields and the three additional fields we added to the* `User` *model.*

Custom Authentication

Due to the increasing importance of cybersecurity and the ever-changing authentication landscape, Django's authentication system is designed to be as secure as possible but remain very generic. This is so the authentication system can be extended by third-party apps that employ the latest security techniques.

For this reason, Django doesn't contain solutions for problems like:

- Non-unique usernames
- Password strength checking
- Throttling of login attempts
- Authentication against third-parties (OAuth, for example)
- Object-level permissions

There are many third-party applications that provide solutions to these problems (e.g., django-allauth[6] for OAuth and OAuth2), but as I want this book to remain about core Django as much as possible, I won't be covering any third-party authentication apps in the book.

It's difficult enough to keep up with Django's punishing release cycle, without having to keep third-party app information up to date as well. There's also a practical aspect too—if I wrote about every cool third-party app available for Django, this book would never get finished!

6 https://django-allauth.readthedocs.io/en/latest/overview.html

Users in the Front End

We're Now Back to the MyClub App

We're returning to the MyClub app for the rest of the chapter, so make sure you're back in the `myclub_root` folder!

A common and important feature of modern websites is to hide content from unregistered users. To demonstrate how to restrict content to registered users in Django, we will implement an example of restricted access—turn the right sidebar menu into a user menu that's only visible to logged in users.

The first step in the process is to create the user registration system so customers can register with the MyClub website. As managing users in the front end is such a common requirement, Django's developers have provided several handy classes and built-in forms and views to make registering and authenticating users a breeze.

To get our authentication system up and running, we need to do three things:

1. Create a customer registration view.
2. Create the authentication templates; and
3. Create new URLconfs to link to the authentication system.

Add the Registration View

Django has built-in generic authentication forms for logging users in and out and resetting or changing passwords. Each of these forms also has a built-in default view, so you don't have to create one.

The `UserCreationForm` (which is used for registering new users with a website) doesn't have a default view—we need to write one. We will create the user registration view with one of Django's generic editing views—`CreateView`. To create our new view, add the following to `myclub_views.py` (new code):

```
# myclub_root\events\views\myclub_views.py

# add the following to the imports at the top of the file
from django.views.generic.edit import CreateView
from django.contrib.auth.forms import UserCreationForm
from django.urls import reverse_lazy

# ...

1  class Register(CreateView):
2      template_name = 'registration/register.html'
3      form_class = UserCreationForm
4      success_url = reverse_lazy('register-success')
5
6      def form_valid(self, form):
7          form.save()
8          return HttpResponseRedirect(self.success_url)
```

If you remember from Chapter 13, `CreateView` is a useful class that makes creating and displaying a blank edit form easy—all you need to do is pass it a template and a form, and it will create a blank edit form on the fly.

First, we need to import `CreateView` and the `UserCreationForm` class into our `events` app's views.

Then, we create the `Register` class. Stepping through this code:

- **Line 1.** The `Register` class declaration. The `Register` class inherits from `CreateView`.
- **Line 2.** The `template_name` attribute tells `CreateView` what template to use. We will create the `register.html` template shortly.
- **Line 3.** Is the form to use with `CreateView`. In this case, we're using the `UserCreationForm` class to create the form.

- **Line 4.** `success_url` is the URL the form will redirect to once the form has been successfully processed. We're using `reverse_lazy()` to return the URL at runtime.
- **Lines 6 to 8.** Our `Register` class has a single method—`form_valid()`. This is a built-in method that will save our new user's information to the database once a valid registration form has been submitted. The `form_valid()` method then redirects to a success page URL set at runtime by reverse lookup.

Create the Templates

Our next task is to create the templates for rendering our registration and login/logout forms. There are three templates that need to be created:

1. **`login.html`**. A template to display the login form.
2. **`register.html`**. A template to display the user registration form; and
3. **`success.html`**. A simple template to tell the user they have successfully registered with the site.

We will also modify `base.html` to show user information at the top of the page.

Before creating the templates, create a new folder called "registration" in your site templates folder.

The Login Template

```
# \myclub_site\templates\registration\login.html

{% extends "base.html" %}

{% block title %}MyClub User Login{% endblock title %}


{% block content %}
<h1>Please Login</h1>
<p>You must be logged in to access the user menu.</p>

```

```
10 <form method="post" action="{% url 'login' %}">
11 <table>
12     {{ form.as_table }}
13     <tr>
14         <td> </td>
15         <td><input type="submit" value="login"></td>
16     </tr>
17 </table>
18 <p>Not registered yet? <a href="{% url 'register' %}">Register
here</a>.</p>
19 <input type="hidden" name="next" value="{{ next }}" />
20 {% csrf_token %}
21 </form>
22 {% endblock content %}
```

This is mostly HTML and Django template code, but there are some lines that need explanation:

- **Lines 10 and 18.** We are using Django's `{% url %}` tag. This tag performs the same function as `reverse_lazy()`; it performs a reverse lookup of the URL name and replaces it with the actual URL when Django renders the template.
- **Line 19.** We've added a hidden field to the form. When a page link is redirected (which is what happens when a user is sent to the login page), Django will save the original destination in the `next` template variable. We're adding the `next` variable, so once the form has been successfully submitted, the value of `next` is preserved, and Django knows where to redirect the user.

The Register Template

```
# \myclub_site\templates\registration\register.html

{% extends "base.html" %}

{% block title %}User Registration{% endblock title %}

{% block content %}
<h1>User Registration</h1>
<p>Enter your username and password to register.</p>

<form method="post" action="">
```

```
<table>
    {{ form.as_table }}
    <tr>
        <td> </td>
        <td><input type="submit" value="register"></td>
    </tr>
</table>
<input type="hidden" name="next" value="{{ next }}" />
{% csrf_token %}
</form>
{% endblock content %}
```

There's nothing new here, so you should find this template code easy to follow.

The Success Template

```
# \myclub_site\templates\registration\success.html

{% extends "base.html" %}

{% block title %}User Registration Success{% endblock title %}

{% block content %}
<h1>User Registration Success</h1>
<p>You have successfully registered.</p>

<p>Click <a href="{% url 'login' %}?next=/">here</a> to log in.</p>
{% endblock content %}
```

Again, nothing new—just note how we are appending `?next=/` to the URL provided by the `{% url %}` tag. It's perfectly legal to concatenate text in this way in Django template code.

Modify the Base Template

Finally, we need to make some changes to `base.html` to display user authentication status at the top of the page (changes in bold):

```
# \myclub_site\templates\base.html

1  <div id="top_menu">
2    Home | Calendar | About |
3    <a href="/contact">Contact Us</a> |
4    {% if user.is_authenticated %}
5      Hello, {{ user.username }}.
6      <a href="{% url 'logout' %}?next=/">Log out</a>.
7    {% else %}
8      Not logged in.
9      <a href="{% url 'login' %}?next=/">Log in</a>.
10   {% endif %}
11 </div>
12 <div id="topbanner"> # ...
```

This is simple to follow—on **line 4** we have an `if` statement that will render a logged in message if the user is logged in, or a logged out message if they are not (**lines 5 and 8**). The template also provides a convenient link to login or logout from the page header.

Create URLconfs

Our last task is to add the URLconfs for our authentication views (changes in bold):

```
# myclub_root\myclub_site\urls.py

# Add the following to the imports at the top of the file
from events.views import TemplateViewDemo, Register

# ...

urlpatterns = [

    # ...

    path(
        'register/success/',
        TemplateView.as_view(template_name="registration/success.html"),
        name ='register-success',
    ),
    path('register/', Register.as_view(), name='register'),
```

```
11     path('', include('django.contrib.auth.urls')),
12 ]
```

Let's have a quick look at what's going on here:

- **Lines 5 to 9.** We are using the `TemplateView` generic class-based view (see Chapter 13) to render a simple template when a user successfully registers with our site.
- **Line 10.** Is the URLconf for our user registration form.
- **Line 11.** We are including Django's authentication URLs which provide the URL and view for our login and logout views. `auth.urls` also provides patterns for changing and resetting passwords. We won't use them here, but if you want to check them out, see the Django documentation[7].

Testing the Authentication System

We have made several changes to the front end, so now it's time to test to see if it all works. Fire up the development server and navigate to `http://127.0.0.1:8000/`. At the top of the page, you should now see the logged out message (Figure 14-8).

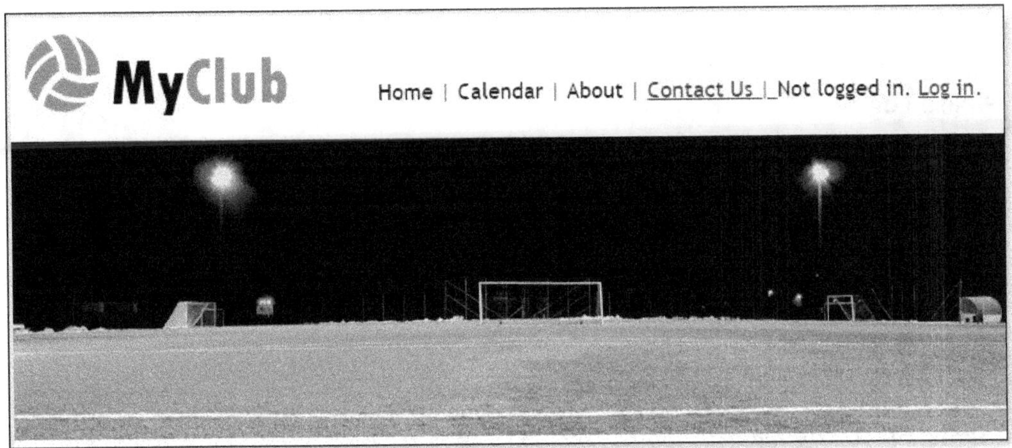

***Figure 14-8.** The top of our modified base template showing the logged out message.*

7 https://docs.djangoproject.com/en/dev/topics/auth/default/#module-django.contrib.auth.views

If you're running the development server from earlier in the chapter and are still logged in as admin, you will see a message like Figure 14-9. If you see this message, click on "Log out" to test the registration views.

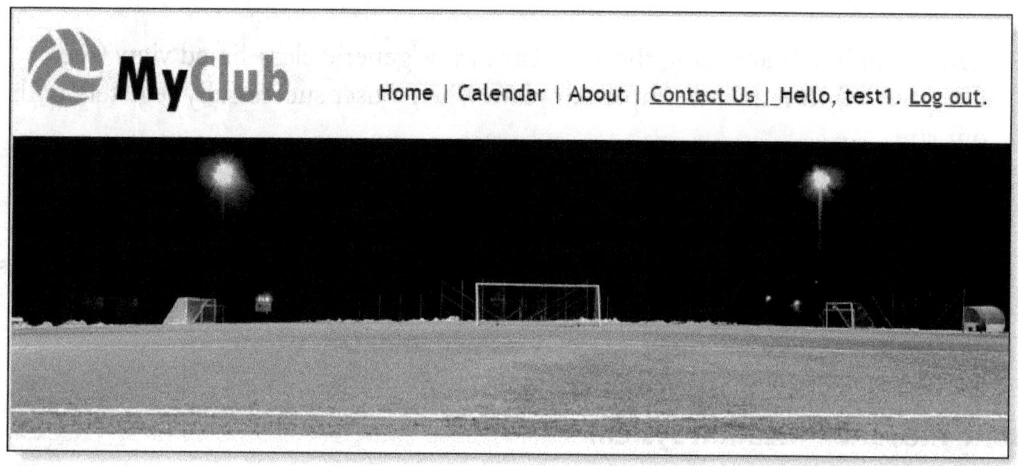

***Figure 14-9.** The top of our modified base template showing the logged in message.*

Click on the "Log in" link in the menu and the site should now redirect to the login page (Figure 14-10).

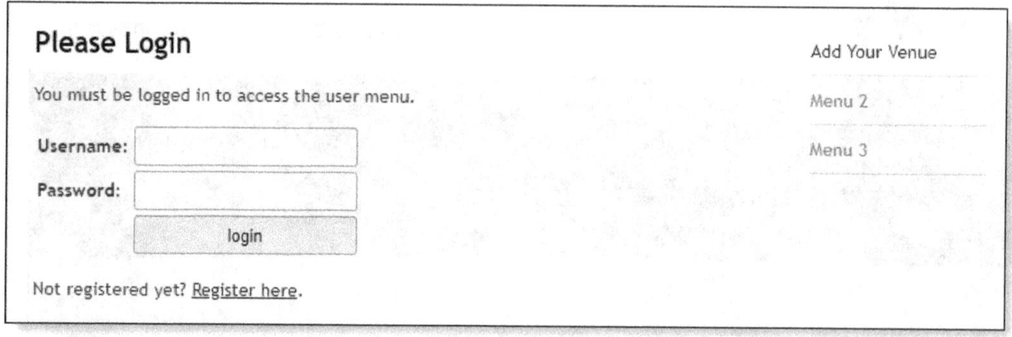

***Figure 14-10.** The login template. Note the link to the registration template at the bottom of the form.*

Finally, on the login form click the "Register here" link and you should see the user registration page (Figure 14-11).

User Registration

Enter your username and password to register.

Username:

Required. 150 characters or fewer. Letters, digits and @/./+/-/_ only.

Password:

- Your password can't be too similar to your other personal information.
- Your password must contain at least 8 characters.
- Your password can't be a commonly used password.
- Your password can't be entirely numeric.

Password confirmation:

Enter the same password as before, for verification.

register

Add Your Venue

Menu 2

Menu 3

Figure 14-11. *The user registration form and its validation logic is generated for you by Django.*

Restricting Content in the Front End

Now we've set up the front end authentication system, we can make the necessary changes to restrict access to the user menu.

The first step is to hide the menu from anonymous users. Make the following changes to your base template (changes in bold):

```
# myclub_root\myclub_site\templates\base.html

1  # ...
2  </header>
3  {% if user.is_authenticated %}
4  <aside id="rightsidebar">
5    <nav id="nav">
6    <ul>
7      <li><a href="/add_venue">Add Venue</a></li>
8      <li><a href="/events">Manage Events</a></li>
9      <li>My Profile</li>
10   </ul>
11   </nav>
12 </aside>
13 {% endif %}
14 <section id="main">
15 # ...
```

I've only reproduced a small part of the template code here. The important line is **line 3** where we're checking the `is_authenticated` attribute of the current user instance. If `is_authenticated` is `True`, the side menu will show.

I've also made some modifications to the menu items in **lines 8 and 9**.

You need not make any more changes to hide the right menu. If you open the website in your browser as an anonymous user, the menu will be hidden.

This is not a complete solution, however. Hiding the menu doesn't secure the venue and events pages—they can still be accessed by URL. For example, if you navigate to `http://127.0.0.1:8000/add_venue/`, you can still add a venue even if you're not logged in (Figure 14-12).

To secure the form, we need to secure the view. Securing a view is straightforward, but the implementation is different for function-based and class-based views. Let's start with the add venue form, which is shown by the function-based view `add_venue`.

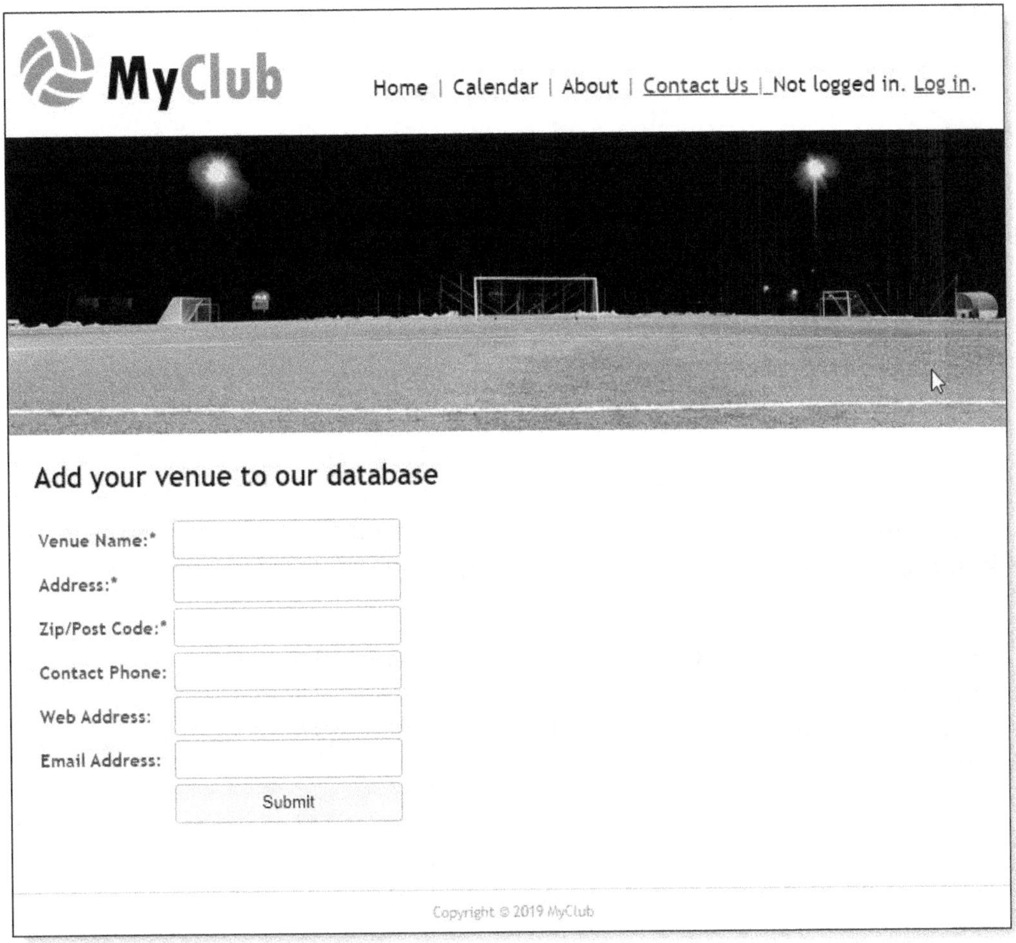

Figure 14-12. Hiding the right menu doesn't secure the venue form; to do this you must secure the view.

To modify `add_venue` we will add a *decorator*. A decorator is a special function that wraps around another function and modifies its behavior. In Python, a decorator function starts with the `@` symbol and must be on the line immediately before the function it modifies.

This concept is easier to understand in practice, so let's modify our add_venue function (changes in bold):

```
# \events\views\myclub_views.py

# Add this import to the top of your file
from django.contrib.auth.decorators import login_required

# ...
@login_required(login_url=reverse_lazy('login'))
def add_venue(request):
    # ...
```

Here we have imported the login_required function and used it to wrap (decorate) the add_venue function. Now, when add_venue is called, login_required first checks if the user is logged in and redirects to the login view if they're not.

Because a decorator is a function, we need to use reverse_lazy() to ensure Django doesn't evaluate the URL until runtime. So, when Django sees reverse_lazy('login'), it will convert it to the URL login/ at runtime and append it to the root URL (in our case http://127.0.0.1:8000/).

In case you were wondering where the login/ URL came from, when we included django.contrib.auth.urls earlier in this chapter, it included URL patterns for several built-in views, including named URLs for the login and logout views. Clever stuff. URL reversing is one of those things about Django you grow to love when you are trying to build portable and scalable applications.

We follow a similar process to secure the events views, except they're class-based views, so we need to use *mixins*. We covered mixins in Chapter 13, but to refresh your memory, a mixin is a special class that contains methods and attributes that can be "mixed in" to other classes without needing to inherit the mixin class.

Lets' make the modifications to the events classes, and then I will explain what's going on (changes in bold):

```
# myclub_root\events\views\demo_views.py

# Add this import to the top of the file
from django.contrib.auth.mixins import LoginRequiredMixin

1  class CreateViewDemo(LoginRequiredMixin, CreateView):
2
3      login_url = reverse_lazy('login')
4      model = Event
5      fields = ['name', 'event_date', 'description']
6      success_url = reverse_lazy('show-events')
7
8
9  class UpdateViewDemo(LoginRequiredMixin, UpdateView):
10
11     login_url = reverse_lazy('login')
12     model = Event
13     fields = ['name', 'event_date', 'description']
14     template_name_suffix = '_update_form'
15     success_url = reverse_lazy('show-events')
16
17
18 class DeleteViewDemo(LoginRequiredMixin, DeleteView):
19
20     login_url = reverse_lazy('login')
21     model = Event
22     context_object_name = 'event'
23     success_url = reverse_lazy('show-events')
```

After importing `LoginRequiredMixin` from `django.contrib.auth.mixins`, the changes to each event view are identical:

- **Lines 1, 9 and 18.** We've added `LoginRequiredMixin` to each event class.
- **Lines 3, 11 and 20.** We've set the `login_url` attribute to the URL of the login page. Like the function-based view, we're using `reverse_lazy()` to retrieve the login URL at runtime.

I haven't restricted access to the list view. This makes sense because anonymous users should be able to see all events, but they shouldn't be able to add, edit or delete events.

Once you save the views, you will find you can navigate to `http://127.0.0.1:8000/events/` as an anonymous user, but if you try to add, edit or delete an event, you will be redirected to the login page.

The view logic is not complete in these examples. For example, there isn't a link on the home page for anonymous users to be able to view events. They do, however, give you an idea of how to restrict content in the front end.

Permission-based Restrictions

You can also add permission-based restrictions to your views. Permission-based restrictions are implemented the same way as user-based restrictions, except you use the `@permission_required` decorator (for function-based views) and the `PermissionRequiredMixin` (for class-based views). More information on permission-based restrictions can be found in the Django documentation[8].

You can also use permissions in templates with `perms.module`, which is a proxy for `User.has_module_perms()`, and `perms.module.perm`, which is a proxy for `User.has_perm()`. For example:

```
# Example only. Don't add to your code.

{% if perms.events %}
  <li><a href="/events">Manage Events</a></li>
{% endif %}
```

In the above example, the menu item will show for all logged in users who have access to the `events` app. In the next example, the menu is visible to users with the `add_event` permission:

8 https://docs.djangoproject.com/en/dev/topics/auth/default/

```
# Example only. Don't add to your code.

{% if perms.events.add_event %}
  <li><a href="/events">Manage Events</a></li>
{% endif %}
```

To explore permission-based restrictions in templates in greater detail, see the Django documentation[9].

Chapter Summary

In this chapter, we dug deeper into user management in Django, starting with exploring the `User` model class and creating users in code.

I then showed you how to extend the user model, design a custom `User` model from scratch, and use an email address instead of a username to login to Django.

We finished with techniques and code for managing users in the front end—hiding content, and restricting access to add and edit forms for your models' views.

In the next chapter, we will explore advanced code and techniques for managing more complex forms.

9 https://docs.djangoproject.com/en/dev/topics/auth/default/#permissions

15

Advanced Forms

In this chapter, we'll dig deeper into Django's forms. We'll start by learning how to customize Django's forms with additional media (style sheets and JavaScript), creating and adding custom widgets, and adding rich-text editing capability to forms in the front end.

Later in the chapter, we'll explore Django's messages framework and how to use the framework in our forms to send messages to users, and then I'll show you how to use formsets to display tabular data in the browser.

Finally, we'll dig into Django's `formtools` app, where you'll learn how to create workflows for multi-part forms and model forms.

Customizing Forms

While the forms we have looked at so far cover most use-cases, there are still plenty of customizations you can make to your forms. Likely customizations boil down to two major types—form appearance and form function.

Form customization is application-specific, so I couldn't possibly cover all of them here, but from experience, there are three customizations you will make most often:

1. Adding media (JavaScript and CSS) to a form to change its appearance and function.
2. Replacing form field widgets with another built-in widget, or a custom widget you've created; and
3. Adding rich-text editing capability to forms in the front end.

We'll cover each of these use-cases in this section of the chapter.

Adding Media to Forms

To add media to a form, we add a `Media` inner class to the form class. For example, let's add some media to the `VenueForm` class (changes in bold):

```
# myclub_root\events\forms.py

1  class VenueForm(ModelForm):
2      required_css_class = 'required'
3      class Meta:
4          model = Venue
5          fields = '__all__'
6
7      class Media:
8          css = {
9              'all': ('form.css',)
10         }
11         js = ('mycustom.js',)
12
13     def clean(self):
14         # ...
```

The new `Media` inner class is in **lines 7 to 11**. `js` is a tuple of all JavaScript files to be loaded with the form. `css` is a dictionary of style sheets. Each dictionary key is a CSS media type so you can have multiple media declarations. For example:

```
# Example only. Don't add to your code

css = {
    'screen': ('form.css', 'pretty.css'),
    'print': ('print.css'),
}
```

For the media to be loaded with our form, we must tell Django to load the media in our templates. As media is usually loaded in the `<head></head>` section of an HTML page, we first must add a new block to `base.html` (change in bold):

```
# myclub_root\myclub_site\templates\base.html

<head>

    # ...

    {% block styles %}{% endblock styles%}
</head>
```

Once `base.html` has been edited, we can override the styles block in our add venue form (change in bold):

```
# \events\templates\events\add_venue.html

{% extends "base.html" %}

{% block title %}Add Venue{% endblock title %}
{% block styles %}{{ form.media }}{% endblock styles%}

{% block content %}

# ...

<td><input id="submit" type="submit" value="Submit"></td>
```

I've also added an id attribute to the submit button so we can style it with CSS.

Django stores the form's media declarations in the `media` attribute of the form class, which we're accessing via the `form.media` template variable. Navigate to `http://127.0.0.1:8000/add_venue/` and look at the page source. Your `head` section should look like this:

```
1 <head>
2 <meta charset="utf-8">
3 <title>Add Venue</title>
4 <link href="/static/main.css" rel="stylesheet" type="text/css">
5 <link href="/static/form.css" type="text/css" media="all"
rel="stylesheet">
6 <script type="text/javascript" src="/static/mycustom.js"></script>
7 </head>
```

You can see in **lines 5 and 6** our form media has been added to the template. Note also the media URL is relative to your `STATIC_URL` setting.

We haven't created either of these media files yet, so your venue form won't look any different.

I'm not going to create a JavaScript file for our template, but you can see from this example how easy it is to add JavaScript to a Django template.

We will, however, create a fresh look for our form by creating `form.css` (new file):

```
# myclub_root\myclub_site\static\form.css

table {
    width: 100%;
}
label {
    display: block;
    text-align: right;
    margin-right: 10px;
}
input, textarea {
    background-color: #f4f4f4;
    border-radius: 6px;
```

```
}
#submit {
    width: 200px;
    display: block;
    margin-left: auto;
    margin-right: auto;
    margin-top: 10px;
    height: 40px;
    border-radius: 20px;
    font: bold;
    color: white;
    background-color: #270c39;
}
```

Once you have saved this new style sheet, refresh your browser, and your form should have a new custom look (Figure 15-1). You might need to clear your browser cached for the new css file to load.

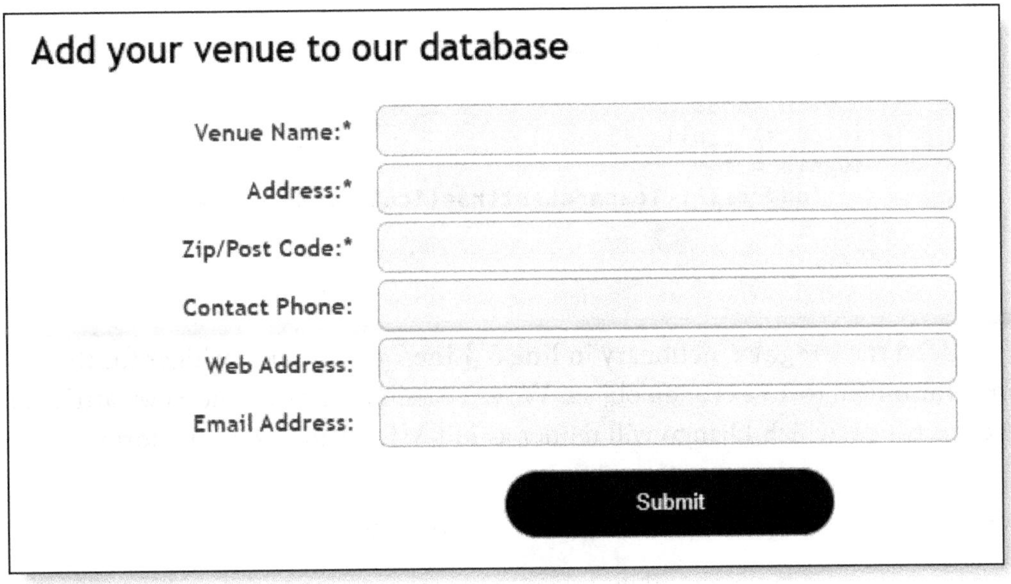

Figure 15-1. *Adding a custom look to a form with the* `Media` *inner class.*

Custom Widgets

Along with adding styles and JavaScript to forms, you can customize individual form fields by changing the default widget to a built-in widget or to a custom widget you create.

To customize widgets, you add the `widgets` attribute to your form class. `widgets` is a dictionary where the key is the form field, and the value contains information on what customizations to make to the field. For example, let's change the `address` field to a three-line textarea (changes in bold):

```
# myclub_root\events\forms.py

# add the following to the imports at the top of the file
from django.forms import ModelForm, Textarea

1 class VenueForm(ModelForm):
2     required_css_class = 'required'
3     class Meta:
4         model = Venue
5         fields = '__all__'
6         widgets = {
7             'address': Textarea(attrs={'cols': 40, 'rows': 3}),
8         }
9         # ...
```

We've added the `widgets` dictionary in **line 6. Line 7** changes the widget for the address form field to a `Textarea` object. We are passing the `cols` and `rows` attributes to the `Textarea`, which Django will render as HTML attributes on the form.

If you refresh the form, it will now look like Figure 15-2.

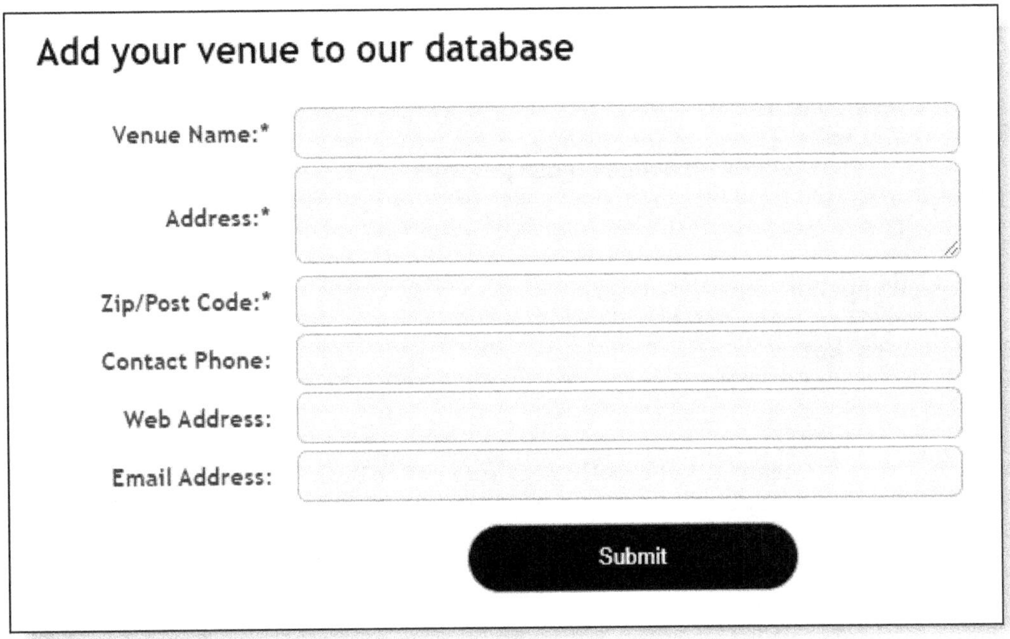

Figure 15-2. *The Address field is now represented by a three-line textarea.*

Django's form widgets are simple objects—each is associated with a small HTML template that renders as an HTML form element. For example, the `TextInput` widget renders as `<input type="text" ...>`. If you're curious and want to explore the built-in widgets, you will find them inside your virtual environment. They're buried pretty deep, so here's the full URL:

```
\Lib\site-packages\django\forms\templates\django\forms\widgets\
```

Creating a custom widget is as easy as adding custom styling and functions to an existing widget. For example, let's create a custom widget for the venue name field (changes in bold):

```
# myclub_root\events\forms.py

1  class MyFormWidget(forms.TextInput):
2      class Media:
3          css = {
4              'all': ('widget.css',)
5          }
6
7
8  class VenueForm(ModelForm):
9      required_css_class = 'required'
10     class Meta:
11         model = Venue
12         fields = '__all__'
13         widgets = {
14             'name': MyFormWidget(attrs={'class': 'mywidget'}),
15             'address': Textarea(attrs={'cols': 40, 'rows': 3}),
16         }
17         # ...
```

Let's have a look at what's going on:

- **Line 1** is our new custom widget. `MyFormWidget` inherits from `forms.TextInput`.
- **Lines 2 to 5** is the `Media` inner class for `MyFormWidget`. Like forms, you can add both CSS and JavaScript to widgets. I've kept it simple and defined a single style sheet for the custom widget.
- **Line 14**. I've added the `name` field to the widgets dictionary and assigned the `MyFormWidget` to the field. I am also adding a `class` attribute to the field so we can apply CSS styling to the field.

So something interesting shows in the browser, we also need to create `widget.css` (new file):

```
# myclub_root\myclub_site\static\widget.css

.mywidget {
    border-width: 2px;
    border-color: black;
}
```

Once you saved the files, refresh the form, and it will now look like Figure 15-3.

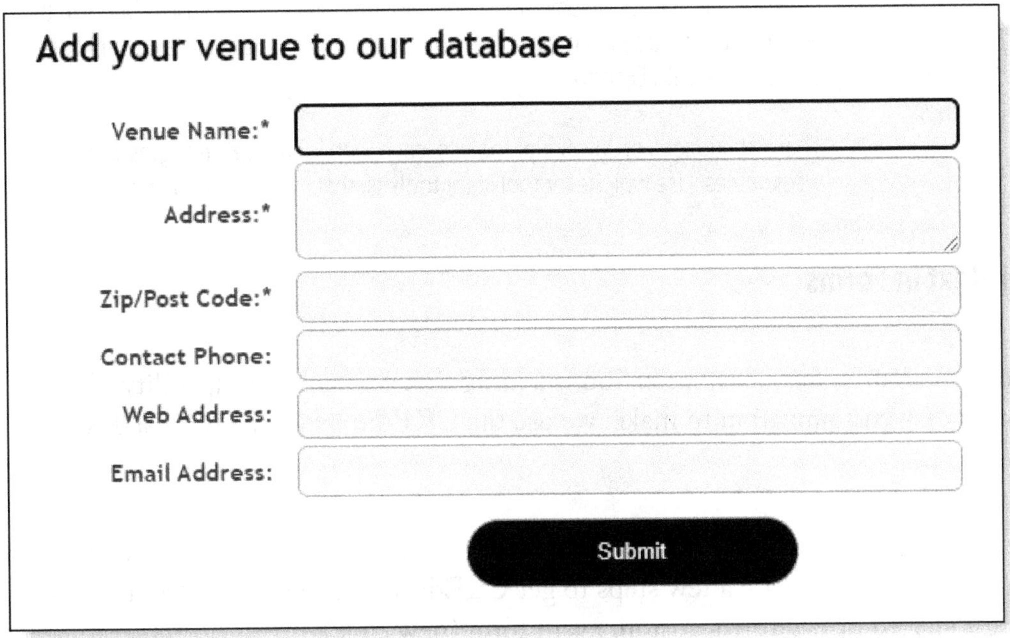

Figure 15-3. *The Venue Name field has been replaced by a custom widget.*

Okay, so a black border is not that interesting, but the principle applies to any customization you would wish to make. For example, you can add JavaScript auto-fill functions to text fields, fancy animations or conditional formatting. Another example would be adding one of the many JavaScript calendar widgets to date fields on your forms.

Which JavaScript Toolkit?

I take the same position as Django's developers: while Django uses jQuery in the admin app, that doesn't mean I recommend jQuery as the only JavaScript library you can use with Django.

There are dozens of JavaScript toolkits, each with individual strengths and weaknesses. Use whichever toolkit (or toolkits) that suit your requirements.

Rich-text in Forms

Another common form customization is adding rich-text editing capability. This is another easy customization to make: we use the CKEditor module we installed in Chapter 12.

To show you how it works, I will change the `description` field on the event forms to a rich-text field. There are a few steps to get CKEditor running in the front end, so let's get started by creating a custom event form (new code):

```
# myclub_root\events\forms.py

# add the following to the imports at the top of the file
from ckeditor.widgets import CKEditorWidget
from .models import Venue, Event

# ...

class EventForm(ModelForm):
    description = forms.CharField(widget=CKEditorWidget())
    class Meta:
        model = Event
        fields = ['name', 'event_date', 'description']
```

This is a new class. After adding the import at the top of the file, add the class to the end of the file.

The only thing new in this class is **line 2**, where I have assigned the `CKEditorWidget` class to the `description` field.

The default sizing for the editor widget is too large for our forms, so the next change we'll make is to CKeditor's settings. Add the settings to the end of your `settings.py` file:

```
# myclub_root\myclub_site\settings.py

# ...

CKEDITOR_CONFIGS = {
    'default': {
        'height': 300,
        'width': 500,
    },
}
```

Next, we must edit the update and create forms to use the custom event form. If you remember, we created these forms when we explored class-based views in Chapter 13, so they should be in the `demo_views.py` file (changes in bold):

```
# myclub_root\events\views\demo_views.py

# add the following to the imports at the top of the file
from events.forms import EventForm

# ...

class CreateViewDemo(LoginRequiredMixin, CreateView):

    login_url = reverse_lazy('login')
    model = Event
    # fields = ['name', 'event_date', 'description']
    success_url = reverse_lazy('show-events')
    form_class = EventForm


class UpdateViewDemo(LoginRequiredMixin, UpdateView):

```

```
12        login_url = reverse_lazy('login')
13        model = Event
14        # fields = ['name', 'event_date', 'description']
15        template_name_suffix = '_update_form'
16        success_url = reverse_lazy('show-events')
17        form_class = EventForm

# ...
```

The modifications to the classes are identical:

- **Lines 5 and 14**. We're using a custom form, so we can't use the `fields` attribute any more—it will throw an error. I've commented the lines here, but you can delete them.
- **Lines 7 and 17**. I've assigned the custom form to each class with the `form_class` attribute.

We've finished changing the forms, now all that's left to do is to tweak the form templates (changes in bold):

```
# \events\templates\events\event_form.html

{% extends "base.html" %}

{% block title %}CreateView Demo{% endblock title %}
{% block styles %}{{ form.media }}{% endblock styles %}
# ...

# \events\templates\events\event_update_form.html

{% extends "base.html" %}

{% block title %}CreateView Demo{% endblock title %}
{% block styles %}{{ form.media }}{% endblock styles %}
# ...

# myclub_root\events\templates\events\event_detail.html

# ...
<tr>
  <td><strong>Description:</strong></td><td>{{ event.description|safe
```

```
}}</td>
</tr>
# ...
```

Pay careful attention; we're modifying three different files here. The changes are as follows:

- **`event_form.html`**. Added form media to the `head` element. This will load CKEditor's CSS and JS into the page.
- **`event_update_form.html`**. Added form media to the `head` element. This will load CKEditor's CSS and JS into the page.
- **`event_detail.html`**. Added a `safe` filter to the description field, otherwise, Django will escape the HTML in the rich-text field.

Once you have finished, the add and update event forms will show with a rich-text editor (Figure 15-4).

Rich-text at Model Level

CKEditor also provides a `RichTextField()` model field, so you can define rich-text capable fields at model level.

If your model defines a rich-text field, **all** forms will try to display the field as rich-text. I tend not to define rich-text fields at model level as you lose flexibility, so I prefer to decide on a form-by-form basis.

As with most things Django, it's up to your personal preference, so I've added this note for completeness. Check out the Django CKEditor documentation[1] if you want to use the model field.

1 https://github.com/django-ckeditor/django-ckeditor#field

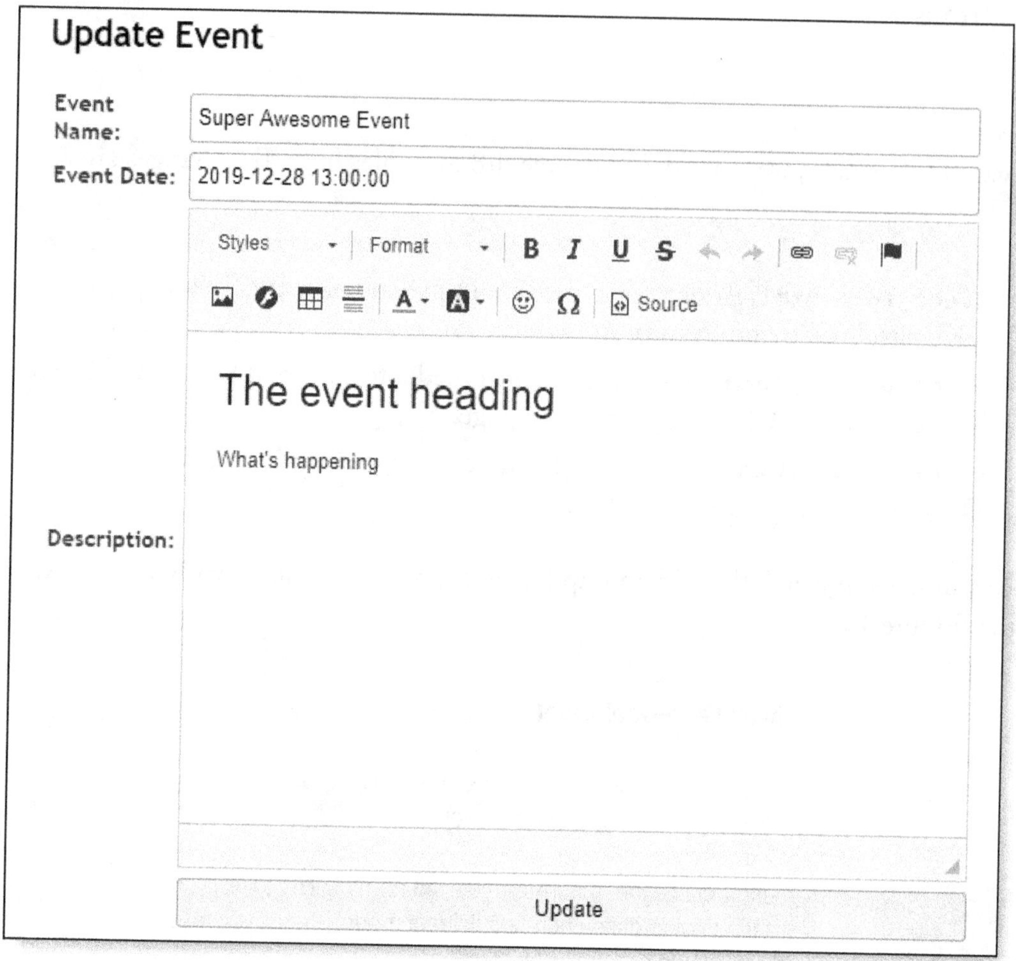

Figure 15-4. The update event form with a rich-text editor for the description field.

The Messages Framework

Notification messages shown on a web page or in a popup window are a common feature of modern websites. In Chapter 8, we wrote a simple notification to show the success message after the contact form was submitted.

Messaging is not just related to forms—messages can be used in any application to inform a user that some event or action has occurred. However, as messaging is most commonly related to form submissions, I will cover it in this chapter. I touch on the messages framework again in Chapter 17, where I show you how to use messages when testing and debugging your apps.

As messaging is so common, Django has full support for both cookie- and session-based messaging, provided via the *messages framework*. The default configuration is to use cookie-based messaging and to fall back to session-based messaging if cookies are disabled or the message is too large for a cookie. You can also change the configuration to use cookie- or session-based messaging exclusively, but the default is best for most applications.

The messages framework provides five message levels:

1. **DEBUG**. Development-related messages that will be ignored (or removed) in production.
2. **INFO**. Informational messages for the user.
3. **SUCCESS**. An action was successful.
4. **WARNING**. Not a failure, but there's a problem.
5. **ERROR**. An action was unsuccessful, or some other failure occurred.

Each of the message levels has a corresponding tag which contains a string representation of the message level in lowercase (e.g., The tag for `DEBUG` is "debug"). Message tags are typically used in CSS classes to style the message based on the message type. For example, if a `SUCCESS` message was passed to a template:

```
<p class="{{ message.tag }}">
```

Would be rendered as:

```
<p class="success">
```

We'll see this in action shortly when we modify the template for the contact form.

Django's messages framework is installed and configured when you run `startproject`, so implementing the messages framework in your apps only requires some small changes to your views and templates.

First, I will modify the `ContactUs()` class-based view we created for the contact page in Chapter 13 (changes in bold):

```
# myclub_root\myclub_site\contact.py

# add the following to the imports at the top of the file
from django.contrib import messages

# ...

class ContactUs(FormView):
    template_name = 'contact/contact.html'
    form_class = ContactForm
    success_url = '/contact'

    # def get(self, request, *args, **kwargs):
    #     context = self.get_context_data(**kwargs)
    #     if 'submitted' in request.GET:
    #         context['submitted'] = request.GET['submitted']
    #     return self.render_to_response(context)

    def form_valid(self, form):
        cd = form.cleaned_data
        con = get_connection('django.core.mail.backends.console.EmailBackend')
        send_mail(
            cd['subject'],
            cd['message'],
            cd.get('email', 'noreply@example.com'),
            ['siteowner@example.com'],
            connection=con
        )
        messages.add_message(
            self.request,
            messages.SUCCESS,
            'Your message was submitted successfully. Thank you.'
        )
```

```
27          return super().form_valid(form)
28
29      def form_invalid(self, form):
30          messages.add_message(
31              self.request,
32              messages.ERROR,
33              'You have errors in your submission'
34          )
35          return super().form_invalid(form)
```

Other than importing `messages` from `django.contrib` at the top of the file, there are four changes to the contact form view:

- **Line 4.** We're no longer using a `GET` parameter to show the success message, so `success_url` can redirect to the contact page without adding "`?submitted=True`" to the URL.
- **Lines 6 to 10.** We don't need the `get()` method now we're using the messages framework. I've commented it out so you can see what I've removed, but you can also delete the method from your code.
- **Lines 22 to 26.** The `add_message()` method of the `messages` class will add the message to the context in a context variable named `messages`. The method requires the current request object, the message level and the message as a string, which is what we are passing in here.
- **Line 29.** We're overriding the `form_valid()` method of the `FormView` class, which allows us to add an error message using the messages framework.
- **Lines 30 to 34.** The error message is added to the context by `add_message()`
- **Line 35** passes the form back to the parent method, which renders the form and modified context. You could also return a response directly, but this way preserves the inheritance chain and avoids potential errors if another class overrides this method in a future version of the app.

The next step is to change the contact template to show any messages passed by the view (changes in bold):

```
# \myclub_site\templates\contact\contact.html

1  {% extends "base.html" %}
2
3  {% block title %}Contact Us{% endblock title %}
4
5  {% block content %}
6  <h1>Contact us</h1>
7
8  {% if messages %}
9    {% for msg in messages %}
10     <p{% if msg.tags %} class="{{ msg.tags }}"{% endif %}>{{ msg
}}</p>
11   {% endfor %}
12 {% endif %}
13
14 <form action="" method="post" novalidate>
15   <table>
16     {{ form.as_table }}
17     <tr>
18       <td> </td>
19       <td><input type="submit" value="Submit"></td>
20     </tr>
21   </table>
22 {% csrf_token %}
23 </form>
24
25 {% endblock content %}
```

In the modified template, I've replaced the `if/else` tag block from the original file with a new `if` block that will display any messages passed to the template (**lines 8 to 12**). There are two things to note with this new code:

- **Line 9.** We're creating a `for` loop because even if there is only one message, you must iterate over the message sequence to clear the message storage.
- **Line 10.** We're using the message tag as the class name for the HTML paragraph. For example, when there is an error, this will render as `<p class="error">`.

Now we've changed the view and the template, there's one more thing to do—we don't have a CSS class for the error message, so let's add it to `main.css` now (change in bold):

```
# myclub_root\myclub_site\static\main.css

# ...

.errorlist li, .error {
    border: 1px solid red;
    color: red;
    # ...
```

Once the changes have been made, when you navigate to `http://127.0.0.1:8000/contact/` and submit an invalid form, your browser should look like Figure 15-5.

Contact us

You have errors in your submission

	This field is required.
Your Name:	
Your e-mail address:	
	This field is required.
Subject:	
	This field is required.
Message:	
	Submit

Figure 15-5. *Showing an error message with Django's messages framework.*

And, once the form has been submitted successfully, your browser should look like Figure 15-6. Notice the blank form shows as well as the message, which is more consistent with how messages are displayed on professional websites.

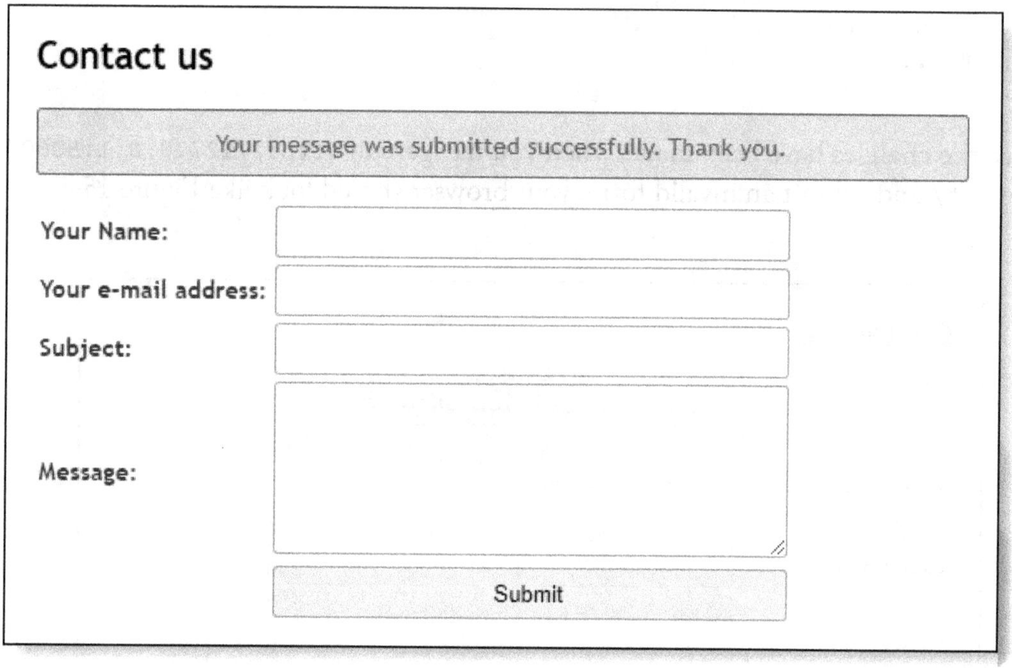

Figure 15-6. Showing a success message with Django's messages framework.

Django Formsets

Formsets in the front end work the same way they do in the admin, except you must create and style them yourself. Django makes creating formsets easier with the `formset_factory` class, which only requires the form you wish to use for the formset.

Let's start with an example. This is a form for adding members to a club committee (new class):

```
# myclub_root\events\forms.py

# ...

class CommitteeForm(forms.Form):
    first_name = forms.CharField()
    last_name = forms.CharField()
    phone = forms.CharField()
```

Now, we need a view to create the formset for us (new view):

```
# myclub_root\events\views\demo_views.py

# add the following to the imports at the top of the file
from events.forms import EventForm, CommitteeForm
from django.forms import formset_factory

# ...

1  def committee_formset(request):
2      committee_formset = formset_factory(CommitteeForm, extra=3)
3      if request.method == 'POST':
4          formset = committee_formset(request.POST)
5          if formset.is_valid():
6              # process the form
7              pass
8      else:
9          formset = committee_formset()
10         return render(request, 'events/committee.html', {'formset':
formset})
```

After importing the `CommitteeForm` from `events.forms` and the `formset_factory` class from `django.forms`, you can see the view looks similar to a view for a single form.

The key line in this code is **line 2**, where we use `formset_factory` to create a formset from the `CommitteeForm` form. The `extra` attribute tells Django how many forms to show on the page.

NOTE: We're not processing this example form (comment in line 6), so don't submit it, otherwise, you will get an error.

To see our formset, we need a template (new file):

```
# \events\templates\events\committee.html

1  {% extends "base.html" %}
2
3  {% block title %}Formset Demo{% endblock title %}
4
5  {% block content %}
6
7  <h1>Club Committee</h1>
8
9  <form action="" method="post" novalidate>
10     {{ formset.management_form }}
11     <table>
12         {% for form in formset %}
13             {{ form }}
14         {% endfor %}
15     </table>
16     {% csrf_token %}
17     </form>
18
19 {% endblock content %}
```

This is a standard Django template, so there's nothing new here, but it's worth digging further into **line 10**. Django uses a few variables to keep track of management data for the formset (the number of forms showing, total forms in the formset, etc.). These management variables must be added to the form, otherwise, Django will raise an exception. Line 10 adds the management variables to the form as hidden fields.

Finally, to show our formset, we need a URLconf (change in bold):

```
# myclub_root\events\urls.py

urlpatterns = [
    # ...
    path('committee/', views.committee_formset, name='committee'),
]
```

Once you've saved all the files, navigate to `http://127.0.0.1:8000/committee/`, and your browser should look like Figure 15-7.

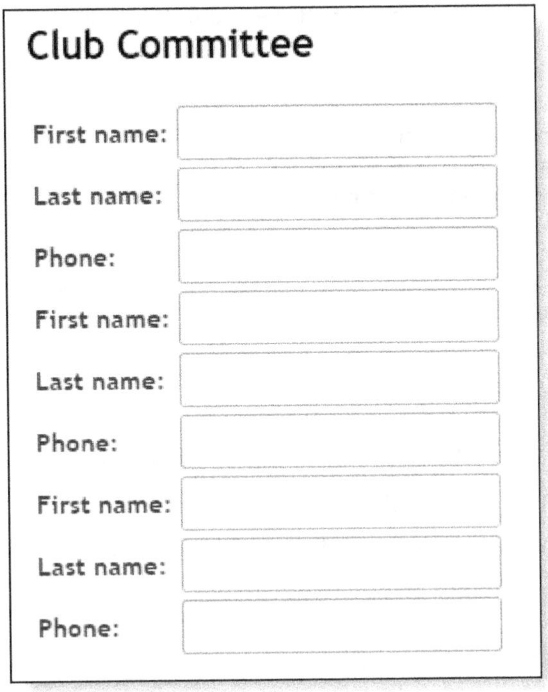

***Figure 15-7.** The simple committee formset showing in the browser.*

If you look at the page source, you can see the management variables in the form too, they're at the top of the form and look like this:

```
<input type="hidden" name="form-TOTAL_FORMS" ... >
<input type="hidden" name="form-INITIAL_FORMS" ... >
```

As you can see from Figure 15-7, Django has done nothing to format the forms for you—it's just stacked them on top of each other. Let's tweak the template code to get the tabular look we want (changes in bold):

```
# \events\templates\events\committee.html

# ...
1  <table>
2  <tr>
3    <th>First Name</th><th>Last Name</th><th>Phone</th>
4  </tr>
5    {% for form in formset %}
6    <tr>
7      <td>{{ form.first_name }}</td>
8      <td>{{ form.last_name }}</td>
9      <td>{{ form.phone }}</td>
10   </tr>
11   {% endfor %}
12 </table>
13 <input id="submit" type="submit" value="Add Members">
14 {% csrf_token %}
# ...
```

To tweak the template, I've added a header row in **lines 2 to 4**, and I've formatted the forms in the formset into individual table rows (**lines 6 to 10**). I've also added a submit button on **line 13** to complete the form, but since we haven't added code to process the form, clicking it will throw an error.

Refresh your browser, and the page will now look like Figure 15-8.

Figure 15-8. *The reformatted committee form now showing in tabular format.*

Remember: we haven't added any form processing code to the committee form view, so the next step would be to add validation and code to process input from the user, but we won't do that here. The basic `formset_factory` class is great, but given most often you will use formsets with models, Django has a better option for working with model formsets—`modelformset_factory`.

With `modelformset_factory` you get `formset.is_valid()` and `formset.save()` methods that behave the same way as `form.is_valid` and `form.save()`.

To show you how to use `modelformset_factory`, we will build a quick edit form for events where a user can quickly change a venue's name and date within a formset that shows in the front end.

As `modelformset_factory` uses the structure of the model directly, we need not create a form, so let's dive in and create the view (new view):

```
# myclub_root\events\views\demo_views.py

# add the following to the imports at the top of the file
from django.core.paginator import Paginator, EmptyPage,
PageNotAnInteger
from django.forms import formset_factory, modelformset_factory

# ...

def all_events(request):
    EventsFormSet = modelformset_factory(
        Event,
        fields=('name', 'event_date'),
        extra=0
    )
    qry = Event.events.all()
    pg = Paginator(qry, 4)
    page = request.GET.get('page')
    try:
        event_records = pg.page(page)
    except PageNotAnInteger:
        event_records = pg.page(1)
    except EmptyPage:
```

```
15            event_records = pg.page(pg.num_pages)
16        if request.method == 'POST':
17            formset = EventsFormSet(request.POST)
18            if formset.is_valid():
19                formset.save()
20                return_url = '/allevents/'
21                if 'page' in request.GET:
22                    return_url += '?page=' + request.GET['page']
23                return HttpResponseRedirect(return_url)
24        else:
25            page_qry = qry.filter(id__in=[event.id for event in event_
records])
26            formset = EventsFormSet(queryset=page_qry)
27
28        context = {'event_records': event_records, 'formset': formset}
29        return render(request, 'events/all_events.html', context)
```

This view is more complicated than the view for the committee, but most of it we've already covered in the book. Let's have a look at the important parts of this code:

- **Lines 2 to 6**. This is the model formset. `modelformset_factory` requires a model name and the model fields to show in the form. `extra` is optional. We're setting `extra` to `0` here, so the formset doesn't show any blank forms. We're not adding any code to process a new record in this example, so we don't want blank forms showing.
- **Line 7**. We're retrieving all event records from the database and storing them in the QuerySet `qry`.
- **Lines 8 to 15**. We're building a paginator for the formset. If you've forgotten how to build a paginator, refer back to Chapter 10.
- **Lines 16 to 23**. Here, we process the POSTed form. If the form is valid, we save it (**line 19**). Notice how we don't have to save individual records as Django manages all records in the formset for us. The extra code in **lines 21 and 22** ensures we stay on the same page in the formset; otherwise when you save the form, the formset will reset to the first page.

  We're not doing anything with the form if it's invalid. As Django adds a dictionary of error messages to the form automatically, an invalid form submission will drop through to **line 28** and re-render the form.

- **Line 25.** If the form isn't POSTed, this line filters the event records so `page_qry` only contains the records for the current page.
- **Line 26.** Creates a formset from the records in `page_qry`.

Now we've got the view done, it's time to create the template (new file):

```
# \events\templates\events\all_events.html

{% extends "base.html" %}

{% block title %}Quick Edit Events{% endblock title %}

{% block content %}
<h1>Quick Edit Events</h1>
{% if formset.errors %}
  <ul>
  {% for error in formset.errors %}
    {{ error }}
  {% endfor %}
  </ul>
{% endif %}
<form action="" method="post" novalidate>
  {{ formset.management_form }}
  <table>
  <tr><th>Event Name</th><th>Event Date</th></tr>
    {% for form in formset %}
    <tr>
      {{ form.id }}
      <td>{{ form.name }}</td>
      <td>{{ form.event_date }}</td>
    </tr>
    {% endfor %}
  </table>
  {% csrf_token %}
  <input style="width: 100px;" id="submit" type="submit" value="Update">
</form>

<div style="padding-top: 20px;">
  {% if event_records.has_previous  %}
    <a href="?page=1">&laquo; first</a>
    <a href="?page={{ event_records.previous_page_number }}">previous</a>
```

```
34    {% endif %}
35    Page {{ event_records.number }} of {{ event_records.paginator.num_pages }}
36    {% if event_records.has_next %}
37      <a href="?page={{ event_records.next_page_number }}">next</a>
38      <a href="?page={{ event_records.paginator.num_pages }}">last &raquo;</a>
39    {% endif %}
40 </div>
41 {% endblock content %}
```

Highlights from this code:

- **Lines 7 to 13** render any errors passed to the template.
- **Line 20.** The record id must be recorded on the form so Django can update the correct record in the database. `form.id` saves the id to a hidden field on the form.
- **Lines 30 to 40.** The formset paginator code. If you want to review this code, see Chapter 10.

All that's left to do now is to add a URLconf (change in bold):

```
# myclub_root\events\urls.py

urlpatterns = [
    # ...
    path('allevents/', views.all_events, name='all-events'),
]
```

Once you've saved the files, navigate to `http://127.0.0.1:8000/allevents/` and your browser should look like Figure 15-9.

Change a few records to see how you can update and save records on each page of the formset. If you submit invalid data on any of the forms, the errors will show as well (Figure 15-10).

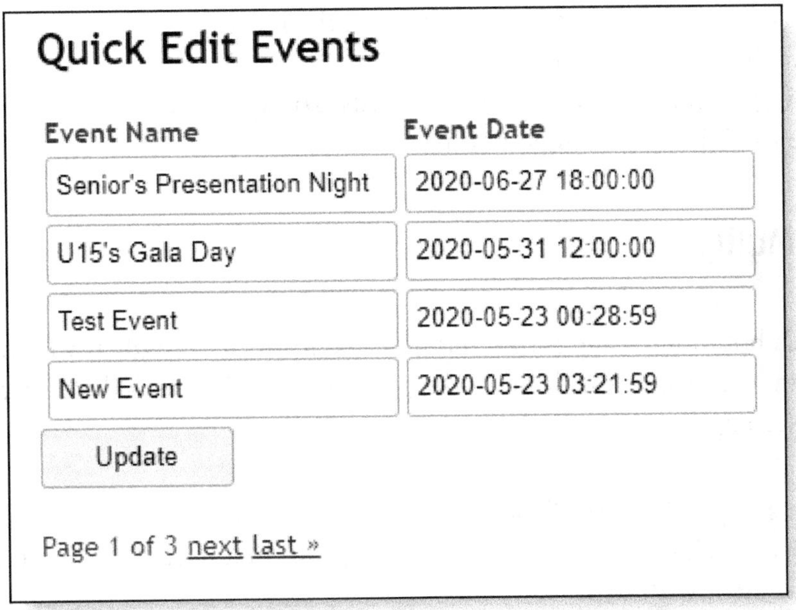

Quick Edit Events

Event Name	Event Date
Senior's Presentation Night	2020-06-27 18:00:00
U15's Gala Day	2020-05-31 12:00:00
Test Event	2020-05-23 00:28:59
New Event	2020-05-23 03:21:59

Update

Page 1 of 3 next last »

Figure 15-9. The event quick edit form showing fields in tabular format.

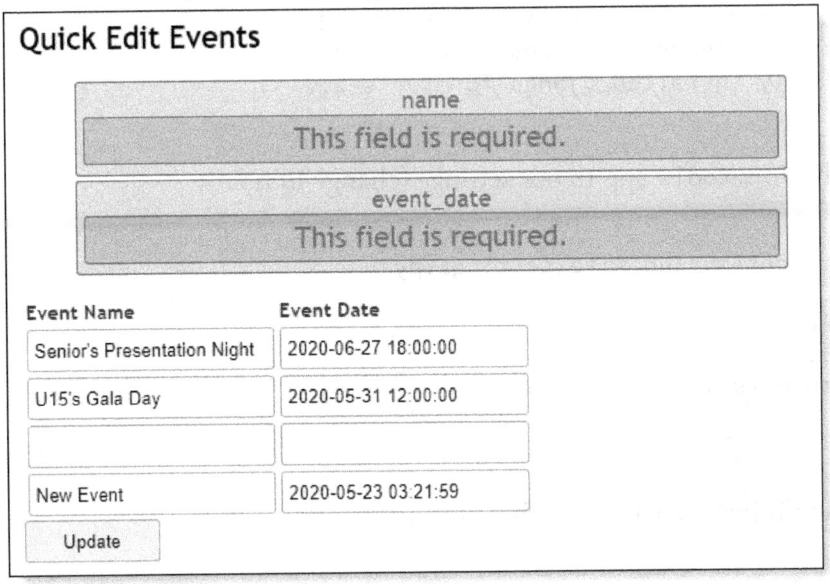

Quick Edit Events

name
This field is required.

event_date
This field is required.

Event Name	Event Date
Senior's Presentation Night	2020-06-27 18:00:00
U15's Gala Day	2020-05-31 12:00:00
New Event	2020-05-23 03:21:59

Update

Figure 15-10. Displaying errors for the formset.

These examples are enough to get you started on the right track, but there's a lot more you can do with formsets and model formsets. This includes adding fields, deleting records, sorting columns and adding new records. To explore the full capabilities of formsets, see the Django documentation[2 3].

Handling Multiple Forms

Working with both multi-step forms and multiple forms in a single workflow is common in modern websites. To make the process easier, Django's developers created the `formtools` app.

Formtools was originally part of core Django, but since Django 1.8, it has existed as a separate project. As it's now separate from Django, we first have to install it into our virtual environment with `pip`:

```
(env_myclub) ...\myclub_root> pip install django-formtools
Collecting django-formtools
Downloading .../django_formtools-2.2-py2.py3-none-any.whl (148kB)
    |##########################| 153kB 2.2MB/s
Installing collected packages: django-formtools
Successfully installed django-formtools-2.2
```

And add the `formtools` app to our settings (change in bold):

```
# myclub_root\myclub_site\settings.py

INSTALLED_APPS = [
    # ...
    'formtools',
]
```

Once the app is installed, it needs three things to work:

2 https://docs.djangoproject.com/en/dev/topics/forms/formsets/
3 https://docs.djangoproject.com/en/dev/topics/forms/modelforms/#model-formsets

1. The forms to load into the wizard.
2. A form wizard class to manage the forms; and
3. A template to display the forms.

To show you how the form wizard works, I will create a simple two-step survey that emails the submitted forms to a site administrator.

Let's start with the forms (new code):

```
# myclub_root\events\forms.py

# ...

class SurveyForm1(forms.Form):
    name = forms.CharField(max_length=100)
    email = forms.EmailField()


class SurveyForm2(forms.Form):
    response1 = forms.CharField(label="What's great about our club?", widget=Textarea)
    response2 = forms.CharField(label="What's not so great about our club?", widget=Textarea)
```

Add the two survey forms to the end of your `forms.py` file. They're standard Django forms, so I will not explain them here. If you want a refresher on standard Django forms, check out Chapter 8.

Now, let's add a new wizard view class (new code):

```
# myclub_root\events\views\demo_views.py

# add the following to the imports at the top of the file
from django.http import HttpResponseRedirect
from formtools.wizard.views import SessionWizardView
from django.core.mail import send_mail, get_connection
from django.contrib import messages
```

```
# ...

1  class SurveyWizard(SessionWizardView):
2      template_name = 'events/survey.html'
3      def done(self, form_list, **kwargs):
4          responses = [form.cleaned_data for form in form_list]
5          mail_body = ''
6          for response in responses:
7              for k,v in response.items():
8                  mail_body += "%s: %s\n" % (k, v)
9          con = get_connection('django.core.mail.backends.console.
EmailBackend')
10         send_mail(
11             'Survey Submission',
12             mail_body,
13             'noreply@example.com',
14             ['siteowner@example.com'],
15             connection=con
16         )
17         messages.add_message(
18             self.request,
19             messages.SUCCESS,
20             'Your survey was submitted successfully. Thank you for
your feedback'
21         )
22         return HttpResponseRedirect('/survey')
```

Digging deeper into this code:

- **Line 1.** Our `SurveyWizard` class subclasses `SessionWizardView`.
- **Line 2.** We're configuring the class to use a custom template which we'll create shortly. The `formtools` app has a built-in default template, but it's basic and not of much use.
- **Line 3.** The `SessionWizardView` class requires you to implement a `done()` method to manage form submissions.
- **Lines 4 to 8.** `form_list` is a list of dictionaries containing the data from each form. We're using standard Python code to parse the responses into a formatted string suitable for an email message.
- **Lines 9 to 16** use the `send_mail()` function to send the email. We're using the console back end again, so the email will be output to the shell.

- **Lines 17 to 21** use the messages framework to add a success message to the response.

The last step is to create the template (new file):

```
# \events\templates\events\survey.html

{% extends "base.html" %}

{% block title %}Club Survey{% endblock title %}
{% block styles %}{{ wizard.form.media }}{% endblock styles %}

{% block content %}
<h1>Please provide some feedback:</h1>

{% if messages %}
    {% for msg in messages %}
    <p{% if msg.tags %} class="{{ msg.tags }}"{% endif %}>{{ msg }}</p>
    {% endfor %}
{% endif %}

<p>Step {{ wizard.steps.step1 }} of {{ wizard.steps.count }}</p>
<form action="" method="post">{% csrf_token %}
<table>
{{ wizard.management_form }}
{% if wizard.form.forms %}
    {{ wizard.form.management_form }}
    {% for form in wizard.form.forms %}
        {{ form }}
    {% endfor %}
{% else %}
    {{ wizard.form }}
{% endif %}
</table>
{% if wizard.steps.next %}
<input type="submit" value="Next"/>
{% else %}
<input type="submit" value="Submit"/>
{% endif %}
{% if wizard.steps.prev %}
<button name="wizard_goto_step" type="submit" value="{{ wizard.steps.
prev }}">Back</button>
{% endif %}
</form>
{% endblock content %}
```

The cool thing about `formtools` is that the wizard object is passed to the template by the `SessionWizardView` class, so there's minimal work needed to create the form workflow. There's nothing else new in this template, so I won't dig any deeper into the code.

Next, I will add some tweaks to the site style sheet to make the form wizard prettier (changes in bold):

```
# myclub_root\myclub_site\static\main.css

input, button, textarea {
    # ...
}
input[type="submit"], button {
    height: 30px;
    width: 150px;
    float: right;
}

# ...
```

Finally, we need a URLconf to load the survey (changes in bold):

```
# myclub_root\events\urls.py

# add the following to the imports at the top of the file
from events.views import SurveyWizard
from events.forms import SurveyForm1, SurveyForm2

urlpatterns = [
    path('survey/', SurveyWizard.as_view([SurveyForm1, SurveyForm2]),
name='survey'),
    # ...
]
```

This is straightforward—`SurveyWizard` is a class-based view, so it implements the `as_view()` method. Here, we're passing a list of forms to use with the wizard.

Once you're done, navigate to `http://127.0.0.1:8000/survey/`, and your browser should look like Figure 15-11.

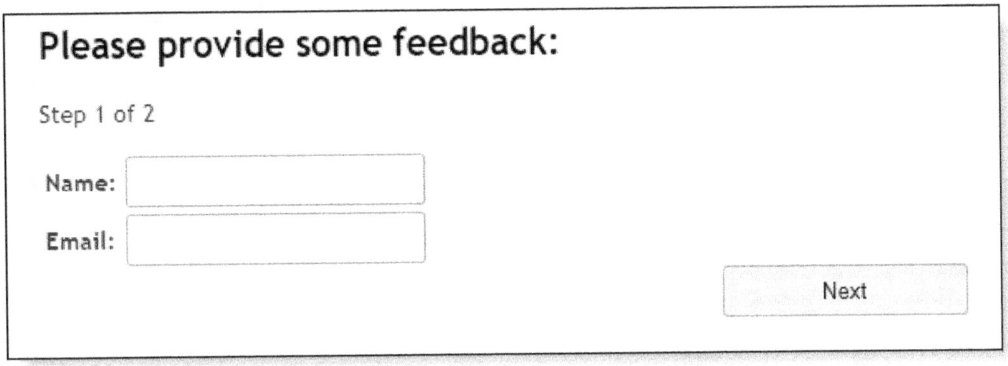

Figure 15-11. *The first page of our simple survey form wizard.*

Fill out the form and click **Next**, and the second survey form will show (Figure 15-12).

Notice how invalid forms are managed by `formtools` without you having to implement validation and error handling in your code.

Once you click **Submit**, the responses from the survey will be sent to the shell. This is what it looks like on my PC:

```
# ...
Subject: Survey Submission
From: noreply@example.com
To: siteowner@example.com
Date: Wed, 01 Jan 2020 23:22:36 -0000
Message-ID: <...@DESKTOP-INQV0G1>

name: nigel
email: me@example.com
response1: everything!
response2: nothing!
-------------------------------------------
```

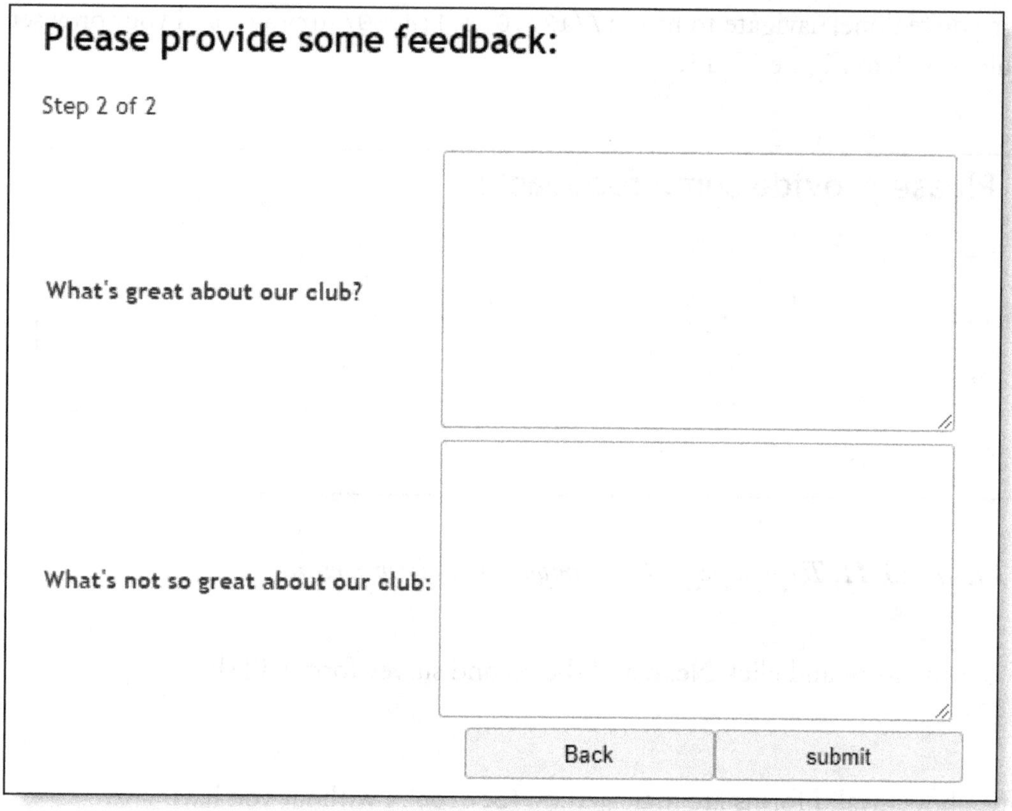

Please provide some feedback:

Step 2 of 2

What's great about our club?

What's not so great about our club:

Back submit

Figure 15-12. The second page of our simple survey form wizard.

Model Form Wizards

You create a form wizard for model forms in the same way as regular forms. To show you how to use a form wizard for model forms, I will use the `EventForm` and `ModelForm` classes we created earlier in the book.

As the forms have already been created, we start by creating the view:

```
# myclub_root\events\views\demo_views.py

# ...

class ModelFormWizard(SessionWizardView):
    template_name = 'events/modelwiz_demo.html'
    def done(self, form_list, **kwargs):
        for form in form_list:
            form.save()
        return HttpResponseRedirect('/')
```

This is a much simpler class because all we're doing is saving each of the forms from the form wizard.

Now for the template (new file):

```
# \events\templates\events\modelwiz_demo.html

{% extends "base.html" %}

{% block title %}Wizard Demo{% endblock title %}
{% block styles %}{{ wizard.form.media }}{% endblock styles%}

{% block content %}
<h1>Model Form Wizard Demo</h1>

{% if messages %}
    {% for msg in messages %}
    <p{% if msg.tags %} class="{{ msg.tags }}"{% endif %}>{{ msg }}</p>
    {% endfor %}
{% endif %}

<p>Step {{ wizard.steps.step1 }} of {{ wizard.steps.count }}</p>
<form action="" method="post">{% csrf_token %}
<table>
{{ wizard.management_form }}
{% if wizard.form.forms %}
    {{ wizard.form.management_form }}
    {% for form in wizard.form.forms %}
        {{ form }}
    {% endfor %}
{% else %}
```

```
    {{ wizard.form }}
{% endif %}
</table>
{% if wizard.steps.next %}
<input type="submit" value="Next"/>
{% else %}
<input type="submit" value="Submit"/>
{% endif %}
{% if wizard.steps.prev %}
<button name="wizard_goto_step" type="submit" value="{{ wizard.steps.
prev }}">Back</button>
{% endif %}
</form>
{% endblock content %}
```

Except for the title and the heading, this template is identical to the survey template.

Finally, we need a URLconf to load the model form wizard (changes in bold):

```
# myclub_root\events\urls.py

# add the following to the imports at the top of the file
from events.views import SurveyWizard, ModelFormWizard
from events.forms import VenueForm, EventForm

urlpatterns = [
    path('new/', ModelFormWizard.as_view([VenueForm, EventForm]),
name='wizard-demo'),
    # ...
]
```

Once you're done, navigate to `http://127.0.0.1:8000/new/` and your browser should look like Figure 15-13.

Fill out the form and click **Next** and the event form will show (Figure 15-14).

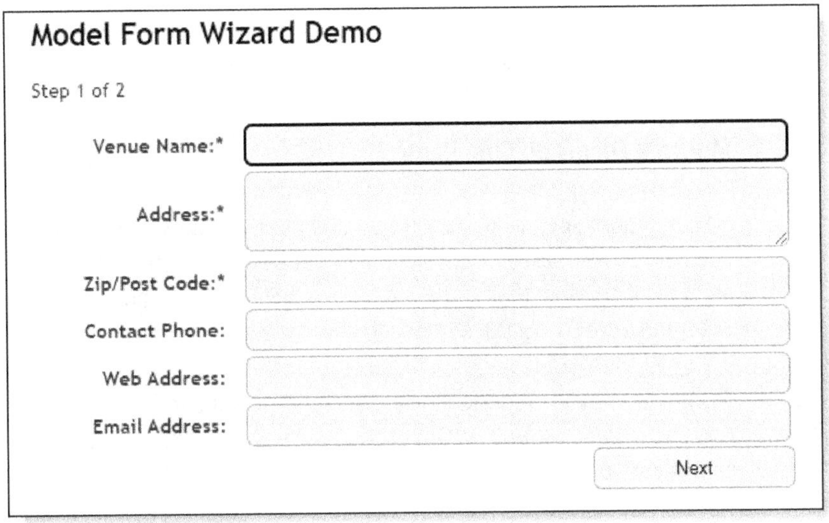

Figure 15-13. The first page of our simple model form wizard.

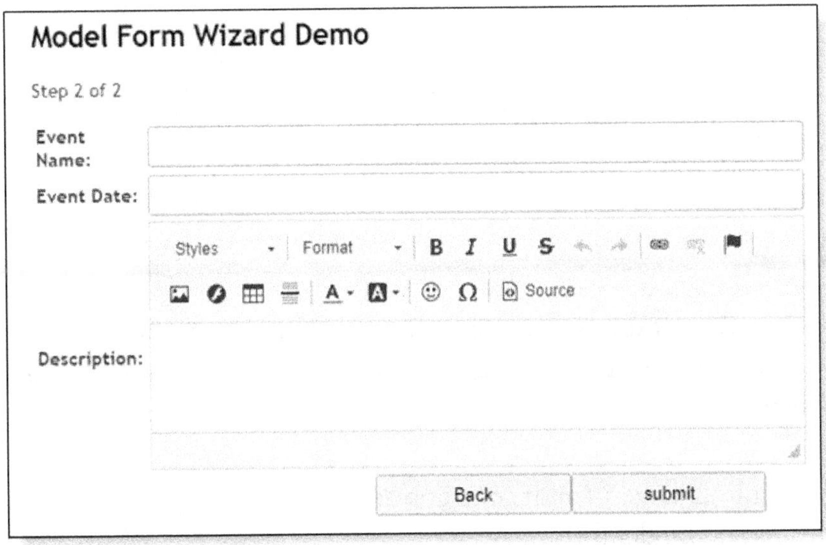

Figure 15-14. The second page of our simple model form wizard.

Clicking **Submit** with valid form data will save a new venue record and a new event record to the database. You can check this out in the admin.

Multiple Forms on One Page

Having more than one HTML form on one page has always been problematic. The nature of HTML makes it difficult to differentiate what form has been submitted, and validating more than one form often requires clunky conditional branching in code and extra JavaScript to manage the forms.

Assuming you can't redesign the app to avoid needing to have multiple forms on one page, Django's form wizard provides an easy solution: put each form on a separate wizard page.

The `formtools` app has many more useful methods and advanced customizations available than what we have covered in this chapter. I encourage you to dig deeper and check out the django-formtools documentation[4].

Chapter Summary

In this chapter, we dug deeper into Django's forms. We started by learning how to customize Django's forms with additional media (style sheets and JavaScript), create and add custom widgets, and how to add rich-text editing capability to forms in the front end.

Later in the chapter, we explored Django's messages framework and how to use the framework in our forms to send messages to users, and then I showed you how to use formsets to display tabular data in the browser.

Finally, we dug into Django's `formtools` app and learned how to create workflows for multi-part forms and model forms.

In the next chapter, we will dig deeper into working with databases in Django.

4 https://django-formtools.readthedocs.io/en/latest/index.html

16

Working With Databases

In this chapter, we will dig deeper into working with databases in Django.

We will start with a tour of the Django management commands useful for working with databases. We'll then look at how to manage migrations, connect to existing databases and solve problems with database connections by fixing migrations and recreating your database.

I'll finish the chapter with detailed instructions on how to connect your Django projects with PostgreSQL, MySQL and MariaDB.

Database Management Commands

`manage.py`, Django's management command utility, has about a dozen management commands for working with databases. In every case, you execute the command with:

```
python manage.py <command>
```

You must be inside the virtual environment for management commands to work.

Many tutorials use `django-admin` for these commands. `manage.py` is a wrapper for `django-admin` that sets `DJANGO_SETTINGS_MODULE` to point to your project's `settings.py` file, so it's OK to use either command.

Some commands (e.g., `flush`) require your settings module to be loaded, so I stick with `manage.py`. That way, I don't have to remember which commands I can use with `django-admin` and which commands need to use `manage.py`.

check

While not strictly a database command, `check` will pick up errors with your database connection, models and migrations, so it's handy as a preliminary check before you run `makemigrations`.

Running `check` will output something similar to this:

```
(env_myclub) ...\myclub_root> python manage.py check
System check identified no issues (0 silenced).
```

dbshell

`dbshell` runs the command-line client for the database you're using with your project. This won't work out of the box if you've been using SQLite as Django comes with a pre-packaged version of SQLite3 (a DLL if you're on Windows).

If you're a fan of command-line clients for databases, this command can be useful. I'm not a fan, so have always used available GUI managers where I can (e.g., DB Browser for SQLite).

dumpdata

The primary use for `dumpdata` is to output database data so it can be loaded into another database. It's not infallible—especially if you have complex models and are exporting from one database engine and importing into another.

The default is to output all data as a single stream to the standard output (which is usually the terminal). This is not much use, so I use two options when using `dumpdata`:

```
(env_myclub) ...> python manage.py dumpdata --indent 4 -o dbdump.json
```

The first option, `--indent`, adds standard 4-space code indentation to the JSON output. The second option, `-o` (that's an O, not zero), outputs to a file named "dbdump.json".

It's a plain text file, so you could use a `.txt` extension, but the `.json` extension ensures the filetype recognition software in most code editors formats it nicely for you. Here's a snippet of the file output:

```
[
{
    "model": "events.venue",
    "pk": 1,
    "fields": {
        "name": "South Stadium",
        "address": "South St",
        "zip_code": "123456",
        "phone": "555-12345",
        "web": "http://southstexample.com",
        "email_address": "southst@example.com"
    }
},
{
    "model": "events.venue",
    "pk": 2,
    "fields": {

# ...
```

There are four other options for `dumpdata` you're likely to need at some stage:

- **`--all`**. Use if you have custom model managers that filter records and want to dump all records.

- **`--natural-foreign`**. Serialize foreign key and many-to-many relationships. If you're dumping permissions and content types, you need this option.
- **`--natural-primary`**. Omits the primary key on serialization so it can be calculated during deserialization.
- **`--exclude`**. Exclude the named application or model from serialization.

flush

To remove all data from your database, use `flush`:

```
(env_myclub) ...\myclub_root> python manage.py flush
You have requested a flush of the database.
This will IRREVERSIBLY DESTROY all data currently in the 'D:\\
OneDrive\\Documents\\myclub_project\\myclub_root\\db.sqlite3' database,
and return each table to an empty state.
Are you sure you want to do this?

    Type 'yes' to continue, or 'no' to cancel:
```

If you want to start from an empty database, it's better to drop and recreate the database and then run your migrations. See the section "Recreating Your Database" for more information.

inspectdb

`inspectdb` is used for database introspection. `inspectdb` is meant as a shortcut, not for definitive model creation as the models it outputs need to be customized. Things that need to be tweaked include:

- `inspectdb` will create an attribute for every field in the table. You may not need every field in your models.
- If `inspectdb` can't map a column type to a Django field type, it will create a `TextField` with a warning comment instead.

- Foreign key and many-to-many relationships are often in the wrong order.
- All relationships will have the `on_delete` attribute set to `models.DO_NOTHING`.
- All models generated are unmanaged, so Django will not manage the database table.

Run `inspectdb` against the existing database with:

```
python manage.py inspectdb
```

This command will output a `models.py` file to the terminal. Here's a snippet from running `inspectdb` against our MyClub project:

```
# ...
class EventsEvent(models.Model):
    name = models.CharField(max_length=120)
    event_date = models.DateTimeField()
    description = models.TextField()
    manager = models.ForeignKey(AuthUser, models.DO_NOTHING,
blank=True, null=True)
    venue = models.ForeignKey('EventsVenue', models.DO_NOTHING,
blank=True, null=True)

    class Meta:
        managed = False
        db_table = 'events_event'

class EventsEventAttendees(models.Model):
    event = models.ForeignKey(EventsEvent, models.DO_NOTHING)
    myclubuser = models.ForeignKey('EventsMyclubuser', models.DO_
NOTHING)

    class Meta:
        managed = False
        db_table = 'events_event_attendees'
        unique_together = (('event', 'myclubuser'),)
# ...
```

If you want the output to go to a file, you can pipe it to a file:

```
python manage.py inspectdb > tables_to_models.py
```

You can also run it against a named database with:

```
python manage.py inspectdb --database <database_name>
```

For this last command to work, your `settings.py` file must contain a valid connection and credentials for the named database.

loaddata

Use `loaddata` to add data exported by `dumpdata` to your database, or to load an initial dataset into a new database:

```
(env_myclub) ...\myclub_root> python manage.py loaddata dbdump.json
Installed 118 object(s) from 1 fixture(s)
```

`loaddata` works with any fixture (i.e., serialized database content) in XML, JSON or YAML format. It can also read compressed fixtures in zip, gz and bz2 format.

I won't explore external fixtures here because it's a fraught process and I could never cover every possible error you will encounter trying to move data from one database to another. Check out the Django documentation[1] if you want to dive deeper into fixtures.

makemigrations

`makemigrations` searches for changes to your models and creates new migrations based on the detected changes. It can be used to search for changes in all your models with:

1 https://docs.djangoproject.com/en/dev/ref/django-admin/#loaddata

```
python manage.py makemigrations
```

Or you can use it to create migrations for specific apps:

```
python manage.py makemigrations app1 app2
```

The latter form is useful for apps that don't have a `\migrations` folder.

migrate

`makemigrations` only creates the migrations; it doesn't apply them. Use the `migrate` command to apply outstanding migrations:

```
python manage.py migrate
```

You can also migrate select apps:

```
python manage.py migrate app1 app2
```

showmigrations

Lists all the migrations in the current project:

```
(env_myclub) ...\myclub_root> python manage.py showmigrations
```

Here's a snippet from the output generated by this command:

```
admin
[X] 0001_initial
[X] 0002_logentry_remove_auto_add
[X] 0003_logentry_add_action_flag_choices
```

```
auth
[X] 0001_initial
[X] 0002_alter_permission_name_max_length
[X] 0003_alter_user_email_max_length
[X] 0004_alter_user_username_opts
[X] 0005_alter_user_last_login_null
# ...
```

sqlflush

Prints the SQL statements for the `flush` command.

sqlmigrate

Prints the SQL statements for a migration. Requires the app name and the migration name. For example:

```
sqlmigrate events 0001_initial
```

squashmigrations

`squashmigrations` will squash all the migrations for an app down to the fewest migrations possible. It's useful for when you've collected dozens (and even hundreds!) of migrations and want to condense them down into only a few migrations.

Let's check it out by first listing all the migrations I have for the `events` app:

```
(env_myclub) ...\myclub_root> python manage.py showmigrations events

events
[X] 0001_initial
[X] 0002_auto_20190819_1509
[X] 0003_auto_20190825_1406
[X] 0004_auto_20190826_0839
```

```
[X] 0005_auto_20190904_1101
[X] 0006_auto_20191112_1940
[X] 0007_auto_20191207_1059
[X] 0008_auto_20191207_1207
[X] 0009_auto_20191229_0923
[X] 0010_auto_20191229_1108
```

We're using the `showmigrations` command to list all the migrations. Note your migration names will be different if you try this code.

Now, let's squash the migrations. `squashmigrations` will squash all migrations up to and including the named migration. For example, let's squash them all:

```
python manage.py squashmigrations events 0010_auto_20191229_1108
```

The output for this command will look like this:

```
Will squash the following migrations:
- 0001_initial
- 0002_auto_20190819_1509
- 0003_auto_20190825_1406
- 0004_auto_20190826_0839
- 0005_auto_20190904_1101
- 0006_auto_20191112_1940
- 0007_auto_20191207_1059
- 0008_auto_20191207_1207
- 0009_auto_20191229_0923
- 0010_auto_20191229_1108
Do you wish to proceed? [yN] y
```

Type "y" and then Enter to squash the migrations. Your output will look like this:

```
Optimizing...
Optimized from 36 operations to 10 operations.
Created new squashed migration ...\events\migrations\0001_
squashed_0010_auto_20191229_1108.py
You should commit this migration but leave the old ones in place;
the new migration will be used for new installs. Once you are sure
```

```
all instances of the codebase have applied the migrations you squashed,
you can delete them.
```

Now, see what changes have been made by running `showmigrations` again:

```
(env_myclub) ...\myclub_root> python manage.py showmigrations events

events
[X] 0001_squashed_0010_auto_20191229_1108 (10 squashed migrations)
```

Pay attention to the notice in the output of the `squashmigrations` command—Django doesn't delete the old migration files, it leaves the old ones in place for you to delete.

Managing Migrations

Keeping your project's models in sync with the database with Django's migrations is usually painless: you change your models, run `makemigrations` and then run `migrate` and everything works.

Real-life programming isn't always smooth sailing, however. Three main problems often pop up to ruin your day:

1. You need your models to match an existing database.
2. The current migrations don't match the database schema.
3. You're migrating from one database back end to another.

Django's migrations documentation[2] and dozens of online resources provide a myriad of solutions to these problems, including:

- Rolling back migrations
- Editing the migrations table in your database

2 https://docs.djangoproject.com/en/dev/topics/migrations/

- Writing your own migrations
- Manually changing migrations
- And so on…

These all translate to one word for me: *nightmare*.

Some of you will have to use these solutions in your career, and for that, you have my sympathy but little advice. I'm not a DBA, have no plans to become a DBA, and if I ever faced such a situation, I would delegate it to smarter people than me.

I do have my own solution to these problems, though. It's a simple, repeatable process:

1. Backup existing database (if it exists).
2. Dump the data (if necessary).
3. Create a new database with makemigrations/migrate.
4. Add data to the new database.

There's plenty of nuance with these steps, and step 4 is never smooth. I also expect it won't work for high load databases and large-scale data migrations. However, for smaller, light to medium load single database installs, it beats the heck out of hacking database tables and migrations in my book.

Feel free to disagree with me (many do). But if you want to follow the same process, here's more specific advice.

Connecting to Existing Databases

Django has its own way of building tables, relationships and indexes. Django's authentication system is also tightly coupled to many aspects of the database schema. Getting a Django project to play nicely with an existing schema always risks putting you into one of the nightmare situations I mentioned before.

My favored option is to start with a new database and import the data from the legacy database. If that's not possible, you can follow another process:

- First step, run `inspectdb` and tidy up the models created. Delete the models you don't need for your Django project. Remember, Django only cares about the tables in the database that relate to the models in your project, so there's no problem having tables in the database that are not mapped to Django models.
- Once you're happy with your models, migrate against a clone of the database and see what breaks. Rinse and repeat as you build out your project.

Migrations Out Of Sync

Migrations are like version control for your database. If a modification is made to the database outside of Django, or a migration file is lost or corrupted, it's possible for the migrations and database to get out of sync.

The simplest fix is to identify the changes to the database, change your models to match the changes, and run `migrate` with the `--fake` option:

```
python manage.py makemigrations
python manage.py migrate --fake
```

The `--fake` option generates the migrations but doesn't run the SQL to change the database schema.

If `--fake` doesn't work, you can either start hacking your migrations, or you can recreate the database from scratch and reload the data into your database tables.

Recreating Your Database

This is my favored option for changing to a new database back end (e.g., when you move from SQLite to Postgres for production). It's also handy for when your database is a mess, or your migrations are out of sync, or when you've been chasing data errors for a week, and a clean start seems a better idea than setting your database server alight and watching it burn.

The process is simple:

1. Run `dumpdata`
2. Drop or delete the database
3. Delete the migrations folder from every Django app in your project
4. Recreate an empty database (unnecessary for SQLite)
5. Run `makemigrations` for each app
6. Run `migrate`
7. Run `loaddata` (and hope it works)

There's more elegant ways to do this, but it not only guarantees a fresh set of migrations and database tables, it can also be cathartic for days when your database server has a tentative appointment with a baseball bat.

First step is to run `dumpdata`. As we're exporting the entire database, I'm using the `--all` option to ensure all records are dumped, `--natural-foreign` to ensure foreign key and many-to-many relationships are recreated, and `--natural-primary` to recalculate primary keys:

```
(env_myclub) ...> python manage.py dumpdata --natural-foreign
--natural-primary --all --indent 4 -o dbdump.json
[...............................................................
......]
```

Next step, jump into Window's Explorer (Finder on a Mac) and:

1. Delete the `db.sqlite3` file from the `\myclub_root` folder; and
2. Delete the `\migrations` folder from the `\events` folder.

Then, make new initial migration for the events app:

```
(env_myclub) ...> python manage.py makemigrations events
Migrations for 'events':
events\migrations\0001_initial.py
    - Create model Venue
    - Create model Subscriber
    - Create model MyClubUser
    - Create model Event
```

Migrate the database:

```
(env_myclub) ...> python manage.py migrate
Operations to perform:
Running migrations:
Applying contenttypes.0001_initial... OK
Applying auth.0001_initial... OK
# lots more migrations
```

And reload the table data:

```
(env_myclub) ...> python manage.py loaddata dbdump.json
Installed 118 object(s) from 1 fixture(s)
```

If you are recreating the database for the same back end, this process is painless most of the time. If you are changing databases, generally the last step is where things go wrong. There is no such thing as 100% compatibility between one database's schema and another. This is as true for open-source database engines as it is for proprietary engines. Patience is an important skill to learn when moving data from one system to another.

Connecting to Other Database Engines

Throughout the book, we've used SQLite for our MyClub website. However, SQLite is not considered a production-ready database for anything but the smallest applications. At some stage, you will need to switch to one of the professional database engines supported by Django.

It's always better if your database is running on a server, either on your local network, or on a remote server, but this isn't always practical or cost-effective.

Luckily, each of the database engines supported by Django can be installed and run locally. In this section of the chapter, I will show you how to install the other open-source databases supported by Django:

- PostgreSQL
- MySQL
- MariaDB (Django 3 only)

Django also offers Oracle support, but as it's a commercial program that requires and Oracle account to access, I won't cover it here.

For each example, I am assuming you have completed the first three steps from the *Recreating Your Database* section:

1. Ran `dumpdata`.
2. Deleted the `db.sqlite3` file; and
3. Delete the `migrations` folder from the `events` app.

The installation instructions are for Windows 10. I can't make any guarantees they will work on earlier versions of Windows as database servers can be notoriously difficult to set up on non-Linux machines.

For macOS users, here's a quick summary of my experiences:

- **PostgreSQL**. Very similar to Windows setup, and quite easy to get running. Fix problems with `psycopg2` by installing with `pip install psycopg2-binary`.
- **MySQL**. I've never got it to work. Some say you can use Homebrew to install both `mysql` and `mysqlclient`, but that hasn't worked for me either. My preference is to set up a free database on PythonAnywhere and connect to that, rather than try to run MySQL on macOS.

- **MariaDB.** MariaDB is a fork of MySQL, so it needs `mysqlclient`. For this reason, I assume it won't be any less painful to get running on macOS. There are also no install packages available for macOS at this time, so you would have to install it from source. As support has only been offered for the first time in Django 3 there are limited tutorials. I have no advice, sorry.

What About NoSQL Databases?

NoSQL databases have been getting a lot of press in the last few years, so some of you may wonder why they're not covered in this book.

The simple answer is they're not core Django, and they're not officially supported by Django's development team, so I won't be covering them.

If you're interested in exploring NoSQL database support options for Django, type "django nosql" into your favorite browser.

PostgreSQL

Download the binary for your OS from `https://www.postgresql.org/download/`.

The installer package for both Windows and Mac is provided by EnterpriseDB, so the install process is identical for each platform (Figure 16-1).

Follow the installation wizard and accept the defaults for each option. You will need to set a password and port number (best to leave the port number alone). Remember to record the password and database port you entered during installation, or you won't be able to access PostgreSQL!

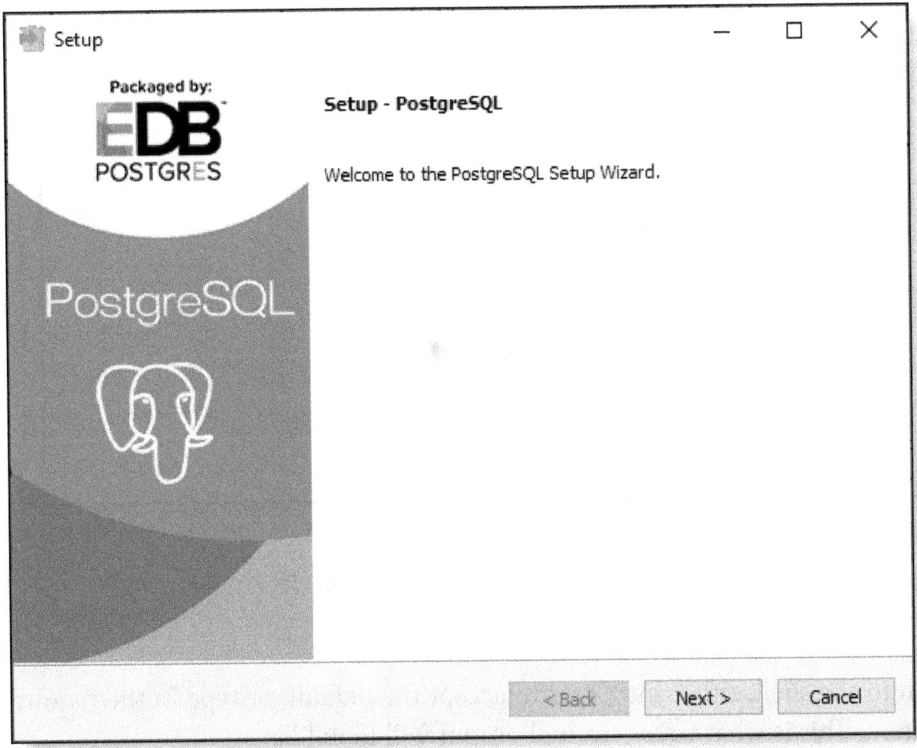

Figure 16-1. The PostgreSQL database installer running on Windows.

Once you have installed PostgreSQL, the easiest way to run the database shell is to type "SQL Shell" into the search bar and hit Enter to open the database shell (Figure 16-2).

Figure 16-2. The PostgreSQL database shell running on Windows.

To log in to the shell, either hit Enter to accept the default, or type in the required information. This is what your terminal output will look like:

```
Server [localhost]: # Hit Enter (return)
Database [postgres]: # Hit Enter (return)
Port [5432]: # Hit Enter (return)
Username [postgres]: # Hit Enter (return)
Password for user postgres: <your password>
psql (12.1)
Type "help" for help.

postgres=#
```

Now we've logged in to the shell, we need to create a database user, a database and grant the user access to the database (typed commands are in bold):

```
postgres=# CREATE USER myclub_user WITH PASSWORD '<your password>';
CREATE ROLE
postgres=# CREATE DATABASE myclub_db;
CREATE DATABASE
```

```
postgres=# GRANT ALL PRIVILEGES ON DATABASE myclub_db TO myclub_user;
GRANT
postgres=#
```

Configuring Django for PostgreSQL

Once the database is set up, it's back over to Django. First, fire up the development server and install the PostgreSQL module for Django:

```
(env_myclub) ...\myclub_root> pip install psycopg2
Collecting psycopg2
Downloading .../psycopg2-2.8.4-cp37-cp37m-win32.whl (983kB)
    |################################| 993kB 3.3MB/s
Installing collected packages: psycopg2
Successfully installed psycopg2-2.8.4
```

On macOS, the install command is:

```
$ pip install psycopg2-binary
```

Next, we need to change your settings to use PostgreSQL. Replace the settings for SQLite with the following:

```
DATABASES = {
    'default': {
        'ENGINE': 'django.db.backends.postgresql',
        'NAME': 'myclub_db',
        'USER': 'myclub_user',
        'PASSWORD': '<your password>',
        'HOST': 'localhost',
        'PORT': '5432',
    }
}
```

Save your settings file, and run the remaining commands to migrate your database from SQLite to PostgreSQL:

```
(env_myclub) ...\myclub_root> python manage.py check
System check identified no issues (0 silenced).

(env_myclub) ...\myclub_root> python manage.py makemigrations events
Migrations for 'events':
events\migrations\0001_initial.py
    - Create model Venue
    - Create model Subscriber
    - Create model MyClubUser
    - Create model Event
(env_myclub) ...\myclub_root> python manage.py migrate
Operations to perform:
Apply all migrations: admin, auth, contenttypes, events, sessions
Running migrations:
# lots of migrations

(env_myclub) ...\myclub_root> python manage.py loaddata dbdump.json
Installed 118 object(s) from 1 fixture(s)
```

Hopefully, this process went ahead without a hitch. Once the database has been migrated to PostgreSQL, open your project admin and you should see all your models and data available in the admin.

You can also check out the database with the `pgAdmin4` app that was installed with PostgreSQL. Type "pgadmin" into the search bar to open the database admin for PostgreSQL. Once you're logged in, navigate down to the tables for your `myclub_db` database (under "Schemas") and you can see that your tables and table data have been migrated to PostgreSQL (Figure 16-3).

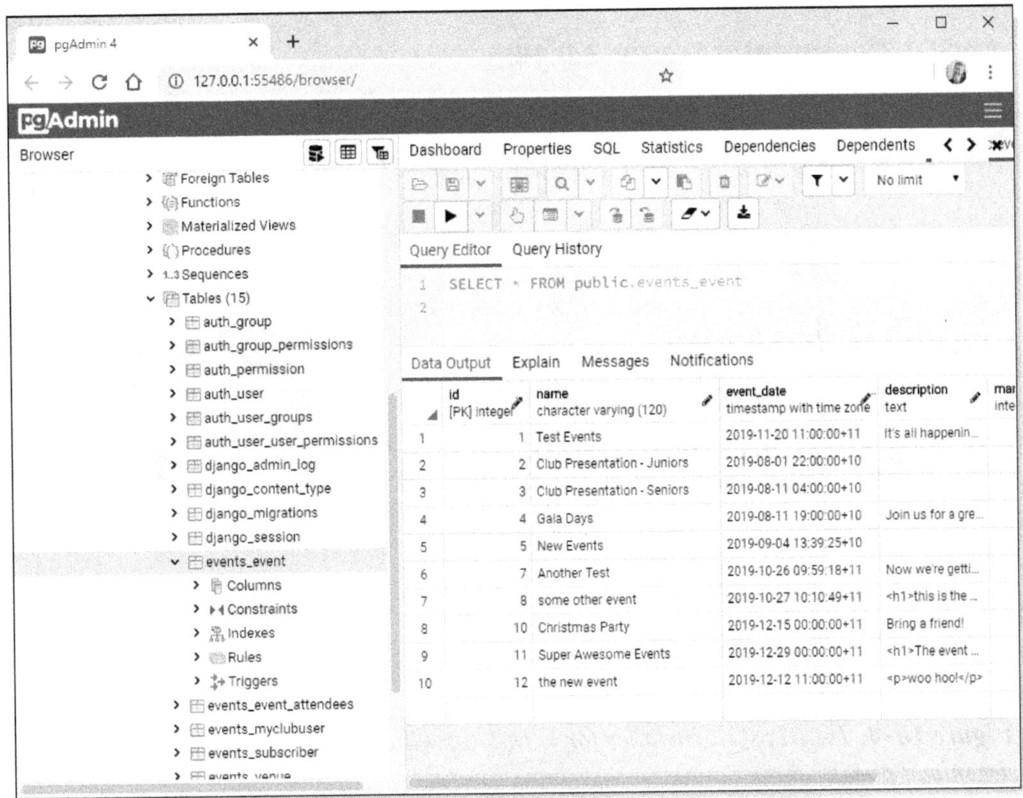

***Figure 16-3.** The MyClub project has been migrated to PostgreSQL.*

MySQL

The first step to running MySQL locally is to download the installer from `https://dev.mysql.com/downloads/mysql/`.

It should autodetect your OS, but if not, select Windows from the dropdown. You must click **Go to Download Page** button to open a new window and then download the installer file (Figure 16-4).

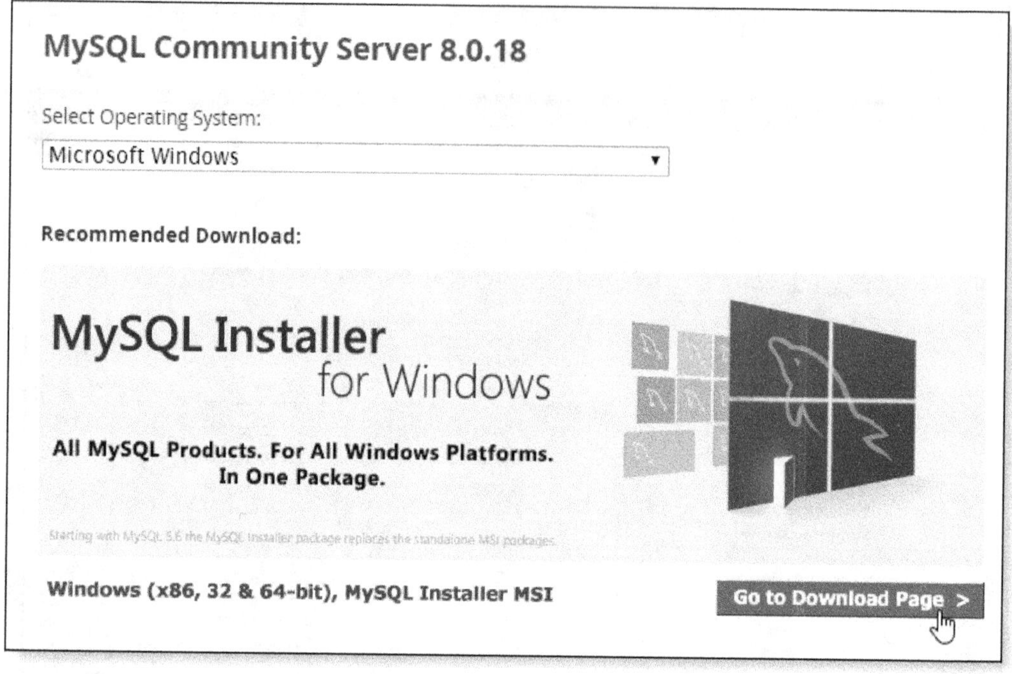

Figure 16-4. *The MySQL installer for Windows. Click on the button to go to the download page.*

Select the community version (`mysql-installer-community-8.0.x.x.msi`), not the online version.

It's best not to use MySQL's default installation option on Windows, as you will end up with about a gig's worth of software bloat you don't need on your machine.

First, change the setup to **Custom** (Figure 16-5).

On the **Select Products and Features** pane, select MySQL server and the Python connector (Figure 16-6).

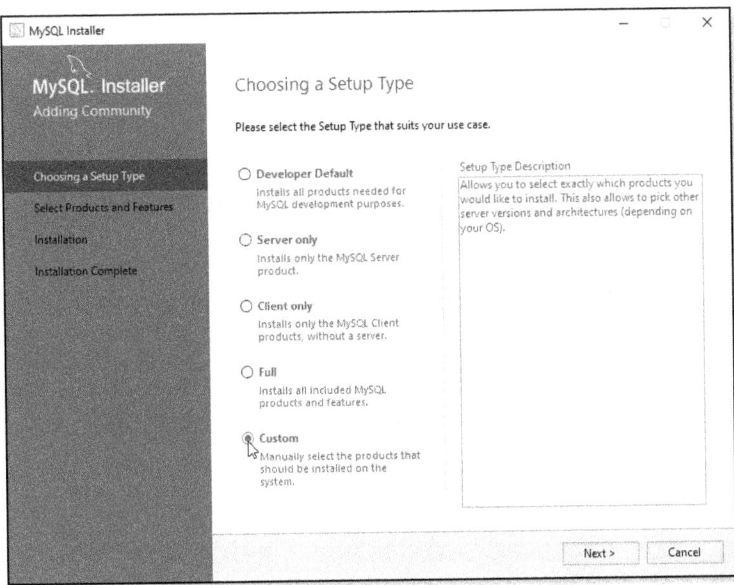

Figure 16-5. *Select the custom setup option, so you don't get a gig's worth of bloat on your computer.*

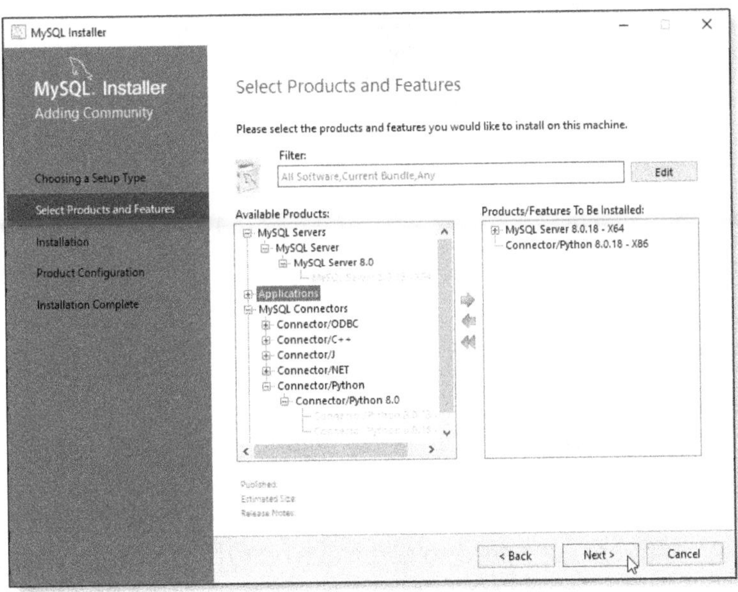

Figure 16-6. *Select only the MySQL server and the Python connector to install.*

After the server has installed, click **Next** to go to the product configuration window. For each panel, select the following:

- **High Availability**—Standalone (default)
- **Type and Networking**—Development Computer(default)
- **Authentication method**—Strong passwords(default)
- **Accounts and Roles**—Set the root password. Don't add a user account
- **Windows Service**—(default)

Once the configuration options are set, the **Apply Configuration** panel opens. Click **Execute** to configure the server (Figure 16-7).

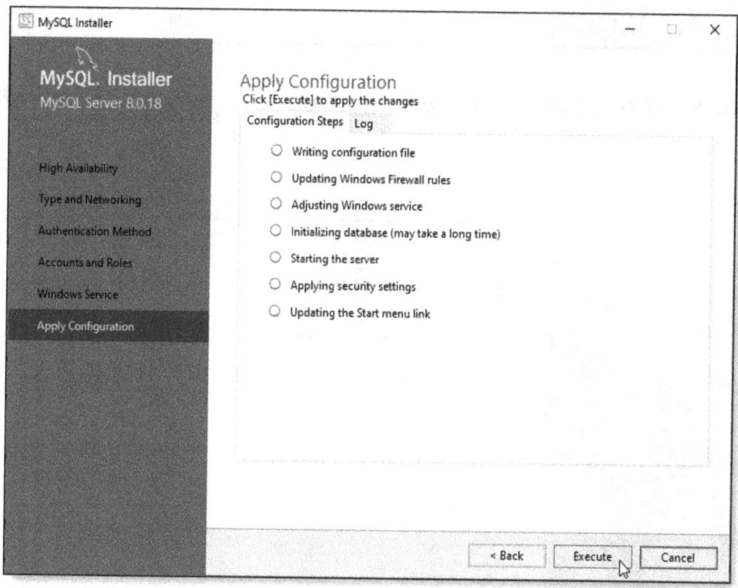

Figure 16-7. *Applying the MySQL server configuration options.*

Once MySQL is configured, we need to add the MySQL database shell to our `PATH` statement so we can use it in PowerShell or at the command prompt.

Start by typing "environment" into the search bar and selecting **Edit the system environment variables**. This will open the System Properties dialog box (Figure 16-8). Click on **Environment Variables**.

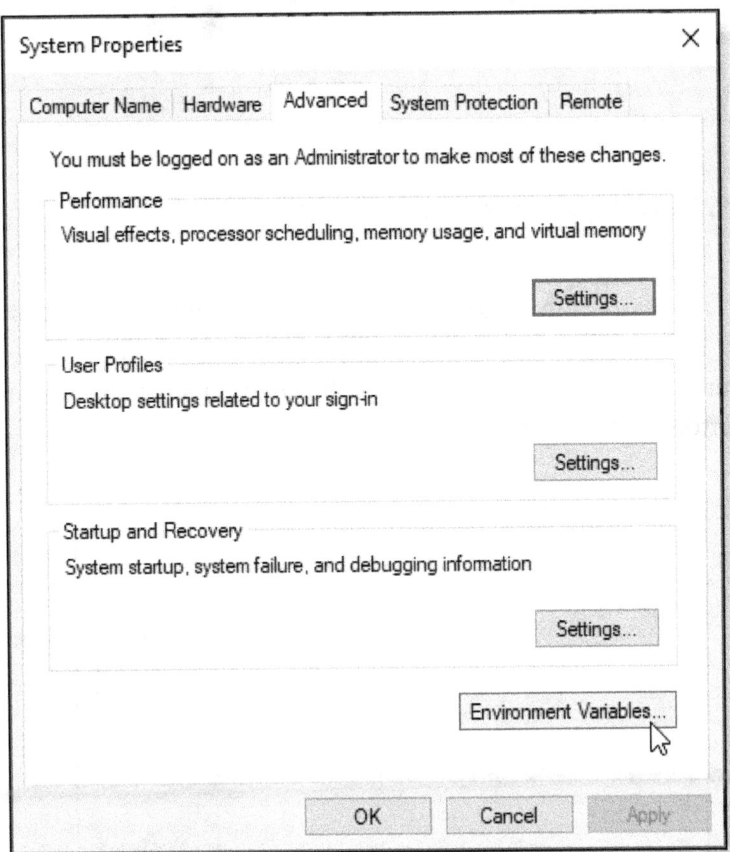

Figure 16-8. *Edit the environment variables in Windows.*

Select the path entry and click **Edit** (Figure 16-9).

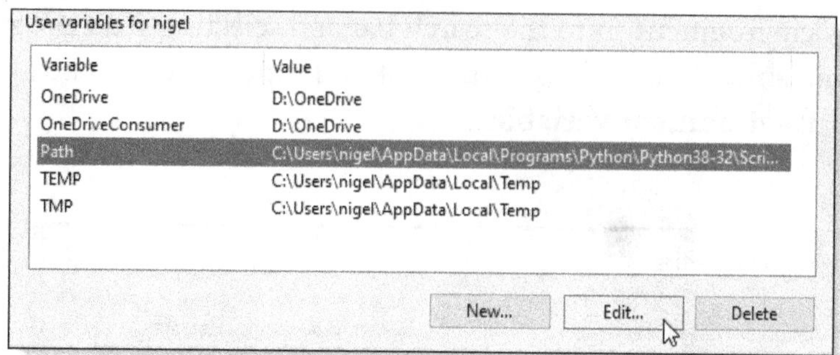

Figure 16-9. *Select the path user variable to edit.*

Click **Browse.** The `mysql` command-line program is in `\Program Files\MySQL\MySQL Server 8.0\bin`. Browse until you find the correct folder and then click **OK**. If you have entered the path correctly, your path statements list should have MySQL added to the bottom of the list (Figure 16-10).

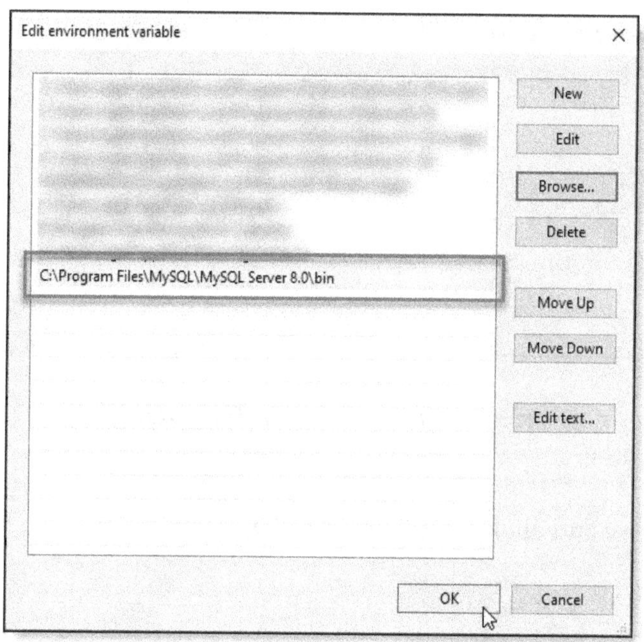

Figure 16-10. *Add the MySQL server monitor command-line client to Windows.*

To log into the database shell open PowerShell (or command prompt) and enter:

```
mysql -u root -p
```

Enter your password, and you should be rewarded with the MySQL database monitor shell prompt:

```
C:\Users\nigel> mysql -u root -p
Enter password: **********
Welcome to the MySQL monitor.  Commands end with ; or \g.
Your MySQL connection id is 14
Server version: 8.0.18 MySQL Community Server - GPL

Copyright (c) 2000, 2019, Oracle and/or its affiliates. All rights
reserved.

Oracle is a registered trademark of Oracle Corporation and/or its
affiliates. Other names may be trademarks of their respective
owners.

Type 'help;' or '\h' for help. Type '\c' to clear the current input
statement.

mysql>
```

Finally, set up your database and database user with the following commands:

```
mysql> CREATE USER 'myclub_user'@'localhost' IDENTIFIED WITH mysql_
native_password BY '<your password>';
Query OK, 0 rows affected (0.12 sec)

mysql> CREATE DATABASE myclub_db;
Query OK, 1 row affected (0.16 sec)

mysql> GRANT ALL ON myclub_db.* TO 'myclub_user'@'localhost';
Query OK, 0 rows affected (0.05 sec)
```

Configuring Django for MySQL

For MySQL to work with Django, you must install the database client `mysqlclient` using `pip` (make sure you're running the virtual environment):

```
(env_myclub) ...\myclub_root> pip install mysqlclient
```

When you run this command, one of two things is likely to happen: It will install OK, or you will get this error:

```
error: Microsoft Visual C++ 14.0 is required.
```

Many of Python's packages use Visual C++ runtime on Windows. If you don't have Visual Studio installed on your computer, this is a common error.

To fix this error, you can:

1. Install Visual Studio; or
2. Install an unofficial binary of `mysqlclient`.

One of the major reasons I now use Microsoft Visual Studio Code instead of Visual Studio is because Visual Studio is a giant bloated monster that can take hours to install and configure. So, we will take the easy option and install the binary file.

First, go to `https://www.lfd.uci.edu/~gohlke/pythonlibs/#mysqlclient` and download the latest wheel (`.whl`) for the installed version of Python. I am running Python 3.7 in my virtual environment, so at the time of writing, this is `mysqlclient-1.4.6-cp37-cp37m-win32.whl`.

Copy this file from your downloads folder to `\myclub_root`, and then run:

```
(env_myclub) ...> pip install mysqlclient-1.4.6-cp37-cp37m-win32.whl
Installing collected packages: mysqlclient
```

```
Successfully installed mysqlclient-1.4.6
```

Next, we need to change your settings to use MySQL. Replace the settings for SQLite with the following:

```
DATABASES = {
    'default': {
        'ENGINE': 'django.db.backends.mysql',
        'NAME': 'myclub_db',
        'USER': 'myclub_user',
        'PASSWORD': '<your password>',
        'HOST': 'localhost',
        'PORT': '3306',
    }
}
```

Save your settings file, and run the remaining commands to migrate your database from SQLite to MySQL:

```
(env_myclub) ...\myclub_root> python manage.py check
System check identified no issues (0 silenced).


(env_myclub) ...\myclub_root> python manage.py makemigrations events
Migrations for 'events':
events\migrations\0001_initial.py
    - Create model Venue
    - Create model Subscriber
    - Create model MyClubUser
    - Create model Event
(env_myclub) ...\myclub_root> python manage.py migrate
Operations to perform:
Running migrations:
    # lots of migrations

(env_myclub) ...\myclub_root> python manage.py loaddata dbdump.json
Installed 118 object(s) from 1 fixture(s)
```

Once the process is completed successfully, you will be up and running on a MySQL database.

MariaDB

MariaDB Only Works in Django 3

If you want to run the following setup, your project needs to be running Django 3.

MariaDB is an open-source fork of MySQL, created to combat Oracle's gradual shift of MySQL to proprietary licensing.

MariaDB can be downloaded from `https://downloads.mariadb.org/`. Download the latest `.msi` for your version of Windows (32 or 64bit). At the time of writing, the latest stable version of MariaDB is 10.4.11 (Figure 16-11).

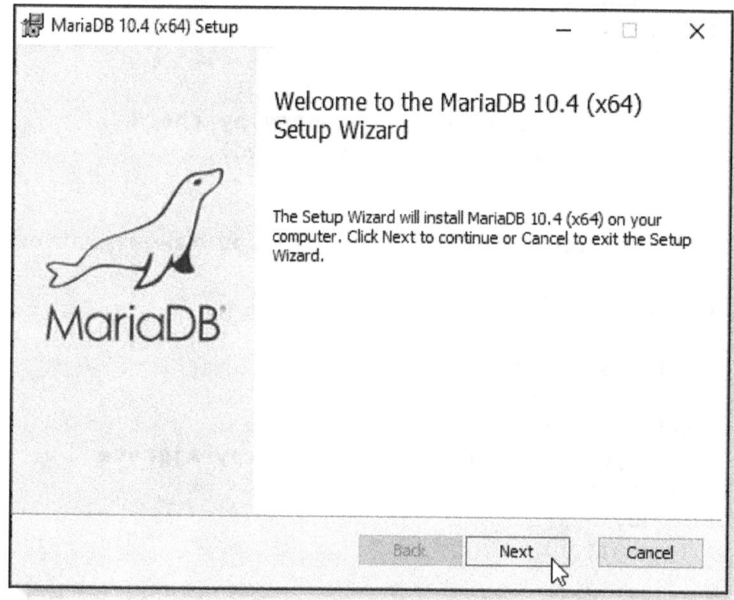

Figure 16-11. *The MariaDB installer for Windows.*

The setup is very similar to MySQL—accept the defaults and set a root password. If you're running MySQL on the same machine, you must change the TCP port number also.

Add MariaDB to the Windows path the same as MySQL. The MariaDB monitor command-line client's default installation path is `C:\Program Files\MariaDB 10.4\bin`, so once you've added the path to Windows, your PATH should look like Figure 16-12.

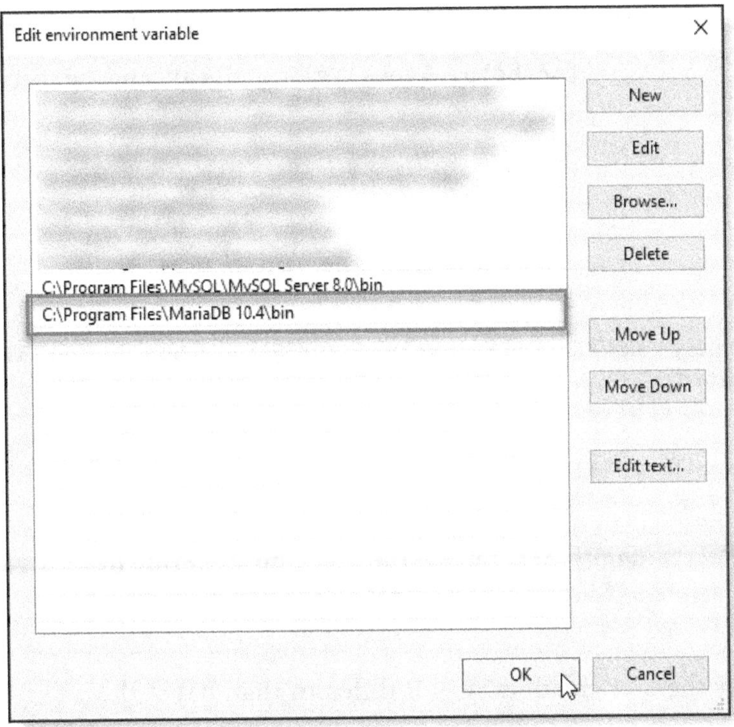

***Figure 16-12.** Adding MariaDB to the path follows the same process as adding MySQL.*

Once the path has been added, you can log into the MariaDB database monitor in PowerShell (or command prompt) with:

```
mariadb -u root -p
```

Enter your password, and you should be rewarded with the MariaDB database shell prompt:

```
C:\Users\nigel> mariadb -u root -p
Enter password: **********
Welcome to the MariaDB monitor.  Commands end with ; or \g.
Your MariaDB connection id is 11
Server version: 10.4.11-MariaDB mariadb.org binary distribution

Copyright (c) 2000, 2018, Oracle, MariaDB Corporation Ab and others.

Type 'help;' or '\h' for help. Type '\c' to clear the current input
statement.

MariaDB [(none)]>
```

Let's create the database and user account while we're here:

```
MariaDB [(none)]> CREATE USER 'myclub_user'@'localhost' IDENTIFIED BY
'<your password>';
Query OK, 0 rows affected (0.002 sec)

MariaDB [(none)]> CREATE DATABASE myclub_db;
Query OK, 1 row affected (0.001 sec)

MariaDB [(none)]> GRANT ALL ON myclub_db.* TO 'myclub_user'@'localhost';
Query OK, 0 rows affected (0.005 sec)
```

You can see only the user creation SQL is different than MySQL.

MariaDB uses the `django.db.backends.mysql` engine and `mysqlclient` module the same as MySQL. If you haven't install `mysqlclient`, see the instructions for MySQL.

The settings for MariaDB are identical to MySQL if you are not running MySQL on the same machine. Otherwise, you need to change the PORT setting to the TCP port number you selected during setup (change in bold):

```
DATABASES = {
    'default': {
        'ENGINE': 'django.db.backends.mysql',
        'NAME': 'myclub_db',
        'USER': 'myclub_user',
        'PASSWORD': 'Password1~',
        'HOST': 'localhost',
        'PORT': '3307',
    }
}
```

The rest of the migration from SQLite to MariaDB is the same as for MySQL:

```
(env_myclub) ...\myclub_root> python manage.py check
System check identified no issues (0 silenced).

(env_myclub) ...\myclub_root> python manage.py makemigrations events
Migrations for 'events':
events\migrations\0001_initial.py
    - Create model Venue
    - Create model Subscriber
    - Create model MyClubUser
    - Create model Event
(env_myclub) ...\myclub_root> python manage.py migrate
Operations to perform:
Running migrations:
    # lots of migrations

(env_myclub) ...\myclub_root> python manage.py loaddata dbdump.json
Installed 118 object(s) from 1 fixture(s)
```

Once the process is completed successfully, you will be up and running on a MariaDB database.

When to Change to a Production Database?

At some point, you must change from SQLite to one of the other database engines, so the question becomes: *When?*

This is another of those situations where looking for the One Best Time is fraught. As with many software development questions, the best answer is: "It depends."

I have always tried to switch to a production database as early in development as possible. If that means right from the beginning, that's OK.

SQLite is great for prototyping (and writing books!), as you don't have to worry about configuring and managing a database server. But if you have access to the production server or have the database software installed locally, there's no reason you can't use PostgreSQL (for example) from the start.

While you're learning from this book, use SQLite. When you build your first production website, make the choice that seems best. Even if you were wrong, you will have learned something.

Chapter Summary

In this chapter, we dug deeper into working with databases in Django.

We started with a tour of the Django management commands useful for working with databases. We then looked at how to manage migrations, connect to existing databases, and solve problems with database connections by fixing migrations and recreating your database.

I finished the chapter with detailed instructions on how to connect your Django projects with PostgreSQL, MySQL and MariaDB.

In the next chapter, we will explore testing and debugging in Django.

17

Debugging and Testing

In this chapter, we will take a look at debugging and testing in Django.

We'll start with a closer look at Django's error page and the wealth of information it contains, and then check out how we can use the messages framework as a debugging tool.

We will finish the chapter with a quick introduction to unit testing in Django.

Using Django's Error Page

Writing any amount of code is certain to introduce bugs and errors in the code, so debugging is a normal part of programming.

At this stage, you would have seen Django's error page many times, so it's worth a digression to have a closer look at it. If you have an error in your code, or you've been using `assert False` to test the output of your application, you will get a page that looks like Figure 17-1.

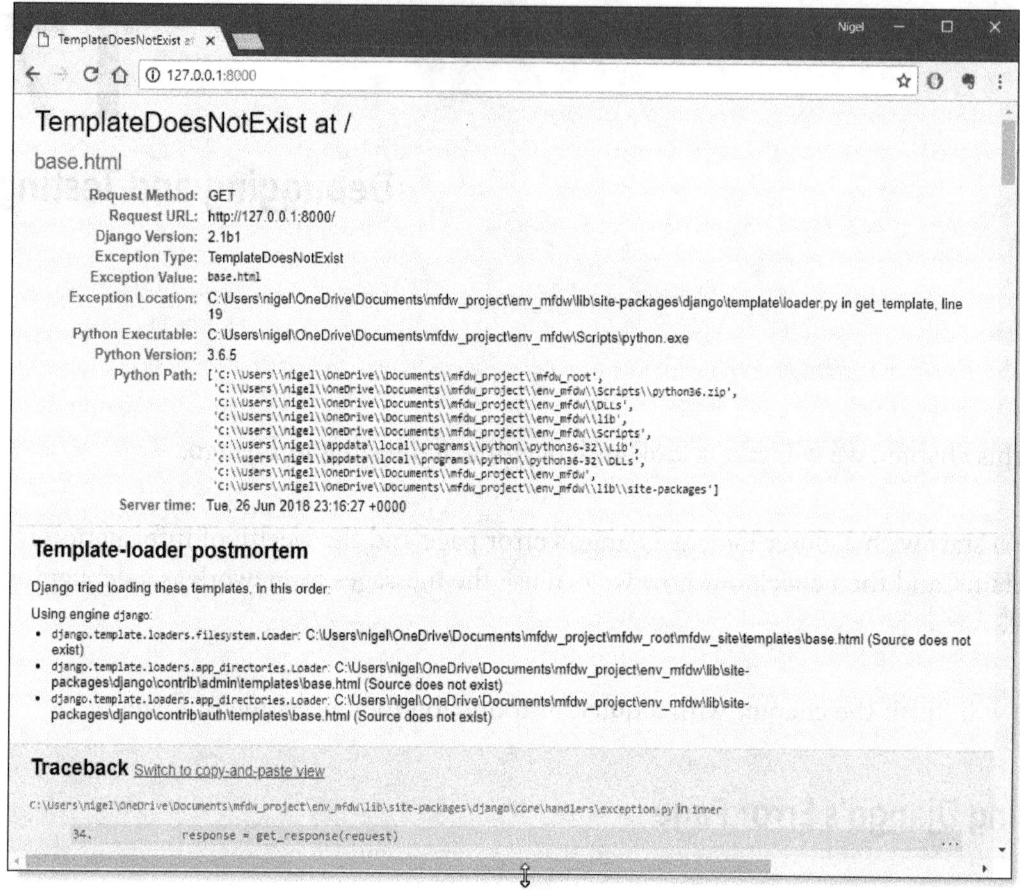

Figure 17-1. *Django's error page provides an enormous amount of useful information when you need to troubleshoot your application.*

Take some time to explore the error page and get to know the various bits of information it gives you. Here are some things to note:

- At the top of the page, you get the key information about the exception: the type of exception, any parameters to the exception (the **TemplateDoesNotExist** message in this case), the file in which the exception was raised and the offending line number.

- As this is a template error, Django will display a **Template-loader postmortem** to show you where things went wrong.
- Under the key exception information, the page displays the full Python traceback for this exception. This is like the standard traceback you get in Python's command-line interpreter, except it's more interactive.
- For each level (frame) in the traceback, Django displays the name of the file, the function/method name, the line number and the source code of that line. Click the line of source code (in dark gray), and you'll see several lines from before and after the erroneous line, to give some context to the code that led to the error.
- Click **Local vars** under any frame in the stack to view a table of local variables and their values in that frame at the exact point in the code at which the exception was raised. This debugging information can be a great help.
- Note the **Switch to copy-and-paste view** text under the **Traceback** header. Click the link, and the traceback will switch to an alternate version that can be copied and pasted. Use this when you want to share your exception traceback with others to get technical support.
- Underneath, the **Share this traceback on a public website** button will do this work for you in just one click. Click it to post the traceback to dpaste[1] where you'll get a unique URL you can share with other people.
- Next, the **Request information** section includes a wealth of information about the incoming Web request that spawned the error: `GET` and `POST` information, cookie values and meta information.
- Below the **Request information** section, the **Settings** section lists all the settings for this particular Django installation.

The Django error page can show a range of different information depending on the error type. You should consider it your number one troubleshooting tool when your Django app is not working.

It's obvious that much of this information is sensitive. As it exposes the innards of your Python code and Django configuration, a malicious person could use it to reverse-engineer your web application.

1 http://dpaste.com/

For security reasons, the Django error page only shows when a Django project is in debug mode. When we created the project with `startproject`, Django put the site in debug mode. This is OK for now; just know you must **never** run a production site in debug mode.

Using the Messages Framework

A problem with using `assert False` and Django's error page to troubleshoot a project is you must stop the code to examine the objects in your application. If you want to step through running code, the usual approach is to use the debugger built into your code editor or third-party apps like the Django Debug Toolbar[2].

Another useful tool for testing and debugging is the messages framework. If you want to review the messages framework, I covered it in Chapter 15.

By default, the messages framework will only add messages at `INFO` level or higher, so we need to make some tweaks to our settings before we can use messages for debugging (changes in bold):

```
# myclub_root\myclub_site\settings.py

# add the following to the imports at the top of the file
from django.contrib.messages import constants as message_constants

# ...

DEBUG = True

ALLOWED_HOSTS = ['127.0.0.1']

if DEBUG:
    MESSAGE_LEVEL = message_constants.DEBUG
else:
    MESSAGE_LEVEL = message_constants.INFO
```

2 https://django-debug-toolbar.readthedocs.io/en/latest/

The first step is to import the message constants from `django.contrib.messages`.

The message constants are numeric values mapped to each of the message levels:

```
DEBUG   => 10
INFO    => 20
SUCCESS => 25
WARNING => 30
ERROR   => 40
```

In **line 3**, I've added the localhost (`127.0.0.1`) to the `ALLOWED_HOSTS` setting. If you want to test using messages and set `DEBUG` to `False`, you must set `ALLOWED_HOSTS`.

Finally, in **lines 5 to 8**, I have added a conditional statement that sets the message level based on whether `DEBUG` is `True` or `False`.

You might wonder why I added the conditional statement. If you think about it, unconditionally setting the message level would be a very bad idea. If you accidentally forget to change the message level back to `INFO` and above, your debug messages will show on your production site!

Now we have the correct settings, we must add the message tags to our base template (changes in bold):

```
# myclub_root\myclub_site\templates\base.html

# ...
<section id="main">
  {% if messages %}
    {% for msg in messages %}
    <p{% if msg.tags %} class="{{ msg.tags }}"{% endif %}>{{ msg }}</p>
    {% endfor %}
  {% endif %}
  {% block content %}
  # ...
```

This is exactly the same code we added to the contact form in Chapter 15. Here, we're iterating through any messages in the message queue and displaying them above the content block on the page.

Now, let's add a message to a view. I will use the `all_events` view again (change in bold):

```
# myclub_root\events\views\demo_views.py

def all_events(request):
    # ...

    context = {'event_records': event_records, 'formset': formset}
    messages.debug(request, qry)
    return render(request, 'events/all_events.html', context)
```

In this example, I've added a debug message to the request that will show the `qry` QuerySet. This is a shortcut method available to the message class and is equivalent to:

```
messages.add_message(
    self.request,
    messages.DEBUG,
    qry,
)
```

If you run the development server and navigate to `http://127.0.0.1:8000/allevents/`, your browser should look like Figure 17-2.

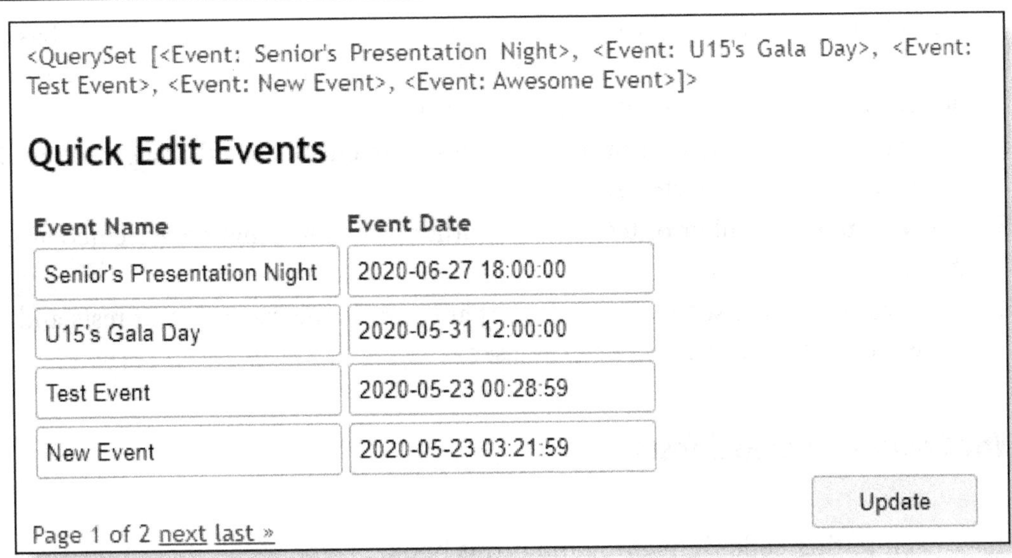

Figure 17-2. *The events page showing a debug message in the page.*

You can add any number of messages to your pages in this way, making it easy to monitor objects and variables in your code without having to interrupt program execution.

Unit Testing

Like all mature programming languages, Django has unit testing capabilities built in. Unit testing is a software testing process where you write code to test individual units of a software application to ensure they do what we expect them to do.

Unit testing can be performed at multiple levels—from testing an individual method to see if it returns the right value and how it handles invalid data, to testing an entire suite of methods to ensure a sequence of user inputs leads to the desired results.

Unit testing is based on four fundamental concepts:

1. A **test fixture** is the setup needed to perform tests. This could include databases, sample datasets and server setup. A test fixture may also include any clean-up actions required after tests have been performed.
2. A **test case** is the basic unit of testing. A test case checks whether a given set of inputs leads to an expected set of results.
3. A **test suite** is a number of test cases, or other test suites, that are executed as a group.
4. A **test runner** is the software program that controls the execution of tests and feeds the results of tests back to the user.

So Why Create Automated Tests?

You have been testing code right throughout this book; maybe without even realizing it. Each time you use the Django shell to see if a function works or to see what output you get for a given input, you are testing your code.

The problem with manual testing is you must repeat the process each time you change the code. Even if you don't change the code you've tested, there's no guarantee another piece of code in your app won't introduce errors (e.g., passing the wrong datatype).

Manual testing might be OK for very simple applications, but even the simplest of websites can be complex behind the scenes. Reducing time-consuming manual testing by replacing it with automated testing is a normal part of professional programming.

With automated testing, you write tests for each important part of your code. When you change the code or change other parts of your app, you can run the same tests to ensure you have not introduced bugs into the app.

Creating automated tests has many advantages:

- **Saves you time.** Manually testing myriad complex interactions between components of a big application is time-consuming and error-prone. Automated tests save time and let you focus on programming.

- **Prevents problems.** Tests highlight the internal workings of your code, so you can see where things have gone wrong.
- **Looks professional.** The pros write tests. If you write code without tests, other professional programmers can't be confident the code you write works as intended.
- **Improves teamwork.** Tests limit the chances that colleagues will inadvertently introduce bugs into your code (and vice versa!).

Unit Testing in Django

Software testing is a deep and detailed subject, and this chapter provides only a basic introduction to unit testing. I have not written tests for any of the code in the book because my aim is to teach you Django. Automated testing is a methodology for producing robust applications; there is nothing Django-specific about unit tests.

There's also a practical aspect to leaving testing out of the sample code: to do justice to professional testing requires a book to itself.

If you want a book on test-driven development in Django, check out Test-Driven Development with Python[3], by Harry Percival.

There are also many resources on the Internet on software testing theory and methods. I encourage you to do your own research on this important topic. For a more detailed discussion on Django's approach to unit testing, see the Django documentation[4].

Running Tests

Automated tests are run using the `test` management command:

```
python manage.py test
```

3 https://www.obeythetestinggoat.com/pages/book.html
4 https://docs.djangoproject.com/en/dev/topics/testing/

If you were to run this command inside your virtual environment now, your terminal output would be:

```
(env_myclub) ...\myclub_root> python manage.py test
System check identified no issues (0 silenced).

----------------------------------------------------------------------
Ran 0 tests in 0.000s

OK
```

Django looks for tests in a file called `tests.py`. When you run `startapp`, Django creates a `tests.py` file automatically. If you look in the `\events` folder, you should find an empty `tests.py` file. Let's add a test to the events app:

```
# myclub_root\events\tests.py

1 from django.test import TestCase
2
3 class BandTest(TestCase):
4
5     def test_not_even_close(self):
6         self.assertEqual('Nickelback', 'Metallica')
```

Tests are Python classes. In Python apps, they're an extension of `unittest.TestCase`. Django extends this class with `SimpleTestCase` which adds Django-specific assertions and the test client. Django then adds its own version of `TestCase` that extends `SimpleTestCase` to add database support.

`django.test.TestCase` is the most common class for writing tests in Django. If you want to avoid database queries in a test, you can use `SimpleTestCase` as database queries are disabled by default.

Our `BandTest` class in **line 3** inherits from `django.test.TestCase`. Each test class should encapsulate test methods for a single class or function where possible (e.g., a model or a view). In our `BandTest` class, we have one method (**line 5**) that uses an assertion to test the equality of two objects (**line 6**).

We've used `assert False` to trigger the Django error page on several occasions in this book. Assertions in tests operate on a similar principle, but there are many assert methods that will either return `True` or `False`. If an assertion returns `True`, the test passes. If it returns `False`, the test fails. Django uses the most common assertions from `unittest.TestCase`, as well as a few Django-specific assertions added by `SimpleTestCase`. The most common assertions in Django tests are in Table 17-1. For more assertions and detailed descriptions, see the Python documentation[5] and the Django documentation[6].

Method	Source	Checks that
`assertEqual`, `assertNotEqual`	`unittest.TestCase`	a == b, a != b
`assertTrue`, `assertFalse`	`unittest.TestCase`	bool(x) is True, False
`assertIs`, `assertIsNot`	`unittest.TestCase`	a is b, a is not b
`assertIsNone`, `assertIsNotNone`	`unittest.TestCase`	x is None, x is not None
`assertIn`, `assertNotIn`	`unittest.TestCase`	a in b, a not in b
`assertIsInstance`, `assertNotIsInstance`	`unittest.TestCase`	isinstance(a, b), not isinstance(a, b)
`assertRaisesMessage`	`SimpleTestCase`	The callable raises the specified exeption and exception message

5 https://docs.python.org/3/library/unittest.html#unittest.TestCase
6 https://docs.djangoproject.com/en/dev/topics/testing/tools/#assertions

Method	Source	Checks that
`assertFormError`	`SimpleTestCase`	A field on a form raises the provided list of errors when rendered on the form
`assertFormsetError`	`SimpleTestCase`	The formset raises the provided list of errors when rendered
`assertContains`, `assertNotContains`	`SimpleTestCase`	The response does/does not produce the given status code and contains the stated text
`assertTemplateUsed`, `assertTemplateNotUsed`	`SimpleTestCase`	A template is/is not used
`assertURLEqual`	`SimpleTestCase`	Two URLs are the same
`assertRedirects`	`SimpleTestCase`	The response returned redirect status
`assertHTMLEqual`, `assertHTMLNotEqual`	`SimpleTestCase`	The HTML strings being compared are equal/not equal
`assertInHTML`	`SimpleTestCase`	The HTML fragment is contained in provided HTML
`assertQuerysetEqual`	`SimpleTestCase`	A QuerySet returns a particular list of values

Table 17-1. *Common assertions for running Django test cases.*

After saving the file, running the `test` command should now produce a result:

```
(env_myclub) ...\myclub_root> python manage.py test
Creating test database for alias 'default'...
System check identified no issues (0 silenced).
F
==================================================
FAIL: test_not_even_close (events.tests.BandTest)
--------------------------------------------------
```

```
Traceback (most recent call last):
File "D:\...\events\tests.py", line 6, in test_not_even_close
    self.assertEqual('Nickelback', 'Metallica')
AssertionError: 'Nickelback' != 'Metallica'
- Nickelback
+ Metallica
----------------------------------------------------
Ran 1 test in 0.001s
FAILED (failures=1)
Destroying test database for alias 'default'...
```

You can see from the output of the test that our assertion failed—Nickelback is not equal to Metallica.

In most cases, test methods are not much more complicated than this. Generally, you are testing for things that seem obvious—two variables are the same, a result is a number, a view returns a response, and so on—but that's where the power of automatic testing lies. Many bugs are introduced when changes to one part of the application breaks something obvious in another.

With a simple test like this, you can develop your band application with confidence, knowing as long as Nickelback is not equal to Metallica, the universe is OK.

Testing Classes and Methods

Our first test, while handy for learning how to write a basic test, is not much use as it tests nothing in our application. You can test classes and their methods by creating an instance of the class, and then writing tests to see what information is returned. For example, let's write a test to see if the string representation of our `Event` class matches what we expect (changes in bold):

```
# myclub_root\events\tests.py

from django.test import TestCase
from datetime import datetime
from .models import Event

```

```
5 class EventsTest(TestCase):
6
7     def test_str_rep(self):
8         event = Event(name="Test Event", event_date=datetime.now())
9         self.assertEqual(str(event), event.name)
```

NOTE: you should delete or comment out the `BandTest` class before continuing so you don't keep getting test failures in your output.

If you remember, back in Chapter 4 we configured the `__str__()` method to return the event name as the string representation for the `Event` class. Here, in **line 8**, I have created an instance of the `Event` class, and in **line 9**, I am checking the string representation of the instance against the event name.

Run the `test` command again, and the `Event` model should pass the test:

```
(env_myclub) ...\myclub_root> python manage.py test
Creating test database for alias 'default'...
System check identified no issues (0 silenced).
.
---------------------------------------------
Ran 1 test in 0.000s

OK
Destroying test database for alias 'default'...
```

Testing other class methods is as simple as adding more tests. For example, let's test the `event_timing()` method of the `Event` class (changes in bold):

```
# myclub_root\events\tests.py

from django.test import TestCase
from datetime import datetime, timedelta
from .models import Event

class EventsTest(TestCase):

    def test_str_rep(self):
```

```
8           event = Event(name="Test Event", event_date=datetime.now())
9           self.assertEqual(str(event), event.name)
10
11      def test_event_timing(self):
12          now = datetime.now()
13          past = now - timedelta(days=2)
14          future = now + timedelta(days=2)
15          event = Event(name="Test Event", event_date=now)
16          self.assertEqual(event.event_timing(now), "Event is on the same day")
17          self.assertEqual(event.event_timing(past), "Event is after this date")
18          self.assertEqual(event.event_timing(future), "Event is before this date")
```

This test class is more detailed, but employs the same principles:

- **Line 11** is the new test method which inherits from `django.test.TestCase`.
- **Lines 12 to 14.** We set up some date values for testing the method.
- **Line 15.** We create an instance of the `Event` class.
- **Lines 16 to 18.** We run some assertions against the `event_timing()` method to ensure we get the results we expect.

Save the file and run the test command again, and you should have two passed tests:

```
(env_myclub) ...\myclub_root> python manage.py test
Creating test database for alias 'default'...
System check identified no issues (0 silenced).
.
---------------------------------------------
Ran 2 tests in 0.001s

OK
Destroying test database for alias 'default'...
```

Testing Views

Testing a view follows a similar process to testing classes, but there is a wrinkle—how do you test the response from the view?

Django provides a *test client* to solve this problem. Django's test client acts as a dummy browser to allow you to test your views. The test client can be instantiated directly:

```
# Example only. Don't add this to your code

from django.test import Client

client = Client()
response = client.get('/get/url/')
```

However, given that each Django `TestCase` class has access to an instance of a Django test client, it's more common to access the client as `self.client`. For example, let's create a new test class to test the `all_events()` view:

```
# myclub_root\events\tests.py

# ...

1 class EventViewTests(TestCase):
2
3     def test_all_events(self):
4         response = self.client.get('/allevents/')
5         self.assertEqual(response.status_code, 200)
```

In this new test class, I am using the `self.client` instance of the `TestCase` class to fetch a response from the `/allevents/` url (**line 4**). Then in **line 5**, the class tests if the `HTTP` status of the response is `200` (OK).

When you run this test, you should get the following output:

```
(env_myclub) ...\myclub_root> python manage.py test
Creating test database for alias 'default'...
System check identified no issues (0 silenced).
...: UnorderedObjectListWarning: Pagination may yield inconsistent
results with an
 unordered object_list: <class 'events.models.Event'> QuerySet.
pg = Paginator(qry, 4)
.
----------------------------------------.
Ran 3 tests in 0.053s

OK
Destroying test database for alias 'default'...
```

The test passes OK, but notice the warning message. If you remember from Chapter 10, Django's QuerySets do not guarantee ordering unless it's explicitly stated. Here, the unordered event list could create a situation where the events are in a different order each time you run the query.

This is the sort of non-obvious bug that should make the value of automated tests self-evident. I didn't introduce this error deliberately to prove my point, by the way. It popped up the first time I wrote the test, and I had an "Oh yeah, that's right!" moment. As they say, every mistake is a learning opportunity.

So, let's fix the bug (change in bold):

```
# myclub_root\events\views\demo_views.py

# ...

def all_events(request):
    EventsFormSet = modelformset_factory(
        Event,
        fields=('name', 'event_date'),
        extra=0
    )
    qry = Event.events.all().order_by('event_date')
    pg = Paginator(qry, 4)
    # ...
```

A simple change—we're ordering the QuerySet before passing it to the `Paginator` class. If you run the test again, the warning will go away.

There are many other tests you can add to ensure your view is operating correctly. For example, you can also test to ensure the formset is being added to the context (changes in bold):

```
# myclub_root\events\tests.py

# ...

1 class EventViewTests(TestCase):
2
3     def test_all_events(self):
4         response = self.client.get('/allevents/')
5         self.assertEqual(response.status_code, 200)
6         self.assertIn('formset', response.context)
```

I've only added one line here. In **line 6**, I've added an `assertIn` test to check to see that the `formset` key has been added to the context.

I'm not going to delve any deeper into automated testing here. You should have a good grasp of how to set up tests, becoming an expert at testing is as simple as adding as many tests as you can think of, and then adding some more, as there is no such thing as too many tests!

Chapter Summary

In this chapter, we looked at debugging and testing in Django.

We started with a closer look at Django's error page and the wealth of information it contains, and then checked out how we can use the messages framework as a debugging tool.

We finished the chapter with a quick introduction to unit testing in Django.

This chapter completes the Essentials part of the book. You have now learned the essential 80% of Django's core functionality that you will regularly use in your programming career.

In the last chapter of the book, I'll address the extras in core Django that, while important to learn, are not as often used in Django development as the content covered so far.

18

Odds and Ends

In this last chapter, I have compiled a few notes on each of the parts of Django that are uncommon, don't fit into another chapter or I simply have nothing to add that isn't in the Django documentation.

The Flatpages App

Not every page on a website needs to be created on the fly by a custom app. There are many pages (e.g., about pages, terms and conditions, and site policies) that only require simple HTML content and don't change often. For small sites with only a few pages, the option not to have to develop a dedicated app for serving pages can also be useful.

Django provides the ability to create and manage simple HTML pages with the `flatpages` app, which is a part of the Django `contrib` packages. To get started, we need to add it to our `INSTALLED_APPS` list in `settings.py` (changes in bold):

```
# myclub_root\myclub_site\settings.py

INSTALLED_APPS = [
    # ...
    'django.contrib.sites',
    'django.contrib.flatpages',
]
```

```
SITE_ID = 1

MIDDLEWARE = [
    # ...
    'django.contrib.flatpages.middleware.FlatpageFallbackMiddleware',
]
```

The flatpages app relies on the sites framework, so we must install it as well. sites is a contrib package that makes working with multiple sites easier. As it's not a common requirement, I won't be covering the sites app in this book. If you want more information, check out the sites framework[1].

SITE_ID must be set when you install the sites framework. As there is only one site, we set SITE_ID to "1".

There are two ways to load flat pages in Django: via a URLconf or with the flatpages middleware. To load a flatpage with a URL, you can load all pages with:

```
path('pages/', include('django.contrib.flatpages.urls')),
```

Use a catchall (which *must* come after all other URLconfs):

```
path('<path:url>', views.flatpage),
```

Or hard-code individual URLs:

```
path('about/', views.flatpage, {'url': '/about/'}, name='about'),
```

But we're not going to use any of these methods because the second implementation option—flatpages middleware—provides a much simpler implementation.

1 https://docs.djangoproject.com/en/dev/ref/contrib/sites/

In the code above, I have added `django.contrib.flatpages.middleware.FlatpageFallbackMiddleware` to the end of our site middleware list. Whenever a 404 (Not found) error is raised, this middleware will check the flatpages database to see if a page matching the URL exists.

This is functionally equivalent to using the catchall URL but has the advantage of keeping the configuration options for flatpages in your settings file. Plus, you don't have to worry about the catchall interfering with URL resolution in your other apps.

Now, we just need to add the tables for the `sites` framework and the `flatpages` app to our database:

```
(env_myclub) ...\myclub_root> python manage.py migrate
Operations to perform:
Apply all migrations: admin, auth, contenttypes, events, flatpages,
sessions, sites
Running migrations:
Applying sites.0001_initial... OK
Applying flatpages.0001_initial... OK
Applying sites.0002_alter_domain_unique... OK
```

Once you have run the `migrate` command, you will see Django has added the `sites` framework and `flatpages` apps to the admin home page (Figure 18-1).

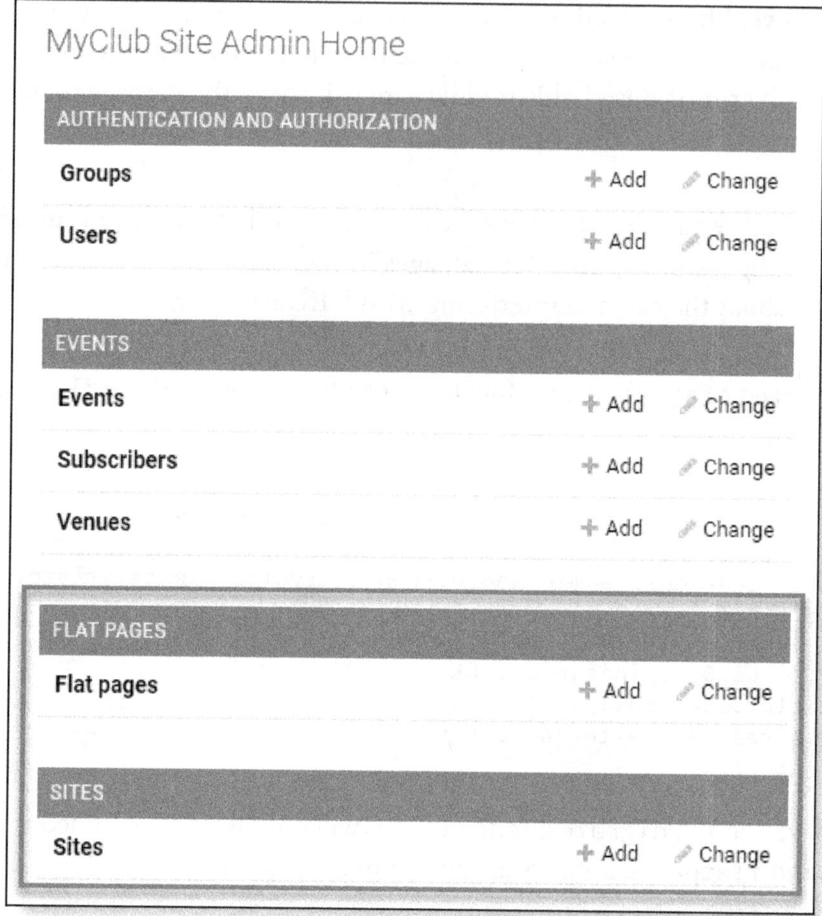

Figure 18-1. *Django has added The Sites framework and the Flat Pages app to the Django admin.*

If you click **Add** next to the Flat pages app, Django will open the "Add flat page" form (Figure 18-2).

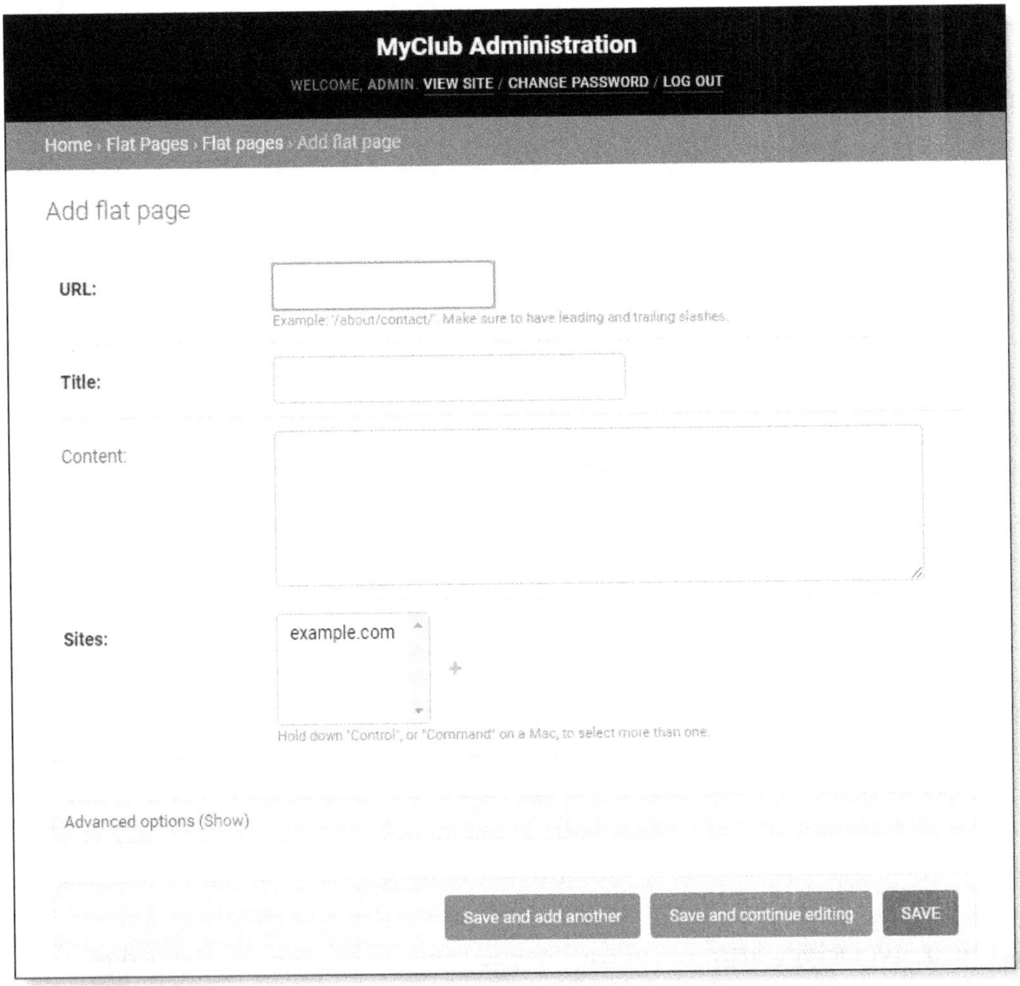

***Figure 18-2.** You can add new flatpages via the admin interface. Note this form lacks a rich-text editor for the page content.*

This is a perfectly acceptable setup, but notice the Content field is plain text. Since the content will be HTML, it would be better if we could add a rich-text editor so we can use WYSIWYG editing on the page content.

We did the hard work in Chapter 12 when we added CKEditor to our project, so all we need to do now is configure the flatpage form to use a custom widget for the content (new code):

```
# myclub_root\events\admin.py

# add the following to the imports at the top of the file
1 from django.db import models
2 from django.contrib.flatpages.models import FlatPage
3 from django.contrib.flatpages.admin import FlatPageAdmin

# ...

4 class FlatPageAdmin(FlatPageAdmin):
5     formfield_overrides = {
6         models.TextField: { 'widget': CKEditorWidget}
7     }

# ...

# add these at the end of the file
8 admin.site.unregister(FlatPage)
9 admin.site.register(FlatPage, FlatPageAdmin)
```

After importing the `FlatPage` model and `FlatPageAdmin` class (**lines 2 and 3**), I've created a new `FlatPageAdmin` class on **line 4**. I've named my custom admin class the same as the default class, so it will override the default class. I've then used the `formfield_overrides` attribute of the class to override the `TextField` widget and replace it with `CKEditorWidget`.

This simple field type override works because the only flatpage model field that uses a `TextField` is the content field.

Save the file and refresh your admin, and the add form should now look like Figure 18-3.

Create a home page (URL = "/") and an about page (URL = "`/about/`"), then add some content to each page before you go on to the next section.

Figure 18-3. *With the CKEditor widget added to the content field, you can now add rich-text content to your flat pages.*

Now the `flatpages` app is set up, and we have some pages to display, we need to add a template to show the content. When looking for a template for displaying flatpage content, Django will look for a file named `default.html` in a folder called `flatpages`.

First, create the `flatpages` folder in your site templates folder. Then add the `default.html` template (new file):

```
# \myclub_site\templates\flatpages\default.html

{% extends "base.html" %}

{% block title %}{{ flatpage.title }}{% endblock title %}

{% block content %}
    {{ flatpage.content }}
{% endblock content %}
```

There's nothing new in this template—the only thing to note is that the `flatpage.title` and `flatpage.content` template variables will be added to the context by the flatpage middleware.

Now, let's modify the site base template to activate the remaining links in the top menu (changes in bold):

```
# myclub_root\myclub_site\templates\base.html

# ...
<div id="top_menu">
    <a href="/">Home</a> | <a href="/calendar">Calendar</a> |
    <a href="/about">About</a> | <a href="/contact">Contact Us</a> |
    {% if user.is_authenticated %}
# ...
```

This is a snippet of the complete `base.html` template, but you can see I've added links for the home page, event calendar, and the about page.

As the `index` view displays the event calendar, we need to change the events URLs (change in bold):

```
# myclub_root\events\urls.py

path('calendar/', views.index, name='index'),
```

This is a small change—the event calendar now displays at the `http://127.0.0.1:8000/calendar/` URL instead of the site root.

You need not do anything to add the URLs for your new home page or the about page because the flatpage middleware will automatically look for them when all other URL comparisons fail (i.e., Django throws a 404). If you navigate to your new home page, the browser should look like Figure 18-4.

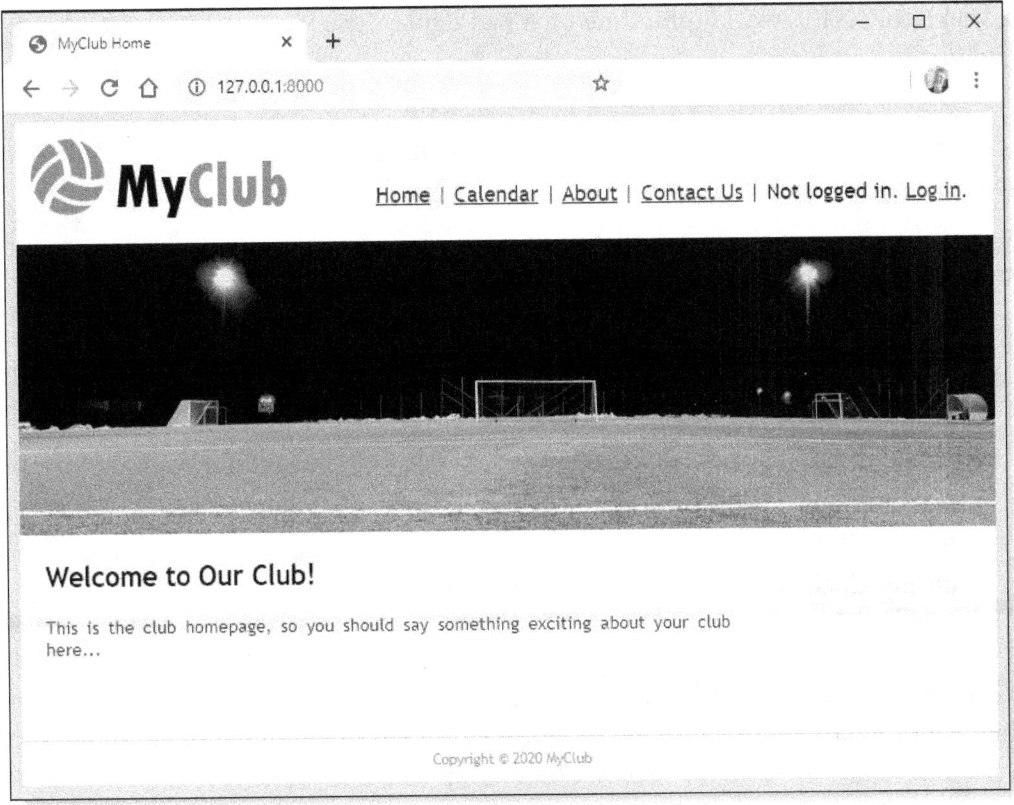

***Figure 18-4.** The MyClub homepage showing flatpage content and live links in the top menu.*

While you are there, click on the "About" link to check out the about page you created with flatpages, and click the "Calendar" link to see the event calendar.

Django's Cache Framework

Django is fast, so caching is something you won't have to implement often unless you're working with medium- to high-traffic sites. This is contrary to the "you should always cache" mantra, but that advice comes from either the PHP world (slow as a wet week), the .NET world (grandma on a bad day) or the Java world (please, shoot me now).

As caching is often unnecessary on a Django website, it's not installed by default—to enable caching you need to add the `CACHES` setting to your settings file.

Django natively supports the following cache back ends:

- **Memcached**[2]—`django.core.cache.backends.memcached.MemcachedCache`
- **Database Caching**—`django.core.cache.backends.db.DatabaseCache`
- **File Caching**—`django.core.cache.backends.filebased.FileBasedCache`
- **Local-memory Caching**—`django.core.cache.backends.locmem.LocMemCache`
- **Dummy Cache (for development)**—`django.core.cache.backends.dummy.DummyCache`

The back end is set with the `BACKEND` setting. For example, configuring a Memcached cache on a local port:

```
CACHES = {
    'default': {
        'BACKEND': 'django.core.cache.backends.memcached.
MemcachedCache',
        'LOCATION': '127.0.0.1:11211',
    }
}
```

2 https://memcached.org/

This is an example for configuring a database cache:

```
CACHES = {
    'default': {
        'BACKEND': 'django.core.cache.backends.db.DatabaseCache',
        'LOCATION': 'myapp_cache_table',
    }
}
```

You can find more examples of the different cache back ends and implementation instructions in the Django documentation[3].

Sessions in Django

Session support is installed when you run `startproject`. It's implemented via the `django.contrib.sessions` app and the `SessionMiddleware`.

By default, Django uses database sessions, which are adequate for most websites. If you require higher performance, you can use cached sessions, but Django's developers recommend you only use Memcached in this instance because local-memory sessions are not persistent.

File- and cookie-based sessions are also available, but you would only use either of these if there is a specific reason you can't use database- or cache-based sessions. This is because file-based sessions are slow and prone to permission errors, and cookie-based sessions are unreliable because many users disable cookies.

When `SessionMiddleware` is active, all views have a `session` attribute, which can be get and set in the view. For example:

```
# SET:

request.session['top_band'] = 'AC/DC'
```

3 https://docs.djangoproject.com/en/dev/topics/cache/

```
# GET:

top_band = request.session['top_band']
```

The `session` attribute is a dictionary-like object, so you can use `keys()` and `items()`, and it also has handy functions for getting and setting session expiration times.

You can find more information on sessions in Django in the Django documentation[4].

System Logging

Django uses Python's built-in `logging` module[5] to log system messages.

To implement the logging module in a Django project requires a few settings, which are detailed in the Django documentation[6].

Syndication Feed Framework

While RSS is still not dead, it's been the walking dead for some time now. Once social and news media companies realized it was hard to control and monetize, services offering RSS and Atom feeds have dwindled.

If you do need to write a syndication framework, don't worry, Django has one built in[7].

4 https://docs.djangoproject.com/en/dev/topics/http/sessions/
5 https://docs.python.org/3/library/logging.html#module-logging
6 https://docs.djangoproject.com/en/dev/topics/logging/#django-logger
7 https://docs.djangoproject.com/en/dev/ref/contrib/syndication/

Internationalization and Localization

The original *Mastering Django:Core* for Django 1.8 had a pretty decent chapter on internationalization and localization in Django. It was originally written for Django 1.1 by Jacob and Adrian (creators of Django), and I tidied it up for Django 1.8.

The issue I have is Jacob and Adrian's content became the Django docs and I, as a native English speaker with English-speaking clients, find myself with very little to add.

I think it's healthy as programmers and teachers to accept our limitations and this is one of mine. If you want to learn more about supporting multiple languages in Django, I refer you to the Django documentation[8] and Django's fantastic global community who are only as far away as typing "django internationalization" into your favorite search engine.

Security in Django

Web security is an important and ever-changing topic. Because of its importance and the risks involved, I'm not covering it in this book because anything I write is likely to be obsolete before the book is published.

For the latest information on security in Django, see the Django documentation[9] on security, and the latest archive of security issues[10] in Django.

8 https://docs.djangoproject.com/en/dev/topics/i18n/
9 https://docs.djangoproject.com/en/dev/topics/security/
10 https://docs.djangoproject.com/en/dev/releases/security/#archive-of-security-issues

Images in Django

Django has no native image handling capabilities; as far as Django is concerned, an image is just another file type.

It's a common misconception, but Django is not a Content Management System (CMS). Yes, the Django admin has some characteristics of a CMS, but the admin has been designed to manage data, models and users, not content.

This doesn't mean there aren't plenty of options for image handling in Django, it's just that they're all third-party apps and therefore out of the scope of this book.

You can use Django to build CMSes. Mezzanine[11], Wagtail[12] and django CMS[13] are examples of CMSes that have been built on Django. I encourage you to check out these projects if you are looking for a straight content management solution based on Django.

Showing thumbnails in the admin is a common requirement. You can find many solutions by typing "show images in django admin" into your favorite browser.

The CKEditor[14] rich-text editor we installed in Chapter 12 can be configured to insert images into your content, but you're going to have to dig into JavaScript plugins to make this work.

There are also many projects on Django Packages[15] that provide solutions for image handling.

Remember too that Django is just Python, so you can use Pillow[16] in your apps.

---

11 http://mezzanine.jupo.org/
12 https://wagtail.io/
13 https://www.django-cms.org/en/
14 https://github.com/django-ckeditor/django-ckeditor
15 https://djangopackages.org/
16 https://python-pillow.org/

Signals

Django includes a built-in signal dispatcher that allows Django's apps to receive notifications of actions that occur elsewhere in the project. Django breaks signal functions up into *senders* and *receivers*.

Django's built-in senders are:

- Model signals
  - `pre_init()`
  - `post_init()`
  - `pre_save()`
  - `post_save()`
  - `pre_delete()`
  - `post_delete()`
  - `m2m_changed()`
  - `class_prepared()`
- Management signals
  - `pre_migrate()`
  - `post_migrate()`
- Request/response signals
  - `request_started()`
  - `request_finished()`
  - `got_request_exception()`
- Test signals
  - `setting_changed()`
  - `template_rendered()`
- Database Wrappers
  - `connection_created()`

You will find more details on the built-in senders in the Django documentation[17]. You can also define custom signals[18].

A receiver is a callback function you connect to a particular signal. You can connect manually, but the easiest way is to use the `@receiver()` decorator. For example:

```
from django.core.signals import post_save
from django.dispatch import receiver

@receiver(post_save)
def my_post_save_callback(sender, **kwargs)
    # do some post-save processing
```

You will find more details on writing receivers in the Django documentation.

Search

While conceptually simple, search is one of the hardest things to do in any web application. Search engines like Google have conditioned us to think search is as simple as typing in a search term and retrieving the results. However, when you sit down to write a search algorithm, you immediately realize it's a lot harder than first thought. For example:

- What database fields should you search?
- How do you sort results by relevance?
- How to search like terms, e.g., "fly" also searches for "flyer", "flying" and "flies"?
- How do you find related terms, e.g., "Queensland" also searches for "QLD" (state abbreviation) and "Brisbane" (Queensland city)?
- How do you account for accented characters? Different languages?

17 https://docs.djangoproject.com/en/dev/ref/signals/
18 https://docs.djangoproject.com/en/dev/topics/signals/#defining-and-sending-signals

Professional search that works as expected is a complicated and ever-changing beast, so it's not something Django implements natively. You can use Django to build some reasonably powerful searches—just don't expect Google-like performance.

At its most basic, search can be performed by looking for the search term in one or more fields in your database. In Django, a simple search can be performed with field lookups like `__icontains`. For example:

```
result = mymodel.objects.filter(db_field__icontains="search_term")
```

You can search multiple fields with `Q` objects. For example:

```
Q1 = Q(db_field1__icontains="search_term")
Q2 = Q(db_field2__icontains="search_term")
result = mymodel.objects.filter(Q1|Q2)
```

We covered field lookups and `Q` objects in Chapter 9. Other lookup filters you can use are `istartswith` and `iendswith`. You can also use `iregex` to use regular expressions for building more complicated searches.

To implement a simple search in Django, you

1. show a `GET` **form** that passes the search term to;
2. a **view** that uses a field lookup or `Q` object. The view then passes the result back to;
3. a **template** that displays the result.

These are all basic Django tasks you should be more than capable of completing at this stage.

There's nothing stopping you searching multiple models in your view and you can prioritize results by ordering the database fields and models in your template.

The next step up in capability (and complexity) is to use the `django.contrib.postgres.search` module to implement PostgreSQL's full-text search engine. This assumes you're running PostgreSQL with your project.

Now, instead of using `Q` objects in your view, you're using classes like `SearchVector()` and `SearchQuery()`. The form-view-template implementation is the same as a simple search.

For more information on using PostgreSQL's full-text search, see the Django documentation[19].

Beyond simple search and using PostgreSQL's full-text search, you only have third-party applications. Here are a few options for you to explore:

- **Django Haystack**[20]—a Django API that allows your apps to implement different search back ends.
- **Whoosh**[21]—a full-text indexing and searching library implemented in pure Python.
- **ElasticSearch**[22] and **Solr**[23]—Dedicated search back end applications.
- **Algolia**[24] and **Swiftype**[25]—hosted search services.

Deploying Django

When I sat down to outline this book, deploying Django was another of those topics where I was left asking "what can I add?".

19 https://docs.djangoproject.com/en/dev/ref/contrib/postgres/search/
20 https://django-haystack.readthedocs.io/en/master/
21 https://github.com/whoosh-community/whoosh
22 https://www.elastic.co/
23 https://lucene.apache.org/solr/
24 https://www.algolia.com/
25 https://swiftype.com/

I've written about deploying a Django project to PythonAnywhere in my beginner's book: *Build a Website with Django 3*. There are also many tutorials online on deploying to PythonAnywhere, Heroku, AWS, DigitalOcean and numerous other hosts.

In my experience, and I am sure it's common with other tutorial writers, the problem with writing these tutorials is that they break. The host might change their deployment process, the tutorial may miss a minor detail, or the person trying to follow the tutorial may make a mistake.

Now Django 3 has added limited support for ASGI servers, the error rate will only increase.

So, rather than write something today that may break tomorrow (which is frustrating for everyone), I'm referring you to the two best sources for Django deployment information:

4. The latest Django documentation[26].
5. Your favorite search engine.

In the latter case, type in "deploy django to".

I just entered this phrase in Google and got an extensive list of hosts including Heroku, AWS, Azure, Google Cloud, and others.

If I do write some deployment tutorials, you will find them on `djangobook.com` where I can update them easily.

While we're still on the subject of deployment, there is something I feel remains relevant is to point out Django was designed to be scalable from the get-go.

Most small to medium websites will run happily on a single server, but once your traffic and your database get larger, it's time to use Django's scaling options.

26 https://docs.djangoproject.com/en/dev/howto/deployment/

The first and easiest scaling option is to put your database on a separate server. To do this, you move your database to the new server and change your `DATABASE_HOST` setting to point to the new database server.

The next scaling option is to host your media (static files) on a separate server. Nginx[27] is by far the most popular option here, but a CDN server is also a good option.

To serve static files from a separate server requires configuration of the `STATIC_FILES` and `STATIC_ROOT` settings. See the Django documentation[28] for more information.

These two scaling options, along with caching with Memcached, are likely to cover all your performance needs unless you start working with global brands with enormous websites. Your options once you start working on sites this big (e.g., load balancing and database replication) are not Django-related and out of the scope of this book.

What's New in Django 3

The two major changes for Django 3 are the addition of MariaDB support and limited support for ASGI (asynchronous) servers.

We covered MariaDB in Chapter 16, and ASGI support is currently very limited, so I will not add any substantial content regarding ASGI until a later edition of the book. If you want info on ASGI, check the `djangobook.com` website because if I do write tutorials on ASGI, that's where they will appear first.

There are numerous small changes in Django 3, but none with a substantial effect on your Django 2 applications. If you want to see all the changes, check out the Django 3 release notes[29].

27 https://www.nginx.com/
28 https://docs.djangoproject.com/en/dev/howto/static-files/deployment/#serving-static-files-in-production
29 https://docs.djangoproject.com/en/3.0/releases/3.0/

And We're Done!

After more than a year of constant writing, I am somewhat relieved to be writing this!

I haven't covered everything I could have covered—that would take several books—but I hope I've covered most of the important stuff and given you a solid start to your Django programming career.

All the best with your programming journey!

Nige

Index

@

A

B

C

D

E

F

G

H

I

J

K

L

M

Q

R

S

T

U

V

W

X

Y

Z

CPSIA information can be obtained
at www.ICGtesting.com
Printed in the USA
FSHW020542011221
86569FS

9 780648 884415